Tzemah L. Yoreh
The First Book of God

Beihefte zur Zeitschrift für die alttestamentliche Wissenschaft

Herausgegeben von
John Barton · Reinhard G. Kratz
Choon-Leong Seow · Markus Witte

Band 402

De Gruyter

Tzemah L. Yoreh

The First Book of God

De Gruyter

ISBN 978-3-11-022167-1
e-ISBN 978-3-11-022168-8
ISSN 0934-2575

Library of Congress Cataloging-in-Publication Data
A CIP catalogue record for this book is available from the Library of Congress.

Bibliographic information published by the Deutsche Nationalbibliothek

The Deutsche Nationalbibliothek lists this publication in the Deutsche
Nationalbibliografie; detailed bibliographic data are available in the Internet
at http://dnb.d-nb.de.

Printing: Hubert & Co. GmbH & Co. KG, Göttingen
∞ Printed on acid-free paper

Printed in Germany

www.degruyter.com

Acknowledgements

This book is dedicated to my mother Tirzah Zehurah Meacham who began reading me bible while *in utero*, and has taught me *Chokhmah VaDaat* ever since. Words cannot convey the debt of gratitude I owe her. My father, Harry Fox, has always been the first reader of my work, my harshest critic, and my most ardent supporter. My father's intellectual honesty, and my mother's rigor are the yardsticks by which I measure myself. I hope I make them both proud.

My Doctor Vater Israel Knohl has supported me since my undergraduate years. There is no teacher who has taught me more. His fearless originality has always inspired me onwards.

My brother Tanhum Yoreh, first translated this book from the original Hebrew, his diligent work formed an excellent starting point for many revisions and reformulations. I look forward to seeing his original work in print in coming years.

My spouse Aviva Richman has lovingly endured the constant rants that have accompanied the lengthy process involved in bringing this book to press, her unstinting support and patience are the solid bulwark upon which I depend.

There are many teachers who have sculpted my untutored knowledge of texts into what I hope is scholarly sensitivity. Leah Mazor was the first to encourage me to unflinchingly follow what I consider to be the truth. Baruch Schwartz taught me more about Pentateuchal criticism than anyone else. Alexander Rofe helped hone my reading strategies. Shalom Paul lent me his enthusiasm. To them and all my other teachers at Hebrew University, I extend a heartfelt thanks.

Many colleagues and friends have read parts of this manuscript or heard the ideas expressed therein and have given me valuable advice and criticism. Particularly worthy of mention are my first students Philip Elman, Julia Andleman, and Miryam Segal, my good friend Seth Sanders, and my *Rav Chaver*, Benjamin Sommer.

I would like to thank Walter de Gruyter for publishing my manuscript. I've read and appreciated many of the books that have appeared in the BZAW series and I consider it a great honor that my book is now part of this collection.

I am sure I've forgotten many people who deserve my gratitude, it was a long journey, and so many of you helped me.

Finally, I must thank Alice Shalvi who went above and beyond the call of duty in her capacity as copy editor of this book. The accuracy and consistency herein are hers, the mistakes are mine.

Contents

Abbreviations

BaRev	*Biblical Archaeology Review*
BASOR	*Bulletin of the American Schools of Oriental Research*
BDB	Francis Brown, S. R. Driver, and Charles A. Briggs, *A Hebrew and English Lexicon of the Old Testament* (Oxford: Clarendon Press, 1907)
BZAW	Beihefte zur *ZAW*
BHS	*Biblica Hebraica Stuttgartensia*
BN	*Biblische Notizen*
BR	*Bible Review*
BTB	*Biblical Theology Bulletin*
BTS	*Bible et Terre Sainte*
BWANT	*Beiträge zur Wissenschaft vom Alten und Neuen Testament*
BZ	*Biblische Zeitschrift*
CBQ	*Catholic Biblical Quarterly*
DBAT	Dielheimer Blätter zum Alten Testament und seiner Rezeption in der Alten Kirche
ETL	Ephemerides Theologicae Lovanienses
EUS	European University Studies
FRLANT	Forschungen zur Religion und Literatur des Alten und Neuen Testaments
HUCA	*Hebrew Union College Annual*
KB	Ludwig Koehler and Walter Baumgartner (eds.) *Lexicon in Veteris Testamenti libros* (Leiden: E. J. Brill, 1953)
JAOS	*Journal of American Oriental Society*
JBL	*Journal of Biblical Literature*
JBQ	*Jewish Bible Quarterly*
JNSL	*Journal of Northwest Semitic Languages*
JR	*Journal of Religion*
JSOT	*Journal for the Study of the Old Testament*
JSOTS	*Journal for the Study of the Old Testament* Supplement Series
JTS	*Journal of Theological Studies*
KHAT	Kurzer Hand-Kommentar zur Alten Testament
OBO	Orbis biblicus et Orientalis
OTL	Old Testament Library
RB	*Revue Biblique*
SBLMS	SBL Monograph Series
TynB	*Tyndale Bulletin*
USQR	*Union Seminary Quarterly Review*
VT	*Vetus Testamentum*
VTSup	*Vetus Testamentum* Supplements
WCJS	World Congress for Jewish Studies
WMANT	Wissenschaftliche Monographien zum Alten und Neuen Testament

1. Introduction

1.1 The Elohistic Source: An Introduction

In 1798 Ilgen identified two bodies of written material embedded within the canonical text of Genesis which used "elohim" to identify the Deity; the two were later referred to as the priestly source (P) and the elohistic source (E).[1] In 1853 Hupfeld distinguished between the two in a convincing manner and finally Graff realized the antiquity of J (the yahwistic source, i.e. the body of material which preferred the name Yhwh) and of E relative to P.[2] Thus the "elohistic source" of modern criticism was first conceived of and isolated. The successful isolation of these literary sources led Documentary scholars, most adequately represented by Julius Wellhausen (1899), to the following conclusions:[3]

> 1) J, E and P (composed in that order) were independent parallel sources combined by a series of redactors, the final product being the present text of Genesis-Numbers.
> 2) E is fragmented (relative to J and P), the most obvious lacunae being the lack of pre-patriarchal narratives and the absence of an Isaac cycle.
> 3) E, as well as J and P, each had its own distinct set of vocabulary and ideas, allowing scholars to identify and delineate the contours of each source.
> 4) In Genesis and through Ex. 3, E uses "Elohim" to identify the Deity. Following this chapter, E also used "Yhwh." This of course made division more perilous and led to the hypothetical combined source JE.

Non-conventional opinions such as Tuch's Supplementary Hypothesis,[4] which posited an elohistic base text supplemented by yahwistic redaction, and Dillmann's antedating of E relative to J[5] fell by the academic

---

1   J. Skinner, *Genesis, A Critical and Exegetical Commentary* (ICC), Edinburgh, foreword XLIII but cf. D. Carr, No Return to Wellhausen, *Biblica* 86 (2005): 107-114.
2   Thus Skinner's description in his foreword.
3   J. Wellhausen, *Die Composition des Hexateuchs und der Historischen Bücher des Alten Testaments*, Berlin, 1899.
4   F. Tuch, *Kommentar über die Genesis*, Halle, 1838.
5   A. Dillmann, *Die Genesis* (Handbuch zum Alten Testament), Leipzig, 1892.

wayside. Wellhausen's coherent presentation of the Documentary Hypothesis and most importantly for this work, his delineation of the E source dominated scholarship until the 1930s when E's existence began to be attacked on a number of different fronts.

The blows inflicted upon the existence E are comparable to the present attack upon the entire Documentary Hypothesis. The catalyst in this case was the position advocated by Gunkel[6] and especially by his student Gressmann,[7] who went so far as to claim that J and E were no more than labels exchanged at will. According to Gunkel and Gressmann, the distinction between J and E could only rarely be carried out with any certainty. Opinions such as these made their mark on scholars of the next generation such as Noth,[8] who did not, however, carry his doubts as far as did Gressmann. Yet he, too, expressed uncertainty regarding scholarship's ability to distinguish between the sources by using the minute differences of vocabulary and style. It was mainly Volz and Rudolph,[9] together with Mowinckel,[10] whom we must credit with the first concentrated attack on E's existence. They insisted that E was no more than an addendum to J and could hardly be called a source.

Another important development was the position of scholars such as Cassuto[11] and afterwards Brichto[12] on the validity of the Deity's names as a criterion for distinguishing between sources. Cassuto suggested a more literary theory, based upon the different aspects of Yhwh and Elohim as found in early Jewish sources (the Midrash and Philo). Although Cassuto stood on the sidelines of biblical criticism, his method was a precursor of new developments. The dismissal of E accelerated after the 1930s and by the 1970s it became an accepted opinion advocated by mainstream scholars such as Claus Westermann.[13] This

---

6   H. Gunkel, *The Legends of Genesis: The Biblical Saga and History* (W. H. Carruth tr.), New York, 1970.

7   H. Gressmann, *Mose und Seine Zeit: Ein Kommentar zu den Mose Sagen*, Göttingen, 1913.

8   M. Noth *A History of Pentateuchal Traditions*, (tr. B.W. Anderson), Englewood Cliffs, New Jersey, 1972.

9   P. Volz and E. Rudolph, *Der Elohist als Erzähler; ein Irrweg der Pentateuch Kritik* (*BZAW* 63), Berlin, 1933.

10   S. Mowinckel, Der Ursprung der Bil'amsage, *ZAW* 48 (1930): 233-271.

11   U. Cassuto, *From Noah to Abraham* (I. Abrahams tr.), Jerusalem, 1964.

12   H. C. Brichto, *The Names of God: Poetic Readings in Biblical Beginnings*, New York, 1998.

13   C. Westermann, *Genesis 1-11, Genesis 12-36, Genesis 37-50: A Commentary* (J. J. Scullion tr.), Minneapolis, 1984-1986.

exegete was joined by influential scholars such as Van Seters,[14] Rendtorff[15] and their students (most notably, Blum 1984[16]), who dismiss the Documentary Hypothesis as a whole (not just E). While all the above-mentioned scholars may represent different paradigms and schools of scholarly endeavor, they all agree on E's non-existence and dismiss the names of the Deity as a valid criterion for distinguishing between sources.

Scholars did not abandon the elohistic source *en masse*, and even today there are a fair number of "backward" scholars who continue to defend it. The researchers who believe in the existence of the elohistic source can be divided into two groups. The first and more conservative group accept the standard version of the Documentary Hypothesis and attempt to defend Wellhausen's fundamental assertions. Members of this group include Wolff,[17] Jenks,[18] McEvenue,[19] Coote[20] and Graupner.[21] The most conservative among them, such as McEvenue, still emphasize language and stylistic indicators in their divisions and refuse to abandon or modify Welhausen's axioms. Most of these researchers do, however, concede somewhat to detractors and thus the "new E" is often streamlined to exclude ostensibly dubious assignments. Thus among the most recent Documentary scholars there is rarely an elohistic plague narrative,[22] and the prophetic texts in Num. 11-12 attributed to E by previous generations of scholars disappear from the newer reconstructions of this corpus (Graupner 2002). The revelation of Yhwh in Ex. 3:13-15 in the early reconstructions of E is also reconsidered by some modern day advocates of the Documentary Hypothesis.

Less conservative scholars responded to the challenge by more radical redefinitions of the elohistic source. The first of the four exegetes to whom I shall refer is Weisman[23] who, in his book *From Jacob to Israel*, sought to prove that the elohistic source is the earliest stratum, at least

---

14 J. Van Seters, Prologue to History: The Yahwist as Historian in Genesis, Louisvile, Kentucky, 1992.

15 R. Rendtorff, *Die Überlieferungsgeschichtliche Probleme des Pentateuch* (BZAW 147), Berlin, 1977.

16 E. Blum, *Die Komposition der Vätergeschichte* (WMANT 57), Neukirchen –Vluyn, 1984.

17 H. W. Wolff, The Elohistic Fragments in the Pentateuch, *Interpretation* 26 (1972): 158-173.

18 A. W. Jenks, *The Elohist and North Israelite Traditions* (SBLMS 22), Missoula, 1977.

19 S. E. McEvenue, The Elohist at Work, *ZAW* 96 (1984): 315-332.

20 R. C. Coote, *In Defense of Revolution: The Elohist History*, Minneapolis, 1991.

21 A. Graupner, *Der Elohist: Gegenwart und Wirksamkeit des transzendenten Gottes in der Geschichte* (WMANT 97), Neukirchen-Vluyn, 2002.

22 F. Kohata, *Jahwist und Priesterschrift in Ex. 3-14* (BZAW 166), Berlin, 1986.

23 Z. Weisman, *From Jacob to Israel* (Hebrew), Jerusalem, 1986.

in the Jacob cycle, this Israeli scholar makes use of Tuch's old Supplementary Hypothesis and claims that the elohistic source was edited by the Yahwist, who had also added most of the Abraham and Isaac narrative cycles. A similar hypothesis was advanced by Lubsczyk[24] in a theoretical article which to the best of my knowledge was not elaborated upon by either himself or others. While one may disagree with both these scholars on their "extreme" opinions regarding the date of E's compilation (the late second millennium B.C.E.), these opinions do, however, offer an important theoretical alternative, independent of the classic "Documentary" paradigm.

According to Weisman, the Elohist was "edited" by a yahwistic source, but according to Schmitt, the elohistic source was the "editor" of yahwistic material.[25] Schmitt tries to show that the elohistic or the "Reuben" stratum of the Joseph cycle (Gen. 37-50) is an editorial layer added to earlier yahwistic material. This hypothesis partially accepts Volz, Rudolph and Mowinckel's criticism (which claimed that E was no more than an addendum to J), but still speaks of E in terms of authorship and source. Following in his teacher's footsteps, Schmitt's student Zimmer[26] attempts to prove that E was the editor of J throughout the Pentateuch (focusing on Gen. 20-22).[27] Zimmer claims that the Elohist was an editor/theologian who added a stratum of prophecy and "hokhmah" (wisdom) to the base narrative. According to Zimmer, the Elohist was active in the final years of the Judean exile (late sixth century B.C.E). One of Zimmer's important observations (pp. 41-42), following Kohata's lead,[28] was his questioning the use of "Yhwh" by the elohistic source after Ex. 3.[29]

1.2 Ex. 3:13-15

In hindsight, the perpetual scholarly vacillation regarding the existence and non-existence of E is not surprising; it follows from the weakness of the axioms described in the opening paragraphs of this essay. How

---

24 H. Lubsczyk, Elohim beim Jahwisten, *SVT* 29, 1978, 226-253.
25 H. C Schmitt, *Die Nichtpriestliche Josephgeschichte* (BZAW 155), Berlin, 1980.
26 F. Zimmer, *Der Elohist als weisheitlich-prophetische Redaktionsschicht: Eine literarische theologiegeschichtliche Untersuchung der sogenannten elohistischen Texte im Pentateuch,* (European University Studies, Series 12, Vol. 656), Frankfurt, 1999.
27 Ch. Levin, *Der Jahwist* (FRLANT 157), Göttingen, 1993, p. 173ff also argues that Gen. 20-22 should be considered distinct though his reconstruction differs radically.
28 F. Kohata, *Ex. 3-14.*
29 Graupner, *Elohist,* also accepts this contention.

can a fragmentary source which cannot be adequately isolated ever stand the test of scholarship? If E's vocabulary and style are unique, why can we not use them to divide texts after Ex. 3? Scholars may have attempted to isolate this source after Ex. 3, but the lack of strict criteria for its determination resulted in diverse opinions with little to recommend one over another. In my opinion, E can be successfully divided and isolated. Serious reconsideration of opinions hitherto almost completely abandoned by scholarship, such as Dillmann's position on E's antiquity and Tuch's supplementary approach, allows us—when applied consistently—to uncover the literarily coherent elohistic text. As one of the most important windows to this corpus, the "hallowed" contention regarding E's use of Yhwh after Ex. 3 must be re-examined.

One of the few common denominators of scholars who dismiss the Documentary approach is the abandonment of the names of the Deity as a valid marker of source division. Rather than stemming from any inherent weakness in the theory itself this abandonment is, in my opinion, no more than a backlash response to the careless and inconsistent use of the indicator. According to the Documentary Hypothesis, there are two sources in Genesis which use the name "Elohim"—E and P—which with few exceptions aid in dividing elohistic and priestly texts from the surrounding J material. Ex. 3 marks the turning point where, according to Wellhausen (*et al.*), E begins to use Yhwh. In view of the sharp criticism of this hypothesis, I maintain that it is simply untenable.

There are three verses (Ex. 3:13-15) which, according to most source theorists, describe the elohistic revelation of the Deity's special name: "But Moses said to God, 'If I come to the Israelites and say to them, "The God of your ancestors has sent me to you," and they ask me, "What is his name?" what shall I say to them?' God said to Moses, 'I AM WHO I AM.' He said further, 'Thus you shall say to the Israelites, "I AM has sent me to you" God also said to Moses, 'Thus you shall say to the Israelites, "The LORD, the God of your ancestors, the God of Abraham, the God of Isaac, and the God of Jacob, has sent me to you": This is my name forever, and this my title for all generations'."

These verses have the distinction of being among the best researched verses of the Bible. Much of the scholarship is devoted to the etymology of the name "Yhwh" (verse 15) and its connection to the root "היה" (to be) which appears three times in verse 13 in the imperfect ("אהיה"). These verses are also at the crux of the disagreement regarding the names of the Deity as a valid criterion for division between biblical texts and sources. One of the strongest claims against the standard opinion is that of Cassuto who points out:[30] "It is precisely in these verses, which are regarded as incontrovertible proof of the existence of an elohistic source according to which the Tetragrammaton was not known to the patriarchs, that it is specifically written (verse 15): Yhwh the God of your fathers *the God of Abraham, the God of Isaac and the God of Jacob.*" Cassuto considers the critical solution which suggests the involvement of a redactor in this verse as "an answer of despair". Indeed, how can one of the cornerstones of source division rely on a redacted verse or verses? As Cassuto's observation indicates (although he himself would never have agreed) *the whole* of verse 15 exhibits all the signs of being secondary: a) It contradicts vs. 13-14, which clearly state that the name of the Deity is "ehyeh"; b) It nevertheless assumes knowledge of the previous verses by its use of the word "עוד" (translated "moreover"); c) Together with verse 16 ("Go and assemble the Elders of Israel, and say to them, 'The LORD, the God of your ancestors, the God of Abraham, of Isaac, and of Jacob, has appeared to me, saying: I have given heed to you and to what has been done to you in Egypt"), a clear redactional theme is apparent, namely, the introduction of the idea of "Yhwh" into the base narrative of Exodus. This was deemed necessary by the J redactor since the purpose of the plague narrative is to ensure Yhwh's fame and glory throughout the land.

What of the similarity in sound and letters of "Yhwh" and the elohistic "Ehyeh" (translated above as "I am")? In this case I must agree with Propp[31] who claims that this similarity has been overstressed. The name "Ehyeh," in my opinion, is simply a play on God's promise in verse 11: "כי אהיה עמך" ("I will be with you.") The absence of an original elohistic assertion regarding the change of names, and the fact that coherent elohistic episodes can be isolated in Ex. 3 and subsequently (in Ex. 18, 19, 20) which exclusively employ the name Elohim (*cf.* the classic divisions of McNeile[32] and Driver[33]), lead us to conclude that E's exclusive name for the Deity was "Elohim" throughout the whole of the Elohistic corpus.

An apparent weakness of this conclusion is the ostensible fragmentary state of the E source, if one posits the exclusive use of Elohim. Indeed, I hope to demonstrate that E is not fragmentary, but rather that

---

30   U. Cassuto, *A Commentary on the Book of Exodus* (I. Abrahams tr.), Jerusalem, 1967, 40.

31   W. H. C. Propp, *Exodus 1-18, A New Translation with Introduction and Commentary* (Anchor Bible), New York, 1998, 224-226.

32   *The Book of Exodus with Introduction and Notes* (Westminster Commentaries), London, 1908.

33   *The Book of Exodus with Introduction and Notes* (The Cambridge Bible for Schools and Colleges), Cambridge, 1953.

the elohistic source has its own unity as a group of story cycles centered around important Israelite figures.

1.3 E as the Basic Source

The standard Documentary theory *à la* Wellhausen consistently dates E after J, relying on such criteria as the decreased anthropomorphism in E (revelation by dreams) in comparison to J. This line of reasoning is, however, based largely on the outdated Hegelian history of ideas. In reality many ideas have cycles. Daniel's visions, that of Trito-Isaiah who addresses God as a warrior (Isaiah chs. 59, 63), and Zachariah's vision of the end of days are certainly more anthropomorphic than E's revelation by dreams. Other chronological schemes were proposed relatively early on in the history of biblical scholarship. Dillmann, for example, reverses the order (putting E before J) and even Skinner (who accepts Wellhausen's chronology) concedes (in his foreword) that it is hard to decide one way or the other and concludes that E is closer than J to the "preliterary stage."

The fact of the matter is that I have not found even one instance where it can clearly be shown that the Elohist is a redactor of J (despite Zimmer's contention of its lateness). On the other hand, I have on any number of occasions found a yahwistic source redacting E: The binding of Isaac, Jacob's ladder, Jethro's meeting, to name but a few. According to the standard Documentary Hypothesis this source is usually JE (the text of the combined J and E sources) or RJE (the redactor who combined the J and E documents). There is, however, no need to resort to questionable sources whose main discernible purpose is to "label" non-attributable passages. In my opinion, these "difficult" passages can be successfully divided. The reason for the failure of scholars to do so hitherto is due to the flawed Documentary methodology, which in many cases was forced upon the text even when it was not appropriate and was further weakened by the inconsistent use of distinguishing criteria.

The following is one example of the superfluity of this supposed RJE source. I accept (more or less) the Documentary division of Gen. 28:10-20 (Jacob's ladder) between J and E, whereby the divine promises and the change of name (Luz to Bethel) are attributed to a late J, while the general revelation and Jacob's oath are attributed to an earlier E. The legitimate question that thus arises is: What difference is there between the Yahwist in this passage and the acknowledged redactional layer of Gen. 22 (Gen. 22:15-18) which exhibits the same characteristics—promises to the fathers—and is usually attributed to RJE? One of my contentions throughout this work is that there is no difference between the early J and the late RJE and that they are in fact one and the same.

1.4 J: Source or Redaction Layer?

In the introduction to his book, Schmitt[34] emphasizes that one of the main problems in critical Bible studies is the differentiation between a source and a redactional layer. In my opinion, Wagner,[35] Dozeman[36] and Van Seters[37] were correct when they postulated that J (or "the pre-priestly redactional layer") was both a source and a redactor. In other words, I propose that a full base elohistic text was supplemented by J. The supplementary approach negates the need to isolate two or three independent and parallel strands: It posits only one base text, thus avoiding one of the major pitfalls of the Documentary Hypothesis. The independent and parallel versions of the documents are often "found" only with great difficulty, after uncalled for manipulation of the text, and more often than not are incomplete. Examples of this faulty Documentary analysis abound, but at this juncture one shall suffice: The birth of Jacob's sons as recounted by Gen. 29-31 is usually divided amongst two sources J and E, based upon the variance of divine names. It is, however, impossible to separate two independent narratives, and if we accept the Documentary division we are left with two very incomplete strands which do not make sense on their own. In contrast, the supplementary analysis of this episode yields highly satisfactory results, and see our analysis below in Chapter 5.

1.5 J and the Divine Sobriquets

As a source, J shows a clear preference for the name Yahweh (Yhwh). However, due to the fact that J is also the editor of E, this source occasionally uses other appellations because of its need to integrate its own

---

34   Schmitt, *Joseph*, 7.

35   N. Wagner, A Response to Professor Rolf Rendtorff, *JSOT* 3 (1977): 57-63.

36   T. Dozeman, *God on the Mountain* (The Society of Biblical Literature Monograph Series), Atlanta, 1989.

37   In his prologue to Genesis in 1992, and in many previous and subsequent scholarly works listed in the Bibliography and throughout this work.

traditions into the existing texts. The use of variant names is noticeable in the yahwistic sections of Gen. 2-6, where the Deity is usually called "Yhwh Elohim" (in English, "the Lord God") e.g. "Then the LORD God formed man from the dust of the ground." After these chapters there are few exceptions to this source's "yahwism." (Appellations such as "El Olam," "El Elyon" and "El Ro'i" are commonly understood as aspects of "Yhwh.") The reason for the variety in the first few chapters of the Pentateuch is the Yahwist's clear desire to identify the specific God of the Israelites with the more general "Elohim" at the beginning of all things. There are other exceptions (to the exclusive use of Yhwh). One is, J's Ex. 3:15 "God (Elohim) also said to Moses, 'Thus you shall say to the Israelites, "The LORD (Yhwh), the God of your ancestors, the God of Abraham, the God of Isaac, and the God of Jacob'"'" (explicated above); Another is Joseph's appeal to Potiphar's wife in Gen. 39:9: "How then could I do this great wickedness, and sin against God (Elohim)?," where the assumption is that the Egyptian woman would not recognize a Hebrew God, much like her fellow Egyptian, Pharaoh, who declares "Who is the LORD (Yhwh), that I should heed him and let Israel go? I do not know the LORD (Yhwh), and I will not let Israel go" (Ex. 5:2).

1.6 J as an Editor

A popular objection to the critical analysis of the Pentateuch is as follows: If the Torah was written and edited by different groups of editors, why did they leave the repetitions and the contradictions intact? One could very well explain that in the ancient Near-East there was a more forgiving attitude towards textual inconsistencies than there is today, and thus editors would not necessarily be bothered by the obvious presence of more than one source. My hypothesis, however, provides a much simpler answer, at least for the texts in question. Even at a glance one can discern that the Yahwist was a very conservative editor, willing to live with obvious textual inconsistencies. The reason for this may well have been the "holiness" he attributed to the inherited text he was editing. After all, he considered it to be the written word of God and as such held it in high regard. The question is precisely how far the Yahwist's esteem extended. If, as I contend, the complete elohistic source was preserved, it would indicate that the Yahwist did not allow himself to delete or edit out any detail of the basic document, restricting himself to supplementation. The alternative solution would be to assume that the yahwistic editor did delete some of the details, but left behind enough of E so that when the process was reversed, as in this study, the basic document isolated still "looked" complete. This type of solution is in many ways weak; firstly, it assumes an editorial process that cannot be documented, and secondly, a simple and more elegant solution is preferable. My hypothesis is neither "mystical" as some would contend, nor a religious justification for biblical criticism. Rather it claims to be the simplest explanation for the facts at hand.

If the Yahwist is restricted to supplementation, what happens when the conservative editor does not agree with his predecessor? Literary history suggests two main options. The first is writing a separate text. As examples of such a process one might consider the book of Deuteronomy, the Temple Scroll, or the book of Jubilees. The second option is inserting one's own point of view into the actual text, as was done by many medieval exegetes in reference to the Babylonian Talmud (see Rabeinu Tam's introduction to Sefer Hayashar). The Yahwist chose the second option. When the Yahwist did not agree with the Elohist, he inserted his opinion into the text, and in order to ensure that his version of the story was the one that readers ultimately accepted, he reiterated and emphasized his agenda in as many ways and as many times as possible. This type of reiteration is but one of the effective editorial techniques employed by the Yahwist. A more thorough examination of this phenomenon is found in the verse by verse analyses.

While I claim that the Yahwist's role is that of a supplementary editor, it is important to emphasize that he was more than that. Like his predecessor the Elohist, the Yahwist had independent traditions at his disposal which he then integrated into his works. Indeed, one of the main reasons the southern Yahwist edited the northern Elohist was the desire to create a single historical document which was also relevant to a Judean audience. In this study I shall focus only on the editorial facet of the Yahwist's work.

1.7 The Bridger

In his seminal examination of the Joseph cycle, Donald Redford posits a final Genesis Redactor, to whom he attributes the latest sections of the book, such as Chapter 38.[38] Rendtorrf[39] also speaks of this final redactor

---

38   D. B. Redford, *A Study of the Biblical Story of Joseph*, SVT 20, Leiden, 1970.

in his analyses of bridging passages such as the concluding verses of the book of Genesis, which bridge between family and nation, exodus and eisodos, and connect the book of Genesis to the Exodus - Numbers complexes and beyond. In my website, www.biblecriticism.com, I refer to this Genesis Redactor as "B" – the Bridger.

A good starting point for the delineation of the B source in the present context is Wenham's intriguing contention of a late J layer in the genealogy of Noah's sons in Gen. 10.[40] The redactional layer is very apparent: While all the original priestly material uses the formula "and the sons of X were," the late redactional layer uses the formula "and "X gave birth to," using יָלַד or יֵלֶד (to give birth) in the qal and the qal passive, as opposed to the regular priestly formulae "הוֹלִיד" and "יִוָּלֵד" (also to give birth) in the nifal and the hifil as found in the unsupplemented lists of Gen. 5, 10 and 11. Wenham's atypical attribution of this redactional stratum to a late J is unlikely, however, and an acknowledged post-priestly source (such as Redford's Genesis Editor) is more probable. An examination of similar non-priestly genealogies helps widen the circle of texts that may be attributed to this author.

The same type of formula (יָלַד / יֵלֶד) is found at the end of Gen. 4 in the short genealogy through Seth. This account (two verses) is cognizant both of the previous narrative (the death of Abel is alluded to) and the subsequent priestly genealogy in Gen. 5 (Adam, Seth, Enosh) and thus (with consideration of its similarity to the post-priestly layer of Gen. 10) is later than both the P list and the J narrative. The same type of formulae are found in the genealogy at the end of Gen. 22, which functions as a bridge between the account of Isaac's binding and the search for Isaac's wife in Gen. 24, in the list of Jacob's descendants in Gen. 46, and in the account of the daughters of man marrying the sons of God in Gen. 6.

Upon examination of these texts one notices the Bridger's ties to ancient non-Israelite myths, such as the Nimrod legend in Gen. 10, the addition of names in order to arrive at the traditional number of seventy nations (echoed in Gen. 46, where the Bridger arrives at seventy Israelite descendants), as well as in the legend of the sons of God in Gen. 6. Perhaps one may conjecture that late texts, such as Abraham defeating five kings with 318 soldiers, or Balaam talking to his donkey (Num. 22), or the legends regarding the previous inhabitants of Canaan (Deut. 2-3), which are all relatively late textually and share a non-

---

39   Rendtorff, *Überlieferung*, 77.
40   G. Wenham, The Priority of P, *VT* 49 (1999): 240-248.

Israelite mythic element rarely found in biblical narrative, were added
to the Pentateuchal fabric by this author.

I have consciously chosen to refrain from anything but approximate
and relative dating of the Pentateuchal sources discussed in this work,
instead relying upon both textual relationships and ideas which were
not very time specific. All I can say about the B source in terms of date
of composition is that it was later than H (the late priestly author),
which is considered by many to be exilic.

I am aware that this short discussion does not qualify as a valid introduction to this redactional stratum. Since many biblical scholars,
however, have referred to similar entities and have attributed some of
the same material to these entities, I feel justified in presenting only a
short sketch of this redactional stratum and in drawing attention to
some of its features which have not previously received attention in
scholarship.

1.8 The New Fragmentary Hypothesis

European scholars responded to Rolf Rendtorff's call (put forth in his
seminal work *Der Überlieferungsgeschichtliche Problem des Pentateuch*,
1977) to examine the evolution of Pentateuchal narrative from the ker-
nels to the entire work without the *a priori* assumption of independent
documents. Such an examination was begun to a certain degree by
Gunkel and especially by Gressmann, who referred to the non-priestly
sources of the Tetrateuch as tags that could be exchanged at will, thus
largely freeing them to engage in the evolution and relative chronology
of Pentateuchal traditions.

Thirty-four years later many scholars have reached very similar
general conclusions, though there is significant divergence in the details among members of what we shall term the tradition cycle school.[41]
It is generally agreed that patriarchal traditions evolved independently
of the Exodus traditions and were connected only at a relatively late
date by priestly and post-priestly authors.[42] The patriarchal traditions
of Abraham, Jacob and Joseph were also independent of one another at
their earliest stages of literary composition, as was the earliest account

---

41 It is generally referred to as the fragmentary hypothesis, which I view as inaccurate
    and somewhat dismissive terminology.
42 See especially, J. Ch. Gertz, *Tradition und Redaktion in der Exoduserzählung: Unter-
    suchungen zur Endredaktion des Pentateuch*, FRLANT 186, Göttingen, 2000; K.
    Schmid, *Erzväter und Exodus : Untersuchungen zur doppelten Begründung der Ursprünge
    Israels innerhalb der Geschichtsbücher des Alten Testaments* (WMANT 81), 1999.

of the primeval history.[43] One of the primary redactional means by which these separate tradition complexes were connected (the patriarchal tradition complexes to one another and then to the Exodus complex) is the promises to the patriarchs added to the text in a number of phases. (The number varies among the proponents of the theories).[44] This theory of evolution uses some of the same nomenclature as the Documentary Hypothesis. Priestly and Deuteronomistic redactors are among the later redactors referred to, though they completely dismiss the earlier non-priestly sources J and E.[45]

Although the above critics do not use the tags J and E, there is actually much in common between the supplementary theory I present in this book and the basic scheme of development outlined in Blum's *Vätergeschichte*. We both accept Weisman's conclusions that the basic Jacob-Joseph complexes are the earliest sections of Genesis (Weisman calls these sections E) and that the majority of the Abraham complex (which Weisman calls J) is relatively later. We both see the promises to the patriarchs as a relatively late addition to pentateuchal texts (although Blum argues for many more stages of development than I do). This stems from an even more basic agreement. Blum and I all accept supplementation or redaction criticism as one of the main ways, if not the main way, in which the Pentateuch developed.

It is, however, difficult to argue the specifics of a source theory with scholars who do not accept the theories' postulates. To put it in the context of this book, it is futile to argue about what verses should be attributed to E with someone who does not accept the existence of E, or even the existence of pentateuchal sources. A meaningful dialogue can occur between members of competing schools of pentateuchal evolution only at the level of basic assumptions and methodology.

David Carr, which in some ways is the American representative of of this growing school, provides the groundwork for such a dialogue in his groundbreaking work: *The Fractures of Genesis*. He begins his discussion by recapitulating what constitutes a textual fracture indicating plurality of authorship. While this may seem very basic, it helps to create a common framework within which scholars who subscribe to divergent paradigms can conduct a fruitful dialogue. While I may

---

43 D. Carr, *Reading the Fractures of Genesis*, Louisville, Kentucky, 1996.
44 In a relatively recent discussion Blum presents some of these layers in the promise text of Gen. 28:10-22: E. Blum, Noch Einmal; Jakobs Traum in Bethel Gen. 28, 10-22, in *Rethinking the Foundations: Historiography in the Ancient World and in the Bible, Essays in Honor of John Van Seters* (S. L. McKenzie, T. Roemer and H. H. Schmid eds.), 2000, 33-54.
45 Blum 1984, refers to these redactors as KD and KP.

not be able to discuss with Carr whether a specific verse is attributable to E and the next to J, I can argue with him whether the divergence that led me to make the distinction is a valid one. This is no small feat and can also help to distinguish between more and less speculative scholarship. Throughout this book my main interaction with tradition cycle critics and others who do not accept source criticism will be at this level.

There are three other areas where I will engage proponents of the new non-documentarians both in this introduction and throughout this work:

1. Their dismissal of the names of the Deity as valid "textual fractures" indicating plurality of authorship.

2. The promises to the patriarchs as a redactional stratum.

3. The ties between the patriarchal traditions and the books of Exodus-Numbers.

1. The dismissal of the names of the Deity as valid textual fractures

A major point of divergence between source critics and the proponents of this tradition cycle hypothesis, is the latter's disregard of the names of the Deity as indicative of textual plurality. I submit that the onus of proving this criterion's irrelevance is upon the tradition cycle critics, since the names Elohim and Yhwh themselves are indicative of different ideas —generality versus specificity—and thus only if one can demonstrate that this divergence is not implied within the texts that use these different names can one conclusively dismiss this criterion. No such rigorous demonstration is made by tradition cycle critics. They, too frequently, rely on the breaches and inconsistent use of this criterion within the Documentary Hypothesis, and thus do not seriously engage this fundamental criterion upon which biblical criticism was founded. The present work applies a new rigor to this distinction and shows how even today, new insight may be gained into the text by its consistent use. See especially my analysis of the Birth of Jacob's children in Gen. 29-30, and the chapter on the Balaam cycle, which provides a sufficient response.

By way of example, one instance of critical dismissiveness may be cited. David Carr goes so far as to admit that there is a definite preference in Gen. 20-22 for the name "Elohim". However, he dismisses this finding, as inconsequential, since he regards these chapters as narratively indistinguishable from Gen. 12-19, which share so many of the same characters, themes and ideas.[46] Carr does not note that one more important feature distinguishes this group of chapters from the rest of the Abraham complex. The promises to the patriarchs are a secondary feature in these texts, as I shall show. According to the logic of the tradition cycle critics, after peeling away the layers of promises one should arrive at the earliest layer of text. I hope to demonstrate in Chapter 3 that this layer is part of the larger E corpus

2. The Promises to the Patriarchs

There is little doubt among scholars that the promises to the patriarchs are occasionally inserted into the texts of Genesis and Exodus. The question is whether they are the glue that binds the tradition complexes together, whether a number of phases of promises are to be discerned and whether the promises are always secondary. Often the promises fit their narrative contexts quite well and the fracture between them and the rest of the narrative is slight or even indiscernible. For example, the promises that Abraham's progeny shall be abundant (a valid interpretation of Gen. 12:2-3) if he follows the Deity's command (12:1) and that they shall inherit the land (Gen. 12:7) are integral to the text of this chapter and separating them would harm the narrative fabric. These two basic promises and the fact that they are dependent upon Abraham's compliance (if Abraham had not heeded the Lord's call, the Lord would not have promised him the land) characterize the vast majority of this genre. The fact that there are numerous variations upon these themes is often indicative of the context in which they exist rather than redactional strata. I will address this further when promises arise in the course of my presentation of E.

3. The Exodus Tradition

One may legitimately ask whether the connections between Genesis and Exodus exist without the patriarchal promises and the priestly and post-priestly redactional layers. While the answer given by tradition cycle critics is a resounding "No," I submit that this answer is not as

---

46   Carr, *Fractures*, 197.

unequivocal as these critics claim. Israel (according to E) arrived in Egypt to live there after a famine, the sons of Israel attempt to leave many years later, Israel lived and traveled in the trans-Jordan and northern Israel, in Num. 21 this is where they return to—a very natural narrative progression which does not necessitate further reinforcement. Elohim promised a descent to Egypt and also a return in 46:1-5. Is this not what occurs? Do we have any right to expect constant reinforcement of narrative connections in the terse pre-priestly narrative complexes?

A more general problem is that very plainly Exodus is not a story of origins. It presupposes a national entity referred to as Israel, but what is Israel, from whence did the nation spring, who were its founding fathers? It is very difficult to read Exodus-Numbers as anything but an advanced chapter in a tale at least partially told. As early as the mid-eighth century the prophet Hosea connected between Jacob and Moses who led the Israelites out of Egypt: 12:12: "Jacob fled to the land of Aram; there Israel served for a wife, and for a wife he guarded sheep. By a prophet the LORD brought Israel up from Egypt, and by a prophet he was guarded."

One could conveniently relegate these verses to a late anonymous redactor, though this section seems to be quite organic to Hosea's prophecy, who wishes to relate the Israelites misdeeds and present circumstances to the history of their ancestors. What Hosea is demonstrating is the very organic logical and literary connection between the patriarchal period and the Egyptian period. If the story of the Israelites began in Canaan and continued in Egypt how else could it have been told? The Israelites come as a family group, time passes they become something more than a family group and concurrently their relationship with the Egyptians changes, how could this have been related without the unevenness between family and nation, and the positive and negative Egyptian attitudes?

This topic will be further discussed in our examination of the first unit of the book of Exodus, which is at the crux of the tradition cycle critics' argument.

1.9 Conclusion

In an article defending the existence of the elohistic source published in 1976, Wolff concludes with the query: "May we not be missing the deepest secret of our lives if we fail to meet the challenge of the Elohist?" In accordance with his implied enthusiastic recommendation, and contrary to popular scholarly opinion ,my own research has led me to posit the literary, thematic and structural unity of the E source. Proof will be provided by means of a systematic examination of the entire Tetrateuch and the isolation of its elohistic material. At the same time I shall seek to demonstrate how the yahwistic source edited and supplemented the elohistic source. Throughout this work, various opinions and paradigms will be critically examined and the advantages of the Supplementary Hypothesis will be demonstrated.

It is impossible to relate to every paradigm and every scholar or even to a majority of them, desirable as this may seem. I have therefore concentrated my efforts on various versions of the Documentary and Supplementary hypotheses, with which I have a common dialogue, and have limited the dialogue with tradition cycle critics which I hope to engage on my website www.biblecriticism.com in the near future.

2. The Book of E

Note: The E source will be presented verse by verse. The translation of the Hebrew follows the NRSV with slight variations. NRSV translates Yhwh as the LORD, and Elohim as God. In the discussion, the English and Hebrew terms are used interchangeably.

Key to the texts

(-)	Words missing from the verse
(+)	Words added or changed
(+ -)	Words added or changed and words missing from the verse
a	Only the first part of the verse appears
b	Only the second part of the verse appears
a(-)	Words missing from the first part of the verse
b(-)	Words missing from the second part of the verse
[_]	Words added for clarity
(_)	Possibly part of the text

2.1 The Abraham Cycle

Abraham and Sarah's Sojourn in Gerar (Gen. 20)

20:1(-) Abraham journeyed toward the region of the Negeb, and settled between Kadesh and Shur. While residing in Gerar as an alien, 2 Abraham said of his wife Sarah, "She is my sister." And King Abimelech of Gerar sent and took Sarah. 3 But God came to Abimelech in a dream by night, and said to him, "You are about to die because of the woman whom you have taken; for she is a married woman. 7 Now then, return the man's wife; for he is a prophet, and he will pray for you and you shall live. But if you do not restore her, know that you shall surely die, you and all that are yours."8 So Abimelech rose early in the morning, and called all his servants and told them all these things; and the men were very much afraid.10 And Abimelech said to Abraham, "What were you thinking of, that you did this thing?"11 Abraham said, "I did it because I thought, There is no fear of God at all in this place, and they will kill me because of my wife. 14(-) Then Abimelech restored Abraham's wife Sarah to him. 15 Abimelech said, "My land is before you; settle where it pleases you." 17 Abraham prayed to God; and God healed Abimelech and also healed his wife and female slaves so that they bore children.

The Birth of Isaac (Gen. 21)

21:2a Sarah conceived and bore Abraham a son in his old age 3(-) Abraham gave the name Isaac to his son whom Sarah bore him. 6 Now Sarah said, "God has brought laughter for me; everyone who hears will laugh with me." 7 And she said, "Who would ever have said to Abraham that Sarah would nurse children? Yet I have borne him a son in his old age." 8 The child grew, and was weaned; and Abraham made a great feast on the day that Isaac was weaned.

The Banishment of Hagar's Son (Gen. 21)

9 But Sarah saw the son of Hagar the Egyptian, whom she had borne to Abraham, playing with her son Isaac. 10 So she said to Abraham, "Cast out this slave woman with her son; for the son of this slave woman shall not inherit along with my son Isaac." 11 The matter was very distressing to Abraham on account of his son. 12a But God said to

Abraham, "Do not be distressed because of the boy and because of your slave woman; whatever Sarah says to you, do as she tells you." 14 So Abraham rose early in the morning, and took bread and a skin of water, and gave it to Hagar, putting it on her shoulder, along with the child, and sent her away. And she departed, and wandered about in the wilderness of Beer-sheba.15 When the water in the skin was gone, she cast the child under one of the bushes. 16 Then she went and sat down opposite him a good way off, about the distance of a bowshot; for she said, "Do not let me look on the death of the child." And as she sat opposite him, she lifted up her voice and wept. 17 And God heard the voice of the boy; and the angel of God called to Hagar from heaven, and said to her, "What troubles you, Hagar? Do not be afraid; for God has heard the voice of the boy where he is." 19 Then God opened her eyes and she saw a well of water. She went, and filled the skin with water, and gave the boy a drink. 20 God was with the boy, and he grew up; he lived in the wilderness, and became an expert with the bow. 21 He lived in the wilderness of Paran; and his mother got a wife for him from the land of Egypt.

The Agreement Between Abraham and Abimelech (Gen. 21)

22(-) At that time Abimelech, said to Abraham, "God is with you in all that you do; 23 now therefore swear to me here by God that you will not deal falsely with me or with my offspring or with my posterity, but as I have dealt loyally with you, you will deal with me and with the land where you have resided as an alien." 24 And Abraham said, "I swear it." 25 When Abraham complained to Abimelech about a well of water that Abimelech's servants had seized, 26 Abimelech said, "I do not know who has done this; you did not tell me, and I have not heard of it until today." 28 Abraham set apart seven ewe lambs of the flock. 29 And Abimelech said to Abraham, "What is the meaning of these seven ewe lambs that you have set apart?" 30 He said, "These seven ewe lambs you shall accept from my hand, in order that you may be a witness for me that I dug this well." 31a Therefore that place was called Beer-sheba;

The Sacrifice of Isaac (Gen. 22)

22:1 After these things God tested Abraham. He said to him, "Abraham!" And he said, "Here I am." 2 He said, "Take your son, your only son Isaac, whom you love, and go to the land of Moriah, and offer him there as a burnt offering on one of the mountains that I shall show you." 3 So Abraham rose early in the morning, saddled his donkey, and took two of his young men with him, and his son Isaac; he cut the wood for the burnt offering, and set out and went to the place in the distance that God had shown him. 4 On the third day Abraham looked up and saw the place far away. 5 Then Abraham said to his young men, "Stay here with the donkey; the boy and I will go over there; we will worship, and then we will come back to you." 6 Abraham took the wood of the burnt offering and laid it on his son Isaac, and he himself carried the fire and the knife. So the two of them walked on together. 7 Isaac said to his father Abraham, "Father!" And he said, "Here I am, my son." He said, "The fire and the wood are here, but where is the lamb for a burnt offering?" 8 Abraham said, "God himself will provide the lamb for a burnt offering, my son." So the two of them walked on together. 9 When they came to the place that God had shown him, Abraham built an altar there and laid the wood in order. He bound his son Isaac, and laid him on the altar, on top of the wood. 10 Then Abraham reached out his hand and took the knife to kill his son (and he killed his son). 11 The angel of God called to him from heaven, and said, "Abraham, Abraham!" And he said, "Here I am." 12(-) He said, "Now I know that you fear God, since you have not withheld your son, your only son, from me." 19 So Abraham returned to his young men, and they arose and went together to Beer-sheba; and Abraham lived at Beer-sheba.

2.2 The Jacob Cycle

Jacob in Bethel (Gen. 28)

10a Jacob left Beer-sheba. 11 He came to a certain place and stayed there for the night, because the sun had set. Taking one of the stones of the place, he put it under his head and lay down in that place. 12 And he dreamed that there was a ladder set up on the earth, the top of it reaching to heaven; and the angels of God were ascending and descending on it. 17 And he was afraid, and said, "How awesome is this place! This is none other than the house of God, and this is the gate of heaven."18 So Jacob rose early in the morning, and he took the stone that he had put under his head and set it up for a pillar and poured oil on the top of it. 19a He called that place Bethel; 20 Then Jacob made a vow, saying, "If God will be with me, and will keep me in this way that

I go, and will give me bread to eat and clothing to wear, 21a so that I come again to my father's house in peace, 22 this stone, which I have set up for a pillar, shall be God's house; and of all that you give me I will surely give one tenth to you."

The Meeting by the Well (Gen. 29)

29:1 Then Jacob went on his journey, and came to the land of the people of the east. 2 As he looked, he saw a well in the field and three flocks of sheep lying there beside it; for out of that well the flocks were watered. The stone on the well's mouth was large,.4a(-) Jacob said to them (the shepherds), 7(-)"Look, it is still broad daylight; it is not time for the animals to be gathered together. Water the sheep, and go, pasture them." 8 But they said, "We cannot until all the flocks are gathered together, and the stone is rolled from the mouth of the well; then we water the sheep."9 While he was still speaking with them, Rachel came with her father's sheep; for she kept them. 10(-) Now when Jacob saw Rachel, and the sheep, Jacob went up and rolled the stone from the well's mouth, and watered the flock. 11 Then Jacob kissed Rachel, and wept aloud. 12(-) And Jacob told Rachel that he was her father's kinsman, and she ran and told her father.13a(-) When Laban heard the news about Jacob, he ran to meet him; he embraced him and kissed him, and brought him to his house.

Jacob and the Daughters of Laban (Gen. 29)

15 Then Laban said to Jacob, "Because you are my kinsman, should you therefore serve me for nothing? Tell me, what shall your wages be?" 16 Now Laban had two daughters; the name of the elder was Leah, and the name of the younger was Rachel. 18 Jacob loved Rachel; so he said, "I will serve you seven years for your younger daughter Rachel." 19 Laban said, "It is better that I give her to you than that I should give her to any other man; stay with me." 20 So Jacob served seven years for Rachel, and they seemed to him but a few days because of the love he had for her.21 Then Jacob said to Laban, "Give me my wife that I may go in to her, for my time is completed." 22 So Laban gathered together all the people of the place, and made a feast. 23 But in the evening he took his daughter Leah and brought her to Jacob; and he went in to her. 25 When morning came, it was Leah! And Jacob said to Laban, "What is this you have done to me? Did I not serve with you for Rachel? Why

then have you deceived me?" 26 Laban said, "This is not done in our country—giving the younger before the firstborn. 27 Complete the week of this one, and we will give you the other also in return for serving me another seven years." 28 Jacob did so, and completed her week; then Laban gave him his daughter Rachel as a wife. 30 So Jacob went in to Rachel also, and he loved Rachel more than Leah. He served Laban for another seven years.

The Birth of Jacob's Sons (Gen. 29-30)

29:32(-) Leah conceived and bore a son, and she named him Reuben; for she said, "surely now my husband will love me." 30:1 When Rachel saw that she bore Jacob no children, she envied her sister; and she said to Jacob, "Give me children, or I shall die!" 2 Jacob became very angry with Rachel and said, "Am I in the place of God, who has withheld from you the fruit of the womb?" 3 Then she said, "Here is my maid Bilhah; go in to her, that she may bear upon my knees and that I too may have children through her." 4(-) So she gave him Bilhah as a wife; and Jacob went in to her. 5 And Bilhah conceived and bore Jacob a son. 6 Then Rachel said, "God has judged me, and has also heard my voice and given me a son"; therefore she named him Dan. 7(-) Bilhah conceived again and bore Jacob a son. 8 Then Rachel said, "With mighty wrestlings I have wrestled with my sister, and have prevailed"; so she named him Naphtali.14 In the days of wheat harvest Reuben went and found mandrakes in the field, and brought them to his mother Leah. Then Rachel said to Leah, "Please give me some of your son's mandrakes." 15 But she said to her, "Is it a small matter that you have taken away my husband? Would you take away my son's mandrakes also?" Rachel said, "Then he may lie with you tonight for your son's mandrakes." 16 When Jacob came from the field in the evening, Leah went out to meet him, and said, "You must come in to me; for I have hired you with my son's mandrakes." So he lay with her that night. 17 And God heeded Leah, and she conceived and bore Jacob a son. 18(-) Leah said, "God has given me my hire"; so she named him Issachar. 19(-) And Leah conceived again, and she bore Jacob a son. 20(-) Then Leah said, "God has endowed me with a good dowry"; so she named him Zebulun. 22 Then God remembered Rachel, and God heeded her and opened her womb. 23 She conceived and bore a son, and said, "God has taken away my reproach"; 24a(-) and she named him Joseph.

Jacob Decides to Leave Laban (Gen. 31)

4 Jacob sent and called Rachel and Leah into the field where his flock was, 5a and said to them, "I see that your father does not regard me as favorably as he did before. 6 You know that I have served your father with all my strength; 7 yet your father has cheated me and changed my wages ten times, but God did not permit him to harm me. 8 If he said, 'The speckled shall be your wages,' then all the flock bore speckled; and if he said, 'The striped shall be your wages,' then all the flock bore striped. 9 Thus God has taken away the livestock of your father, and given them to me. 10 During the mating of the flock I once had a dream in which I looked up and saw that the male goats that leaped upon the flock were striped, speckled, and mottled. 11(-) Then God said to me in the dream, 'Jacob,' and I said, 'Here I am!' 12 And he said, 'Look up and see that all the goats that leap on the flock are striped, speckled, and mottled; for I have seen all that Laban is doing to you. 13 I am the God of Bethel, where you anointed a pillar and made a vow to me. Now leave this land at once and return to the land of your birth.'" 14 Then Rachel and Leah answered him, "Is there any portion or inheritance left to us in our father's house? 15 Are we not regarded by him as foreigners? For he has sold us, and he has been using up the money given for us. 16 All the property that God has taken away from our father belongs to us and to our children; now then, do whatever God has said to you."

Jacob Escapes Laban (Gen. 31)

17 So Jacob arose, and set his children and his wives on camels; 19 Now Laban had gone to shear his sheep, and Rachel stole her father's household gods. 20 And Jacob deceived Laban the Aramean, in that he did not tell him that he intended to flee. 21 So he fled with all that he had; starting out he crossed the Euphrates, and set his face toward the hill country of Gilead. 22 On the third day Laban was told that Jacob had fled. 23 So he took his kinsfolk with him and pursued him for seven days until he caught up with him in the hill country of Gilead. 24 But God came to Laban the Aramean in a dream by night, and said to him, "Take heed that you say not a word to Jacob, either good or bad." 25 Laban overtook Jacob. Now Jacob had pitched his tent in the hill country, and Laban with his kinsfolk camped in the hill country of Gilead. 26 Laban said to Jacob, "What have you done? You have deceived me, and carried away my daughters like captives of the

sword. 27 Why did you flee secretly and deceive me and not tell me? I would have sent you away with mirth and songs, with tambourine and lyre. 28 And why did you not permit me to kiss my sons and my daughters farewell? What you have done is foolish. 30b Why did you steal my gods?" 31 Jacob answered Laban, "Because I was afraid, for I thought that you would take your daughters from me by force. 32 But anyone with whom you find your gods shall not live. In the presence of our kinsfolk, point out what I have that is yours, and take it." Now Jacob did not know that Rachel had stolen the gods. 33 So Laban went into Jacob's tent, and into Leah's tent, and into the tent of the two maids, but he did not find them. And he went out of Leah's tent, and entered Rachel's. 34 Now Rachel had taken the household gods and put them in the camel's saddle, and sat on them. Laban felt all about in the tent, but did not find them. 35 And she said to her father, "Let not my lord be angry that I cannot rise before you, for the way of women is upon me." So he searched, but did not find the household gods.

The Alliance between Jacob and Laban (Gen. 31)

36 Then Jacob became angry, and upbraided Laban. Jacob said to Laban, "What is my offense? What is my sin, that you have hotly pursued me? 37 Although you have felt about through all my goods, what have you found of all your household goods? Set it here before my kinsfolk and your kinsfolk, so that they may decide between us two. 38 These twenty years I have been with you; your ewes and your female goats have not miscarried, and I have not eaten the rams of your flocks. 39 That which was torn by wild beasts I did not bring to you; I bore the loss of it myself; of my hand you required it, whether stolen by day or stolen by night. 40 It was like this with me: by day the heat consumed me, and the cold by night, and my sleep fled from my eyes. 42b(-) God saw my affliction and the labor of my hands."43 Then Laban answered and said to Jacob, "The daughters are my daughters, the children are my children, the flocks are my flocks, and all that you see is mine. But what can I do today about these daughters of mine, or about their children whom they have borne? 44 Come now, let us make a covenant, you and I; and let it be a witness between you and me." 45 So Jacob took a stone, and set it up as a pillar. 50b [And he said] "see that God is witness between you and me." 51(-) Then Laban said to Jacob, "See this pillar, which you have set between you and me. 52(-) This pillar is a witness, that I will not pass beyond this pillar and you will not pass beyond this pillar to me, for harm." 54 and Jacob offered a

sacrifice on the height and called his kinsfolk to eat bread; and they ate bread and tarried all night in the hill country. 55 Early in the morning Laban rose up, and kissed his grandchildren and his daughters and blessed them; then he departed and returned home.

Jacob's Struggle with the Angel (Gen. 32)

1 Jacob went on his way and the angels of God met him; 2a and when Jacob saw them he said, "This is God's camp!" 24 Jacob was left alone; and a man wrestled with him until daybreak. 25 When the man saw that he did not prevail against Jacob, he struck him on the hip socket; and Jacob's hip was put out of joint as he wrestled with him. 26 Then he said, "Let me go, for the day is breaking." But Jacob said, "I will not let you go, unless you bless me." 27 So he said to him, "What is your name?" And he said, "Jacob." 28 Then the man said, "You shall no longer be called Jacob, but Israel, for you have striven with God and with humans, and have prevailed." 29 Then Jacob asked him, "Please tell me your name." But he said, "Why is it that you ask my name?" And there he blessed him. 30 So Jacob called the place Peniel, saying, "For I have seen God face to face, and yet my life is preserved."

Jacob Reunion with Esau (Gen. 33)

1a Now Jacob looked up and saw Esau coming, and four hundred men with him. 3(-). So, he proceeded towards them, until he came near his brother. 4 Esau ran to meet him, and embraced him, and fell on his neck and kissed him, and they wept. 5 When Esau looked up and saw the women and children, he said, "Who are these with you?" Jacob said, "The children whom God has graciously given your servant." 10 Jacob said, "No, please; if I find favor with you, then accept a present from my hand; for truly to see your face is like seeing the face of God— since you have received me with such favor. 11(-) Please accept my gift because God has dealt graciously with me, and because I have everything I want." So he urged him, and he took it. 16 So Esau returned that day on his way to Seir. 18(-) and Jacob came safely to the city of Shechem, and he camped before the city.

2.3 Jacob's Return to Bethel (Gen. 35)

35:2 Jacob said to his household and to all who were with him, "Put away the foreign gods that are among you, and purify yourselves, and change your clothes; 3 then come, let us go up to Bethel, that I may make an altar there to the God who answered me in the day of my distress and has been with me wherever I have gone." 4 So they gave to Jacob all the foreign gods that they had, and the rings that were in their ears; and Jacob hid them under the oak that was near Shechem. 6(-) Jacob came to Bethel, which is in the land of Canaan, he and all the people who were with him, 7a and there he built an altar and called the place El-bethel, 16 Then they journeyed from Bethel; and when they were still some distance from Ephrath, Rachel was in childbirth, and she had hard labor. 17 When she was in her hard labor, the midwife said to her, "Do not be afraid; for now you will have another son." 18 As her soul was departing (for she died), she named him Ben-oni; but his father called him Benjamin. 19 So Rachel died, and she was buried on the way to Ephrath (that is, Bethlehem), 20 and Jacob set up a pillar at her grave; it is the pillar of Rachel's tomb, which is there to this day.

The Joseph Cycle

Joseph and His Brothers (Gen. 37)

3 Now Israel loved Joseph more than any other of his children, because he was the son of his old age; and he had made him a long robe with sleeves. 4 But when his brothers saw that their father loved him more than all his brothers, they hated him, and could not speak peaceably to him. 5 Once Joseph had a dream, and when he told it to his brothers, they hated him even more. 6 He said to them, "Listen to this dream that I dreamed. 7 There we were, binding sheaves in the field. Suddenly my sheaf rose and stood upright; then your sheaves gathered around it, and bowed down to my sheaf." 8 His brothers said to him, "Are you indeed to reign over us? Are you indeed to have dominion over us?" So they hated him even more because of his dreams and his words. 12 Now his brothers went to pasture their father's flock near Shechem. 13 And Israel said to Joseph, "Are not your brothers pasturing the flock at Shechem? Come, I will send you to them." He answered, "Here I am." 14b So he sent him from the valley of Hebron and he came to Shechem, 18 They saw him from a distance, and before he came near to them, they conspired to kill him. 19 They said to one another, "Here comes

this dreamer. 20 Come now, let us kill him and throw him into one of the pits; then we shall say that a wild animal has devoured him, and we shall see what will become of his dreams." 21 But when Reuben heard it, he delivered him out of their hands, saying, "Let us not take his life." 22 Reuben said to them, "Shed no blood; throw him into this pit here in the wilderness, but lay no hand on him"—that he might rescue him out of their hand and restore him to his father. 23 So when Joseph came to his brothers, they stripped him of his robe, the long robe with sleeves that he wore; 24 and they took him and threw him into a pit. The pit was empty; there was no water in it. 28(-) When some Midianite traders passed by, they drew Joseph up, lifting him out of the pit, And they took Joseph to Egypt.29 When Reuben returned to the pit and saw that Joseph was not in the pit, he tore his clothes. 30 He returned to his brothers, and said, "The boy is gone; and I, where can I turn?" 36 Meanwhile the Midianites had sold him in Egypt to Potiphar, the captain of the guard.

The Ministers' Dreams (Gen. 40)

1 Some time after this, the cupbearer of the King of Egypt and his baker offended their lord the King of Egypt. 3a and he put them in custody in the house of the captain of the guard 4 The captain of the guard charged Joseph with them, and he waited on them; and they continued for some time in custody. 5(-) One night they both dreamed—the cupbearer and the baker of the King of Egypt—each his own dream, and each dream with its own meaning. 6 When Joseph came to them in the morning, he saw that they were troubled. 7 So he asked Pharaoh's officers, who were with him in custody in his master's house, "Why are your faces downcast today?" 8 They said to him, "We have had dreams, and there is no one to interpret them." And Joseph said to them, "Do not interpretations belong to God? Please tell them to me."9 So the chief cupbearer told his dream to Joseph, and said to him, "In my dream there was a vine before me, 10 and on the vine there were three branches. As soon as it budded, its blossoms came out and the clusters ripened into grapes. 11 Pharaoh's cup was in my hand; and I took the grapes and pressed them into Pharaoh's cup, and placed the cup in Pharaoh's hand." 12 Then Joseph said to him, "This is its interpretation: the three branches are three days; 13 within three days Pharaoh will lift up your head and restore you to your office; and you shall place Pharaoh's cup in his hand, just as you used to do when you were his cupbearer. 14 But remember me when it is well with you;

please do me the kindness to make mention of me to Pharaoh, and so get me out of this place. 15a For in fact I was stolen out of the land of the Hebrews." 16 When the chief baker saw that the interpretation was favorable, he said to Joseph, "I also had a dream: there were three cake baskets on my head, 17 and in the uppermost basket there were all sorts of baked food for Pharaoh, but the birds were eating it out of the basket on my head." 18 And Joseph answered, "This is its interpretation: the three baskets are three days; 19 within three days Pharaoh will lift up your head—from you!—and hang you on a pole; and the birds will eat the flesh from you."20 On the third day, which was Pharaoh's birthday, he made a feast for all his servants, and lifted up the head of the chief cupbearer and the head of the chief baker among his servants. 21 He restored the chief cupbearer to his cupbearing, and he placed the cup in Pharaoh's hand; 22 but the chief baker he hanged, just as Joseph had interpreted to them. 23 Yet the chief cupbearer did not remember Joseph, but forgot him.

Pharaoh's Dreams (Gen. 41)

1 After two whole years, Pharaoh dreamed that he was standing by the Nile, 2 and there came up out of the Nile seven sleek and fat cows, and they grazed in the reed grass. 3 Then seven other cows, ugly and thin, came up out of the Nile after them, and stood by the other cows on the bank of the Nile. 4 The ugly and thin cows ate up the seven sleek and fat cows. And Pharaoh awoke. 5 Then he fell asleep and dreamed a second time; seven ears of grain, plump and good, were growing on one stalk. 6 Then seven ears, thin and blighted by the east wind, sprouted after them. 7 The thin ears swallowed up the seven plump and full ears. Pharaoh awoke, and it was a dream. 8 In the morning his spirit was troubled; so he sent and called for all the magicians of Egypt and all its wise men. Pharaoh told them his dreams, but there was no one who could interpret them to Pharaoh. 9 Then the chief cupbearer said to Pharaoh, "I remember my faults today. 10 Once Pharaoh was angry with his servants, and put me and the chief baker in custody in the house of the captain of the guard. 11 I dreamed on the same night, he and I, each having a dream with its own meaning. 12 A young Hebrew was there with us, a servant of the captain of the guard. When we told him, he interpreted our dreams to us, giving an interpretation to each according to his dream. 13 As he interpreted to us, so it turned out; I was restored to my office, and the baker was hanged."14(-) Then Pharaoh sent for Joseph, when he had shaved himself and changed his

clothes, he came in before Pharaoh. 15 And Pharaoh said to Joseph, "I have had a dream, and there is no one who can interpret it. I have heard it said of you that when you hear a dream you can interpret it." 16 Joseph answered Pharaoh, "It is not I; God will give Pharaoh a favorable answer." 17 Then Pharaoh said to Joseph, "In my dream I was standing on the banks of the Nile; 18 and seven cows, fat and sleek, came up out of the Nile and fed in the reed grass. 19 Then seven other cows came up after them, poor, very ugly, and thin. Never had I seen such ugly ones in all the land of Egypt. 20 The thin and ugly cows ate up the first seven fat cows, 21 but when they had eaten them no one would have known that they had done so, for they were still as ugly as before. Then I awoke. 22 I fell asleep a second timea and I saw in my dream seven ears of grain, full and good, growing on one stalk, 23 and seven ears, withered, thin, and blighted by the east wind, sprouting after them; 24 and the thin ears swallowed up the seven good ears. But when I told it to the magicians, there was no one who could explain it to me."25 Then Joseph said to Pharaoh, "Pharaoh's dreams are one and the same; God has revealed to Pharaoh what he is about to do. 26 The seven good cows are seven years, and the seven good ears are seven years; the dreams are one. 27 The seven lean and ugly cows that came up after them are seven years, as are the seven empty ears blighted by the east wind. They are seven years of famine. 28 It is as I told Pharaoh; God has shown to Pharaoh what he is about to do. 29 There will come seven years of great plenty throughout all the land of Egypt. 30 After them there will arise seven years of famine, and all the plenty will be forgotten in the land of Egypt; the famine will consume the land. 31 The plenty will no longer be known in the land because of the famine that will follow, for it will be very grievous. 32 And the doubling of Pharaoh's dream means that the thing is fixed by God, and God will shortly bring it about. 33 Now therefore let Pharaoh select a man who is discerning and wise, and set him over the land of Egypt. 34 Let Pharaoh proceed to appoint overseers over the land, and take one-fifth of the produce of the land of Egypt during the seven plenteous years. 35 Let them gather all the food of these good years that are coming, and lay up grain under the authority of Pharaoh for food in the cities, and let them keep it. 36 That food shall be a reserve for the land against the seven years of famine that are to befall the land of Egypt, so that the land may not perish through the famine."37 The proposal pleased Pharaoh and all his servants. 38 Pharaoh said to his servants, "Can we find anyone else like this—one in whom is the spirit of God?" 39 So Pharaoh said to Joseph, "Since God has shown you all this, there is no one so discerning and wise as you. 40 You shall be over my house, and all my people shall order themselves as you command; only with regard to the throne will I be greater than you." 41 And Pharaoh said to Joseph, "See, I have set you over all the land of Egypt." 42 Removing his signet ring from his hand, Pharaoh put it on Joseph's hand; he arrayed him in garments of fine linen, and put a gold chain around his neck. 43 He had him ride in the chariot of his second-in-command; and they cried out in front of him, "Bow the knee!" Thus he set him over all the land of Egypt. 44 Moreover Pharaoh said to Joseph, "I am Pharaoh, and without your consent no one shall lift up hand or foot in all the land of Egypt." 45(a) Pharaoh gave Joseph the name Zaphenath-paneah; and he gave him Asenath daughter of Potiphera, priest of On, as his wife. 46(b) And Joseph went out from the presence of Pharaoh, and went through all the land of Egypt. 47 During the seven plenteous years the earth produced abundantly. 48 He gathered up all the food of the seven years when there was plenty in the land of Egypt, and stored up food in the cities; he stored up in every city the food from the fields around it.

Joseph's Brothers Beg (Gen. 41-42)

41:56 And since the famine had spread over all the land, Joseph opened all that was in them (in the cities) and sold to the Egyptians, for the famine was severe in the land of Egypt. 57 Moreover, all the world came to Joseph in Egypt to buy grain, because the famine became severe throughout the world. 42:5 Thus the sons of Israel were among the other people who came to buy grain, for the famine had reached the land of Canaan. 6 Now Joseph was governor over the land; it was he who sold to all the people of the land. And Joseph's brothers came and bowed themselves before him with their faces to the ground. 7 When Joseph saw his brothers, he recognized them, but he treated them like strangers and spoke harshly to them. "Where do you come from?" he said. They said, "From the land of Canaan, to buy food." 9b He said to them, "You are spies; you have come to see the nakedness of the land!" 10 They said to him, "No, my lord; your servants have come to buy food. 11 We are all sons of one man; we are honest men; your servants have never been spies." 12 But he said to them, "No, you have come to see the nakedness of the land!" 13(-) They said, "We are the sons of a certain man in the land of Canaan; the youngest, however, is now with our father, and one is no more." 14 But Joseph said to them, "It is just as I have said to you; you are spies! 15 Here is how you shall be tested: as Pharaoh lives, you shall not leave this place unless your youngest brother comes here!" 17 And he put them all together in prison for three days.18 On the third day Joseph said to them, "Do this and you will live, for I fear God: 19 if you are honest men, let one of your brothers stay here where you are imprisoned. The rest of you shall go and carry grain for the famine of your households, 20 and bring your youngest brother to me. Thus your words will be verified, and you shall not die." And they did so. 26 They loaded their donkeys with their grain, and departed. 35 As they were emptying their sacks, there in each one's sack was his bag of money. When they and their father saw their bundles of money, they were dismayed.

Joseph's Brothers Return (Gen. 43)

15(-) So the men took the present as well as Benjamin. Then they went on their way down to Egypt, and stood before Joseph. 16 When Joseph saw Benjamin with them, he said to the steward of his house, "Bring the men into the house, and slaughter an animal and make ready, for the men are to dine with me at noon." 17 The man did as Joseph said, and brought the men to Joseph's house. 26 When Joseph came home, they brought him the present that they had carried into the house, and bowed to the ground before him. 27 He inquired about their welfare, and said, "Is your father well, the old man of whom you spoke? Is he still alive?" 28 They said, "Your servant our father is well; he is still alive." And they bowed their heads and did obeisance. 29 Then he looked up and saw his brother Benjamin, his mother's son, and said, "Is this your youngest brother, of whom you spoke to me? God be gracious to you, my son!" 30 With that, Joseph hurried out, because he was overcome with affection for his brother, and he was about to weep. So he went into a private room and wept there. 31 Then he washed his face and came out; and controlling himself he said, "Serve the meal." 33 When they were seated before him, the firstborn according to his birthright and the youngest according to his youth, the men looked at one another in amazement. 34 Portions were taken to them from Joseph's table, but Benjamin's portion was five times as much as any of theirs. So they drank and were merry with him.

The Silver Goblet (Gen. 44-45)

3 As soon as the morning was light, the men were sent away with their donkeys. 4 When they had gone only a short distance from the city,

Joseph said to his steward, "Go, follow after the men; and when you overtake them, say to them, 'Why have you returned evil for good? Why have you stolen my silver cup? 5 Is it not from this that my lord drinks? Does he not indeed use it for divination? You have done wrong in doing this.'"6 When he overtook them, he repeated these words to them. 7 They said to him, "Why does my lord speak such words as these? Far be it from your servants that they should do such a thing! 9 Should it be found with any one of your servants, let him die; moreover the rest of us will become my lord's slaves." 10 He said, "Even so; in accordance with your words, let it be: he with whom it is found shall become my slave, but the rest of you shall go free." 12(-) He searched, beginning with the eldest and ending with the youngest; and the cup was found. 13 At this they tore their clothes. Then each one loaded his donkey, and they returned to the city. 15 Joseph said to them, "What deed is this that you have done? Do you not know that one such as I can practice divination?" 16(-+) And they said, "What can we say to my lord? What can we speak? How can we clear ourselves? God has found out the guilt of your servants; here we are then, my lord's slaves, both we and also the one in whose possession the cup has been found." 45:1 Then Joseph could no longer control himself before all those who stood by him, and he cried out, "Send everyone away from me." So no one stayed with him when Joseph made himself known to his brothers. 2 And he wept so loudly that the Egyptians heard it, and the household of Pharaoh heard it. 3 Joseph said to his brothers, "I am Joseph. Is my father still alive?" But his brothers could not answer him, so dismayed were they at his presence.4a Then Joseph said to his brothers, "Come closer to me." And they came closer. 14 Then he fell upon his brother Benjamin's neck and wept, while Benjamin wept upon his neck. 15 And he kissed all his brothers and wept upon them; and after that his brothers talked with him.

Pharaoh's Benevolence (Gen. 45)

16 When the report was heard in Pharaoh's house, "Joseph's brothers have come," Pharaoh and his servants were pleased. 17 Pharaoh said to Joseph, "Say to your brothers, 'Do this: load your animals and go back to the land of Canaan. 18 Take your father and your households and come to me, so that I may give you the best of the land of Egypt, and you may enjoy the fat of the land.' 19 You are further charged to say, 'Do this: take wagons from the land of Egypt for your little ones and for your wives, and bring your father, and come. 20 Give no thought to

your possessions, for the best of all the land of Egypt is yours.'" 21 The sons of Israel did so. Joseph gave them wagons according to the instruction of Pharaoh, and he gave them provisions for the journey. 22 To each one of them he gave a set of garments; but to Benjamin he gave three hundred pieces of silver and five sets of garments. 23 To his father he sent the following: ten donkeys loaded with the good things of Egypt, and ten female donkeys loaded with grain, bread, and provision for his father on the journey. 24 Then he sent his brothers on their way, and as they were leaving he said to them, "Do not quarrel along the way."25(-) So they went up out of Egypt and came to their father in the land of Canaan. 26 And they told him, "Joseph is still alive! He is even ruler over all the land of Egypt." He was stunned; he could not believe them. 27a(-) And when he saw the wagons that Joseph had sent to carry him. 28 Israel said, "Enough! My son Joseph is still alive. I must go and see him before I die."

The Revelation at Beer-sheba (Gen. 46)

1(-) When Israel set out on his journey with all that he had and came to Beer-sheba, he offered sacrifices to the God of his father. 2 God spoke to Israel in visions of the night, and said, ("Jacob, Jacob." And he said, "Here I am." 3 Then he said,) "I am God, the God of your father; do not be afraid to go down to Egypt, for I will make of you a great nation there. 4 I myself will go down with you to Egypt, and I will also bring you up again; and Joseph's own hand shall close your eyes."

Joseph and Israel's First Encounter (Gen. 46-47)

29(-) Joseph made ready his chariot and went up to meet his father Israel. He presented himself to him, fell on his neck, and wept on his neck a good while. 30 Israel said to Joseph, "I can die now, having seen for myself that you are still alive." 47:5 Then Pharaoh said to Joseph, "Your father and your brothers have come to you. 6(-) The land of Egypt is before you; settle your father and your brothers in the best part of the land; and if you know that there are capable men among them, put them in charge of my livestock." 11(-) Joseph settled his father and his brothers, in the best part of the land, in the land of Rameses, as Pharaoh had instructed. 12 And Joseph provided his father, his brothers, and all his father's household with food, according to the number of their dependents.

The Second Meeting (Gen. 47)

29 When the time of Israel's death drew near, he called his son Joseph and said to him, "If I have found favor with you, put your hand under my thigh and promise to deal loyally and truly with me. Do not bury me in Egypt. 30 When I lie down with my ancestors, carry me out of Egypt and bury me in their burial place." He answered, "I will do as you have said." 31 And he said, "Swear to me"; and he swore to him. Then Israel bowed himself on the head of his bed.

Israel's Blessing (Gen. 48)

1 After this Joseph was told, "Your father is ill." So he took with him his two sons, Manasseh and Ephraim. 2b Israel summoned his strength and sat up in bed. 8 When Israel saw Joseph's sons, he said, "Who are these?" 9 Joseph said to his father, "They are my sons, whom God has given me here." And he said, "Bring them to me, please, that I may bless them." 10 Now the eyes of Israel were dim with age, and he could not see well. So Joseph brought them near him; and he kissed them and embraced them. 11 Israel said to Joseph, "I did not expect to see your face; and here God has let me see your children also." 12 Then Joseph removed them from his father's knees, and he bowed himself with his face to the earth. 13 Joseph took them both, Ephraim in his right hand toward Israel's left, and Manasseh in his left hand toward Israel's right, and brought them near him. 14 But Israel stretched out his right hand and laid it on the head of Ephraim, who was the younger, and his left hand on the head of Manasseh, crossing his hands, for Manasseh was the firstborn. 17 When Joseph saw that his father laid his right hand on the head of Ephraim, it displeased him; so he took his father's hand, to remove it from Ephraim's head to Manasseh's head. 18 Joseph said to his father, "Not so, my father! Since this one is the firstborn, put your right hand on his head." 19 But his father refused, and said, "I know, my son, I know; he also shall become a people, and he also shall be great. Nevertheless his younger brother shall be greater than he, and his offspring shall become a multitude of nations." 20 So he blessed them that day, saying, "By you Israel will invoke blessings, saying, 'God make you like Ephraim and like Manasseh.'" So he put Ephraim ahead of Manasseh.

Israel's Death and Burial (Gen. 50)

49:33(-) He drew up his feet into the bed, breathed his last, and was gathered to his people. 1 Then Joseph threw himself on his father's face and wept over him and kissed him. 2 Joseph commanded the physicians in his service to embalm his father. So the physicians embalmed Israel; 3 they spent forty days in doing this, for that is the time required for embalming. And the Egyptians wept for him seventy days. 4 When the days of weeping for him were past, Joseph addressed the household of Pharaoh, "If now I have found favor with you, please speak to Pharaoh as follows: 5 My father made me swear an oath; he said, 'I am about to die. In the tomb that I hewed out for myself in the land of Canaan, there you shall bury me.' Now therefore let me go up, so that I may bury my father; then I will return." 6 Pharaoh answered, "Go up, and bury your father, as he made you swear to do."7 So Joseph went up to bury his father. With him went up all the servants of Pharaoh, the Elders of his household, and all the Elders of the land of Egypt, 8a as well as all the household of Joseph, his brothers, and his father's household. 9 Both chariots and charioteers went up with him. It was a very great company. 10 When they came to the threshing floor of Atad, which is beyond the Jordan, they held there a very great and sorrowful lamentation; and he observed a time of mourning for his father seven days. 14 After he had buried his father, Joseph returned to Egypt with his brothers and all who had gone up with him to bury his father.

After Israel's Death (Gen. 50)

15 Realizing that their father was dead, Joseph's brothers said, "What if Joseph still bears a grudge against us and pays us back in full for all the wrong that we did to him?" 16 So they approached Joseph, saying, "Your father gave this instruction before he died, 17 Say to Joseph: 'I beg you, forgive the crime of your brothers and the wrong they did in harming you.' Now therefore please forgive the crime of the servants of the God of your father." Joseph wept when they spoke to him. 18 Then his brothers also wept, fell down before him, and said, "We are here as your slaves." 19 But Joseph said to them, "Do not be afraid! Am I in the place of God? 20 Even though you intended to do harm to me, God intended it for good, in order to preserve a numerous people, as he is doing today. 21 So have no fear; I myself will provide for you and your little ones." In this way he reassured them, speaking kindly to them.

22a So Joseph remained in Egypt, he and his father's household; 26(-)
And Joseph died and he was embalmed and placed in a coffin in Egypt.

2.4 The Moses Cycle

The New King (Ex. 1)

8 Now a new king arose over Egypt, who did not know Joseph. 9 He
said to his people, "Look, the Israelite people are stronger and more
powerful than we. 10 Come, let us deal shrewdly with them, or they
will increase and, in the event of war, join our enemies and fight
against us and escape from the land." 15 The King of Egypt said to the
Hebrew midwives, one of whom was named Shiphrah and the other
Puah, 16 "When you act as midwives to the Hebrew women, and see
them on the birthstool, if it is a boy, kill him; but if it is a girl, she shall
live." 17 But the midwives feared God; they did not do as the King of
Egypt commanded them, but they let the boys live. 18 So the King of
Egypt summoned the midwives and said to them, "Why have you
done this, and allowed the boys to live?" 19(-) The midwives said,
"Because the Hebrew women are not like the Egyptian women; for they
are vigorous and give birth before the midwife comes to them." 21.
And because the midwives feared God, he gave them families.

Moses' Mission (Ex. 3)

1(-) Moses was keeping the flock of his father-in-law Jethro, the priest
of Midian; he led his flock beyond the wilderness, to the mountain of
God. 2b He looked, and a bush was blazing, yet it was not consumed. 3
Then Moses said, "I must turn aside and look at this great sight, and
see why the bush is not burned up." 4b God called to him out of the
bush, "Moses, Moses!" And he said, "Here I am." 5 Then he said,
"Come no closer! Remove the sandals from your feet, for the place on
which you are standing is holy ground." 6(-) He said further, "I am the
God of your father," And Moses hid his face, for he was afraid to look
at God. 9(-+) (And he said)"Behold, the cry of the Israelites has now
come to me; I have also seen how the Egyptians oppress them. 10(-+) So
come, I will send you to the King of Egypt to bring my people, the
Israelites, out of Egypt." 11(-+) But Moses said to God, "Who am I that I
should go to the King of Egypt, and bring the Israelites out of Egypt?"
12 He said, "I will be with you; and this shall be the sign for you that it

is I who sent you: when you have brought the people out of Egypt, you shall worship God on this mountain."13 But Moses said to God, "If I come to the Israelites and say to them, 'The God of your ancestors has sent me to you,' and they ask me, 'What is his name?' what shall I say to them?" 14 God said to Moses, "I AM WHO I AM." He said further, "Thus you shall say to the Israelites, 'I AM has sent me to you.' " 18(-) They will listen to your voice; and you and the Elders of Israel shall go to the King of Egypt and say to him, 'The the God of the Hebrews, has met with us; let us now go a three days' journey into the wilderness, so that we may sacrifice to our God.' 19 I know, however, that the King of Egypt will not let you go even if compelled by a mighty hand.

Moses Returns to Egypt (Ex. 3-4)

18 Moses went back to his father-in-law Jethro and said to him, "Please let me go back to my kindred in Egypt and see whether they are still living." And Jethro said to Moses, "Go in peace." 20(-) So Moses took his wife and his sons, put them on a donkey and Moses carried the staff of God in his hand. 27(-+) And Aaron went; and met him at the mountain of God and kissed him. 29 Then Moses and Aaron went and assembled all the Elders of the Israelites. 3(+) Then they said to the King of Egypt, "The God of the Hebrews has revealed himself to us; let us go a three days' journey into the wilderness to sacrifice to the LORD our God, or he will fall upon us with pestilence or sword." 4 But the King of Egypt said to them, "Moses and Aaron, why are you taking the people away from their work? Get to your labors!"

The Three Plagues (Ex. 9-10)

The Plague of Hail (Ex. 9)

23a(-) Then Moses stretched out his staff toward heaven; 24 there was hail with fire flashing continually in the midst of it, such heavy hail as had never fallen in all the land of Egypt since it became a nation. 25 The hail struck down everything that was in the open field throughout all the land of Egypt, both human and animal; the hail also struck down all the plants of the field, and shattered every tree in the field.

The Plague of Locusts (Ex. 10)

13(-) So Moses stretched out his staff over the land of Egypt, and when morning came, the east wind had brought the locusts. 14 The locusts came upon all the land of Egypt and settled on the whole country of Egypt, such a dense swarm of locusts as had never been before, nor ever shall be again. 15 They covered the surface of the whole land, so that the land was black; and they ate all the plants in the land and all the fruit of the trees that the hail had left; nothing green was left, no tree, no plant in the field, in all the land of Egypt.

The Plague of Darkness (Ex. 10)

22 So Moses stretched out his hand toward heaven, and there was dense darkness in all the land of Egypt for three days. 23a People could not see one another, and for three days they could not move from where they were.

The Exodus (Ex. 12-14)

33 The Egyptians urged the people to hasten their departure from the land, for they said, "We shall all be dead." 34 So the people took their dough before it was leavened, with their kneading bowls wrapped up in their cloaks on their shoulders. 5(a) The King of Egypt was told that the people had fled; 7 he took six hundred picked chariots and all the other chariots of Egypt with officers over all of them. 9(-) The Egyptians pursued them, and they overtook them camped by the sea. 19a(-) The angel of God moved and went behind them; 20a He came between the army of Egypt and the army of Israel. 21(-) Then Moses stretched out his hand over the sea. and turned the sea into dry land; and the waters were divided. 22 The Israelites went into the sea on dry ground, the waters forming a wall for them on their right and on their left. 23(-) The Egyptians pursued, and went into the sea after them. 27a So Moses stretched out his hand over the sea, and at dawn the sea returned to its normal depth. 28(-) The waters returned and covered the chariots and the chariot drivers, not one of them remained.

Water Shortages (Ex. 15)

22 Then Moses ordered Israel to set out from the Red Sea, and they went into the wilderness of Shur. They went three days in the

wilderness and found no water. 23a When they came to Marah, they could not drink the water of Marah because it was bitter. 24 And the people complained against Moses, saying, "What shall we drink?" 27 Then they came to Elim, where there were twelve springs of water and seventy palm trees; and they camped there by the water.

The War with Amalek (Ex. 17)

8 Then Amalek came and fought with Israel at Rephidim. 9 Moses said to Joshua, "Choose some men for us and go out, fight with Amalek. Tomorrow I will stand on the top of the hill with the staff of God in my hand." 10 So Joshua did as Moses told him, and fought with Amalek, while Moses, Aaron, and Hur went up to the top of the hill. 11 Whenever Moses held up his hand, Israel prevailed; and whenever he lowered his hand, Amalek prevailed. 12 But Moses' hands grew weary; so they took a stone and put it under him, and he sat on it. Aaron and Hur held up his hands, one on one side, and the other on the other side; so his hands were steady until the sun set. 13 And Joshua defeated Amalek and his people with the sword.

Jethro Aids Moses (Ex. 18)

1a Jethro, the priest of Midian, Moses' father-in-law, heard of all that God had done for Moses and for his people Israel. 5(-) Jethro, Moses' father-in-law, came into the wilderness where Moses was encamped at the mountain of God. 6a He sent word to Moses, "I, your father-in-law Jethro, am coming to you." 7(-) Moses went out to meet his father-in-law; he bowed down and kissed him; each asked after the other's welfare. 12 And Jethro, Moses' father-in-law, brought a burnt offering and sacrifices to God; and Aaron with all the Elders of Israel came to eat bread with Moses' father-in-law in the presence of God. 13 The next day Moses sat as judge for the people, while the people stood around him from morning until evening. 14 When Moses' father-in-law saw all that he was doing for the people, he said, "What is this that you are doing for the people? Why do you sit alone, while all the people stand around you from morning until evening?" 15 Moses said to his father-in-law, "Because the people come to me to inquire of God. 16 When they have a dispute, they come to me and I decide between one person and another, and I make known to them the statutes and instructions of God." 17 Moses' father-in-law said to him, "What you are doing is not

good. 18 You will surely wear yourself out, both you and these people
with you. For the task is too heavy for you; you cannot do it alone. 19
Now listen to me. I will give you counsel, and God be with you! You
should represent the people before God, and you should bring their
cases before God; 20 teach them the statutes and instructions and make
known to them the way they are to go and the things they are to do.
21(-) You should also look for able men among all the people, men who
fear God, are trustworthy, and hate dishonest gain and set such men
over them. 22 Let them sit as judges for the people at all times; let them
bring every important case to you, but decide every minor case
themselves. So it will be easier for you, and they will bear the burden
with you. 23 If you do this, and God so commands you, then you will
be able to endure, and all these people will go to their home in peace."
24 So Moses listened to his father-in-law and did all that he had said. 27
Then Moses let his father-in-law depart, and he went off to his own
country.

Preparing for Revelation (Ex. 19)

3(-) Then Moses went up to God; who called him 10(-) and said: "Go to
the people and consecrate them today and tomorrow. Have them wash
their clothes 11a and prepare for the third day." 14 So Moses went
down from the mountain to the people. He consecrated the people, and
they washed their clothes. 15 And he said to the people, "Prepare for
the third day; do not go near a woman."16 On the morning of the third
day there was thunder and lightning, as well as a thick cloud on the
mountain, and a blast of a trumpet so loud that all the people who were
in the camp trembled. 17 Moses brought the people out of the camp to
meet God. They took their stand at the foot of the mountain. 19 As the
blast of the trumpet grew louder and louder, Moses would speak and
God would answer him in thunder.

The Seven Commandments (Ex. 20)

1 Then God spoke all these words: 3 You shall have no other gods
before me. 4a(-) You shall not make for yourself an idol of any form. 13
You shall not murder. 14 You shall not commit adultery.15 You shall
not steal.16 You shall not bear false witness against your neighbor.17a
You shall not covet your neighbor's house. 18 When all the people
witnessed the thunder and lightning, the sound of the trumpet, and the

mountain smoking, they were afraid and trembled and stood at a distance, 19 and said to Moses, "You speak to us, and we will listen; but do not let God speak to us, or we will die." 20 Moses said to the people, "Do not be afraid; for God has come only to test you and to put the fear of him upon you so that you do not sin." 21 Then the people stood at a distance, while Moses drew near to the thick darkness where God was.

The Golden Calf (Ex. 24, 32)

13 So Moses set out with his assistant Joshua, and Moses went up into the mountain of God. 14 To the Elders he had said, "Wait here for us, until we come to you again; for Aaron and Hur are with you; whoever has a dispute may go to them." 15a Then Moses went up on the mountain.

32:1 When the people saw that Moses delayed to come down from the mountain, the people gathered around Aaron, and said to him, "Come, make gods for us, who shall go before us; as for this Moses, the man who brought us up out of the land of Egypt, we do not know what has become of him." 2 Aaron said to them, "Take off the gold rings that are on the ears of your wives, your sons, and your daughters, and bring them to me." 3 So all the people took off the gold rings from their ears, and brought them to Aaron. 4 He took the gold from them, formed it in a mold, and cast an image of a calf; and they said, "These are your gods, O Israel, who brought you up out of the land of Egypt!" 6 They rose early the next day, and offered burnt offerings and brought sacrifices of well-being; and the people sat down to eat and drink, and rose up to revel. 15 Then Moses turned and went down from the mountain, carrying (the) two tablets in his hands, tablets that were written on both sides, written on the front and on the back. 16 The tablets were the work of God, and the writing was the writing of God, engraved upon the tablets. 17 When Joshua heard the noise of the people as they shouted, he said to Moses, "There is a noise of war in the camp." 18 But he said, "It is not the sound made by victors, or the sound made by losers ;it is the sound of revelers that I hear."19 As soon as he came near the camp and saw the calf and the dancing, Moses' anger burned hot, and he threw the tablets from his hands and broke them at the foot of the mountain. 20 He took the calf that they had made, burned it with fire, ground it to powder, scattered it on the water, and made the Israelites drink it.

The Waters of Meribah (Num. 20)

1a(-) And the people stayed in Kadesh. 2a(-) and there was no water 3(-
) so the people quarreled with Moses and said: 5(-)"Why have you
brought us up out of Egypt, to bring us to this wretched place? It is no
place for grain, or figs, or vines, or pomegranates; and there is no water
to drink." 10b He said to them, "Listen, you rebels, shall *I* bring water
for you out of this rock?"11(-) Then Moses lifted up his hand and struck
the rock twice with his staff; water came out abundantly.

The Bronze Snake (Num. 21)

4b The people became impatient on the way 5(-) and the people spoke
against God and against Moses, "Why have you brought us up out of
Egypt to die in the wilderness? For there is no food and no water." 6(-)
And poisonous serpents bit the people, so that many Israelites died.
7a(-) The people came to Moses and said, "We have sinned." 9 So
Moses made a serpent of bronze, and put it upon a pole; and whenever
a serpent bit someone, that person would look at the serpent of bronze
and live.

The Conquest (Num. 21)

21 Then Israel sent messengers to King Sihon of the Amorites, saying,
22 "Let me pass through your land; we will not turn aside into field or
vineyard; we will not drink the water of any well; we will go by the
King's Highway until we have passed through your territory." 23 But
Sihon would not allow Israel to pass through his territory. Sihon
gathered all his people together, and went out against Israel to the
wilderness; he came to Jahaz, and fought against Israel. 24 Israel put
him to the sword, and took possession of his land from the Arnon to
the Jabbok, as far as to the Ammonites; for the boundary of the
Ammonites was strong. 25 Israel took all these towns, and Israel settled
in all the towns of the Amorites, in Heshbon, and in all its villages. 32
Moses sent to spy out Jazer; and they captured its villages, and
dispossessed the Amorites who were there. 33 Then they turned and
went up the road to Bashan; and King Og of Bashan came out against
them, he and all his people, to battle at Edrei. 35 So they killed him, his
sons, and all his people, until there was no survivor left; and they took
possession of his land.

2.5 The Balaam Cycle

The Summons (Num. 22)

2 Now Balak son of Zippor saw all that Israel had done to the Amorites. 3(-) Moab was in great dread of the people, (indeed) Moab was overcome with fear of the People of Israel. 5(-) He sent messengers to Balaam son of Beor at Pethor, which is on the Euphrates, in the land of Amaw, to summon him, saying, "A people has come out of Egypt; and they have settled next to me. 6 Come now, curse this people for me, since they are stronger than I; perhaps I shall be able to defeat them and drive them from the land; for I know that whomever you bless is blessed, and whomever you curse is cursed." 9 God came to Balaam and said, "Who are these men with you?" 10 Balaam said to God, "King Balak son of Zippor of Moab, has sent me this message: 11'A people has come out of Egypt and has spread over the face of the earth; now come, curse them for me; perhaps I shall be able to fight against them and drive them out. ' " 12 God said to Balaam, "You shall not go with them; you shall not curse the people, for they are blessed." 13(a) So Balaam rose in the morning, and said to the officials of Balak, "Go to your own land." 14 So the officials of Moab rose and went to Balak, and said, "Balaam refuses to come with us." 15 Once again Balak sent officials, more numerous and more distinguished than these. 16 They came to Balaam and said to him, "Thus says Balak son of Zippor: 'Do not let anything hinder you from coming to me; 17 for I will surely do you great honor, and whatever you say to me I will do; come, curse this people for me.'" 20 That night God came to Balaam and said to him, "If the men have come to summon you, get up and go with them; but do only what I tell you to do." 21 So Balaam got up in the morning, saddled his donkey, and went with the officials of Moab.

The First Blessing (Num. 22-23)

36 When Balak heard that Balaam had come, he went out to meet him at Ir-moab, on the boundary formed by the Arnon, at the farthest point of the boundary. 37 Balak said to Balaam, "Did I not send to summon you? Why did you not come to me? Am I not able to honor you?" 39 Then Balaam went with Balak, and they came to Kiriath-huzoth. 40 Balak sacrificed oxen and sheep, and sent them to Balaam and to the officials who were with him. 23:1 Then Balaam said to Balak, "Build me seven altars here, and prepare seven bulls and seven rams for me." 2

Balak did as Balaam had said; and Balak and Balaam offered a bull and a ram on each altar. 4a Then God met Balaam; 18 Then Balaam uttered his oracle, saying: "Rise, Balak, and hear; listen to me, O son of Zippor: 19 God is not a human being, that he should lie, or a mortal, that he should change his mind. Has he promised, and will he not do it? Has he spoken, and will he not fulfill it? 22 God, who brings them out of Egypt, is like the horns of a wild ox for them.23 Surely there is no enchantment against Jacob, no divination against Israel; now it shall be said of Jacob and Israel, 'See what God has done!'24 Look, a people rising up like a lioness, and rousing itself like a lion! It does not lie down until it has eaten the prey and drunk the blood of the slain."

The Second Blessing (Num. 23-24)

27 So Balak said to Balaam, "Come now, I will take you to another place; perhaps it will please God that you may curse them for me from there." 28 So Balak took Balaam to the top of Peor, (which overlooks the wasteland.) 29 Balaam said to Balak, "Build me seven altars here, and prepare seven bulls and seven rams for me." 30 So Balak did as Balaam had said, and offered a bull and a ram on each altar. 24:2 Balaam looked up and saw Israel camping tribe by tribe. Then the spirit of God came upon him, 3 and he uttered his oracle, saying: "The oracle of Balaam son of Beor, the oracle of the man whose eye is clear, 4 the oracle of one who hears the words of God, who sees the vision of the Almighty, who falls down, but with eyes uncovered: 5 How fair are your tents, O Jacob, your encampments, O Israel! 6(-) Like palm groves that stretch far away, like gardens beside a river, like cedar trees beside the waters.7 Water shall flow from his buckets, and his seed shall have abundant water, his king shall be higher than Agag, and his kingdom shall be exalted. 8 God who brings him out of Egypt, is like the horns of a wild ox for him;he shall devour the nations that are his foes and break their bones. He shall strike with his arrows. 9 He crouched, he lay down like a lion, and like a lioness; who will rouse him up? Blessed is everyone who blesses you, and cursed is everyone who curses you."

The Third Blessing (Num. 24)

10(-) Then Balak's anger was kindled against Balaam, and he struck his hands together. Balak said to Balaam, "I summoned you to curse my enemies, but instead you have blessed them. 11 Now be off with you!

Go home!" 12a And Balaam said to Balak, 14 "I am going to my people; let me advise you what this people will do to your people in days to come." 15 So he uttered his oracle, saying: "The oracle of Balaam son of Beor, the oracle of the man whose eye is clear, 16 the oracle of one who hears the words of God, and knows the knowledge of the Most High, who sees the vision of the Almighty, who falls down, but with his eyes uncovered: 17 I see him, but not now; I behold him, but not near—a star shall come out of Jacob, and a scepter shall rise out of Israel; it shall crush the borderlandsd of Moab, and the territory of all the Shethites.18 Edom will become a possession, Seir a possession of its enemies, while Israel does valiantly.19 One out of Jacob shall rule, and destroy the survivors of Ir."20 Then he looked on Amalek, and uttered his oracle, saying: "First among the nations was Amalek, but its end is to perish forever." 21 Then he looked on the Kenite, and uttered his oracle, saying: "Enduring is your dwelling place, and your nest is set in the rock; 22 yet Kain is destined for burning. How long shall Asshur take you away captive?" 23 Again he uttered his oracle, saying: "Alas, who shall live when God does this? 24 But ships shall come from Kittim and shall afflict Asshur and Eber; and he also shall perish forever."25 Then Balaam got up and went back to his place, and Balak also went his way.

3. The Elohistic Abraham Cycle

Note: The elohistic text is presented in regular font. The italics and smaller fonts indicate supplementary additions.

3.1 Abraham and Sarah's Sojourn in Gerar (Gen. 20)

20:1 *From there* Abraham journeyed toward the region of the Negeb, and settled between Kadesh and Shur. While residing in Gerar as an alien, 2 Abraham said of his wife Sarah, "She is my sister." And King Abimelech of Gerar sent and took Sarah. 3 But God came to Abimelech in a dream by night, and said to him, "You are about to die because of the woman whom you have taken; for she is a married woman." 4 *Now Abimelech had not approached her; so he said, "Lord, will you destroy an innocent people? 5 Did he not himself say to me, 'She is my sister'? And she herself said, 'He is my brother.' I did this in the integrity of my heart and the innocence of my hands." 6 Then God said to him in the dream, "Yes, I know that you did this in the integrity of your heart; furthermore it was I who kept you from sinning against me. Therefore I did not let you touch her.* 7 Now then, return the man's wife; for he is a prophet, and he will pray for you and you shall live. But if you do not restore her, know that you shall surely die, you and all that are yours."8 So Abimelech rose early in the morning, and called all his servants and told them all these things; and the men were very much afraid. 9 *Then Abimelech called Abraham, and said to him, "What have you done to us? How have I sinned against you, that you have brought such great guilt on me and my kingdom? You have done things to me that ought not to be done."* 10 And Abimelech said to Abraham, "What were you thinking of, that you did this thing?" 11 Abraham said, "I did it because I thought, There is no fear of God at all in this place, and they will kill me because of my wife. 12 *Besides, she is indeed my sister, the daughter of my father but not the daughter of my mother; and she became my wife. 13 And when God caused me to wander from my father's house, I said to her, 'This is the kindness you must do me: at every place to which we come, say of me, He is my brother.'"* 14 Then Abimelech *took sheep and oxen, and male and female slaves, and gave them to Abraham, and* restored his [Abraham's] wife Sarah to him. 15 Abimelech said, "My land is before you; settle where it pleases you." 16 *To Sarah he said, "Look, I have given your brother a thousand pieces of silver; it is your exoneration before all who are with you; you are completely vindicated."* 17 Then Abraham prayed to God; and God healed Abimelech and also healed his wife and female slaves so that they bore children. 18 *For the LORD had closed fast all the wombs of the house of Abimelech because of Sarah, Abraham's wife.*

3.1.1 Source Division

According to many Documentary scholars, the parallel narratives of Gen. 12:10-20, Gen. 20 (and Gen. 26) are one of the clearest examples of J and E's basic similarity.[1] (Gen. 12:10-20 recounts that when Abraham and Sarah descended to Egypt because of a famine. Abraham presented Sarah as his sister to the Egyptian monarch, the patriarch is thus protected and granted property; in Gen. 26, Isaac attempts the same ruse with Rebeccah, with less success). The opinion more common today,[2] however, is that 20:1-18 is dependent upon 12:10-20 and subsequent episodes. Accordingly, Van Seters submits that verses 1-18 address the questions and/or the moral dilemmas arising from the first episode with Pharaoh.[3] The first proof of this dependency, according to Van Seters, is verse 1 "From there Abraham journeyed toward the region of the Negeb and settled between Kadesh and Shur. While residing in Gerar as an alien...". Van Seters maintains that the lack of an explicit reason and the general reference to previous journeys—"From there"— is one of the many signs indicating that the narrative in question is secondary and dependent upon Chapter 12:10-20. This reasoning, however, assumes that the narrator is required to provide some sort of explanation for Abraham's sojourn in Gerar. Such an assumption is baseless since the biblical narrator does not give a reason for other stages of Abraham's journey in Canaan; for example, "From there he moved on to the hill country on the east of Bethel, and pitched his tent, with Bethel on the west and Ai on the east" (12:8) or "So Abram moved his tent, and came and settled by the oaks of Mamre, which are at Hebron" (13:18). The phrase "From there," much like "after these things" at the

---

1   J. Skinner, *Genesis*, 215, 315, 363.
2   R. Smend, *Die Erzählung des Hexateuch auf ihre Quellen Untersucht*, Berlin, 38; Volz and Rudolph, 34, S. Mowinckel *Erwägungen zur Pentateuchquellen Frage*, Oslo, 1964, 100; J. Van Seters, *Abraham in History and Tradition*, Yale University, 1975, 171; Y. Zakovitch, *Abram and Sarai in Egypt, Genesis 12:10-20, in the Bible, in the Translations and in Early Jewish Commentaries* (Hebrew), 1983; Blum, *Va☐tergeschichte*, 406. Ch. Levin, *Jahwist*, 173 goes so far as to name this section the Abraham Midrash – as an allusion to its lateness.
3   Van Seters, *Abraham*, 171-175.

beginning of Chapter 22 (and elsewhere.) is more likely a general redactional expression used to link this chapter to non-specific previous
narratives and at most indicates the chapter's connection to the previous narratives of the Abraham cycle.

Van Seters explains that verse 2 is a summary of the previous story:
"Abraham said of his wife Sarah, "She is my sister." And King Abimelech of Gerar sent and took Sarah" and assumes knowledge of Abraham's previous subterfuge with Pharaoh as well as Abimelech's reason
for taking her. Van Seters concedes, however, that the reason for Abraham's lie is mentioned in later verses (20:11), and allows that the absence of an explicit reason for Abimelech's "seizure" of Sarah is simply
a literary lacuna, similar to the many gaps of Chapter 12:10-20 which
the author (advertently or inadvertently) permits the reader to fill in. A
good example of this literary device is the absence of any explicit indication regarding Pharaoh's sexual contact with Sarah, a critical issue in
Chapter 20 as well. Possibly, the author is brief at this juncture because
other aspects of the narrative are more important to him (e.g. Abimelech's dream). Moreover, the spare style exhibited in these first verses is
in accordance with E's terseness throughout his entire work. This
terseness allowed subsequent redactors to fill in literary gaps and mold
the story to their hearts' content.[4]

The following is a list of the remainder of difficulties, questions or
lacunae that arise from the previous narrative of Chapter 12 which,
according to Van Seters, are addressed in Chapter 20.

1. How did the monarch in question know that Sarah was Abraham's
wife? – The information was revealed in a dream 20:3: "You are about
to die because of the woman whom you have taken; for she is a married
woman."
2. Abraham's moral position vis-à-vis the ruler is discussed in 20:4-7; cf.
also Abraham's excuse for deceiving Abimelech (20:11-13)—"there is
no fear of God, she is my half-sister"—and Abimelech's payment to
Sarah and the right to reside in the land of Gerar (20:15-16).
3. Was the payment the ruler gave Abraham in exchange for sexual
relations with Sarah? Chapter 20:4 mentions explicitly that Abimelech
did not approach Sarah in any way. (He did, however, "take her" in
verse 2, a verb which in biblical contexts often alludes to sexual relations). According to 20:14,16, (additional) payment was made when
Sarah was returned to Abraham.

---

4   For literary lacunae and their purpose, see Auerbach's classic article in Mimesis
      (1946).

This supposed reliance, on Chapter 20 does not, however, address all the textual difficulties, one must contend with the repetitions throughout the chapter which are often an indication of textual plurality.

Verse 3: "But God came to Abimelech in a dream;"
Verse 6: "Then God said to him in the dream."

Westermann[5] explains that following the judicial interlude in verses 3-5 it is apparently necessary to repeat the fact that the dialogue occurs in a dream (verse 6). In other words, Westermann is hinting that the judicial discussion comes from a background different from that of the bulk of the account and is foreign to the context of the dream. The author was aware of this incongruity (and of the rarity of dialogues in dream contexts) and thus repeated: "Then God said to him in the dream" (verse 6).[6] Note also the contradiction between what is said in the dream and the situation described in verse 2: Abraham referred to Sarah as "my sister", whereas according to Abimelech Sarah also maintained that Abraham was her "brother." Perhaps the author was merely accentuating Abimelech's claim, but the fact remains that these are also the classic indicators of a textual insertion: repetition, stylistic disparity and contradiction[7] According to my analysis, the direct continuation of verse 3 is verse 7, which omits the unusual dialogue and reiterates the divine warning.

Verse 9: "Then Abimelech called Abraham, and said to him, 'What have you done to us? How have I sinned against you, that you have brought such great guilt on me and my kingdom? You have done things to me that ought not to be done.'"
Verse 10: "And Abimelech said to Abraham, 'What were you thinking of, that you did this thing? '"

Verse 9 mentions a "great guilt" (חטאה גדלה)—an allusion to the moral dimension absent from vs. 10, and present only in vss. 4-6 and other additions. Thus, verse 10 is probably the original query, while

5   Westermann, *Genesis*, 1985, 323.
6   R. Killian, *Dir Vorpriesterlichen Abrahams-Überlieferungen*, Bonn, 1966, 198; Zimmer, *Elohist*, 50, 56.
7   P. Weimar (*Untersuchungen zur Redaktiongeschichte des Pentateuch* [BZAW 146], Berlin, 67) also attributes Sarah's quoted claim to a secondary layer.

verse 9 is an expansion addressing the moral concerns, Van Seters relates to, in his book.[8]

Verse 11:   "Abraham said, 'I did it because I thought, There is no fear of God at all in this place, and they will kill me because of my wife.'"

Verses 12-13:   "[Besides], she is indeed my sister, the daughter of my father but not the daughter of my mother; and she became my wife. And when God caused me to wander from my father's house, I said to her, 'This is the kindness you must do me: at every place to which we come, say of me, He is my brother.'"

Verses 12-13 allude to Abimelech's protest, which I have already identified as secondary. The phrase "He is my brother" appears in verse 5 and again in verse 13, in contrast to Abraham's claim in verse 2: "She is my sister" (without mention of any complementing claim on Sarah's part). Note also the opening word of the sentence "Besides..." which indicates authorial awareness of the fact that this is an additional excuse.[9]

Verse 14 tells us of Sarah's return to Abraham, a critical precondition to Abimelech's wellbeing (and *cf.* verse 7). The verse also mentions an additional gift of "sheep and oxen, and male and female slaves"—an expression of wealth which appears elsewhere in the yahwistic narrative (e.g. Gen. 12:16; 30:43).[10] It would seem therefore that the gift is an editorial addition authored by J.[11] The additional gifts of verse 16 (Sarah's "hush money") are in all likelihood also foreign to the narrative. The verse alludes to Abraham's second response to Abimelech in verse 12, in which Abraham claimed "she is indeed my sister," since in this verse Abimelech refers to Abraham as Sarah's brother.[12]

If this analysis is correct, the result is a shorter narrative (1[-]-3, 7-8, 10-11, 14[-]-15, 17), in which the majority of the answers to Van Seters's "questions" are not addressed, in particular, the most important ques-

---

8   P. Weimar, *Untersuchungen*, 67.

9   Cf. Weimar, *Untersuchungen*, 67, Kilian, *Abrahams U☐berlieferung*, 199, who both attribute the verses to a redactional layer.

10   *Cf.* the yahwistic substantive "שפחה" (handmaiden, female slave), contra the elohistic "אמה" (also handmaiden) – an indicator often employed by Documentary scholars (and see further examples of the elohistic אמה in Gen. 21 as opposed to Gen. 16, where the same handmaiden – Hagar – is referred to as a shifẖah by J).

11   Cf. Weimar, *Untersuchungen*, 67; Kilian, *Abrahams-Überlieferungen*, 201.

12   Cf. Weimar, *Untersuchungen*, 67; Kilian, *Abrahams-Überlieferungen*, 199.

tion: Did Abimelech have sexual relations with Sarah?[13] The "answers"
that do remain, such as the dream in which Sarah's identity is revealed
to Abimelech, are integral to the narrative account. The dream as vehicle of communication between the Deity and his human subjects appears in other elohistic narratives (Jacob, Laban and Balaam are all addressed in dreams) and is in no way anomalous. The answers to Van
Seters' questions, i.e. the noted insertions, do indicate familiarity with
12:10-20 and interpret them. Without the insertions, however, an ac-
quaintance with and reliance upon Gen.12:10-20 is not a necessary conclusion.[14]

This analysis follows the lead of Weimar and Killian who, in their
examination of the chapter, identified a basic narrative stratum and two
editorial layers. However, as Blum shows,[15] (especially with regard to
Weimar's division), their analyses are overly complicated and unconvincing. Scholars such as Van Seters have identified a number of the
difficulties in this chapter, but preferred to understand the episode as a
continuous narrative. The onus is, of course, not on Van Seters, since
most researchers before him saw the narrative as continuous, in part
because of the consistent use of "Elohim" until (but not including)
verse 18. The use of "Elohim" throughout this narrative does not, however, necessarily indicate cohesion when there are other textual issues
such as those delineated above. According to my analysis, the verses
belonging to a later non-yahwistic redactor are verses 4-6 (the dialogue
between Elohim and Abimelech), verses 12-13 (Abraham's second response) which also use "Elohim," and finally verse 16, which alludes to
verse 12. The Yahwist added both verse 9, which mentions Abraham's
"great guilt," an expression which repeats itself in the yahwistic expansion to the Golden Calf episode (Ex. 32:30-31), and the list in verse 14.
The third yahwistic insertion is, of course, verse 18, which is attributed
to J on the basis of the divine name (Yhwh) used only in this verse.[16]

3.1.2 Yahwistic Commentary

I shall begin with a short analysis of the yahwistic insertions in Chapter
20 and then proceed to examine the broader yahwistic supplementation

---

13 Cf. M. Weinfeld, Sarah in the House of Abimelech [Hebrew], *Tarbiz* 52,(1983), 639-
    642.
14 Although *cf.* Zimmer, *Elohist*, 1999, 50ff, who also identifies a basic E layer
    supplemented by a redactor, but sees E as relatively later than J.
15 Blum, *Va☐tergeschichte*, 406-407.
16 Zimmer, *Elohist*, 1999, 52.

of and commentary on, this chapter. The "great guilt" of verse 9 is part of a frequently encountered editorial theme, namely a more realistic representation of the one-dimensional characters which seem to be the elohistic norm. According to the Elohist, Abraham merely wanted to protect himself and possibly his wife from the potentially dangerous natives (the elohistic source will subsequently examine whether this fear was justified). The Yahwist, however, describes Abraham's action as a "great guilt." Abraham does not improve his moral standing vis-à-vis Abimelech when (according to J) he accepts reparations (verse 14: "Then Abimelech took sheep and oxen, and male and female slaves, and gave them to Abraham, and restored his wife Sarah to him"). Abimelech is blameless, the transgression is not his. In the broader context, the Yahwist presents Abraham's lie as part of a recurring ruse. In the yahwistic "parallel" (12:10-20), Abraham acts in the same manner and finds that it is worth his while financially. Thus, when the story repeats itself in our chapter (and with the help of the yahwistic insertions), a pattern of behavior is established and Abraham is presented as a base opportunist who would sell his wife to her great detriment and to his gain.

Gen. 12:10-20

According to many scholars,[17] Gen. 12:10-20 is one of the better examples (and perhaps the only example) of a "typical" yahwistic epsiode. According to these exegetes, Gen. 12:10-20 is an independent unit and belongs to the earliest layers of yahwistic composition. (Van Seters attributes this episode to a pre-yahwistic early version of the Abraham tradition.) I do not deny the exemplary form of this episode and I agree with its attribution to J.[18] In my opinion, however, J is a later source and thus the story belongs to a later editorial stratum. One possible editorial/supplementary function of this story, already mentioned, is the magnification of Abraham's transgression. It is possible to make the facile claim that Gen.12:10-20 belongs to an early yahwistic source, and that the editorial verses in Chapter 20 reminiscent of J actually belong to RJE. According to this argument, 12:10-20 is parallel to, but completely independent of, the episode in Chapter 20. As I claimed in the

---

17 Van Seters, *Prologue*, 246.
18 R. Aharoni, Concerning Three Similar Narratives in the Book of Genesis (Hebrew), *Beit Miqra* 24, 1979, 213-222.

Introduction, however, it is difficult to accept the existence of an "RJE" source.

In my opinion, Gen.12:10-20 does not belong to an "early layer" of biblical narrative, but is rather part of the same editorial source that supplemented Gen. 20. In his Genesis commentary, Cassuto[19] demonstrates that, similarly to what is stated in Midrash, many of the patriarchal accounts (Abraham, Isaac, Jacob, Joseph etc.) allude to later narrative. This marked tendency is referred to as "The deeds of the fathers are a sign [for the deeds] of the sons." The relocation of Abraham (or as he was known then, "Abram") to Egypt in 12:10-20 prefigures a multitude of events in the continuation of the book and later, the following allusions are a mere sample: 1) Both Abraham and the Israelites immigrate to Egypt because of a famine; 2) Joseph is made chancellor of Egypt, ultimately because of his handsome appearance, thus paralleling Abraham's rise to prominence because of Sarah's beauty; 3) Pharaoh banishes Abraham as well as the People of Israel after the Deity inflicts "grave diseases" upon him; 4) both Abraham and Israel, with Pharaoh's men close behind, are sent to the desert where they call upon the Lord; 5) Abraham, returns to Canaan through the desert, and worships the Lord on the way. The multiple allusions to other texts usually indicate a relatively late date. A text which is considered "pure" J and yet has many such allusions, leads one to believe that the entire source is later than texts which do not demonstrate such intertextuality. When a narrative is so obviously connected to many different texts it is usually considered by critical scholarship to be a relatively late composition.[20]

The later non-yahwistic redactor tries to rehabilitate the moral stature of Abraham that was slandered in the yahwistic narrative. Consequently, this author inserted verses 12-13, which reinterpret Abraham's/Abram's ruse of Chapter 12 and portray him as a truthful individual: "[Besides], she is indeed my sister, the daughter of my father but not the daughter of my mother; and she became my wife." The insertions also justify Abimelech's actions and quash any suspicions regarding Abimelech's intimate relations with Sarah by citing heavenly/divine intervention: "It was I who kept you from sinning against me. Therefore I did not let you touch her" (verse 6). According to this redactional stratum, Abimelech even gives Sarah "hush money" (verse 16). Thus, the entire episode is presented by this final redactor as an unfortunate misunderstanding: Abimelech sincerely regrets his actions

---

19   U. Cassuto, *Genesis* and *its Structure* (Hebrew), Jerusalem, 1990, 258.
20   Thus in agreement with Weimar above, who also argues for 12:10-20 as the latest of the three parallel episodes.

and Abraham is presented as an honest but fearful man. A likely candidate for the addition of the above verses is the Bridger, the final redactor of the Pentateuch. The supplementer in this case is clearly non-priestly and non-deuteronomistic, while J is eliminated as an author due to the use of "Elohim" in vss. 6 and 12. However, it is clear from his bridge to Chapters 12:10-20 and Chapter 26 that this author is cognizant of the Abraham and Isaac narrative complexes. He is also concerned that no suspicion fall on Sarah regarding her chastity, a concern most prominent in non-biblical Midrashic sources. His ardent desire to exonerate Abraham leads him to posit an incestuous relationship between Abraham and Sarah, which perhaps betrays his mythic non-nomian background (apparent in many of his other additions), since other instances of incest (such as those of Lot and Noah) are derided in their literary settings.

3.2 The Birth of Isaac (Gen. 21)

21:1 *The LORD dealt with Sarah as he had said, and the LORD did for Sarah as he had promised.* 2 Sarah conceived and bore Abraham a son in his old age *at the time which God had spoken to him* 3 Abraham gave the name Isaac to his son, *who was born to him*, whom Sarah bore *him*. 4 *And Abraham circumcised his son Isaac when he was eight days old, as God had commanded him. 5 Abraham was a hundred years old when his son Isaac was born to him.* 6 Now Sarah said, "God has brought laughter for me; everyone who hears will laugh with me." 7 And she said, "Who would ever have said to Abraham that Sarah would nurse children? Yet I have borne him a son in his old age." 8 The child grew, and was weaned; and Abraham made a great feast on the day that Isaac was weaned.

3.2.1 Source Division

The first verse of Chapter 21, which alludes to the three angels and their tidings to Sarah (Gen. 18), employs the divine name Yhwh, and is assigned to the yahwistic source.[21] The end of verse 2 ("at the time which God had spoken with him") is an allusion to the priestly narrative of Chapter 17 (in which God makes a covenant with Abraham, changes his name and promises him that he shall bear a son by the name of Isaac), since only there did *God (Elohim)* promise him progeny.

---

21 *Cf.* Driver's (*Genesis*, 209) assignment of 1a to J (and not the whole verse), which is difficult since it ignores the parallelism in the verse as a whole

The simple statement in verse 2a informing the reader that Sarah bore Abraham a son, with no allusion to either of the promise narratives (Gen. 17,18), should be attributed to the basic elohistic source. Verse 3, which informs the reader of Isaac's name, is elohistic apart from the words "Who was born to him," and "him" at the end of the verse, assigned to the priestly editor, who is addressing the issue of paternity (and see below). The etiology in verse 6 is also assigned to E.[22] According to the priestly source, Abraham is simply commanded to call his son Isaac (17:19), while according to the Yahwist the reason is that Sarah laughed when she heard the angels' tidings in Chapter 18. Verse 7 is the obvious continuation of verse 6, and the weaning feast in verse 8 is appropriate to the occasion and thus should also be attributed to the original text.[23] Verse 4 alludes to the priestly commandment of circumcision. Verse 5, in which Abraham's age is given, is once more, usually attributed to the priestly source and its chronology.

3.2.2 The Yahwistic Commentary

The priestly and yahwistic insertions are obvious as such. The yahwistic insertions: verse 1 (The LORD dealt with Sarah as he had said, and the LORD did for Sarah as he had promised), verse 2b ("at the time of which God had spoken to him"), as well as the tidings to which they allude, all fill another important function. They emphasize a theme found in the redactional layers of Chapter 20 and attempt to assure us yet again that Abraham, and not Abimelech, is Isaac's biological father. The theme is reiterated at this juncture since Sarah's sojourn in Abimelech's household and the birth of Isaac are adjacent; hence the threefold redactional emphasis upon paternity in verse 3: "Abraham gave the name Isaac to his son, who was born to him, whom Sarah bore him" (only one of which is essential to the coherence of the verse). The priestly source mentions Sarah's chastity explicitly in Chapter 20:4: "Now Abimelech had not approached her," while the Yahwist only hints at the probability that Sarah was not impregnated by Abimelech by adding verse 18, which states that Yhwh acted as a divine birth controller. In Gen. 12:10-20 the question is irrelevant, since according to the Yahwist Sarah was barren (*cf.* Gen. 11:30: "Now Sarai was barren; she

---

22 E. Speiser, *Genesis, Introduction, Translation and Notes* (Anchor Bible), New York, 1964, 153.

23 Verses 8ff are often attributed to E, and see Skinner, *Genesis*, 320-321.

had no child" and Gen. 16:2 ["The Lord has prevented me from having children."])

According to the elohistic source the issue is not at all clear: The basic narrative of Chapter 20 narrates the following: Abimelech took Sarah into his house as a concubine, an act of which the natural outcome is assumed to be engaging in sexual intercourse. The only verse in the elohistic source that in any way suggests that Abimelech was not Isaac's biological father is Gen. 20:17, which hints that the punishment imposed on Abimelech and his maidservants respectively was barrenness and/or impotence. Did this barrenness, however, exist before Abimelech slept with Sarah, or did it occur afterwards? Was Sarah also barren or only Abimelech's other "handmaidens?" The Elohist does not answer these questions. J makes matters a little clearer in verse 18 and steers the reader towards understanding that Sarah was included, since the Lord had closed *all* wombs of the house of Abimelech. (J's abstention from totally alleviating our suspicions is part and parcel of his elliptic story-telling technique, thus heightening narrative tension.) In E's version of Chapter 21 the impression that Abimelech is responsible for fathering Isaac is strengthened. A new son is born to the aged Abraham, who until now had not provided Sarah with any children. This momentous event occurs soon after the time Abimelech "took" Sarah into his household. The continuation of the elohistic narrative deals with the important question of Isaac's fate.

3.3 The Banishment of Hagar's Son (Gen. 21)

9 Sarah saw the son of Hagar the Egyptian, whom she had borne to Abraham, playing with her son Isaac. 10 So she said to Abraham, "Cast out this slave woman with her son; for the son of this slave woman shall not inherit along with my son Isaac." 11 The matter was very distressing to Abraham on account of his son. 12 But God said to Abraham, "Do not be distressed because of the boy and because of your slave woman; whatever Sarah says to you, do as she tells you; *for it is through Isaac that offspring shall be named for you. 13 As for the son of the slave woman, I will make a nation of him also, because he is your offspring."* 14 So Abraham rose early in the morning, and took bread and a skin of water, and gave it to Hagar, putting it on her shoulder, along with the child, and sent her away. And she departed, and wandered about in the wilderness of Beersheba.15 When the water in the skin was gone, she cast the child under one of the bushes. 16 Then she went and sat down opposite him a good way off, about the distance of a bowshot; for she said, "Do not let me

look on the death of the child." And as she sat opposite him, she lifted up her voice and wept. 17 And God heard the voice of the boy; and the angel of God called to Hagar from heaven, and said to her, "What troubles you, Hagar? Do not be afraid; for God has heard the voice of the boy where he is. 18 *Come, lift up the boy and hold him fast with your hand, for I will make a great nation of him."* 19 Then God opened her eyes and she saw a well of water. She went, and filled the skin with water, and gave the boy a drink. 20 God was with the boy, and he grew up; he lived in the wilderness, and became an expert with the bow. 21 He lived in the wilderness of Paran; and his mother got a wife for him from the land of Egypt.

3.3.1 Source Division

It is accepted wisdom among scholars of source criticism that verses 9-19 of Chapter 21 belong uniformly to the elohistic source.[24] However, Gen. 21:12: "But God said to Abraham, 'Do not be distressed because of the boy and because of your slave woman; whatever Sarah says to you, do as she tells you; for it is through Isaac that offspring shall be named for you'," appears to indicate that, according to the elohistic source, Isaac had progeny, contrary to our claim in the Introduction. (There is no elohistic Isaac cycle.) Nevertheless, a brief analysis of the above narrative will show that the verse fragment "For it is through Isaac that offspring shall be named for you" probably belongs to an editorial layer.[25] My analysis begins with the tension between verses 18 and 19. Hagar is commanded in verse 18: "Come, lift up the boy and hold him fast with your hand, for I will make a great nation of him." Verse 19, however, does not accord with this command: here Hagar does not carry her son, but rather fills the water skin and gives him a drink from it. Her son does not move from his place in the bushes (verse 15). This is an indication that verse 18 is a secondary insertion into the story, a claim that gains credence if we examine the continuation of the verse, which promises that her son will one day achieve greatness and father a nation, an event that is not mentioned elsewhere in any elohistic passage.[26] The promise is connected to Elohim's statement "For it is through Isaac that offspring shall be named for you" in verse 12, and

---

24   Driver, *Genesis*, 210-212.

25   Thus Gunkel (*Genesis*, 1997, 226-227) assigns verses 11-13 to a redactor, basing himself on the form of the revelation.

26   Compare the assignment by Westerman (*Genesis*, 1985, 342) of verse 17 and most of verse 18 to a redactor.

especially that in verse 13: "As for the son of the slave woman, I will make a nation of him also, because he is your offspring." It is reminiscent of Elohim's words in Chapter 17:19 (which is unanimously attributed to P), "God said, 'No, but your wife Sarah shall bear you a son, and you shall name him Isaac. I will establish my covenant with him as an everlasting covenant for his offspring after him. As for Ishmael, I have heard you; I will bless him and make him fruitful and exceedingly numerous; he shall be the father of twelve princes, and I will make him a great nation'" (verses 19-20). In my opinion, the promises in Chapter 21 belong to this same source and were inserted in the present context in order to connect the banishment of Hagar and her son to the other priestly passages in Genesis, such as Chapter 17, and to Ishmael's genealogy in Chapter 25.[27] The elohistic source does not make any long term promises to the forefathers. Such promises are either yahwistic or occasionally priestly. [28]

3.3.2 The Yahwistic Commentary

J does not add any material to this episode. A yahwistic parallel of sorts does exist in Chapter 16, which attempts to shed some light on Sarah's unexplained hostility towards Hagar in this chapter, names Hagar's anonymous son and explains his origin. Barren Sarai (the name is changed to Sarah only in Chapter 17) gave Hagar to her husband so that Sarai could vicariously provide Abram (whose name is similarly changed to Abraham only in Chapter 17) with children. The plan backfires when her now-pregnant maidservant flaunts her pregnancy and grows haughty. Sarai succeeds in driving her maidservant away by making her life unbearable. After fleeing to the desert, Hagar is graced with a revelation, is urged to return to her mistress, and is promised that she will give birth to a son and become the mother of a great nation (16:10 "I will so greatly multiply your offspring that they cannot be counted for multitude"). She therefore returns. It is natural that Chapter 16 (in contrast to Chapter 20) names the youth Ishmael because the chapter tells of his birth. The reason for his name: "for the LORD has given heed (שׁמע) to your affliction" (16:11) recalls the angel's statement in Chapter 21: "God has heard (שׁמע) the voice of the boy where he is" (21:17). We cannot know for certain whether the elohistic source was

---

27   Driver, *Genesis*, 1904, 211 also recognized the parallel.

28   This lack of elohistic promises is seen in Boorer's survey (S. Boorer, *The Promise of the Land as Oath* (BZAW 205), Berlin, 1992, 41).

familiar with the name Ishmael: the anonymity of Chapter 20 points one way, while the possible allusion to the name points the other way. Even if the Elohist is unfamiliar with the name "Ishmael" the Yahwist obviously based his etiology on the (elohistic) verse in 21:17. Chapter 16 is the second example (the first being 12:10-20) of the editorial technique (adopted from the Midrash): "The deeds of the fathers hint to the deeds of their descendants" or, more accurately in this case, "the deeds of the fathers hint to further deeds of the fathers." Such an addition saves the Yahwist the time and effort involved in searching for a new narrative paradigm, allowing him to concentrate on other aspects of his storytelling.

Abraham unwillingly banishes his slave wife and his biological son to the wilderness at Sarah's behest, which is reinforced by God's urging him to heed her. Sarah, who undoubtedly enjoys her status as chief wife, is surely entitled to request that Abraham's wealth not be divided with the slave child. Hovering in the background is that laughter root צ.ח.ק, this time used as piel which has both the meaning of laughter and possibly the meaning of scorn. Was the slave son casting doubt on Isaac's paternity, forcing Sarah to silence him by banishing him?

3.4 The Agreement between Abraham and Abimelech (Gen. 21)

22 At that time Abimelech *and Phicol the commander of his army* said to Abraham, "God is with you in all that you do; 23 now therefore swear to me here by God that you will not deal falsely with me or with my offspring or with my posterity, but as I have dealt loyally with you, you will deal with me and with the land where you have resided as an alien." 24 And Abraham said, "I swear it." 25 When Abraham complained to Abimelech about a well of water that Abimelech's servants had seized, 26 Abimelech said, "I do not know who has done this; you did not tell me, and I have not heard of it until today." 27 *So Abraham took sheep and oxen and gave them to Abimelech, and the two men made a covenant.* 28 Abraham set apart seven ewe lambs of the flock. 29 And Abimelech said to Abraham, "What is the meaning of these seven ewe lambs that you have set apart?" 30 He said, "These seven ewe lambs you shall accept from my hand, in order that you may be a witness for me that I dug this well." 31 Therefore that place was called Beer-sheba; *because there both of them swore an oath.* 32 *When they had made a covenant at Beer-sheba, Abimelech, with Phicol the commander of his army, left and returned to the land of the Philistines.* 33 *Abraham planted a tamarisk tree in Beer-sheba, and*

called there on the name of the LORD, the Everlasting God. 34 *And Abraham resided as an alien many days in the land of the Philistines.*

3.4.1 Source Division

That this narrative is mainly elohistic is apparent in the use of Elohim in verses 22-23.[29] Moreover, Abimelech alludes to the boon he granted Abraham in Gen. 20:15 (E), i.e. the right to reside wheresoever he desired. The appearance of Abimelech's general on the scene is probably a yahwistic insertion (see below in the J commentary). The narrative continues until verse 26 without an outside interruption. Verse 27, which speaks of an "alliance" between Abimelech and Abraham, is in all likelihood a yahwistic insertion: It interrupts the E dialogue concerning wells (resumed in verses 28-30) and inserts the issue of an alliance. The addition of Phicol, Abimelech's army commander, is probably in the same vein.[30] Both the second part of verse 31 and verse 32a are etiological and allude to the alliance of verse 27: "…Because there both of them swore an oath. When they had made a covenant at Beer-sheba, Abimelech, with Phicol the commander of his army, left and returned to the land of the Philistines." E's Beersheba etiology is connected to the seven sheep and not the oath; the Hebrew terms for "seven" (שבע) and "to swear" (ש.ב.ע) are derived from homonymous roots. Verse 33 is yahwistic, since it uses "Yhwh", the planting of the tamarisk in this verse is comparable to the erection of altars in Gen. 12 and 13 (both of which are yahwistic chapters). A further indication of the secondary nature of Verses 32 and 34 is the reference to the "land of the Philistines," which clearly contradicts 20:2, in which Abimelech is referred to as the King of Gerar.[31] Abimelech is a Philistine only according to J, here in vss. 32, 34 and in Gen. 26:8 ("King Abimelech of the Philistines").

3.4.2 The Yahwistic Commentary and the Elohistic Context

The Yahwist "upgraded" the E narrative, initially an agreement concerning wells, into an alliance between the Philistines and Abraham, who seemingly represents the People of Israel. It is likely that the

---

29   Wellhausen, *Hexateuch,* 17-18.
30   Gunkel, *Genesis,* 231.
31   Many scholars find secondary elements in vss. 32-34, e.g. Skinner, *Genesis,* 325.

Yahwist turned Abimelech into a Philistine and added an alliance between him and Abraham in order to explain the Philistine presence in
the Promised Land. Abraham promised the Philistines rights over certain parts of Canaan, and there they stayed. Indeed, in his commentary
to the book of Genesis, the medieval commentator Rashbam finds a
connection between this "unfortunate" pact and the sacrifice of Isaac:
he claims that because Abraham made an alliance with the inhabitants
of the land and promised them rights over it (a decidedly negative act),
Elohim punished him with the test.

What, however, is the place of this narrative in the overall context
of the elohistic Abraham cycle? Let us begin with Abimelech's somewhat confusing statement (21:23), "now therefore swear to me here by
God that you will not deal falsely with me or with my offspring or with
my posterity, but as I have dealt loyally with you, you will deal with
me and with the land where you have resided as an alien." A biblical
agreement between two people is usually binding upon subsequent
generations. Abimelech, however, mentions his own progeny and does
not mention Abraham's. Is this exclusion mere chance? Since the two
previous chapters deal with offspring and the ability to procreate, as
does all of the next chapter, any mention of offspring or lack thereof
may be significant. I have more than once mentioned that according to
the E narrative Isaac's paternity is in doubt and that he may indeed be a
bastard. One must of course question why Abraham and Sarah were
"graced" with such a son. I should like to venture that this may be part
of Abraham's punishment for doubting the belief of the people of Gerar
in the religious principle "fear of Elohim"; Abraham himself did not
"fear God" sufficiently nor trust in his ability to protect him, an abrogation of E's most important tenet: "Fear God and live" (which will be
discussed in greater detail at the end of this chapter). E proves that
Abraham's doubts were out of place (20:8): "So Abimelech rose early in
the morning, and called all his servants and told them all these things;
and the men were very much afraid." In 21:22: ("God is with you in all
that you do") Abimelech desires Abraham's goodwill because he
knows that Elohim is with him, thus once again proving that he fears
God. Perhaps the elohistic statement quoted concerning the oath above
(21:23) hints at the fact that Abimelech may have grandchildren and
great- grandchildren, but that Abraham will not, because he sent his
firstborn son into the wilderness, while it is entirely likely that his
second son is a bastard. A more cynical reading would be that Abimelech is asking grace for his bastard son and binding Abraham to protect
him. Abraham's fidelity to his oath in Elohim's name is about to be
tested by Elohim.

3.5 The Sacrifice of Isaac (Gen. 22)

22:1 After these things God tested Abraham. He said to him, "Abraham!" And he said, "Here I am." 2 He said, "Take your son, your only son Isaac, whom you love, and go to the land of Moriah, and offer him there as a burnt offering on one of the mountains that I shall show you." 3 So Abraham rose early in the morning, saddled his donkey, and took two of his young men with him, and his son Isaac; he cut the wood for the burnt offering, and set out and went to the place in the distance that God had shown him. 4 On the third day Abraham looked up and saw the place far away. 5 Then Abraham said to his young men, "Stay here with the donkey; the boy and I will go over there; we will worship, and then we will come back to you." 6 Abraham took the wood of the burnt offering and laid it on his son Isaac, and he himself carried the fire and the knife. So the two of them walked on together. 7 Isaac said to his father Abraham, "Father!" And he said, "Here I am, my son." He said, "The fire and the wood are here, but where is the lamb for a burnt offering?" 8 Abraham said, "God himself will provide the lamb for a burnt offering, my son." So the two of them walked on together. 9 When they came to the place that God had shown him, Abraham built an altar there and laid the wood in order. He bound his son Isaac, and laid him on the altar, on top of the wood. 10 Then Abraham reached out his hand and took the knife to kill his son. 11 The angel of God / (Yhwh) called to him from heaven, and said, "Abraham, Abraham!" And he said, "Here I am." 12 He said, *"Do not lay your hand on the boy or do anything to him, for* now I know that you fear God, since you have not withheld your son, your only son, from me." 13 *And Abraham looked up and saw a ram, caught in a thicket by its horns. Abraham went and took the ram and offered it up as a burnt offering instead of his son. 14 So Abraham called that place "The LORD will provide"; as it is said to this day, "On the mount of the LORD it shall be provided." 15 The angel of the LORD called to Abraham a second time from heaven, 16 and said, "By myself I have sworn, says the LORD: Because you have done this, and have not withheld your son, your only son, 17 I will indeed bless you, and I will make your offspring as numerous as the stars of heaven and as the sand that is on the seashore. And your offspring shall possess the gate of their enemies, 18 and by your offspring shall all the nations of the earth gain blessing for themselves, because you have obeyed my voice."* 19 So Abraham returned to his young men, and they arose and went together to Beer-sheba; and Abraham lived at Beer-sheba.

3.5.1 Source Division

The source division of Gen. 22 according to most critical scholars is quite simple: Verses 1-13, 19 are attributed to the primary elohistic source and verses 15-18 to a redactional yahwistic source. Verse 14 is the only verse over which there is disagreement. Some see it as integral to the narrative;[32] others claim that all of it or part of it was altered by a redactor;[33] while still others regard it as a later etiological tradition explaining the equation between the mountain in the land of Moriah and Jerusalem.[34] However, this division is not as straightforward as may seem from such a general summary, which ignores the fact that verse 11 uses Yhwh and not E's customary Elohim. Scholarship has suggested many solutions to this quandary. Some propose an acceptance of the Syriac's variant "Elohim" as correct and original (over the Masoretic text's Yhwh). This proposal is difficult to accept, since it clearly negates the philological rule: "*lectio difficilior preferendum est.*" The non-conformist reading i.e. "the angel of the LORD (Yhwh)," is preferable to the conformist reading: "The angel of God (Elohim)". Another proposal emphasizes that since "Yhwh" and "Elohim," the two names of the Deity, appear with equal frequency throughout Gen. 22, the appearance of "the angel of Yhwh" in verse 11 presents no difficulty.[35] This type of solution is hard to accept, since it dismisses the divine names as a source-critical criterion. A third opinion suggests that since the expression "angel of Elohim" is infrequent, even this "elohistic" narrative would use the more common "angel of Yhwh".[36] This proposal resembles an excuse rather than an actual solution, since the expression "the angel of Elohim" does indeed occur at other points in Genesis (28:12; 31:11; 32:1). Finally, there are those who claim that the first revelation (verses 11-13) is also a secondary addition[37] but this too is problematic, since verse 12: "Now I know that your fear God" is a typical elohistic sentiment and fits well with the elohistic account. Excising it from the narrative merely because it belongs to a problematic revelation is irresponsible. In fact, none of the solutions proposed by scholarship is convincing.

---

32 And disregard the fact that the verse uses Yhwh instead of Elohim, Skinner, *Genesis*, 327-352.

33 Dillmann, *Genesis*, 291, 293-294; Westermann, *Genesis*, 1985, 363.

34 L. Kundert, *Die Opferung/Bindung Isaaks*, Neukirchen-Vluyn, 1998, 32.

35 J. C. Crenshaw, *A Whirlpool of Torment: Israelite Traditions about God as an Oppressive Presence*, Philadelphia, 1984, 13.

36 Westermann, *Genesis*, 1985, 361.

37 Kundert, *Opferung*, 1-12.

A further difficulty is the role of verses 15-18 (the second revelation of the angel). Van Seters suggests that had there been a second appearance of the angel of Yhwh, the only appropriate place for it would have been verses 15-18 and as such these verses should be regarded as original.[38] This solution is also unacceptable, since it discounts the names of God as a valid source-critical tool. However, Van Seters' argument, underscores the weak point of the Documentary source division: Why should verse 11, which also uses "Yhwh," be assigned to E (the source which uses Elohim) while verses 15-18 are relegated to a secondary status?

The last, and in my opinion most serious, problem, is literary. The elohistic source concludes with verse 19: "and Abraham returned [alone] to his servants." This verse contrasts starkly with verses 6 and 8 ("The two of them walked together") both of which emphasize that Abraham and Isaac walked together.[39] The obvious question here— why Isaac is not mentioned in verse 19—has also not been adequately answered by the frequent analyses of this episode.[40]

The aforementioned difficulties lead us to emend the division suggested above. Firstly, if God's names are to be accepted as a valid source-critical criterion, not only verses 15-18 (the second revelation) but also verse 11 (which uses Yhwh) should be attributed to an editorial layer. If verse 11 is to be understood as an insertion, it is necessary to understand verse 12 in the same way, since this verse ("Do not raise your hand...") is the obvious continuation of the angel's speech. The second part of verse 12, however, "You fear God"—an elohistic phrase par excellence (and cf. Gen. 20:11: "fear of God")—should be attributed to E. A possible solution to this contradictory evidence is that the editor adapted the originally elohistic formulation in verses 11-12 and created a new revelation involving the angel of "Yhwh" instead of God "Elohim."[41] I would suggest that the reason for the rewriting of this verse is that according to the original story, Isaac is sacrificed by Abraham. The yahwistic editor, who could not accept such an outcome,

---

38   Van Seters, *Prologue*, 261-263.

39   We find it very difficult to accept Levin's claim (*Jahwist*, 176) that vss. 6-8, are to be attributed to a second author, or perhaps even to more than one author – there are no fractures that would indicate plurality.

40   Coats's suggestion (G. W. Coats, *Genesis with Introduction to Narrative Literature*, Grand Rapids, Michigan, 1983, 158) that this verse be attributed to an itinerary source is unsatisfactory.

41   Boehm (O. Boehm, The Binding of Isaac: An Inner Biblical Polemic on the Question of "Disobeying" a Manifestly Illegal Order, *VT* 52, 2002, 1-12) assigns verses 11-12 in their entirety to the redactor but fails to account for the use of Elohim in the second half of verse 12.

altered the narrative and turned a story of ultimate sacrifice into a story of redemption.[42] The addition of verse 12a ("Do not raise your hand") and verse 13 (the substitution) elegantly reverses the meaning of the original elohistic revelation.

Admittedly, the division suggested above does have one weak point: There does not seem to be any explicit mention of Isaac's sacrifice. In my opinion, however, there is no need for an elaborate reconstruction. Nothing is really missing. Verse 10: "He picked up his knife to slay his son" can be understood as elliptic; the "missing" words "and he slew his son" are implied and not written, since they are basically a repetition of the extant clause: "to slay his son." Thus verse 10b could conceivably be translated: "And Abraham took the knife to slay his son (and he slew his son)." Since the omission of such clauses is well documented, this proposed reading is in no way anomalous. The commendation in verse 12b "I know that you fear God, since you have not withheld your son, your only son, from me," as well as verse 19 (Abraham's return to Beersheba without Isaac) are now understood in a different and perhaps more sinister light.[43] The constant repetition of "my father" and "my son" is ironic.

One has still to explain why the Yahwist preferred to change the text and substitute "Yhwh" for the original "Elohim" in verse 11. This is best answered by Knohl (1998) in his article on Gen. 22:[44] "According to the narrator, the rational and ethical dimension symbolized by the name YHWH overrules the numinous (irrational and immoral) dimension symbolized by the name Elohim-God".

Knohl claims that the text in Gen. 22 is yahwistic in its entirety and that the debate on the different aspects of the Deity is internal to the scripture. I agree with my teacher regarding the different character of the names in Gen. 22, but take a more critical approach, considering the different names of the Deity as a sign of the composite character of the text. The yahwistic editor was entirely aware that the name Elohim was part and parcel of elohistic theology. Thus, when he altered the meaning of the text to conform with his more "rational" and merciful con-

---

42 Kundert, *Opferung*, 32, 42-43 also argues that the sacrifice was performed in the original account.

43 Verse 19 is the basis of later midrashim which allude to Isaac's actual sacrifice and death and *cf.* S. Spiegel, *The Last Trial, on the Legends and Lore of the Command to Offer Isaac as a Sacrifice*, New–York, 1967.

44 I. Knohl, In the Face of Death: Mortality and Religious Life in the Bible, in Rabbinic Literature, and in the Pauline Letters, in *Self, Soul, and Body in Religious Experience* (Studies in the History of Religion 78), Boston, 1998, 87-95.

ception, he also changed the name which was part of a different and "more numinous" one.

3.5.2 Implications

This analysis accords with subsequent elohistic narratives and narrative cycles. After Gen. 22, Isaac simply does not appear in any elohistic narrative. E takes no part in the so-called Isaac cycle. Isaac is not a character for E after Gen. 22. Any mention of "Elohim" in the so-called Isaac cycle can usually be attributed to P (as in Gen. 25:11, 28:4). All other supposed appearances of Isaac in elohistic narrative may be explained as supplementary additions (as I shall explain below, *passim*).

If my analysis is correct, it affects the critical study of the Pentateuch in important ways. The claim that Abraham sacrificed his son according to the original elohistic story undermines the traditional Documentary Hypothesis. If Isaac was sacrificed (and died), then there is indeed no need for a story-cycle devoted to him. The "gap" referred to in the Introduction is no longer mysterious. In fact no real gap exists if we regard the elohistic source as a collection of five story cycles whose focus is the great personalities of ancestors and heroes connected to the Israelite nation.

The role the redactor plays in this composition is critical. Simply put, through his redaction, he transformed this tale of ultimate sacrifice to one of redemption. He saved Isaac so that he could connect Abraham with Jacob and produce a coherent account of early Israelite "history." But what of E? If what we say is correct, then what is Abraham's role according to the Elohist? (He is not an Israelite patriarch, since his connection to the Israelite line was severed by sacrificing Isaac.) To answer this question, one must determine the purpose of the sacrifice in its original elohistic context.

Many scholars have dealt with the theology of the elohistic source and all agree that "the fear of Elohim" is central to an understanding of E.[45] As I have contended, Abraham causelessly doubted the people of Gerar's "fear of God," and thus his own fear of God was put in doubt. Moreover, he ignored the mores of righteous behavior by prostituting his wife. In Chapter 22, Abraham proves that he still fears God by sacrificing his son of questionable origin. This sacrifice (despite all its modern moral repugnance) solves the difficulty of Isaac's questionable origin. The product of Abraham's sin is sacrificed in expiation. By

---

45   Cf. Wolff, 1972, one of the staunchest defenders of the Elohistic source.

sacrificing Isaac Abraham proves that his fear of Elohim is exemplary. His brief appearance at the beginning of the elohistic source is an example of the degree of "reverence" one should aspire to. Although Abraham is not the biological father of Israel according to E, it is quite likely that he was seen as the theological father.

3.6 A Summary of the Elohistic Narrative

While the internal unity of Abraham's stories has been demonstrated a review of the plot is in order so as to enable one to see how all the pieces fit together. Abraham the prophet moves with his wife to the land of Gerar. His fear that the people of Gerar do not fear Elohim (and are therefore covetous of their neighbors' wives) leads him to claim that his wife is in fact his sister and consequently Abimelech the King of Gerar takes Sarah as his concubine. Elohim warns Abimelech on pain of death to return Sarah to Abraham, which he does. As time goes by, Sarah gives birth to a son whose lineage is questionable, and names him Isaac (laughter – ephemerality). Regardless of his questionable origins, Sarah of course wants her son to be the sole inheritor, and in a twist of supernatural irony Elohim agrees. Abraham banishes his legitimate son and the mother of this son (but not Isaac) into the desert, where with the help of Elohim the son flourishes. Abraham's elder son has done no wrong; it is Abraham who is being punished and this separation from his legitimate son is the first part of the expiation for his sin of doubting whether the inhabitants of Gerar were God-fearing.

After witnessing Abraham's power, Abimelech wisely extracts a promise to show favour to himself and his descendants, and together they are responsible for the founding of Beersheba, where Abraham establishes residence. Abraham's foundation of the city will however benefit him and his offspring very little since, with a last turn of the screw, Elohim "tests" Abraham and requires him to sacrifice his second "son" Isaac. Finally, Abraham returns to Beersheba devoid of offspring, but free of sin.

The above analysis of the episodes may appear somewhat eisegetical (reading into the text) as opposed to exegetical (reading from the text), but in fact nothing has been added or interpreted in a less than straightforward manner. The events are entirely consistent with the theology of the elohistic source, as I will attempt to demonstrate in the appendix to this chapter.

3.6.1 Structure

Outwardly, it would appear that the four episodes of the Abraham cycle (the division into five was for convenience's sake) are arranged in an A-B-A'-B' structure (thus Deurloo 1992).[46] More specifically, Chapter 20 is parallel to the end of Chapter 21 (verses 22-32): both deal with Abimelech and his relations with Abraham, whereas the beginning of Chapter 21 and the entire Chapter 22 deal with the separation of Abraham from his offspring.[47]

There is, however, another, not necessarily contradictory, possibility: Fokkelman claims that the whole of the Abraham cycle is chiastic or circular.[48] I maintain that the elohistic Abraham cycle, too, was organized in this way. The structure is hinted at in the first and last verses of the cycle: "Abraham journeyed toward the region of the Negeb, and settled between Kadesh and Shur. While residing in Gerar as an alien" (20:1), "And they arose and went together to Beersheba; and Abraham lived at Beersheba" (22:19). Chapter 20 is parallel to the beginning of Chapter 22: the first episode deals with Abraham's doubts and his sin, while the second deals with his faith and his atonement. Both sections discuss the death of one of the main characters (Isaac and Abimelech [20:3]) and in both cases servants are explicitly mentioned and play the role of "silent witnesses."

The beginning of Chapter 21 is parallel to its end: both episodes deal with genealogy and the expected inheritance, the first—with Abraham's offspring, and the second with those of Abimelech. In both stories wells are critically important: in the first episode an anonymous well provides succor, while in the other, the well marks the foundation of a city. Finally, the verb "to hear" is important both at the beginning of the chapter and at its end: Abraham hears what Sarah has to say, Elohim hears the cries of Hagar. Abimelech, however, had not heard that his servants had requisitioned Abraham's well.

The conflicting evidence regarding the structure of these four episodes is not particularly bothersome. Both structures can exist side by side, since they serve different purposes: On the one hand, the parallel structure reflects the storyteller's art, and perhaps a wish to contrast the respective fates of Abraham's two sons. On the other hand, the chiasm is indicative of the Elohist's desire to maintain a uniformity of structure

---

46   K. A. Deurloo, Beerseba; Genesis 21, 22-34, *Amsterdamse Cahiers* 11 (1992): 7-13.

47   C. Leviant, Ishmael and Hagar in the Wilderness; a Parallel Akedah, *Midstream* 43:8, 1997, 17-19.

48   J. P. Fokkelman, Time and the Structure of the Abraham cycle, *Oudtestamentische Studiën* 25 (1989): 96-109.

throughout his narrative since, as I hope to prove, all subsequent cycles are structured in the same way.

3.6.2 The Yahwistic Commentary: Summary

According to the above analysis, the Yahwist's burden as the editor of E was indeed weighty. First, he had to turn a story of child-sacrifice into a story of redemption. Secondly, he had to link the Abraham cycle with the remaining stories of the forefathers. I demonstrated the manner in which he intervened internally with the story of the sacrifice. His invasive intervention, however, occurs both before and after the episode in question. As I have already discussed, the Yahwist emphasizes Abraham's legitimate fatherhood through the insertion of tidings and other allusions (*cf.* 20:18, 21:1). Another interesting fact is that in comparison with Jacob, Abraham receives more than his share of promises for posterity, even though the yahwistic Jacob cycle and the yahwistic Abraham cycle (which includes E) are of similar length. This repeated emphasis may, of course, be understood as part of the overall editorial theme connecting Abraham to the Israelite genealogy, as opposed to the Elohist, who cuts off Abraham's line in Chapter 22.

3.7 Appendix: Theology and Sacrifice

The claim that, according to E, Abraham sacrificed Isaac and that Jacob (and not Abraham) was the founding father, may be difficult to accept. Although I stand by my textual analysis, more proof should be brought to bear. The absence of an elohistic Isaac cycle was noted in the Introduction; the majority of the Isaac narratives are concentrated in one chapter (Gen. 26) and are based upon previous narratives (the frequent divine promises of land and progeny to Abraham, the well narratives [Gen. 21:22-34], and Abraham's ruse in Gen. 20). In the two additional chapters that mention Isaac (Chapter 24 and Chapter 27), Isaac is not the main character. Thus Hunter states simply:[49] "Every narrative concerning Isaac has parallels elsewhere in the patriarchal legends." While a thorough analysis of the Isaac-cycle is unwarranted, one should note that, according to Lubsczyk (1978), Weisman (1984) and others, the

---

49   A. G. Hunter, Father Abraham: A Structural and Theological Study of the Yahwists Presentation of the Abraham Material, *JSOT* 35 (1986): 3-27.

cycle is relatively late and is primarily yahwistic.[50] In subsequent chapters, I shall attempt to prove that Isaac's name is not mentioned at all by the elohistic source after Gen. 22. The task is not formidable, since the verses challenging my theory are but few and it is possible to demonstrate that most of them belong to one or other of the editorial strata.

The strongest proof for the validity of my analysis, however, emerges from an examination of the theology of the two sources (E and J) involved in the composition of Chapter 22.

3.7.1 According to the Elohistic source, why would Abraham sacrifice Isaac?

I claim that Abraham's behavior is consistent with the theology of the elohistic source, but what is this theology? It can be summed up in one sentence: "Do this and you will live, I fear God" (Gen. 42:18): if a character fears God, he prospers; if not, he dies. This simple theology, which is not directly bound to morality, is elaborated upon by Rofe, who explains a number of the tales in the Elishah and Elijah cycles in this way. His most striking examples are the murder of the forty-two children who humiliate Elishah (II Kgs. 2:23-25) and the killing of the emissaries who come to deliver Elijah to the king (II Kgs. 1:9-14). The overriding aim of these actions is to prove Elohim's might. Hence, in the words of Rofe:[51]

> The ethical categories of good and evil are [not] relevant here… The Man of God is a holy figure (2Kgs. 4:9) and as such must be treated with veneration, just as one behaves towards the divine and the objects associated to with the Divine. These youths profaned the Holy Man of God, and like the sons of Aaron (Lev. 10:1-3) or Uzza (2 Sam. 6:6-7), who acted with no intent of malice, their punishment is swift and terrible….

Such a theology is manifest in all the interactions between the Deity and humanity in the Genesis source:

1. Elohim threatens to kill Abimelech, King of Gerar, in spite of his innocence (Gen. 20). Abimelech, who takes Elohim's warning very

---

50 Contra M. Noth, *A History of Pentateuchal Traditions*, (tr. by B.W. Anderson tr.), Englewood Cliffs, New Jersey, 1968, 102-115; Rendtorff, *U☐berlieferung*, 32, who see parts of the Isaac narratives as early.

51 A. Rofe, *Introduction to Prophetic Literature* (tr. J. A. Seeligman), London, 15.

seriously, is rewarded and "signs" a treaty with Abraham, "fearer of Elohim" par excellence.[52]

2. In accordance with Sarah's request, corroborated by Elohim, Abraham sends his son and maidservant into the desert with a water skin and little else (a manifestly unethical act). The child survives and flourishes as a result of "Elohim's" watchful presence and due to Abraham's faith in the Deity.

3. Jacob is frightened by the divine presence in Bethel (Gen. 28:10-20) and vows that if the Deity comes to his aid, he will worship him. In accordance with this promise, Elohim saves him from Laban on more than one occasion, and Jacob returns to Bethel and fulfills his vow.

4. Although casting Joseph into the pit is an immoral act by all standards, Joseph's brothers are not punished, because Elohim made good use of the act. Elohim "forgives" unethical actions if and when they coincide with his own plans and do not harm his inscrutability. In this case the text hints that, as a result, Joseph's brothers ended up "fearing Elohim." ("Say to Joseph: 'I beg you, forgive the crime of your brothers and the wrong they did in harming you. Now therefore please forgive the crime of the servants of the God of your father.' Joseph wept when they spoke to him.... But Joseph said to them, 'Do not be afraid! Am I in the place of God?'") (Gen. 50:17, 50:19).

5. The killing of one of Pharaoh's slaves and the saving of the other (Gen. 40:21-22) raise the question of morality yet again. But the morality or immorality of the acts is not considered. They fit in with Elohim's master plan.

6. "Disturbed" by dreams, Pharaoh calls on Joseph to interpret them. Joseph's interpretation of the dreams points toward an impending famine. Pharaoh heeds the warning and thus saves his people and the population of surrounding countries from starvation.

7. In a verse already quoted (42:18), Joseph states unequivocally "Do this and you will live, I fear God." It follows that if one does not fear Elohim, death is a likely outcome.

8. The midwives who feared Elohim were rewarded, even though they lied to the King of Egypt. The King of Egypt, who malevolently commanded the midwives to kill all Israelite males, dies at sea.

---

52   Note Zimmer's emphasis (206) that fear of God is a commandment incumbent on all of humanity and is not restricted to the Israelites.

9. Moses proclaims to the King of Egypt that if the People of Israel do not worship Elohim in the desert, Elohim will kill them all (Ex. 5:3). Why would this be the case? The People of Israel are subject to the whim of their rulers and do not have the ability to leave Egypt. Moses' statement describes a Deity apparently ungoverned by logic or morality.

10. The People of Israel are forbidden to climb or touch the Mountain of God since such an action would be disrespectful, an infringement on the holy. All transgressors are to be punished by death.

11. The People of Israel are literally "frightened unto death" ("Do not let God speak to us, or we will die" Ex. 20:19), but Moses calms them and impresses upon them that God spoke to them in this way so as "to put the fear of him upon you so that you do not sin" (verse 20).

12. According to E, the Israelites are punished for the molding of the Golden Calf by having to drink water tainted with the burnt residue of ashes. J, however, is not satisfied and adds two lethal punishments of his own. Why is E so lenient? Elohim recognizes the purity of Israelite intentions: the Golden Calf was a worship modus (God's chariot or mount); since their indiscretion did little to damage Elohim's prestige, it was not considered a serious sin.

13. In Num. 21:4-10, when the People of Israel complain "Why have you brought us up out of Egypt to die in the wilderness? For there is no food and no water," Elohim sends snakes to kill them. Why such a harsh punishment? When the Israelites complained at other desert stations such as Shur and Masah (Ex. 15:22-27, Num. 20), they received what they asked for (at Shur they were led to a water source and at Masah Moses hit the rock with his staff and water gushed out). The difference lies in the manner in which they voiced their complaint. In this instance, the People of Israel spoke against God, and thus, even though the complaint may have been justified, they got their just desserts as far as E is concerned.

In summary:

For E, fear of Elohim is the primary demand, overriding morality. However, E is not completely devoid of moral considerations and at times moral behavior is part and parcel of fearing God (cf. the midwives' prevention of the wholesale murder of children in Ex. 1). Nevertheless, when the two principles (morality and the fear of Elohim) clash, morality is at a distinct disadvantage.

3.7.2 J's Theology

The main thrust of J's theology is easily summarized.[53] As mentioned in the Introduction, one of J's main objectives is the aggrandizement of Yhwh. Thus, according to J the Deity saves many of the biblical protagonists, especially those essential to the spread of Yhwh's name and fame, even though their death would often have been justified.

1. Adam and Eve are spared from death, though they sinned by transgressing against Yhwh's first command: "But of the tree of the knowledge of good and evil you shall not eat, for in the day that you eat of it you shall die" (Gen. 2:17). However, without this first transgression, the world as we know it would not exist and Yhwh's name would have remained unknown. Compare the daring midrash in *Genesis Rabbah* 1, which compares the creation of the world to the construction of a palace built upon garbage and sewage.

2. Yhwh does not kill Cain instantly after the murder of his brother; rather, he grants him protection. Moreover, Cain's punishment: "You will be a fugitive and a wanderer on the earth" (Gen. 4:12) is never implemented. In point of fact, Cain is not a wanderer, but the world's first builder of a permanent settlement. He must be saved since, according to J, Cain was "the father of humanity", founder of the following genealogy: Adam, Cain, Enoch, Irad, Mehujael, Methushael, Lamech, and Noah. It should be noted that the genealogy through Shet is or was a priestly innovation.[54]

3. Noah is saved from the flood, despite the fact that Yhwh decreed death to all humans. Without some survivors, Yhwh would have remained alone in his grandeur. Noah himself was by no means righteous, as is demonstrated by the vineyard episode in Gen. 9:18-29. Petersen notes that finding favour (Gen. 6:8 "Noah found favour in the eyes of the Lord") has no necessary connection to rectitude.[55]

4. Abraham, who "sells" his wife to Pharaoh in exchange for goods, is not punished; rather, it is Pharaoh who is smitten. Yhwh ensured Abraham's wellbeing, since according to the Yahwist he is part of the unbroken chain of patriarchs (and note "the unbroken chain" of Rabbinic apologetics for Abraham's acts; thus Radak on this verse). J certainly did not spare Abraham because of his moral integrity.

---

53   See Rendtorff's survey in R. Rendtorff, Der "Jahwist" als Theologe, zum Dilemna Der Pentateuchkritik, *SVT* (Congress Volume), Leuven,158-166.

54   I. Knohl, Cain the Father of Humanity, in *Festschrift Weinfeld*, 2004, 63-67.

55   D. L. Petersen, The Yahwist on the Flood, *VT* 21 (1971): 197-208.

5. Although Yhwh decreed that Sodom and Gomorrah would be razed, Abraham's nephew Lot is spared. Was it because of Lot's connection to Abraham or was it in order to demonstrate Yhwh's terrible power to the inhabitants of the region?

6. The command to sacrifice Isaac and his redemption or resuscitation at the last moment (*cf.* the above analysis).

7. Jacob (whose name means "he will sin") is saved from his brother Esau, who planned to kill him, for the same reason that his ancestors were saved: He is a critical link in the Israelite chain.

8. The most extreme example of "crime but no punishment" is that of Jacob's sons in Shechem. Although they slaughter the inhabitants of Shechem and loot their property and the women, they are not punished in any way since they are the "Children of Israel."[56]

9. Pharaoh decrees that all the male children should be put to death, but Moses is saved, in order to redeem the People of Israel from slavery, take them out of Egypt, and triumphantly announce to the world: "Yhwh is God and there is no other beside him" (Deut. 4:35).

10. Moses repeatedly intercedes on Israel's behalf and convinces the Deity to stay his hand. The reason given for sparing his stiff-necked people is because otherwise the nations may say: "It is because the LORD was not able to bring this people into the land he swore to give them that he has slaughtered them in the wilderness" (Num. 14:15).

According to my analysis of E, Abraham needed to be punished, since he did not believe Elohim would protect him and therefore lied to Abimelech and doubted his rectitude. As a result, Elohim punishes Abraham with the death of "his" son, just as he punishes all those who do not fear him. Elohim demands that Abraham sacrifice "his" son—an act that is ironically appropriate, since Isaac was in all probability the unlucky spawn of the adulterous relationship between Abimelech and Sarah. Abraham sacrifices his son and Elohim once again recognizes Abraham as a true fearer of Elohim. The account thus matches E's theology perfectly. The merciful Yahwist modified that account and saved Isaac from death, in the same way he saved every other major representative of the Israelite family tree. As Knohl (1998) claims, "the name YHWH [consistently] overrules the numinous [irrational and immoral] dimension symbolized by the name Elohim."

---

56 According to our analysis of the episode [to be published shortly] the sin of the "Children of Israel" is literally inexcusable, since the rape is a late addition to the text.

Even if I have not succeeded in convincing all readers of the validity of my analysis regarding the sacrifice of Isaac, my thesis concerning the unity and coherence of the elohistic source stands. For even if Abraham did not sacrifice Isaac, it does not follow that there was any connection between Isaac and Jacob according to E. As I hope to demonstrate throughout this book, the "sandwiched" forefather is not mentioned again in E after Gen. 22, and the connection between him and Jacob is a yahwistic novelty. According to E, Jacob, not Abrahram, was the founder of Israel.

4. The Elohistic Jacob Cycle

4.1 Jacob in Bethel (Gen. 28)

10 Jacob left Beer-sheba *and went toward Haran.* 11 He came to a certain place and stayed there for the night, because the sun had set. Taking one of the stones of the place, he put it under his head and lay down in that place. 12 And he dreamed that there was a ladder set up on the earth, the top of it reaching to heaven; and the angels of God were ascending and descending on it. *13 And the LORD stood beside him and said, "I am the LORD, the God of Abraham your father and the God of Isaac; the land on which you lie I will give to you and to your offspring; 14 and your offspring shall be like the dust of the earth, and you shall spread abroad to the west and to the east and to the north and to the south; and all the families of the earth shall be blessed in you and in your offspring. 15 Know that I am with you and will keep you wherever you go, and will bring you back to this land; for I will not leave you until I have done what I have promised you." 16 Then Jacob woke from his sleep and said, "Surely the LORD is in this place—and I did not know it!"* 17 And he was afraid, and said, "How awesome is this place! This is none other than the house of God, and this is the gate of heaven." 18 So Jacob rose early in the morning, and he took the stone that he had put under his head and set it up for a pillar and poured oil on the top of it. 19 He called that place Bethel; *but the name of the city was Luz at the first.* 20 Then Jacob made a vow, saying, "If God will be with me, and will keep me in this way that I go, and will give me bread to eat and clothing to wear, 21 so that I come again to my father's house in peace, *then the LORD shall be my God,* 22 *and* this stone, which I have set up for a pillar, shall be God's house; and of all that you give me I will surely give one tenth to you."

4.1.1 Source Division

If one examines the various analyses of Gen. 28:10-22 one discovers a curious phenomenon: although the chapter has been the focus of many studies in recent years,[1] one must agree with Wenham,[2] who suggests

---

1   R. Rendtorff, Jakob in Bethel, Beobachtungen zum Aufbau und zur Quellenfrage in Gen 28:10-22, ZAW 94 (1982): 511-523; A. Rofe, *Introduction to the Composition of the Torah, Jerusalem* (Hebrew), 1994; J. M. Husser, Les Metamorphoses d'un Songe:

that the new analyses do not in fact represent a real break with classical
source criticism;[3] and that ultimately the textual fractures discovered by
these new approaches are very similar to those of the classic analyses.
The real difference between the tradition-cycle or fragmentary interpreters as represented by Blum and Rofe seems to be in the number of
sources (proponents of the fragmentary or tradition cycle school argue
for a larger number of authors). For Blum (1984), Gen. 28:10-22 is the
kernel from which the Jacob complex grew and he identifies no fewer
than six (!) authors in this short section, ranging from the original cul-
tic-foundation story with an independent existence to the latest redactors, who sought to connect the patriarchal complexes one to another,
and then to the Exodus complex. Wynn-Williams, in his comparison of
Noth and Blum's analyses of the Jacob cycle, shows quite convincingly
how this veritable shattering of the narrative is not exegetically benefi-
cial, and that Noth's Documentary analysis of Gen. 28:10-22 is preferable. Since there is no reason to offer a recapitulation of Wynn-Williams
criticism,[4] and since for the most part I accept the Documentary division of Gen. 28:10-22, my analysis will be fairly succinct.

The second half of the opening verse (verse 10), which designates
Haran as Jacob's destination, is consistent with the yahwistic version of
events wherein Abraham's extended family took up residence in Haran
(24; 27:43; hence Skinner [376] attributes the entire verse to this source).
According to the Elohist, Jacob's destination is "the land of the sons of
the east" (Gen. 29:1).[5] The priestly source also has a different tradition
regarding Jacob's destination: after Jacob's conflict with Esau, Isaac
advises his son to go to Padan Aram (Gen. 28:2). There is no reason to
assume, however, that the first part of verse 10 should not be attributed
to the Elohist. The fact of the matter is that Beersheba was the last place
cited by E (Gen. 22:19: "So Abraham returned to his young men, and
they arose and went together to Beersheba; and Abraham lived at Beer-

Critique Littéraire de Genèse 28,10-22, RB 98 (1991): 321-342; G. Fleischer, Jakob
träumt – eine Auseinandersetzung mit E. Blum Methodischen Ansatz am Beispiel
von Gen. 28, 10-22, BN 76 (1995): 82-102; J. Van Seters, Divine Encounter at Bethel
Gen. 28, 10-12, in Recent Literary Critical Study of Genesis, ZAW 110 (1998): 503-513;
E. Blum, Noch Einmal; Jakobs Traum in Bethel Gen. 28, 10-22, in Rethinking the
Foundations: Historiography in the Ancient World and in the Bible, Essays in Honor of John
Van Seters (S. L. McKenzie, T. Roemer and H. H. Schmid eds.), 2000, 33-54.

2   G. Wenham, Genesis 16-50 (World Biblical Commentary Vol. 2), Dallas, 1994, 220.

3   Wellhausen, Hexateuch, 30-32; S. E, McEvenue, A Return to Sources in Genesis 28,10-
     22, ZAW 106 (1994): 375-389.

4   D. J. Wynn-Williams, The State of the Pentateuch (BZAW 249), Berlin.

5   Dillmann, Genesis, 339.

sheba"), so that by mentioning that Jacob originated there, the Elohist forges a clear literary connection with the Abraham cycle.

Verse 11 describes Jacob choosing a stone on which to sleep. The verse is thus connected to the erection of the elohistic "מצבה" (= pillar) in verse 18 and should most likely be assigned to the same source. Verse 12 is a dream revelation common to E (*cf.* the dream revelation in Chapter 20:3: "But God came to Abimelech in a dream by night, and said to him, 'You are about to die because of the woman whom you have taken; for she is a married woman.'"). Verses 13-15, however, are a typical yahwistic promise narrative (as in Gen. 22:17-18: "I will indeed bless you, and I will make your offspring as numerous as the stars of heaven and as the sand that is on the seashore. And your offspring shall possess the gate of their enemies...") and includes the common yahwistic promises to Jacob and his progeny. Verse 16, which declares: "Surely the LORD is in this place and I did not know it!," alludes to the specific revelation of verses 13-15 and not to the more general revelation of verse 12, making it yahwistic as well. Verse 17 repeats the idea of the sky-gate from verse 12 (E) and is therefore elohistic. Verse 18 speaks of the consecration of Bethel by erecting an elohistic pillar. Following the consecration, the obvious act is one of naming and thus verse 19a is also of elohistic origin. Verse 19b, "but the name of the city was Luz at the first," is etiological and as such is probably a secondary gloss. Jacob's vow to Elohim in verses 20-21a is parallel to the yahwistic revelation and essentially repeats the Deity's promises. This is of course unnecessary and indicates that the verses belong to a different source, probably E. Finally, verse 21b, "then the LORD shall be my God," alludes to the detailed revelation attributed to J. The above analysis purposely did not use the names of God as a source-critical criterion, but the appearances of the two names coincide with my division and help demonstrate that the God-names are an invaluable aid to the critical examination of pentateuchal texts.

4.1.2 The Yahwistic Commentary

Even advocates of the Documentary model, such as Skinner,[6] admit that in this case J is the later source. In my opinion, however, not only is J the later source, but it also supplemented or commented upon the

---

6   Skinner, *Genesis*, 379.

earlier elohistic source.[7] In other words, J's contribution to the story displays familiarity with the elohistic text and is dependent upon it. Wellhausen conceded that the yahwistic verses of Gen. 28:10-22 could not stand on their own,[8] but his observation does not necessitate the adoption of the supplementary model. It is also possible that the elohistic story was the basic text with which the editor worked and that he inserted yahwistic verses at the appropriate junctures. To prove that the supplementary model is the more likely in this case, one must demonstrate the Yahwist's familiarity with the elohistic text.

The Yahwist's verse 13: "And the LORD stood beside him and said, 'I am the LORD, the God of Abraham your father and the God of Isaac...'" assumes knowledge of the previous verse by using a pronominal suffix עָלָיו (translated by NRSV as "[beside] him") whose referent is unknown; it could be the ladder or it could be Jacob. In any case the suffix refers to a person or an object from the previous elohistic verse and is dependent upon it. The specific promises of vastly increasing Jacob's progeny and of protection in verses 13 – 15 were molded to fit in with the surrounding narratives of the Jacob cycle in the same manner as the promise narratives in the other story cycles of Genesis. Jacob arrived in Bethel alone. Therefore, the *beginning* of both of the promises in verses 13 and 14 is addressed to Jacob, but since he will be accompanied by eleven children on his return (Chapter 35), the word "זַרְעוֹ" (his offspring) is appended to the end of vss. 13 and 14. While this may seem syntactically awkward,[9] it can be more simply explained as a reframing of the Lord's blessing to Abraham to fit the present context. In fact, Abraham is purposely alluded to in vs. 13, precisely in order to cement the connection to Gen. 12:1-9.

Verse 15 is parallel to the elohistic verses 20-21a. Yhwh promises: "Know that I am with you and will keep you wherever you go, and will bring you back to this land; for I will not leave you until I have done what I have promised you," while in E Jacob vows "If God will be with me, and will keep me in this way that I go, and will give me bread to eat and clothing to wear, so that I come again to my father's house in peace...". It appears that one source is quoting or alluding to the other, but which one? The answer lies in the yahwistic verse 21b: "then the LORD shall be my God" which alludes to Yhwh's promises in verses

---

7   Cf. R. Couffingal, Le Songe de Jacob; Approches Nouvelles de Genèse 28: 10-22, *Biblica,* 58 (1977): 582-597, who conceded that the Tetragrammaton was added in a number of places in this pericope.

8   Wellhausen, *Hexateuch,* 30-32.

9   Which is what Blum and other tradition cycle critics rely upon in their attribution of vss. 13-15 to three authors, or according to Levin, *Jahwist,* 217-220, two authors.

13-15.   Verse 21b reinforces the impression that Jacob had already heard the promises of the Deity, while the very fact that he is making a vow is evidence that Jacob was not familiar with the words of Yhwh.

On the one hand, verse 16 ("Then Jacob woke from his sleep and said, 'Surely the LORD is in this place—and I did not know it!'") acts as an alternative yahwistic declaration which contrasts with verses 17-18; on the other hand, it functions as a resumptive repetition (a repetition of a verse or a part of a verse for clarity) and provides for a smooth transition to verse 17 ("And he was afraid, and said, 'How awesome is this place! This is none other than the house of God, and this is the gate of heaven'") Verse 19b: "but the name of the city was Luz at the first," is an etiological tradition and is beyond the limited scope of the narrative which deals with the *Bethel (= House of God)* and its consecration. It is entirely possible that the gloss is an attempt by the Yahwist to blur the connection between the name of the place and the godly stone, which is too close to paganism for comfort. By mentioning that the city had a different name the Yahwist is emphasizing that Bethel was not the Deity's particular residence and that he could have chosen any place to reveal himself to Jacob. Another possible interpretation of the evidence is, of course, the assumption of a third editorial source (JE or RJE). This is entirely unnecessary, however, since I have demonstrated that *all* verses of the later stratum display familiarity in one way or another with the elohistic account.

4.2 The Meeting by the Well (Gen. 29)

29:1 Then Jacob went on his journey, and came to the land of the people of the east. 2 As he looked, he saw a well in the field and three flocks of sheep lying there beside it; for out of that well the flocks were watered. The stone on the well's mouth was large, 3 *and when all the flocks were gathered there, the shepherds would roll the stone from the mouth of the well, and water the sheep, and put the stone back in its place on the mouth of the well. 4 Jacob said to them [the shepherds], "My brothers, where do you come from?" They said, "We are from Haran." 5 He said to them, "Do you know Laban son of Nahor?" They said, "We do." 6 He said to them, "Is it well with him?" "Yes," they replied, "and here is his daughter Rachel, coming with the sheep." 7 He said, "Look, it is still broad daylight; it is not time for the animals to be gathered together. Water the sheep, and go, pasture them." 8 But they said, "We cannot until all the flocks are gathered together, and the stone is rolled from the mouth of the well; then we water the sheep." 9 While he was still speaking with them, Rachel came with her father's sheep; for she kept them. 10 Now when Jacob saw Rachel, *the daughter of his mother's brother Laban,*

and the sheep of his *mother's brother Laban,* Jacob went up and rolled the
stone from the well's mouth, and watered the flock *of his mother's brother
Laban.* 11 Then Jacob kissed Rachel, and wept aloud. 12 And Jacob told
Rachel that he was her father's kinsman, *and that he was Rebekah's son;* and she
ran and told her father. 13 When Laban heard the news about *his sister's
son* Jacob, he ran to meet him; he embraced him and kissed him, and
brought him to his house. *Jacob told Laban all these things,* 14 *and Laban said to him,
"Surely you are my bone and my flesh!" And he stayed with him a month.*

4.2.1 Source Division

Today most critical scholars will agree that Gen. 29:1-15 is a one-source
narrative.[10] This consensus, however, is recent. At the end of the nine-
teenth century Dillmann[11] and many others[12] distinguished between the
first verse of Chapter 29 and the rest of the episode. They argued that in
the first verse Jacob's final destination was "the land of the people of
the east," while later verses indicate that Jacob arrived in Haran (29:4).
Dillmann maintained that this first verse belonged to E while the rest of
the chapter was yahwistic. But Dillmann's division and most modern
scholarship ignore textual difficulties, which may point to multiple
sources even after 29:1.

After telling of Jacob's arrival in the east (verse 1-2), the beginning
of the episode is interrupted by verse 3: "And when all the flocks were
gathered there, the shepherds would roll the stone from the mouth of
the well, and water the sheep, and put the stone back in its place on the
mouth of the well." One could view this verse as unnecessarily foreshadows verse 8, verse 2 already states more subtly: "The stone on the
well's mouth was large" without repeating the reasoning of verse 8.[13] In
my opinion,[14] verse 3 is an expansion of verse 2's short proleptic statement. I readily agree with the much-repeated observation regarding the
importance of repetitions in ancient near eastern literature, but these
repetitions usually serve a stylistic or rhythmic purpose and in this case

---

10 Although there is some argument concerning the source in question (and see
    Wenham, *Genesis,* 229).
11 Dillmann, *Genesis,* 339.
12 E.g. Gunkel, *Genesis,* 1997, 317.
13 Cf. Westermann, *Genesis,* 1985, 464-465.
14 Cf. H. Holzinger, *Einleitung in den Hexateuch: Mit Tabellen über die Quellenscheidung,*
    Freiburg and Leipzig, 1893, 194.

verse 3's statement serves no stylistic purpose and makes for a "less interesting" account.[15]

Verses 4-6 present a dialogue between the shepherds of Haran and Jacob; in my opinion these verses are also secondary. In verse 6 the shepherds point Rachel out to the inquiring Jacob, but in verse 7 Jacob ignores this revelation and instead asks about the stone on top of the well. This disregard is very surprising considering the extreme joy Jacob expresses in verses 10-11 when he meets Rachel. The inconsistency points to the verses' secondary nature. But what is the reason for this interpolation? Verse 6 explains how Jacob knew the identity of the maiden just arriving with the sheep of Laban—a person he had supposedly never seen in his life—but what of the other two verses? Their function is obvious: they establish the setting of the episode in Haran. If the verses are secondary, as we claim, verse 1's land of the eastern tribes is the original, *contra* Dillmann.

But is this the full extent of the editorial layer? The close familial connection between Jacob and Laban (that of uncle and nephew) is clear to every reader of Genesis. The first thirteen verses of Gen. 29 emphasize the relationship no less than six times (including three times in verse 10 alone), and the connection is alluded to on many additional occasions. Why such zeal in an otherwise frugally written narrative? Let us begin the answer with an analogy from the legal world. Any jurist will claim that there is no point in prohibiting an act unless there is good reason to believe that the action would be committed. Similarly, there should be no reason to emphasize a known fact, especially in a sparsely written narrative such as the Bible, unless there is good reason to believe that without the emphasis we would understand otherwise. Such is the case in question. I submit that the familial relationship between Laban and Jacob is emphasized precisely because Chapter 29 suggests a closer relationship between the so-called uncle and nephew.

What then is the relationship between them? In verse 12 Jacob mentions to Rachel that he is her father's brother and the term is used reciprocally by Laban in verse 15. Now, the term was always understood here in the broader context as "relative," which is the meaning in scripture in approximately half of the occasions in which it occurs. But is this necessarily the case here? Our understanding of this term is based on familial relationships as expounded by the Yahwist (Chapters 12, 24, 27), but must every source tell the same story? Scholars such as Weisman (1984) maintain that the Jacob narratives as a whole are earlier than the rest of the patriarchal narratives. As such, this earlier source, E

---

15   Gunkel, *Genesis*, 317.

or any other *grundschrift*, may have told a different story here,[16] which the Yahwist in his editorial capacity altered to fit his world of ideas.

If Jacob was originally Laban's brother in the *grundschrift*, then the exaggerated emphasis on their uncle-nephew relationship must be redactional. The Yahwist wished to conform the earlier tradition to his own idea of the patriarchal family tree. Jacob's query of verse 4: "Where are you from my brothers?," can now be understood as a feat of editorial subtlety: the word "brother," clearly used in its more general sense, affects our subsequent understanding of the term in verses 12 and 15, i.e. Laban and Jacob are not brothers, but only relatives.

If my analysis is thus far correct, there should be a more profound reason for the thorough editorial interference, since one might well ask why the editor did not vary his own traditions instead of altering our understanding of the earlier narrative. I submit that his ulterior motive was the protection of Israel's purity (*cf.* the Yahwisitic injunction, Ex. 19:8 "You shall be a kingdom of priests and a holy nation"). Marriage of an uncle to his nieces verged uncomfortably close to consanguinity. Lev. 18 prohibits a similar relationship, that of an aunt and her nephew. A union between cousins was perhaps more acceptable (although not all problems are solved, since Jacob is still marrying two sisters).

The final outcome of this short analysis is a basic story with a number of editorial interpolations in the yahwistic "spirit:" a) The proleptic insertion of verse 3; b) The dialogue between Jacob and his "brothers," the shepherds of Haran; c) The addition of the familial details six times in verses 10-13; d) Verse 13b "Jacob told Laban all these things," which very likely belongs to the same yahwistic redactional source, since it connects this story with the previous confrontation with Esau, an account which does not appear in the elohistic source. As in previous cases, the multiplication of entities is avoided and since the redactional layer conforms with yahwistic ideas, it will be assumed that it is indeed yahwistic.

The difference between elohistic narrative and yahwistic interpolation needs to be emphasized. Elohistic narrative assumes that the audience of readers or listeners is familiar with the characters concerned—Laban, Jacob, Esau and Rachel—a reasonable assumption with regard to the famous figures in Israelite folklore. The Yahwist, whose goal was to compose a story of origins of potential use to future generations, cannot make the assumption of familiarity and therefore needs to present all the facts and figures.

---

16   Indeed Wellhausen, *Hexateuch* 35, claims the episode is elohistic.

4.3 Jacob and the Daughters of Laban (Gen. 29)

15 Then Laban said to Jacob, "Because you are my kinsman, should you therefore serve me for nothing? Tell me, what shall your wages be?" 16 Now Laban had two daughters; the name of the elder was Leah, and the name of the younger was Rachel. 17 *Leah's eyes were lovely, and Rachel was graceful and beautiful.*18 Jacob loved Rachel; so he said, "I will serve you seven years for your younger daughter Rachel." 19 Laban said, "It is better that I give her to you than that I should give her to any other man; stay with me." 20 So Jacob served seven years for Rachel, and they seemed to him but a few days because of the love he had for her.21 Then Jacob said to Laban, "Give me my wife that I may go in to her, for my time is completed." 22 So Laban gathered together all the people of the place, and made a feast. 23 But in the evening he took his daughter Leah and brought her to Jacob; and he went in to her 24 *Laban gave his maid Zilpah to his daughter Leah to be her maid.* 25 When morning came, it was Leah! And Jacob said to Laban, "What is this you have done to me? Did I not serve with you for Rachel? Why then have you deceived me?" 26 Laban said, "This is not done in our country—giving the younger before the firstborn. 27 Complete the week of this one, and we will give you the other also in return for serving me another seven years." 28 Jacob did so, and completed her week; then Laban gave him his daughter Rachel as a wife. 29 *Laban gave his maid Bilhah to his daughter Rachel to be her maid.* 30 So Jacob went in to Rachel also, and he loved Rachel more than Leah. He served Laban for another seven years.

4.3.1 Source Division

The majority of the text may be assigned to the basic elohistic source.[17] The interpolations into the text are verse 14 (mentioned above) and verses 17, 24, and 29. Verse 17 mentions Rachel's beauty as compared to Leah's mundane looks. The beauty of the matriarchs is a recurring yahwistic theme (*cf.* J's Gen. 12:11: "I know well that you are a woman beautiful in appearance"; Rebecca receives similar praise in Gen. 24:16: "The girl was very fair to look upon, a virgin, whom no man had known." Thus it is befitting that Rachel is endowed with beauty just like her predecessors, Sarah and Rebecca.) Verses 24 and 29 present the maidservants that Jacob was given along with the daughters of La-ban—details that are not pertinent to the basic story but are relevant to

---

17   Wellhausen, *Hexateuch*, 35ff; Speiser, *Genesis*, 226-227.

the subsequent episode, in which the maidservants play an important role.[18] Another indicator that verses 24 and 29 are yahwistic and not elohistic is the preference for the term "שפחה" as opposed to the elohistic "אמה", both of which denote handmaiden (This was and is a common distinguishing criterion between the sources. Compare the usage of אמה in E's Gen. 21, used to describe Sarah's handmaiden, as opposed to J's Gen. 16 use of שפחה for the same individual.)

4.3.2 The Yahwistic Commentary

Verses 24 and 29, which mention the maidservants, are yet another proof of the Yahwist's preoccupation with names and familial details. These details help link the five story cycles of Genesis, molding them into a whole. This chronistic theme is even more widespread in the later priestly author who is responsible for the majority of the Pentateuch's genealogical lists.

4.4 The Birth of Jacob's Sons (Gen. 29-30)

29:31 *When the LORD saw that Leah was unloved, he opened her womb; but Rachel was barren.* 32 Leah conceived and bore a son, and she named him Reuben; for she said, *"Because the LORD has looked on my affliction;* surely now my husband will love me." 33 *She conceived again and bore a son, and said, "Because the LORD has heard that I am hated, he has given me this son also"; and she named him Simeon.* 34 *Again she conceived and bore a son, and said, "Now this time my husband will be joined to me, because I have borne him three sons"; therefore he was named Levi.* 35 *She conceived again and bore a son, and said, "This time I will praise the LORD"; therefore she named him Judah; then she ceased bearing.* 30:1 When Rachel saw that she bore Jacob no children, she envied her sister; and she said to Jacob, "Give me children, or I shall die!" 2 Jacob became very angry with Rachel and said, "Am I in the place of God, who has withheld from you the fruit of the womb?" 3 Then she said, "Here is my maid Bilhah; go in to her, that she may bear upon my knees and that I too may have children through her." 4 So she gave him *her maid* Bilhah as a wife; and Jacob went in to her. 5 And Bilhah conceived and bore Jacob a son. 6 Then Rachel said, "God has judged me, and has also heard my voice and given me a son"; therefore she named him Dan. 7 *Rachel's maid* Bilhah conceived again and bore Jacob a *second* son. 8 Then Rachel said, "With mighty wrestlings I have wrestled with

---

18   Cf. Dillmannn's (*Genesis*, 341) attribution to a Priestly editor.

my sister, and have prevailed"; so she named him Naphtali. 9 *When Leah saw that she had ceased bearing children, she took her maid Zilpah and gave her to Jacob as a wife. 10 Then Leah's maid Zilpah bore Jacob a son. 11 And Leah said, "Good fortune!" so she named him Gad. 12 Leah's maid Zilpah bore Jacob a second son. 13 And Leah said, "Happy am I! For the women will call me happy"; so she named him Asher.* 14 In the days of wheat harvest Reuben went and found mandrakes in the field, and brought them to his mother Leah. Then Rachel said to Leah, "Please give me some of your son's mandrakes." 15 But she said to her, "Is it a small matter that you have taken away my husband? Would you take away my son's mandrakes also?" Rachel said, "Then he may lie with you tonight for your son's mandrakes." 16 When Jacob came from the field in the evening, Leah went out to meet him, and said, "You must come in to me; for I have hired you with my son's mandrakes." So he lay with her that night. 17 And God heeded Leah, and she conceived and bore Jacob a *fifth* son. 18 Leah said, "God has given me my hire *because I gave my maid to my husband*"; so she named him Issachar. 19 And Leah conceived again, and she bore Jacob a *sixth* son. 20 Then Leah said, "God has endowed me with a good dowry; *now my husband will honor me, because I have borne him six sons*"; so she named him Zebulun. 21 *Afterwards she bore a daughter, and named her Dinah.* 22 Then God remembered Rachel, and God heeded her and opened her womb. 23 She conceived and bore a son, and said, "God has taken away my reproach"; 24 and she named him Joseph, *saying, "May the LORD add to me another son!"*

4.4.1 The Division into Sources and the Yahwistic Commentary[19]

In my opinion there exist two keys to the division of this text. The first is the differing names for the Deity:[20] the verses containing etioligies involving "Elohim" belong to E (Dan, Naphtali, Issachar, Zebulun and Joseph), while those etiologies which invoke the name "Yhwh" belong to J (Reuben, Simeon, Judah and Joseph). It stands to reason that the story surrounding the birth of the elohistic sons also belongs to E, i.e. Rachel's complaint to Jacob in Gen. 30:1-3 (which contain the elohistic features—the name "Elohim" [God] and the substantive "אמה" [maid] as the yahwistic synonym for "שפחה") and the mandrake episode in 30:14-18,[21] which functions as a prologue to the births of Issachar and

19 This section is a revision of my ZAW article: T. Yoreh, How many Sons Did Jacob have According to E?, *ZAW* 118 (2006): 264-268.
20 *Contra* Blum, Va□tergeschichte, 111; Westermann, *Genesis*, 1985, 472-473, who claim that this criterion is invalid here and elsewhere.
21 Speiser, *Genesis*, 299.

Zebulun. This division can be refined if we include a second key, double etiologies.[22] Three of Jacob's sons are named twice. The obvious ones are Joseph (30:23-24: "God has taken away [אסף] my reproach"; and "May the LORD add to me (יוסף) another son!") and Zebulun (30:20: "God has endowed me (זבדני) with a good dowry", and "Now my husband will honor me (יזבלני), because I have borne him six sons"). The less obvious occurrence of a double etiology is in the case of Reuben, but as Wenham has pointed out,[23] "Surely now my husband will love me" (29:32) can function as an etiology on its own, since "יאהבני" (will love me) contains three out of four of the consonants of Reuben's name (the aleph, the beth and the nun). In my opinion, this etiology is elohistic, as opposed to the first obviously yahwistic etiology: "because the LORD [Yhwh] has looked on my affliction (ראה יהו-ה בעניי)" (29:32).[24] As we shall soon see Reuben plays a pivotal role in the elohistic Joseph cycle.

What can be said with regard to the function of J material in this section? In my opinion, the secondary character of J in these chapters is obvious. Joseph's name is explained by J: "may the LORD [Yhwh] give me another son" (30:24), which hints at the subsequent birth of Benjamin in Gen. 35:16-18. The function of the yahwistic Reuben etiology: "because the LORD [Yhwh] has looked on my affliction" (29:32), is the provision of a clearer etiology than the elohistic "יאהבני" (29:32). (The yahwistic etiology "ראה יהו-ה בעניי" contains all the letters of the Hebrew Reuben.) A similar function is performed by the second Zebulun etiology: "God has endowed me with a good dowry; now my husband will honor me" (30:20).[25] The Hebrew "יזבלני" contains the four primary letters of Zebulun's name, whereas the elohistic (זבדני) contains only three. I should like to conjecture, following Ockham's razor (i.e. reducing the needless multiplying of entities to explain a process), that this etiology is also yahwistic.

Another function of this second yahwistic etiology is to number Jacob's children. According to this half-verse, Zebulun was Leah's sixth child. This is true only if we include Simeon, Levi and Judah —sons

---

22 For a more literary method which tries to understand the doubling as part of the message cf. A. Strus, Étymologie des noms propres dans Gen. 29,32-30,24, *Salesianum* 40 (1978): 57-72.

23 Wenham, *Genesis*, 243.

24 Lehming (S. Lehming, Geburt der Jakobsöhne, *VT* 13 (1963): 80.), is of the opinion that this double etiology is in fact one and that its function is to add a theological element to the simple etiology reu – ben!

25 Cf. the innovative understanding offered by M. David, Zabal (Gen. XXX 20), *VT* 1, (1951): 69 –70, regarding the root zabal and its Assyrian cognates.

who were not born to Jacob, according to the existing E source.[26] On the
basis of the Zebulun etiology, I would like to suggest that the entire
numbering scheme belongs to J and is secondary. In my opinion, the
numbering scheme is intended to emphasize that Jacob had eleven
sons, as opposed to the six we have counted thus far according to E.
The southern tribes, Simeon, Levi and Judah, were added by J when the
northern E document arrived in Judah after the fall of the northern
kingdom.[27] An additional sign that the birth of the three southern tribes
is secondary to the original text is Rachel's comment after the birth of
Naphtali: "With mighty wrestlings I have wrestled with my sister, and
have prevailed" (30:8).[28] If the text is read as it stands, Leah gave birth
to four sons, while Rachel's handmaiden gave birth to only two sons.
Rachel is still far behind in this battle! Only if we assume that the birth
of the southern tribes is secondary, i.e. does not belong to the elohistic
source, does the text make sense. In that case Rachel has indeed tri-
umphed since at this point in the narrative Leah has given birth to only
one son (Reuben), whereas Bilhah has given birth to two (Dan and
Naphtali). Note also that the language in Gen. 30:23, "God has taken
away my reproach," emphasizes Rachel's relief at her ability to contribute to the reproductive competition with her sister. Her birthing of
Joseph evens the tally. This supplementary paradigm offers a simpler
model than supposing two independent fragmentary documents combined by a third redactor.

I shall now attempt to identify further yahwistic material in this
chapter. The Issachar etiology presents conflicting evidence: It begins
with an obviously elohisitic etiology: "God [Elohim] has given me my
hire" (30:18), but the subsequent clause: "because I gave my maid
[שפחתי] to my husband" employs the yahwistic "שפחה." In my opinion,
this last clause is yahwistic and redactional and attempts to obscure the
elohistic assertion that the Deity condones the use of magical mandrakes. This addition also foreshadows further yahwistic material —the
birth of Gad and Asher, Zilpah's sons, in 30:9-13. The addition of Gad
and Asher's births parallels the elohistic verses narrating the birth of
Bilhah's sons, Dan and Naphtali. Further evidence is the consistent use
of the yahwistic "שפחה" in 30:9-13 (three times). I submit that the use of
"שפחה" throughout the narrative is yahwistic. When the term is used in

---

26 Westermann, *Genesis*, 1985, 273, dismisses the possibility that we can learn from this
    story regarding the actual number of tribes, but the fact that the numbering is
    emphasized suggests otherwise.

27 A widely accepted theory, and see for example, J. E. Carpenter, *The Composition of the
    Hexateuch: An Introduction with a Select List of Words and Phrases*, London, 1902, 331.

28 See F. I. Andersen, Note on Genesis 30,8, *JBL* 88 (1969): 200.

elohisitic material such as verses 4 and 8, it is secondary, with the function (perhaps) of emphasizing the legal standing of Bilhah as an inferior wife. The addition of this term is inconsistent and in verse 5 Bilhah is not identified as a "שפחה". Zilpah, on the other hand is always identified as Leah's "שפחה." Finally there is the birth of Dinah, which is usually considered a later addition to the story.[29] I hold no firm position on the source of the only girl born to Jacob, but see no reason to posit a third author in this narrative.

In summary: The original E story told of the birth of six sons: Reuben, Dan, Naphtali, Issahchar, Zebulun and Joseph. J added the three southern tribes — Simeon, Levi and Judah, and the sons of Zilpah — Gad and Asher, and a daughter, Dinah. In order to emphasize this new figure J adds his own numbering system. Other J additions are the term "שפחה" and the relative clause after the Issachar etiology which seeks to obscure the Deity's approval of the mandrakes.

Presented thus, the E narrative is primarily a story of sibling rivalry,[30] rather than a list of Jacob's sons and the order of their birth. In many ways the original story parallels the rivalry between Sarah and Hagar in the J source (Gen. 16) and perhaps this story in Gen. 29-30 was J's inspiration for Gen. 16. The phrase "that she may bear upon my knees" (30:3) emphasizes such a connection, since it appears only here and in Gen. 16:2.

According to E, the sum total of Jacob's sons, including Benjamin, is seven. (J mimics this to give Leah seven children of her own.) Do we find evidence of this more original number elsewhere? One can answer in the affirmative, based on two verses in the Joseph Cycle. Twice, Joseph gives Benjamin five times more presents than the rest of the brothers: Gen. 43:34: "Portions were taken to them from Joseph's table, but Benjamin's portion was five times as much as any of theirs;" and Gen. 45:22: "To each one of them he gave a set of garments; but to Benjamin he gave three hundred pieces of silver and five sets of garments." If the number of Joseph's brothers is eleven this fivefold preference has no special significance. If, however, Joseph had only six brothers, Benjamin receives exactly the same amount of gifts as all the remaining brothers combined (excepting of course Joseph, who presents the gifts). This endowment is symbolic and reflects Joseph's evaluation of Benjamin in comparison with all his other brothers combined. This equation is supported by the Joseph Cycle as a whole, since only Benjamin's presence allows the other brothers to survive. This division is further

---

29   Skinner, *Genesis*, 385.
30   Cf. Westermann, *Genesis*, 1985, 472.

supported by studies claiming that the southern tribes are additions to Gen. 49,[31] as well as by the absence of the southern tribes in the song of Deborah.

4.4.2 Ramifications

This short study has important ramifications for pentateuchal criticism. If my division is correct, it could provide an important key for source critics. It strongly supports the claim that the Judah layer of the Joseph Cycle is secondary.[32] This investigation goes further in that it claims that Judah never existed in the E-source, a reasonable position since Judah and Israel were indeed separate entities for most of their history.

If E did not include the southern tribes among the sons of Jacob, then every mention of Simeon, Levi and Judah does not belong to the E source. Some of the episodes which need to be re-examined in light of this hypothesis include: the rape of Dinah in Gen. 34, the imprisonment of Simeon in Gen. 42, the birth of Moses in Ex. 2, the sin of the Golden Calf in Ex. 32, the spy episode in Num. 14, and every place where the number twelve is mentioned or implied with regard to the tribes of Israel.

Finally, I would like to use this investigation to strengthen the case for the use of the name of the Deity as a criterion in source division. This and similar episodes (Ex. 3, Ex. 19, Num. 22-24) have been justifiably used as ammunition against this criterion, since until now no one who offered a division of this chapter has successfully made use of it. Nevertheless, I submit that this criterion is still useful and that the fault lies in the Documentary method.

4.5 Jacob Decides to Leave Laban (Gen. 30-31)

25 *When Rachel had borne Joseph, Jacob said to Laban, "Send me away, that I may go to my own home and country.* 26 *Give me my wives and my children for whom I have served you, and let me go; for you know very well the service I have given you."* 27 *But Laban said to him, "If you will allow me to say so, I have learned by divination that the LORD has blessed me because of you;* 28 *name your wages, and I will give it."* 29 *Jacob said to him, "You yourself know how I have served you, and how your cattle have fared with me.* 30 *For you had little before I came, and it has in-*

---

31   Levin, *Jahwist*, 66.

32   S. E. Loewenstamm, Reuben and Judah in the Cycle of Joseph Stories, in *From Babylon to Canaan* (S. E. Loewenstammm ed.), Jerusalem, 1992, 35-41.

creased abundantly; and the LORD has blessed you wherever I turned. But now when shall I *provide for my own household also?"* 31 *He said, "What shall I give you?" Jacob said, "You shall* *not give me anything; if you will do this for me, I will again feed your flock and keep it:* 32 *let me* *pass through all your flock today, removing from it every speckled and spotted sheep and every* *black lamb, and the spotted and speckled among the goats; and such shall be my wages.* 33 *So my* *honesty will answer for me later, when you come to look into my wages with you. Every one that* *is not speckled and spotted among the goats and black among the lambs, if found with me, shall be* *counted stolen."* 34 *Laban said, "Good! Let it be as you have said."* 35 *But that day Laban re-* *moved the male goats that were striped and spotted, and all the female goats that were speckled and* *spotted, every one that had white on it, and every lamb that was black, and put them in charge of* *his sons;* 36 *and he set a distance of three days' journey between himself and Jacob, while Jacob was* *pasturing the rest of Laban's flock.*37 *Then Jacob took fresh rods of poplar and almond and plane,* *and peeled white streaks in them, exposing the white of the rods.* 38 *He set the rods that he had* *peeled in front of the flocks in the troughs, that is, the watering places, where the flocks came to* *drink. And since they bred when they came to drink,* 39 *the flocks bred in front of the rods, and so* *the flocks produced young that were striped, speckled, and spotted.* 40 *Jacob separated the lambs,* *and set the faces of the flocks toward the striped and the completely black animals in the flock of* *Laban; and he put his own droves apart, and did not put them with Laban's flock.* 41 *Whenever the* *stronger of the flock were breeding, Jacob laid the rods in the troughs before the eyes of the flock,* *that they might breed among the rods,* 42 *but for the feebler of the flock he did not lay them there;* *so the feebler were Laban's, and the stronger Jacob's.* 43 *Thus the man grew exceedingly rich, and* *had large flocks, and male and female slaves, and camels and donkeys.* 31:1 *Now Jacob heard that* *the sons of Laban were saying, "Jacob has taken all that was our father's; he has gained all this* *wealth from what belonged to our father."* 2 *And Jacob saw that Laban did not regard him as* *favorably as he did before.* 3 *Then the LORD said to Jacob, "Return to the land of your ancestors* *and to your kindred, and I will be with you."* 4 So Jacob sent and called Rachel and Leah into the field where his flock was, 5 and said to them, "I see that your father does not regard me as favorably as he did before. *But the God* *of my father has been with me.* 6 You know that I have served your father with all my strength; 7 yet your father has cheated me and changed my wages ten times, but God did not permit him to harm me. 8 If he said, 'The speckled shall be your wages,' then all the flock bore speckled; and if he said, 'The striped shall be your wages,' then all the flock bore striped. 9 Thus God has taken away the livestock of your father, and given them to me. 10 During the mating of the flock I once had a dream in which I looked up and saw that the male goats that leaped upon the flock were striped, speckled, and mottled. 11 Then *the angel of* God said to me in the dream, 'Jacob,' and I said, 'Here I am!' 12 And he said, 'Look up and see that all the goats that leap on the flock are striped, speckled, and mottled; for I have seen all that Laban is doing to you. 13 I am the God of Bethel,o where you anointed a pillar and made a vow to me. Now leave this land at once and return to the land of your birth.'" 14

Then Rachel and Leah answered him, "Is there any portion or inheritance left to us in our father's house? 15 Are we not regarded by him as
foreigners? For he has sold us, and he has been using up the money
given for us. 16 All the property that God has taken away from our
father belongs to us and to our children; now then, do whatever God
has said to you."

4.5.1 Source Division

Scholars generally agree that Chapter 31 (at least verses 4-16, if not the
entire chapter) can be attributed to one source. [33] Wenham maintains
that this source is J, but the appearance of the elohistic "Elohim" or God
and "מצבה" (pillar) seem to suggest otherwise.[34] I agree that the majority
of verses should be attributed to one source, namely E, albeit with two
important reservations. The first pertains to verse 2: "And Jacob saw
that Laban did not regard him as favorably as he did before," which is
generally assigned to the elohistic source, or in any case to the same
source as verse 5 "And [Jacob] said to them, 'I see that your father does
not regard me as favorably as he did before'".[35] Verse 2 and verse 5a,
however, are doublets and it seems likely that one of them is secondary. Verse 2 is clearly proleptic, i.e. it reveals a detail at an early point in
the narrative and disrupts the fabric and narrative tension of the episode, much like Gen. 29:3: "And when all the flocks were gathered
there, the shepherds would roll the stone from the mouth of the well,
and water the sheep, and put the stone back in its place on the mouth
of the well." The following verse (verse 3: "Then the LORD [Yhwh]
said to Jacob, 'Return to the land of your ancestors and to your kindred,
and I will be with you'") is also a proleptic addition, since the actual
revelation begins only in verse 11. The yahwistic editor, however, dis-
satisfied with Jacob's account of the revelation, was impelled to record
its actual occurrence.

The second break in continuity is verse 5b: "But the God of my father has been with me." A glaring non-sequitur, this verse is clearly
another proleptic gloss, functioning as an introduction to the revelation
of verse 11. The bulk of verses 6-16 do, however, constitute a unity,

---

33 In agreement with Volz and Rudolph, *Irrweg*, 88, who claim that if it were not for the
    documentary hypothesis than this chapter would have never been divided, and see
    also Wenham, *Genesis*, 254, who claims that the complexity of this chapter is due to
    the subject matter.

34 *Cf.* Speiser, *Genesis*, 248.

35 Gunkel, *Genesis*, 331.

except perhaps for the addition by the Yahwist or a later editor of "the angel of" to "Elohim" in verse 11. Whereas in verse 13 the divine figure identifies Himself as "El" (God) and not as an angel, the addition of this "diminishing" angel is a common editorial strategy which prevents anthropomorphism (*cf.* similar interpolations by the Septuagint in Jud. 6:12-24).

4.5.2 The Yahwistic Commentary

The yahwistic supplementation of this account begins with the previous Chapter (30:25), when Jacob asks Laban for permission to leave Haran after the birth of his sons and the fulfillment of his contract. Laban, however, proposes that Jacob name his price and continue working for him. Jacob accedes and through guile and astute animal husbandry succeeds in procuring a significant portion of Laban's flock. This story performs two main functions. The first is etiological: the episode is part of an etymological *leitmotif* concerning Jacob's Hebrew name "יעקב" and its connection to deceit and trickery, which also appears in Hos. 12:4 ("In the womb he tried to cheat [עקב] his brother"). Jacob now requites Laban for replacing Rachel with Leah on the wedding night. The yahwistic author builds the narrative of Gen. 30:25ff on the basis of verse 7b: "but God did not permit him to harm me" and other elohistic excerpts later in Chapter 31 (31:42 "God saw my affliction and the labor of my hands"), clearly arguing that God does not help someone who does not help himself. The second function of the long yahwistic interpolation is to explain why Jacob decides to stay with Laban after the first fourteen years he owed him for his daughters—a detail that the Elohist glosses over. The Yahwist explains that Jacob stayed in Haran because Laban offered him good conditions. In this story, the Yahwist presents the other side of Jacob's personality, a theme I have previously identified with J in the Abraham cycle. The protagonists in E are one-dimensional and the Yahwist took it upon himself to fill in the picture, thus creating well-rounded human characters.

In contrast, Zakovitz claims (in an oral communication) that a late Elohist simply summarized the yahwistic episode concerning Jacob's treachery and that the elohistic statements (quoted above) were in fact a justification of Jacob's actions. I do not accept Zakowitz's position. As I have emphasized in the Introduction and throughout this work, I have not found a single instance where the Elohist is familiar with yahwistic narrative. The Elohist characters are for the most part one-dimensional, but here Zakowitz attributes a sophistication to Jacob that is noticeably absent in this source. Zakowitz's claim and general methodology is more appropriate to a canonical approach (*cf.* above regarding his explanation of Gen. 12 and 20) than to source criticism.

4.6 Jacob Escapes Laban (Gen. 31)

17 So Jacob arose, and set his children and his wives on camels; 18 *and he drove away all his livestock, all the property that he had gained, the livestock in his possession that he had acquired in Paddan-aram, to go to his father Isaac in the land of Canaan.* 19 Now Laban had gone to shear his sheep, and Rachel stole her father's household gods. 20 And Jacob deceived Laban (the Aramean)*, in that he did not tell him that he intended to flee. 21 So he fled with all that he had; starting out he crossed the Euphrates, and set his face toward the hill country of Gilead.22 On the third day Laban was told that Jacob had fled. 23 So he took his kinsfolk with him and pursued him for seven days until he caught up with him in the hill country of Gilead. 24 But God came to Laban the Aramean in a dream by night, and said to him, "Take heed that you say not a word to Jacob, either good or bad."25 Laban overtook Jacob. Now Jacob had pitched his tent in the hill country, and Laban with his kinsfolk camped in the hill country of Gilead. 26 Laban said to Jacob, "What have you done? You have deceived me, and carried away my daughters like captives of the sword. 27 Why did you flee secretly and deceive me and not tell me? I would have sent you away with mirth and songs, with tambourine and lyre. 28 And why did you not permit me to kiss my sons and my daughters farewell? What you have done is foolish. 29 *It is in my power to do you harm; but the God of your father spoke to me last night, saying, 'Take heed that you speak to Jacob neither good nor bad.'* 30 *Even though you had to go because you longed greatly for your father's house,* why did you steal my gods?" 31 Jacob answered Laban, "Because I was afraid, for I thought that you would take your daughters from me by force. 32 But anyone with whom you find your gods shall not live. In the presence of our kinsfolk, point out what I have that is yours, and take it." Now Jacob did not know that Rachel had stolen the gods. 33 So Laban went into Jacob's tent, and into Leah's tent, and into the tent of the two maids, but he did not find them. And he went out of Leah's tent, and entered Rachel's. 34 Now Rachel had taken the household gods and put them in the camel's saddle, and sat on them. Laban felt all about in the tent, but did not find them. 35 And she said to her father, "Let not my lord be angry that I cannot rise before you, for the way of

women is upon me."So he searched, but did not find the household gods.

*It is possible that Laban's nationality is an editorial gloss – an allusion to Padan Aram or Aram Naharayim (Laban's home towns according to P and J); it is not out of the question, however, that this defining adjective is original, since undoubtedly "the Land of the Sons of the East" is part of the Aramean sphere.

4.6.1 Source Division

Chapter 31:18 "and he drove away all his livestock, all the property that he had gained, the livestock in his possession that he had acquired in Paddan-aram, to go to his father Isaac in the land of Canaan" is usually attributed to P. (Compare the similar phraseology of Gen. 12:5: "Abram took his wife Sarai and his brother's son Lot, and all the possessions that they had gathered, and the persons whom they had acquired in Haran; and they set forth to go to the land of Canaan. When they had come to the land of Canaan..." also commonly regarded as priestly[36]). The priestly source introduces the Jacob cycle in Gen. 28:1-9 and this is the first subsequent recurrence of the source. After 31:18, the elohistic narrative, identified as such by the dream revelation of verse 24, continues uninterrupted until Laban's complaints (verses 26ff).

Verse 28 ends with the statement "What you have done is foolish." In fact, Jacob's flight was not foolishness, but prudence. Had he allowed Laban to kiss his grandchildren, Jacob would never have been able to leave. There is, however, an act of foolishness in the text at hand, namely the pilfering of Laban's idols by Rachel, in verse 30b: "Why did you steal my gods?"[37] This indicates that the direct continuation of verse 28b is 30b, with an intervening yahwistic interpolation. Another indicator that verses 29-30a are of a secondary nature is the allusion to Jacob's father (29: "The God of your father;" 30a: "You longed greatly for your father's house"), a character with whom only the Yahwist is familiar. According to the Elohist, the Divinity who appeared to Laban during the night was "Elohim" (and not the God of Jacob's father) and the reason for Jacob's escape is not that he yearned for his father's house, as the Yahwist puts it in verse 30. Jacob left Haran (or more accurately the "lands of the eastern tribes") without in-

---

36 Skinner, *Genesis*, 396.

37 For a bibliographical selection on Laban's idols and the significance of Rachel's "heist" see Westermann, *Genesis*, 1985, 485.

forming his father-in-law because he was commanded to do so by "Elohim" or, according to his response in verse 31, because he was afraid that Laban would take back his daughters.

4.6.2 The Yahwistic Commentary

The supplementary themes are quite clear in this case. As in previous narratives, the Yahwist attempts to strengthen the connections to family. He does this by alluding to the past, specifically to Jacob's father. As I have already mentioned, the Elohist has no interest in Jacob's father, who for him is an anonymous and unimportant figure. Verse 29 ensures that Jacob is made cognizant of the divine intervention in his life (*cf.* the leitmotif of the plague narratives, which are intended to enhance the divine prestige). Furthermore, by putting a justification for Jacob's behaviour in Laban's mouth, the Yahwist rounds out Laban's character and makes him more compassionate. This is further evidence of the Yahwist's desire to present a fuller and more human account of events.

4.7 The Alliance between Jacob and Laban (Gen. 31)

36 Then Jacob became angry, and upbraided Laban. Jacob said to Laban, "What is my offense? What is my sin, that you have hotly pursued me? 37 Although you have felt about through all my goods, what have you found of all your household goods? Set it here before my kinsfolk and your kinsfolk, so that they may decide between us two. 38 These twenty years I have been with you; your ewes and your female goats have not miscarried, and I have not eaten the rams of your flocks. 39 That which was torn by wild beasts I did not bring to you; I bore the loss of it myself; of my hand you required it, whether stolen by day or stolen by night. 40 It was like this with me: by day the heat consumed me, and the cold by night, and my sleep fled from my eyes. 41 *These twenty years I have been in your house; I served you fourteen years for your two daughters, and six years for your flock, and you have changed my wages ten times. 42 If the God of my father, the God of Abraham and the Fear of Isaac, had not been on my side, surely now you would have sent me away empty-handed.* God saw my affliction and the labor of my hands, *and rebuked you last night.*" 43 Then Laban answered and said to Jacob, "The daughters are my daughters, the children are my children, the flocks are my flocks, and all that you see is mine. But what can I do today about these daughters of mine, or about their children whom they have borne? 44

Come now, let us make a covenant, you and I; and let it be a witness between you and me." 45 So Jacob took a stone, and set it up as a pillar. 46 *And Jacob said to his kinsfolk, "Gather stones," and they took stones, and made a heap; and they ate there by the heap. 47 Laban called it Jegar-sahadutha: but Jacob called it Galeed. 48 Laban said, "This heap is a witness between you and me today." Therefore he called it Galeed, 49 and the pillar Mizpah, for he said, "The LORD watch between you and me, when we are absent one from the other. 50 If you ill-treat my daughters, or if you take wives in addition to my daughters, though no one else is with us,* [And he said] see that God is witness between you and me." 51 Then Laban said to Jacob, "See this *heap and see the* pillar, which you* have set between you and me. 52 This *heap is a witness, and the* pillar is a witness, that I will not pass over *this heap* to you, and you will not pass over *this heap and* this pillar to me, for harm. 53 *May the God of Abraham and the God of Nahor"—the God of their father—"judge between us." So Jacob swore by the Fear of his father Isaac,* 54 and Jacob offered a sacrifice on the height and called his kinsfolk to eat bread; and they ate bread and tarried all night in the hill country. 55 Early in the morning Laban rose up, and kissed his grandchildren and his daughters and blessed them; then he departed and returned home.

*Note the widely accepted emendation of the Hebrew original which reads "which I have set".

4.7.1 Source Division

According to many Documentary scholars, the final verses of Chapter 31, the alliance between Jacob and Laban, pose a problem.[38] The difficulty with these verses stems from the persistent and fruitless attempts to isolate two complete narratives that are parallel to one another. This persistence has its roots in the apparent repetitions.[39] The attempts end in failure and, beginning with Volz, there has been a push to attribute the entire text to one source. In this case, however, any attempt to attribute the whole text to one source is clearly harmonistic, since even

---

38 The problem was apparent to the author of the Septuagint, and note the different order of the verses in the Greek, for further discussion see N. Leiter, The Translator's Hand in Transpositions? Notes on the LXX of Genesis 31, *Textus* 14 (1988): 105-130; H. Seebass LXX und MT in Gen. 31,44-53, *BN* 34 (1986): 30-88; M. Zippor, The Story of Laban's Pursuit after Jacob as Reflected in the Septuagint, *Beit Miqra* 46 (2001): 1-27.

39 This persistence has its roots in the apparent repetitions: the two names Mizpah and Gilad [vss. 48, 49]; twice the God/s bear witness [vss 49, 53]; the sides take part in two ceremonial meals [vss 46, 54]; and there are two sets of conditions – cf. Skinner, *Genesis*, 399.

a not particularly discerning reader can perceive the difficulties in reading this text as an uninterrupted unity.

As I have indicated with regard to several instances, many of the difficulties disappear when only one basic narrative and various supplementary sources are assumed. I propose that this is what applies in Gen. 31 as well. The yahwistic redaction in the case of Gen. 31:36-55 is extensive. The interpolations begin with verses 41-42a.[40] Verse 41 repeats verse 38, describing the type of work Jacob performed in his twenty years with Laban ("These twenty years I have been in your house; I served you fourteen years for your two daughters, and six years for your flock..."). Verse 42a uses the non-elohistic divine sobriquets "the God of Abraham and the Fear of Isaac," in contrast to "Elohim" in verse 42b (compare Westermann 1985, 497).[41] The phrase "And rebuked you last night" at the end of verse 42 is also secondary: it alludes to Laban's dream, an incident which was revealed to Jacob only according to the yahwistic interpolation (verses 29-30a). In addition, verses 41-42a expand on verse 42b, which speaks of Jacob's poverty and exhaustion: Jacob was protected by the Deity's intercession on his behalf whenever Laban attempted to cheat him out of his rightful wages (verse 42: "If the God of my father, the God of Abraham and the Fear of Isaac, had not been on my side, surely now you would have sent me away empty-handed").

In verse 45, Jacob sets up a pillar or a stele. Skinner[42] mentions that the Yahwist had an aversion to pillars and preferred altars (*cf.* my appendix on the Yahwist and cult). In order to blur the function of the pillar, the Yahwist suggests an alternative ceremony with a "skein" or "mound" (verses 46-50a). He adds an element of authenticity to his ceremony by naming the mound both in Hebrew and Aramaic (verse 47). The Yahwist makes sure to emphasize that this mound is not inherently sacrosanct, since Jacob and Laban eat on top of it (verse 46). In the elohistic narrative, the eating occurs after the pact in verse 54. According to the Yahwist, the mound is nothing more than the symbolic evidence of an alliance. The yahwistic mound and its function are in contradiction to the elohistic pillar, which is "Elohim's" presence on earth, as we see in verses 45 and 50b: "So Jacob took a stone, and set it up as a pillar... See that God is witness between you and me." The Yahwist also involves deities, but their role is more abstract. In verse 53 the "God of Abraham", the "God of Nahor" and the "Fear of Isaac" are

---

40   Cf. however Wellhausen *Hexateuch*, 42; Gunkel, *Genesis*, 336, whose attributions are
     diametrically opposed to our own.
41   Thus Westermann, *Genesis*, 1985, 497.
42   Skinner, *Genesis*, 399.

the treaty's guarantors. Verse 53 is attributed to J, who mentioned "the Fear of Isaac" in verses 41-42b. Verses 49-50a are also assigned to J: verse 49 uses "Yhwh" ("The LORD (Yhwh) [will] watch between you and me, when we are absent one from the other"); and verse 50a ("If you ill-treat my daughters, or if you take wives in addition to my daughters, though no one else is with us") because it connects to the previous verse (The reference to Mizpah in verse 49 remains obscure.) With an elegant editorial flourish, the Yahwist puts the originally elohistic words "remember that God is witness between you and me" (verse 50b) in Laban's mouth and thus disconnects the statement from the dedication of the pillar. Verse 45 was followed by verse 50b in E's account, thereby juxtaposing the dedication of the pillar and the calling upon God as a witness.[43] In the present context the statement attests to the fact that God is a guarantor, but not to the presence of the Deity in the pillar. The Yahwist is so enthusiastic regarding his "mound" that he squeezes it into his supplements no less than four times in verses 51-52.[44]

4.7.2 The Yahwistic Commentary

Little needs to be added to my analysis of the previous section. Verse 41 detailed the type of work Jacob did throughout the twenty years mentioned in verse 38, as part of the Yahwist's tendency to provide the reader with more of the details of daily life and relationships, as in J's numbering of Jacob's sons. The Yahwist presents an alternative alliance (in verses 46-50a), because it is important for him to blur the cultic function of the pillar. In verse 50, the Yahwist adds more compassion to Laban's character. Laban's main stipulation in his alliance with Jacob is the care of his daughters, which plainly contradicts statements made by Rachel and Leah in a previous E text: "Then Rachel and Leah answered him, 'Is there any portion or inheritance left to us in our father's house? Are we not regarded by him as foreigners? For he has sold us, and he has been using up the money given for us'" (31:14-15). As in any other text, the Yahwist makes sure to link the narrative to other Patriarchal stories and thus (once again) mentions Jacob's extended family antecedents, Abraham, Isaac and Nahor, in verses 42 and 53.

---

43 Driver, *Genesis*, 288, divides the text in much the same way except for vs. 50b which he attributes to J – despite the appearance of God / Elohim in this half verse.

44 Note the tendency to attribute the mound to a third author and cf. Westermann, *Genesis*, 1985, 500.

4.8 Jacob's Struggle with the Angel (Gen. 32)

(Note: The final verse of the previous chapter is sometimes counted as the first verse of this chapter)

32:1 Jacob went on his way and the angels of God met him; 2 and when Jacob saw them he said, "This is God's camp!" *So he called that place Mahanaim.*

3 Jacob sent messengers before him to his brother Esau in the land of Seir, the country of Edom, 4 instructing them, "Thus you shall say to my lord Esau: Thus says your servant Jacob, 'I have lived with Laban as an alien, and stayed until now; 5 and I have oxen, donkeys, flocks, male and female slaves; and I have sent to tell my lord, in order that I may find favor in your sight.' " 6 The messengers returned to Jacob, saying, "We came to your brother Esau, and he is coming to meet you, and four hundred men are with him." 7 Then Jacob was greatly afraid and distressed; and he divided the people that were with him, and the flocks and herds and camels, into two companies, 8 thinking, "If Esau comes to the one company and destroys it, then the company that is left will escape." 9 And Jacob said, "O God of my father Abraham and God of my father Isaac, O LORD who said to me, 'Return to your country and to your kindred, and I will do you good,' 10 I am not worthy of the least of all the steadfast love and all the faithfulness that you have shown to your servant, for with only my staff I crossed this Jordan; and now I have become two companies. 11 Deliver me, please, from the hand of my brother, from the hand of Esau, for I am afraid of him; he may come and kill us all, the mothers with the children. 12 Yet you have said, 'I will surely do you good, and make your offspring as the sand of the sea, which cannot be counted because of their number.' " 13 So he spent that night there, and from what he had with him he took a present for his brother Esau, 14 two hundred female goats and twenty male goats, two hundred ewes and twenty rams, 15 thirty milch camels and their colts, forty cows and ten bulls, twenty female donkeys and ten male donkeys. 16 These he delivered into the hand of his servants, every drove by itself, and said to his servants, "Pass on ahead of me, and put a space between drove and drove." 17 He instructed the foremost, "When Esau my brother meets you, and asks you, 'To whom do you belong? Where are you going? And whose are these ahead of you?' 18 then you shall say, 'They belong to your servant Jacob; they are a present sent to my lord Esau; and moreover he is behind us.' " 19 He likewise instructed the second and the third and all who followed the droves, "You shall say the same thing to Esau when you meet him, 20 and you shall say, 'Moreover your servant Jacob is behind us.' " For he thought, "I may appease him with the present that goes ahead of me, and afterwards I shall see his face; perhaps he will accept me." 21 So the present passed on ahead of him; and he himself spent that night in the camp. 22 The same night he got up and took his two wives, his two maids, and his eleven children, and crossed the ford of the Jabbok. 23 He took them and sent them across the stream, and likewise everything that he had. 24 Jacob was left alone; and a man wrestled with him until daybreak. 25 When the man saw that he did not prevail against Jacob, he struck him on the hip socket; and Jacob's hip was put out of joint as he wrestled with him. 26 Then he said, "Let me go, for the day is breaking." But Jacob said, "I will not let you go, unless you bless me." 27 So he said to him, "What is your name?" And he said, "Jacob." 28 Then the man said, "You shall no longer be called Jacob, but Israel, for you have striven with God and with humans, and have prevailed." 29 Then Jacob asked him, "Please tell me your name." But he said, "Why is it that you ask my name?" And there he blessed him. 30 So Jacob called the place Peniel, saying, "For I have seen God face to face, and yet my life is preserved."

4.8.1 Source Division[45]

The first verses of Gen. 32 (Gen. 32:1-2: "Jacob went on his way and the angels of God met him; and when Jacob saw them he said, "This is God's camp!" So he called that place Mahanayim") have puzzled exegetes for many years. There are those who would connect these stranded verses, at least stylistically, with the previous narrative, which ends: "Then he [Laban] departed and returned home" (31:55), which is parallel to "Jacob went on his way." Indeed, such is the division of the Masoretic *parshiyot*.[46] Another possibility tentatively explored by scholarship is to read these verses as an introduction to the upcoming narrative of Chapter 32, which also deals with companies— companies of cattle and of men.[47]

A third option favoured by many scholars is viewing these verses as an independent etymological tradition, perhaps a remnant of an ancient anthropomorphic tale which a later redactor eliminated.[48] All these explanations are unconvincing, since there is no real connection between these two verses and either of the surrounding narratives. The popular idea that this *"Mahanayim"* tradition is a remnant of a larger story is, in my view, spurious. The two verses pose enough of an anthropomorphic problem in and of themselves.

The solution to this quandary is quite simple, indeed almost trivial, when viewed through the eyes of the supplementary method. Gen. 32: 4-23, Jacob's prayer to God and division into camps, is generally attributed by modern exegetes to the Yahwist.[49] Such is also the case with much of the subsequent episode, Jacob's struggle with the mystery man

---

45 This section is a revision of my Z.A.W article, T. Yoreh, Jacob's Struggle, *ZAW* 117 (2005): 95-97.

46 Speiser, *Genesis*, 252.

47 Wellhausen, *Hexateuch*, 43-44.

48 Skinner, *Genesis*, 405.

49 Driver, *Genesis*, 291-294 does not think the resumptive repetition in verse 23 is not a sign of more than one source, rather it is a necessary tool used by the ancient author, cf. M. Anbar, La Reprise, *VT* 38 (1988): 385-398.

in Gen. 32: 24-30.[50] The main reason for attributing a large portion of Jacob's struggle to the Yahwist, contrary to obvious evidence (i.e. the twofold appearance of "Elohim") is Wellhausen's contention that according to the Elohist, God appears to mankind only in dreams.[51] Coupled with the dismissal of the Elohist as a source, attributing at least part of this episode to the Yahwist has gained a virtual consensus.[52] Yet I remain unconvinced: contrary to Wellhausen, God or his messengers appear at least three times in elohistic texts while the human subject is awake (Gen. 21:12, 17; 22:11). For this reason I prefer to adopt the minority position as put forth by Dillmann[53] and most recently advocated by Weisman[54] and Schmitt.[55]

To summarize our source division: 32:1-2a and 32:24-30 belong to the Elohist, while the intervening verses (following the present consensus) are yahwistic. This means that in the original E source Jacob's struggle with the mystery man immediately follows Jacob's encounter of angels. If this is the case there is no reason to assume that these verses (the *Mahanayim* tradition and Jacob's wrestling match) were not originally part of the same episode.[56] In an attempt to restore some semblance of meaning to the stranded verses, the Yahwist or a later redactor added the etymology of 32:2b "So he called that place Mahanayim".

4.8.2 The Yahwistic Commentary

As in previous narratives, the Yahwist presents the less impressive aspects of Jacob's personality. According to the J tradition Jacob, the hero who battles against the angel of Elohim, is described in the yahwistic addition as a coward who sends bribes or atonement offerings

50   Driver, *Genesis*, 294-297.
51   Wellhausen, *Hexateuch*, 44.
52   There are a whole range of divisions here, but all of them prominently involve the Yahwist, and see Holzinger, *Genesis*, 209-210; Skinner, *Genesis*, 407; Levin, *Jahwist*, 68.
53   Dillmann, *Genesis*, 362ff.
54   Weisman, *Jacob*, 76.
55   H. C. Schmitt, Der Kampf Jakobs mit Gott in Hos. 12, 3ff und in Gen. 32, 23ff: zum Verstaendnis der Verborgenheit Gottes im Hoseabuch und im Elohistischen Geschichtwerk, in *"Ich Bewirke das Heil und erschaffe das Unheil"* (B. Willnes and F. Diedrich eds.), Würzburg: 397-430; and see also F. Van Trigt, La Signifacation de la Lutte de Jacob Pres de Yabboq, *Oudtestamentische Studien* 12 (1958): 280-309, following Vriezen in a communication to the former.
56   Already Bennett, *Genesis*, 309 and Gunkel, *Genesis*, 347ff noted the connection between the two narratives, but did not draw the necessary conclusions.

for stealing his birthright to his brother in order that his brother do him
no harm. In the yahwistic interpolation, Jacob always uses the self-
effacing formal address "my lord Esau," and the size of the bribe that
Jacob sends him is enormous. The yahwistic narrative assumes that
Esau wants to harm Jacob in revenge for stealing his blessing (Ch. 27).
Jacob, the coward, knows this and is afraid that when Esau comes to
him with four hundred men, he will exact his revenge. The Elohist is
not familiar with this hostility, as we shall see below.

Why did the Yahwist separate the two parts of this fragmented episode? The answer, in my opinion, is simple: According to 32:24-30,
Jacob wrestles with a mystery "man," whose identity is in doubt. There
are those who argue even today that, at least metaphorically, this
"man" represents Esau and not an angel.[57] However, this ambiguity is
resolved once one adds 32:1-2a. If immediately before the struggle Jacob encounters a company of angels, it must be assumed that this
"man" is one of the company. The Yahwist added verses 32:3-23 specifically in order to introduce ambivalence into this highly anthropomorphic text, which no doubt was problematic for him. Verses 3-23 give the
impression that Jacob was a coward, yet how could a coward hope to
defeat an angel of God?

4.9 Jacob's Reunion with Esau (Gen. 33)

33:1 Now Jacob looked up and saw Esau coming, and four hundred
men with him. *So he divided the children among Leah and Rachel and the two maids. 2 He
put the maids with their children in front, then Leah with her children, and Rachel and Joseph last
of all.* 3 He himself went on ahead of them, *bowing himself to the ground seven
times,* until he came near his brother. 4 But Esau ran to meet him, and
embraced him, and fell on his neck and kissed him, and they wept. 5
When Esau looked up and saw the women and children, he said, "Who
are these with you?" Jacob said, "The children whom God has graciously given your servant." *6 Then the maids drew near, they and their children, and
bowed down; 7 Leah likewise and her children drew near and bowed down; and finally Joseph and
Rachel drew near, and they bowed down. 8 Esau said, "What do you mean by all this company
that I met?" Jacob answered, "To find favor with my lord." 9 But Esau said, "I have enough, my
brother; keep what you have for yourself."* 10 Jacob said, "No, please; if I find favor
with you, then accept my present from my hand; for truly to see your

---

57   And not an angel – and cf. J. Kodell, Jacob Wrestles with Esau Gen. 32,23-32, *BTB* 10
     (1980): 65-70, S. Molen, The Identity of Jacob's Opponent; Wrestling with Ambiguity
     in Gen. 32:23-32, *Shofar* 11 (1993): 16-29.

face is like seeing the face of God—since you have received me with such favor. 11 Please accept my gift *that is brought to you*, because God has dealt graciously with me, and because I have everything I want." So he urged him, and he took it. 12 *Then Esau said, "Let us journey on our way, and I will go alongside you."* 13 *But Jacob said to him, "My lord knows that the children are frail and that the flocks and herds, which are nursing, are a care to me; and if they are overdriven for one day, all the flocks will die.* 14 *Let my lord pass on ahead of his servant, and I will lead on slowly, according to the pace of the cattle that are before me and according to the pace of the children, until I come to my lord in Seir."* 15 *So Esau said, "Let me leave with you some of the people who are with me." But he said, "Why should my lord be so kind to me?"* 16 So Esau returned that day on his way to Seir. 17 *But Jacob journeyed to Succoth,a and built himself a house, and made booths for his cattle; therefore the place is called Succoth.* 18 and Jacob came safely to the city of Shechem, *which is in the land of Canaan, on his way from Paddan-aram;* and he camped before the city.

4.9.1 Source Division

As in previous instances, a basic elohistic narrative with yahwistic supplementation can be identified. Scholars since Wellhausen[58] have correctly recognizes the majority of the text as yahwistic, but—contrary to Driver[59] and Westermann[60]—the elohistic contribution does exist and is apparent in verses 5, 10, and 11, which use the name Elohim (*cf.* the repetition in verse 5: "Who are these with you" and vs. 8: "What do you mean by all the company that I met?" which to me indicates a plurality of sources). These verses, together with the introduction in verse 1, most of verse 3 (without the seven bows), and the kiss in verse 4 constitute the bulk of the elohistic episode.[61] The "deployment" of the children in preparation for Esau's arrival is similar to the organization of the camps and the strategic thinking of the yahwistic interpolation in 32:7-8: "Then Jacob was greatly afraid and distressed; and he divided the people that were with him, and the flocks and herds and camels, into two companies, thinking, 'If Esau comes to the one company and destroys it, then the company that is left will escape.'" Similarly we see in verse 18: "They belong to your servant Jacob; they are a present sent to my lord Esau; and moreover he is behind us." The same sensitivity to the camps is found in 33:13: "Let my lord pass on ahead of his ser-

---

58 Wellhausen, *Hexateuch*, 45.
59 Driver, *Genesis*, 297-298.
60 Westermann, *Genesis*, 1985, 523-524.
61 Gunkel, *Genesis*, 353-355.

vant, and I will lead on slowly, according to the pace of the cattle that are before me and according to the pace of the children, until I come to my lord in Seir." The term "שפחה" (in 33:2) for handmaiden as opposed to "אמה" is another sign of yahwistic authorship. The way Jacob "panders" to Esau through his seven bows (verse 3) is consistent with the extensive yahwistic interpolation of the previous chapter, and probably belongs to this source. The same is true of verses 6-7 with the wives and the sons bowing, and verse 8 "Esau said, 'What do you mean by all this company that I met?' Jacob answered, 'To find favor with my lord.'" Verses 12-15 are a further elaboration upon Jacob's dishonesty and cravenness. He promises to visit his brother in Seir, a promise which he does not plan to keep, as will be made clear in subsequent chapters. The only verse in this part of the chapter which may be elohistic is Esau's return to Seir (verse 16). If the verses that describe Jacob's servile behaviour are excised, one discovers a basic narrative, which briefly describes an emotional meeting between two long-separated brothers.

Many of the nineteenth-century scholars attributed verses 18-20 to E (Wellhausen 1899, 47-48).[62] Their evidence is, however, unconvincing: the erection of an altar in verse 20 is not an elohistic indicator. The verses are in fact, similar to the yahwistic erection of the altars in Gen. 12, 13 and 21:34, emphasizing ownership over the land, (cf. the appendix on yahwistic cult). Throughout the Jacob Cycle (or for that matter anywhere else except perhaps for the Mountain of God) the Elohist does not sanctify a place of worship other than Bethel. In fact, Jacob deliberately "desecrates" Shechem (a competing sanctuary?) by burying idols there (cf. Gen. 35:4 "So they gave to Jacob all the foreign gods that they had, and the rings that were in their ears; and Jacob hid them under the oak that was near Shechem.")[63] The only verse of this section that may be elohistic is verse 19, which mentions Jacob's arrival in Shechem. This detail connects us to the next and last elohistic episode, which begins in the same locale.

---

62   Wellhausen, *Hexateuch*, 47-48.

63   J. Soggin, Jacob in Shechem and in Bethel Gen. 35, 1-7, in *Shaarei Talmon* (M. Fishbane and E. Tov eds.), Winona Lake, 1910, 195-198, attributes this desecration to late anti-Samaritan tendencies.

4.9.2 The Yahwistic Commentary

By means of his many additions, the Yahwist alters a simple story describing an emotional meeting between brothers who have not seen one another for at least twenty years, into a meeting between a hunter with four hundred men of war and the hunted coward who tries to escape his brother's justified anger. The elohistic story does not truly introduce Esau except in passing in verse 3. Since, according to E, readers are familiar with biblical protagonists there is no real need to fully identify them. In previous yahwistic narratives, Esau is portrayed as a murderous and vengeful character (Gen. 27). The Yahwist, as he is prone to do, now presents Esau's more humane dimension. This is actually a fairly simple expansion since the Yahwist is able to build upon Esau's positive traits as presented in the basic E story. In the J expansion, Esau takes pity upon his brother Jacob and is even willing to escort and protect him. Jacob repays him with a false promise to visit him.

4.10 Jacob's Return to Bethel (Gen. 35)

35:1 *God said to Jacob, "Arise, go up to Bethel, and settle there. Make an altar there to the God who appeared to you when you fled from your brother Esau."* 2 Jacob said to his household and to all who were with him, "Put away the foreign gods that are among you, and purify yourselves, and change your clothes; 3 then come, let us go up to Bethel, that I may make an altar there to the God who answered me in the day of my distress and has been with me wherever I have gone." 4 So they gave to Jacob all the foreign gods that they had, and the rings that were in their ears; and Jacob hid them under the oak that was near Shechem. 5 *As they journeyed, a terror from God fell upon the cities all around them, so that no one pursued them* 6 Jacob came to Luz *that is* Bethel, which is in the land of Canaan, he and all the people who were with him, 7 and there he built an altar and called the place El-bethel, *because it was there that God had revealed himself to him when he fled from his brother. 8 And Deborah, Rebekah's nurse, died, and she was buried under an oak below Bethel. So it was called Allon-bacuth. 9 God appeared to Jacob again when he came from Paddan-aram, and he blessed him. 10 God said to him, "Your name is Jacob; no longer shall you be called Jacob, but Israel shall be your name." So he was called Israel. 11 God said to him, "I am God Almighty: be fruitful and multiply; a nation and a company of nations shall come from you, and kings shall spring from you. 12 The land that I gave to Abraham and Isaac I will give to you, and I will give the land to your offspring after you." 13 Then God went up from him at the place where he had spoken with him. 14 Jacob set up a pillar in the place where he had spoken with him, a pillar of stone; and he poured out a drink offering on it, and poured oil on it. 15 So Jacob called the place where God had spoken with him*

Bethel. 16 Then they journeyed from Bethel; and when they were still some distance from Ephrath, Rachel was in childbirth, and she had hard labor. 17 When she was in her hard labor, the midwife said to her, "Do not be afraid; for now you will have another son." 18 As her soul was departing (for she died), she named him Ben-oni; but his father called him Benjamin. 19 So Rachel died, and she was buried on the way to Ephrath (that is, Bethlehem), 20 and Jacob set up a pillar at her grave; it is the pillar of Rachel's tomb, which is there to this day.

4.10.1 Source Division

In this narrative, which is the last of the elohistic Jacob Cycle, P makes his first contribution to the redaction of the E narrative since Gen. 31:18 (an itinerary verse on the eve of Jacob's departure from Aram). P participates in the composition/redaction of Gen. 34, which tells of Dinah's rape and the subsequent massacre of the male inhabitants of Shechem, but Gen. 34 is not elohistic since Dinah, the protagonist and the subject of the chapter is not an E character (her birth was attributed to J in my analysis above). It is more difficult to identify the priestly redaction of E than it is to identify J's redaction of the same source, since both P and E use "Elohim," which obfuscates matters. The first P addition is the opening verse of the chapter: "God said to Jacob, 'Arise, go up to Bethel, and settle there. Make an altar there to the God who appeared to you when you fled from your brother Esau.' " There is little doubt that this verse is secondary to the basic narrative.[64] According to E, God had already commanded Jacob to return to his homeland (31:13). Moreover, Jacob had promised that when he returned, Bethel would be transformed into a house of God (28:22). Jacob does not need an additional directive to return to Bethel or to sanctify it. This verse is probably a "proleptic command" since P shies away from any human initiative in cultic matters (consider the death of Aaron's sons in Leviticus 10 because of their cultic innovation). According to the E narrative, Jacob resides in Bethel only as a temporary resident. In verse 16 he resumes his travels and reaches Bethlehem, thus disobeying God's command to settle in Bethel. It is possible that the priestly command to establish residence in Bethel is an attempt to harmonize the following verses with the second Priestly revelation in this locale (verse 9ff on the change of name and the reconsecration of Bethel), a revelation which may imply more than a short stay. According to the E narrative, Jacob

---

64   Westermann, *Genesis*, 1985, 550.

never needed to escape his brother Esau. Their only meeting (in Chapter 33) is amicable and any mention of an escape is secondary (Jacob's fraud in Gen. 27 is a yahwistic narrative). Another Priestly addition is verse 5: "As they journeyed, a terror from God fell upon the cities all around them, so that no one pursued them." This is an allusion to the sacking of Shechem in Gen. 34, another narrative with which E is unfamiliar.[65] Lastly, one must mention the Priestly revelation of 35:9-15. No detailed analysis of this unit is required, since verses 9-15 are saturated with Priestly indicators, such as the name El-Shaddai, Padan Aram, etc.

J also participates in the composition of this chapter. Verse 6 states: "Jacob came to Luz that is, Bethel, which is in the land of Canaan, he and all the people who were with him." The name "Luz" is first mentioned in J's Gen. 28:19: "He called that place Bethel; but the name of the city was Luz at the first," where I claimed that it was an attempt to obfuscate Bethel's inherently sacred character. This editorial theme is repeated here as well; the original elohistic verse probably read: "Jacob came to Bethel, he and all the people that were with him."[66] J also desecrates sacrosanct Bethel in verse 8 by burying Deborah under a famous tree in the holy locale.[67] This interpolation once again connects us to the general patriarchal context by mentioning Rebecca's wet nurse.

4.10.2 Priestly Supplementation

Most of the supplementary material in this narrative is Priestly. The supplementation in verses 1, 5 and 7 has been analyzed and only the revelation in verses 9-15 needs to be addressed. In this episode, God reveals himself as El Shaddai, changes Jacob's name to Israel, and promises him progeny and the inheritance of the land. In response, Jacob raises a "Matzebah" or pillar and anoints it with oil.[68] Finally, he names the place "Bethel." This short and compact episode is a Priestly reworking of the revelation at Bethel in Chapter 28:10-22 and Jacob's name change in Chapter 32, especially verse 28. The function of this text is to "amend" the revelation at Bethel and Jacob's name change,

65 Skinner, Genesis, 424, who follows Kuenen's attribution of these verses to a redactor / later stratum of E (A. Kuenen, *Historisch-Kritische Einleitung in die Bücher des A.T. Hinsichtlich ihrer Enstehung und Sammlung*, Leipzig, 1887, 65).

66 Cf. Gunkel's division of this verse (*Genesis*, 365-366).

67 Cf. G. A. Rendsburg, Notes on Gen. 35, *VT* 34 (1984): 361-364.

68 Cf. Driver *Genesis*, 310 who attributes the anointment to J – this is however highly unlikely, just as we have indicated above, J distances himself from pillars (מצבות).

purging them of unwanted elements. In the priestly version of events
there is no reason to suspect God is actually present in a stone (as in the
elohistic version in Chapter 28). Here the pillar is no more than a cultic
object. In the priestly version Jacob's name does not change because he
"wrestled" with Elohim as in Chapter 32, but rather because Elohim
commanded it. In order to create the impression that the version in
Chapter 35 was the original and true version, the priestly editor purposely appended it to the end of the Jacob Cycle, thus making a lasting
impression.[69]

4.11 Summary

4.11.1 The Elohistic Jacob Cycle

Just as in the Abraham Cycle, here too, the E text was divided into
small sections for reasons of convenience. The elohistic Jacob Cycle,
however, is a continuous narrative without contradictions or gaps:[70]
The account begins with Elohim's revelation to Jacob in Bethel. Jacob
makes a vow that if and when he returns, the place will be transformed
into a house of Elohim. From Bethel Jacob arrives at the land of his
brother Laban, where he encounters Laban's daughter Rachel near the
well and demonstrates his emotions by lifting the heavy stone from the
mouth of the well. Jacob stays to live with Laban and agrees to work
for him for seven years in order to win Rachel's hand in marriage, but
Laban tricks him and gives him Leah. Jacob agrees to work for Laban
for a further seven years in exchange for Rachel. A rivalry develops
between Rachel and Leah, the issue at stake being who will bear more
sons for Jacob. Jacob in the meantime continues to work, acquiring
wealth at Laban's expense. Jacob notices his brother's uneasiness and
when he receives a divine command to return he decides to escape.
Rachel steals her father's idols. Laban overtakes Jacob, but Elohim
warns Laban not to harm him. Laban does not find the idols and decides to depart in peace, a non-aggression pact being agreed to upon
his departure. On the way back to Bethel Jacob meets an angel of Elohim and wrestles with him, but does not succeed in vanquishing him.
In return for his release, the angel blesses Jacob and changes his name

---

69 Cf. J. Van Seters, Divine Encounter at Bethel Gen. 28, 10-12, in Recent Literary
    Critical Study of Genesis, *ZAW* 110 (1998): 503-513.

70 The account I isolate is complete, as opposed to Noth's account whose gaps are
    apparent. *cf.* Wynn-Williams, *Pentateuch*, 60-70.

to Israel. After all these adventures, Jacob encounters Esau, who is surprised to see him after so long a time. Finally, Jacob fulfills his vow and returns to Bethel. Upon leaving Bethel, Benjamin is born and his favourite wife Rachel dies.

The elohistic stories of Jacob are more than just continuous: the extensive yahwistic commentary conceals a well thought out literary structure. The Elohist organized his Jacob Cycle chiastically: the first episode of the Jacob cycle is parallel to the last episode, the second episode parallels the penultimate episode and so on (My division into sections was for the purpose of clarity and does not always coincide with the episodic structure below.) [71] In Gen. 28 Elohim reveals himself to Jacob in Bethel and Jacob returns in Gen. 35, thus fulfilling his promise. In the second episode, Jacob meets his brother Laban or, at the very least, his relative, and in the parallel episode Jacob encounters his brother Esau. In the third unit Laban tricks Jacob when, cloaked in darkness, he exchanges his daughters. Jacob consummates his marriage. The deception is discovered in the morning. In the parallel story, Jacob struggles with a mysterious figure throughout the night. Only when the sun rises does he discover that he was actually wrestling with a divine being. Here too the character does not "play fair," striking Jacob in his thigh (perhaps a euphemism for the genitals). In the fourth story, Rachel is the one who takes the initiative and exchanges her night with Jacob for Reuben's mandrakes. In the chiastic parallel, Laban pursues Jacob because Rachel stole his idols. Both stories deal with Jacob's children: in Chapters 29-30 they are born and in Chapter 31 their status as Jacob's children is guaranteed. At the centre of this structure, Elohim reveals himself to Jacob and commands him to return to his homeland.

Apart from the remarkable chiastic structure, other indicators of the Elohist's handiwork are apparent. Jacob passes through seven stops on his long journey: a) Bethel, b) the land of B'nei Kedem, c) Mount Gilad, d) Pniel, e) Shechem, f) Bethel, g) Derech Efrata. The fourth and middle stop, Peniel, is the place where the angel of Elohim changes his name. At the seventh and final stop Rachel gives birth to Jacob's seventh and last son.

---

71   Note the affinity with – M. Fishbane, Composition and Structure in the Jacob Cycle Gen. 25:19-35:22, *Journal of Jewish Studies* 26 (1975): 15-38; S. K. Sherwood, "Had God not Been on My Side", An Examination of the Narrative Technique of the Story of Jacob and Laban: Gen. 29.1-32.2 (European Union Studies 23/400), Frankfurt am Main, 1990 – who find similar structures.

The Chiastic Structure

The Revelation at Bethel (28:10-22)	The Return to Bethel (35:1-20)
The Meeting by the Well (29:1-14)	The Meeting between Jacob and Esau (33:1-18)
Laban's Ruse (29:15-30)	Jacob's struggle with the angel (32:1-32)
The Procreative Competition (29:32-30:24)	The Flight from Laban and the Agreement (31:17-55)

Chiasmus
The revelation to Jacob while keeping Laban's sheep (31:1-16)

4.11.2 Summary: The Yahwistic Commentary

The yahwistic supplementation of the elohistic Jacob Cycle is characterized by the following features:

Links to Previous Patriarchal Narratives

The elohistic source assumes that the readers are familiar with the Israelite heroes and sees no reason to introduce them or provide background information. In contrast, J, who is attempting to compose an historical document, needs to introduce the characters and provide the reader with a background to create continuity. Most of this background work is done in previous story cycles. The Yahwist therefore need only allude to the background of the characters in question. The way he does this is by "name dropping:" At every opportunity, the Yahwist mentions Jacob's ancestors: Abraham and Isaac, his mother Rebecca, Laban's father Nahor—all characters with whom we are familiar from earlier patriarchal narratives.

Making Characters More "Human"

The portrayal of characters in the elohistic source is generally one-dimensional:[72] Jacob is presented as a hard worker, a strong man, and generous to his relatives. In contrast, Laban is presented as a thankless cheater. The yahwistic interpolations "fill out" the protagonists' cha-

---

72   Cf. Speiser's observations in his commentary, *Genesis*, 42.

racters: Jacob, the good worker, cheats his employer and causes the sheep to give birth to lambs of a certain colour (end of Chapter 30); Jacob the mighty hero is a coward when it comes to meeting Esau (Chapter 32). According to the Elohist, Laban may be a thankless chea- ter, but the Yahwist lets us know that he is also a good father to his daughters, since Laban's main stipulation in the alliance with Jacob (31:50) is their security.

The Refining of Unacceptable Elohistic Cult

In my opinion, since the elohistic source is, the earliest source of the Pentateuch, it stands to reason that his religious ideas were not always palatable to a later generation of composers. The elohistic cult in Bethel disturbed both J and P and both schools attempt to influence the read- er's understanding.[73] The Yahwist twice mentions that Bethel was not always sacrosanct and was once called Luz (28:19, 35:6). The Yahwist is thus attempting to demonstrate that the sanctity of Bethel is not inhe- rent, but rather stems from the fact that Yhwh *decided* to reveal himself there. The Yahwist even attempts to "desecrate" Bethel by informing the reader that Rebecca's wet nurse, Deborah, was buried there (35:8). According to the Elohist, Jacob wrestled with the angel and was more than his match. The Yahwist lets us understand that the victory was not necessarily over an angel. He does this by separating the two parts of the original elohistic episode and by implying that Jacob was craven and could not possibly have defeated an angel. The alliance between Jacob and Laban (31:45) takes place in the proximity of a pillar which, according to the text, is a sign of the divine. The pillar is, however, per- ceived as a pagan element by later authors and, in accord with Deut. 16:22, is despised by Yhwh. Instead of the pillar, the Yahwist several times refers to a mound, a neutral non-problematic symbol.

The priestly source deals with the problematic aspects of the Bethel revelation and the name-change by presenting his own version of events at the conclusion of the Jacob cycle (35:9-15), thereby ensuring that the last thing we remember of this cycle is the priestly scheme of events.

---

73 Weisman, *Jacob*, throughout the book.

Correction of "Mistakes"

At times, the yahwistic source wished to "correct" a detail of the basic
elohistic story. As I mentioned in the Introduction, evidence suggests
that because the Yahwist did not dare omit sections of the holy text
before him, the only way to correct details in the text was through supplementation. This he does, and at times with great sophistication. To
cite a number of the most obvious examples: according to the elohistic
story, Laban and Jacob are brothers or, at the very least, the familial
relationship between them is stated generally and remains unspecified.
The Yahwist, who had already established the connection between
Laban and Jacob in Gen. 24, emphasizes (no less than six times) the
uncle-nephew relationship. Moreover, he uses the term "brother" in a
non-familial context in the same narrative (verse 4) in order to disasso-
ciate the word from its basic meaning. Finally he adds verse 14: "And
Laban said to him, 'Surely you are my bone and my flesh,'" which in
my opinion is an attempt to alter the reader's understanding of verse 15
(where the original elohistic relationship is mentioned), letting us understand that the "brotherhood" in verse 15 should be understood generally and not specifically. Another point of contention between the
basic source and J concerns the exact number of Jacob's sons. According to the Elohist, Rachel, Bilhah and Leah bore only seven sons (Chapters 29, 30 and 35). The Yahwist amends this impression and adds five
sons (and a daughter) to the narrative of Chapters 29-30, emphasizing
the new figure of twelve throughout the continuation of the elohistic
narrative.

Thickening the Plot

Under this heading I include the deliberate allusion to future events
and repetition of past events. The purpose of this type of supplementation was to present the reader with a more logical and coherent text
according to the standards of the times. However, it is often difficult to
identify, since repetition of events is also a literary technique. One way
to identify "superfluous repetition" is to determine whether a specific
allusion eliminates the internal suspense of an episode. Two examples
will suffice: a) Gen. 31:3 is a proleptic insertion ("Then the LORD said
to Jacob, 'Return to the land of your ancestors and to your kindred, and
I will be with you.'"). The divine revelation is "revealed" to the reader
only in verse 10 of the same chapter. The Yahwist, however, wanted to
emphasize (perhaps) that the revelation actually occurred (and was not
merely a rhetorical ploy to convince Jacob's wives). He therefore in-

serted a short statement regarding the revelation before the actual speech. b) The proleptic description of the gathering of the shepherds of Haran (29:3) decreases the narrative tension and makes the shepherds' answer to Jacob in verse 8 seem repetitious. It is an additional example of a "superfluous proleptic repetition" in the style of J.

5. The Elohistic Joseph Cycle

5.1 Joseph and His Brothers (Gen. 37)

1 *Jacob settled in the land where his father had lived as an alien, the land of Canaan.* 2 *This is the story of the family of Jacob. Joseph, being seventeen years old, was shepherding the flock with his brothers; he was a helper to the sons of Bilhah and Zilpah, his father's wives; and Joseph brought a bad report of them to their father.* 3 Now Israel loved Joseph more than any other of his children, because he was the son of his old age; and he had made him a long robe with sleeves. 4 But when his brothers saw that their father loved him more than all his brothers, they hated him, and could not speak peaceably to him.5 Once Joseph had a dream, and when he told it to his brothers, they hated him even more. 6 He said to them, "Listen to this dream that I dreamed. 7 There we were, binding sheaves in the field. Suddenly my sheaf rose and stood upright; then your sheaves gathered around it, and bowed down to my sheaf." 8 His brothers said to him, "Are you indeed to reign over us? Are you indeed to have dominion over us?" So they hated him even more because of his dreams and his words. 9 *He had another dream, and told it to his brothers, saying, "Look, I have had another dream: the sun, the moon, and eleven stars were bowing down to me."* 10 *But when he told it to his father and to his brothers, his father rebuked him, and said to him, "What kind of dream is this that you have had? Shall we indeed come, I and your mother and your brothers, and bow to the ground before you?"* 11 *So his brothers were jealous of him, but his father kept the matter in mind.* 12 Now his brothers went to pasture their father's flock near Shechem. 13 And Israel said to Joseph, "Are not your brothers pasturing the flock at Shechem? Come, I will send you to them." He answered, "Here I am." 14 *So he said to him, "Go now, see if it is well with your brothers and with the flock; and bring word back to me."* So he sent him from the valley of Hebron and he came to Shechem, 15 *and a man found him wandering in the fields; the man asked him, "What are you seeking?"* 16 *"I am seeking my brothers," he said; "tell me, please, where they are pasturing the flock."* 17 *The man said, "They have gone away, for I heard them say, 'Let us go to Dothan.'"* So Joseph went after his brothers, and found them at Dothan. 18 They saw him from a distance, and before he came near to them, they conspired to kill him. 19 They said to one another, "Here comes this dreamer. 20 Come now, let us kill him and throw him into one of the pits; then we shall say that a wild animal has devoured him, and we shall see what will become of his dreams." 21 But when Reuben heard it, he delivered him out of their hands, saying, "Let us not take his life." 22 Reuben said to them, "Shed no blood; throw him into this pit here in

the wilderness, but lay no hand on him"—that he might rescue him out of their hand and restore him to his father. 23 So when Joseph came to his brothers, they stripped him of his robe, the long robe with sleeves that he wore; 24 and they took him and threw him into a pit. The pit was empty; there was no water in it. 25 *Then they sat down to eat; and looking up they saw a caravan of Ishmaelites coming from Gilead, with their camels carrying gum, balm, and resin, on their way to carry it down to Egypt. 26 Then Judah said to his brothers, "What profit is it if we kill our brother and conceal his blood? 27 Come, let us sell him to the Ishmaelites, and not lay our hands on him, for he is our brother, our own flesh." And his brothers agreed.* 28 When some Midianite traders passed by, they drew Joseph up, lifting him out of the pit, *and sold him to the Ishmaelites for twenty pieces of silver.* And they took Joseph to Egypt. 29 When Reuben returned to the pit and saw that Joseph was not in the pit, he tore his clothes. 30 He returned to his brothers, and said, "The boy is gone; and I, where can I turn?" 31 *Then they took Joseph's robe, slaughtered a goat, and dipped the robe in the blood. 32 They had the long robe with sleeves taken to their father, and they said, "This we have found; see now whether it is your son's robe or not." 33 He recognized it, and said, "It is my son's robe! A wild animal has devoured him; Joseph is without doubt torn to pieces." 34 Then Jacob tore his garments, and put sackcloth on his loins, and mourned for his son many days. 35 All his sons and all his daughters sought to comfort him; but he refused to be comforted, and said, "No, I shall go down to Sheol to my son, mourning." Thus his father bewailed him.* 36 Meanwhile the Midianites had sold him in Egypt to Potiphar, *Pharaoh's officer* the captain of the guard.

5.1.1 Source Division

Following my source division of Gen. 32 (i.e. E's authorship of the meeting between Jacob and the angel and the subsequent change of name to Israel), this chapter's working hypothesis is that throughout the elohistic Joseph cycle, Joseph's father is known as "Israel" as distinct from the yahwistic "Jacob." The Yahwist kept this name because he was uncomfortable with the anthropomorphism of the elohistic etiology in Gen. 32:28: "Then the man said, 'You shall no longer be called Jacob, but Israel, for you have striven with God and with humans, and have prevailed.'"[1] Since all Documentary scholars believe the opposite to be true, my assumption that E uses Israel and J uses Jacob flies in the face of consensus and one of my main tasks will be to prove this revolutionary hypothesis over the course of the stories of Joseph.[2]

---

1   Cf. Holzinger's observation on this verse, H. Holzinger, (Nachprüfung von B. D. Eerdmans, *Die Komposition der Genesis*, ZAW 31 (1911): 56): "…der name Israel mit El nicht mit Jahwe zusammengesetzt sei".

2   Note also the prevalence of the name Jacob in Driver's J (*Genesis*, 1904).

Chapter 37 is usually divided between J and E and many see it as an exemplary case of Documentary division.[3] I disagree with this conclusion because some of the key criteria by which this chapter was divided are unfounded (e.g. the use of Jacob/Israel by the three sources). Once more it becomes apparent that the supplementary model is preferable.[4] As in previous instances, Chapter 37 is composed of one basic source (E) and subsequent interpolations.

The introductory verses of the Joseph Cycle 1-2aα [the small "a" refers to the division of the half verse]: "Jacob settled in the land where his father had lived as an alien, the land of Canaan. This is the story of the family of Jacob" are priestly (based upon the terms "אלה תולדות" [this is the story] and "מגורי" [had lived as an alien]) and comparable to the introduction to the Isaac Cycle "This is the story of the family of Isaac, Abraham's son: Abraham was the father of Isaac" (Gen. 25:19). Wenham[5] claims that the second introductory verse is yahwistic, but his arguments are unconvincing. 2aβ continues to exhibit priestly characteristics: Joseph's age is mentioned and Bilhah and Zilpah are referred to as "Jacob's wives."[6] 2b is either the yahwistic introduction to the narrative – Joseph as a slanderer fits J's usual mode of rounding off characters – or the end of the priestly introduction. (The term "דבה" = slander is used elsewhere by P, e.g. Num. 14:32.)

The elohistic narrative begins with verse 3 and immediately reveals the issue which will lead to strife between the brothers: "Now Israel loved Joseph more than any other of his children, because he was the son of his old age; and he had made him a long robe with sleeves."[7] The Elohist continues his story with Joseph's sheaf dream. Joseph's second dream (verses 9-11) is probably secondary[8] a) In Joseph's second dream, the sun and the moon, which represent his father and mother, bow down to Joseph, an occurrence with no basis in (narrative) reality.

---

3   E.g. Gunkel, *Genesis*, 387.
4   Following Redford, *Joseph*, 1970; L. Ruppert, Zum Neuren Diskussion um die Josefsgeschichte der Genesis, *BZ* 33 (1989): 92-97; Loewenstamm, *Joseph*, 1992; Carr, *Fractures*, 1996; but the basis for these observations is Gressmann, Ursprung und Entwicklung der Joseph-sage, in *Eucharisterion: Studien zur Religion und Literatur des Alten und Neuen Testaments* (H. Schmidt ed.), Göttingen, 1923, 11–note Schmitt's argument for an opposite relationship between J and E in his 1980 commentary.
5   G. Wenham, The Priority of P, *VT* 49 (1999): 240-248.
6   Cf. Wellhausen, *Hexateuch*, 51 – the pre-priestly terms are either "אמה" [E] or "שפחה" [J] – both of which denote handmaiden.
7   This verse is usually attributed to J by Documentary scholars, thus Driver *Genesis*, 322.
8   Smend, *Hexateuch*, 101, Levin, *Jahwist*, 69 and note Gressmann's comments on both dreams (Gressmann, *Joseph*, 19-20).

His first dream, however, is an allusion to the beginning of Chapter 42 (the prostration of the brothers); b) According to the second dream, Joseph's brethren number eleven, whereas according to the Elohist, Joseph is blessed with only six brothers. c) The terminology of the second dream is different from the rest of the story: following the first dream his brothers "hate" (שׂ.נ.א) him (verses 5 and 8), but after the second dream his brothers are jealous of him (ק.נ.א) (verse 11). For these reasons I attribute the second dream to a secondary source, in this case J. The addition of this dream is intended to add symmetry to the Joseph Cycle as a whole: Joseph interprets two dreams while waiting on two courtiers and Pharaoh, too, dreams two dreams. It is only fitting that the dreamer *par excellence* dream two dreams.[9]

My division of the first eleven verses of Chapter 37 differs markedly from the Documentary analysis which claims that an independent yahwistic garment narrative and an independent elohistic dream narrative were intertwined throughout Chapter 37.[10] According to the analysis presented above, the second dream was added by J and the verses that mention the sleeved garment are in all likelihood elohistic. (In verse 3, Joseph's father is Israel.)

Joseph's dream sets the stage and now the elohistic version of the story quickly unfolds. Joseph's brothers are tending the sheep in the environs of Shechem (verse 12) and Israel sends Joseph to see if all is well with them.[11] Verse 14a: "So he said to him, 'Go now, see if it is well with your brothers and with the flock; and bring word back to me'" is secondary: the verse repeats Israel's general request (verse 13) and explains that Joseph was sent to inquire after the welfare of his brothers and their herds. It should be noted that repetition while adding details is a common editorial technique. Verses 15-17, in which Joseph wanders the fields in search of his brothers, who in the meantime have moved with their sheep to Dothan, are probably also secondary. The move to Dothan does not fulfill any discernible function if it is attributed to E, but attributing the verses to J makes a great deal of sense. According to the Yahwist, Joseph's brothers looted Shechem and killed all the males as a result of the Dinah episode (Gen. 34). It is unlikely that they would want to further antagonise the inhabitants of the area and tend their flocks specifically in the environs of Shechem.[12] The

---

9 This symmetry is also noted by the documentary approach which attributes **both** dreams to E, cf. Driver, *Genesis*, 322.

10 Thus Gunkel, *Genesis*, 387-388.

11 Once again J according to Driver, *Genesis*, 323, *et al.*

12 There is little argument regarding J's compilation of parts of Gen. 34, the existence of an E version of the tale is however hotly contested and see Driver's division between

Yahwist addressed the problem by "transferring" Joseph's brothers to Dothan.

The elohistic story continues in verse 18: Joseph's brothers see him from afar and plot to kill him. At this point, the eldest son, Reuben, intervenes and convinces his fellow brothers not to kill Joseph, but rather to throw him into a pit. This would enable him eventually to save Joseph from their clutches (verses 21-24). Verses 25-27 tell of a meal at which Joseph's brothers, with Judah at their head, decide to sell Joseph to the Ishmaelites instead of killing him. I concur with the majority of scholars, who distinguish between verses 21-24, in which Reuben is the main character and verses 25-27, in which Judah plays the leading role. Verses 25-27 are clearly non-elohistic since E does not recognize Judah as one of Jacob's sons. The verses are usually attributed to the Judean layer of the Joseph Cycle, namely "J."

Following verse 27, my division is identical to that of Driver's,[13] the rationale being as follows. In verse 28a the elohistic narrative is resumed: Midianite merchants find Joseph and take him out of the pit. Verse 28b acts as a bridge between the tradition that Judah and his brothers sold Joseph to the Ishmaelites and the tradition that the Midianites pulled Joseph out of the pit themselves. The verbs are anonymous and the reader can deduce one of two possibilities when reading the canonical version: Either the Midianites sold Joseph to the Ishmaelites without the brothers being in any way involved or, the brothers pulled Joseph out of the pit and sold him to the Ishmaelites, with the Midanites merely helping to pull him out. (The second option is less likely, since the Midianites would then have no real role). The elohistic narrative resumes in verse 30, where Reuben returns to the pit but does not find Joseph. Verses 31-35 describe how the brothers dip Joseph's coat in blood and bring it to Jacob, causing their father to mourn for many days. These verses are without a doubt a yahwistic interpolation ("Jacob," "Sheol" and the very human dimension, which is usually not elaborated upon in E texts). The elohistic narrative is found again in verse 36, the first part of which is a resumptive repetition, which repeats 28b and tells of Joseph's arrival in Egypt. The second half of verse 36 adds that Joseph is sold to "Potiphar, one of Pharaoh's officials, the captain of the guard." In my opinion, this is original, except perhaps for the yahwistic expression "סריס" (translated by NRSV as official); the Elohist prefers the term "שר" (translated by NRSV as captain).

J and P (Driver, *Genesis*, 302), and Skinner's (*Genesis*, 418) division between Jx and Ex – (the x indicates uncertainty).

13   *Genesis*, 325-326.

5.1.2 The Yahwistic Commentary

The yahwistic tradition, in which Judah and the Ishmaelites are the protagonists, causes a considerable number of textual difficulties. At first glance, it appears that two different traditions were combined mechanically (especially verses 28 and onwards), rather than there being a basic text supplemented by a redactor. Even if the late Yahwist knew of an independent tradition with Judah and the Ishmaelites as protagonists, why must it be emphasized at the expense of coherence? Why was it impossible to be satisfied with the Reuben-Midianite version, thus sparing the reader all the textual difficulties?

The emphasis of the Ishmaelites over the Midianites is relevant and serves a literary function: the progeny of the son that Abraham banished following a divine command has achieved success and is the instrument employed to banish Israel's son, who will also become exceptionally successful. Judah's intervention on behalf of Joseph is also important, since according to the Yahwist, Judah is the most important son. Thus, Judah also pleads Benjamin's case before Joseph in 44:18 and onwards. Similarly, Judah is the emissary whom Joseph sends in order to show his father the way to Goshen (46:28). Why then did Judah suggest selling Joseph to the Ishmaelites? This does not seem to fit the image of a responsible son and future leader. As I attempt to demonstrate, the Yahwist was a conservative redactor who refused to excise any piece of the basic elohistic text. According to E, Reuben had already intervened and thus J had to find another way of involving Judah. He therefore initiates Joseph's sale. The decision to sell Joseph during a meal underlines the cruelty of Joseph's brothers, for which they later receive their just desserts. They do not know that in a number of years they will be begging for food from the brother who is now trapped in a pit.

Although Chapter 37 is presented as a good example of a merger between two documents, it is difficult to find two completely independent sources. It is clear that the Yahwist is familiar with the basic elohistic story: Judah's decision to sell Joseph indicates that he (Joseph) is already in the brothers' power. Once more the supplementary model is preferable.

5.2 The Ministers' Dreams (Gen. 40)

1 Some time after this, the cupbearer of the King of Egypt and his baker offended their lord the King of Egypt. 2 *Pharaoh was angry with his two officers, the chief cupbearer and the chief baker,* 3 and he put them in custody in the house of the captain of the guard, *in the prison where Joseph was confined.* 4 The captain of the guard charged Joseph with them, and he waited on them; and they continued for some time in custody. 5 One night they both dreamed—the cupbearer and the baker of the King of Egypt, *who were confined in the prison*—each his own dream, and each dream with its own meaning. 6 When Joseph came to them in the morning, he saw that they were troubled. 7 So he asked Pharaoh's officers, "Why are your faces downcast today?" 8 They said to him, "We have had dreams, and there is no one to interpret them." And Joseph said to them, "Do not interpretations belong to God? Please tell them to me."9 So the chief cupbearer told his dream to Joseph, and said to him, "In my dream there was a vine before me, 10 and on the vine there were three branches. As soon as it budded, its blossoms came out and the clusters ripened into grapes. 11 Pharaoh's cup was in my hand; and I took the grapes and pressed them into Pharaoh's cup, and placed the cup in Pharaoh's hand." 12 Then Joseph said to him, "This is its interpretation: the three branches are three days; 13 within three days Pharaoh will lift up your head and restore you to your office; and you shall place Pharaoh's cup in his hand, just as you used to do when you were his cupbearer. 14 But remember me when it is well with you; please do me the kindness to make mention of me to Pharaoh, and so get me out of this place. 15 For in fact I was stolen out of the land of the Hebrews; *and here also I have done nothing that they should have put me into the dungeon."* 16 When the chief baker saw that the interpretation was favorable, he said to Joseph, "I also had a dream: there were three cake baskets on my head, 17 and in the uppermost basket there were all sorts of baked food for Pharaoh, but the birds were eating it out of the basket on my head." 18 And Joseph answered, "This is its interpretation: the three baskets are three days; 19 within three days Pharaoh will lift up your head—from you!—and hang you on a pole; and the birds will eat the flesh from you." 20 On the third day, which was Pharaoh's birthday, he made a feast for all his servants, and lifted up the head of the chief cupbearer and the head of the chief baker among his servants. 21 He restored the chief cupbearer to his cupbearing, and he placed the cup in Pharaoh's hand; 22 but the chief baker he hanged, just as Joseph had interpreted to them. 23 Yet the chief cupbearer did not remember Joseph, but forgot him.

5.2.1 Source Division

Between Chapter 37 and the resumption of elohistic narrative in Chapter 40 there are two interpolations. The first is the story of Judah and Tamar in Chapter 38, which (according to many indicators) may be assigned to a relatively late source.[14] Following the lead of Redford,[15] who attributes the chapter to the Genesis editor, a final supplementary redactor parallel to B, I attribute it to B or a post-J editor.[16]

E's narrative, which begins in verse one of Chapter 40, is cut off immediately in verse 2 by a second introduction: "Pharaoh was angry with his two officers, the chief cupbearer and the chief baker." Both the use of "his officers" (סריסיו) instead of simply "his cupbearer" or "baker" (as in verse 1) and "Pharaoh" instead of "the King of Egypt" (as in verse 1) indicate a second source.[17] An attribution to J seems likely (and compare the use of "סריס" in Gen. 37:36), in light of the following interpolations. The second part of verse 3 ("in the prison where Joseph was confined"), the second part of verse 5 ("who were confined in the prison"), most of 7a ("Who were with him in custody in his master's house") and the second half of verse 15 ("and here also I have done nothing that they should have put me into the dungeon") are all yahwistic interpolations linking this narrative to its predecessor in Gen. 39.[18] According to E, Joseph's first and primary job was serving Pharaoh's servants in jail, while according to J Joseph fell from grace and was incarcerated because of the attempted seduction. The remainder of Chapter 40 is attributed to the original elohistic narrative.

---

14 This chapter is widely acknowledged as foreign to J, and see Gunkel, *Genesis*, 395; H. C. Schmitt, Die Hintergrunde der "neuesten Pentateuchkritik" und der literarische Befund der Josefsgeschichte Gen. 37-50, *ZAW* 97, 1985, 161-179; but cf. A. J. Lambe, Judah's Development; the Pattern of Departure-Return-Transition, *JSOT* 83 (1999): 53-68.

15 Redford, *Joseph*, 183.

16 The account is alluded to again only in B glosses to priestly genealogies and narratives. *cf.* Gen. 46:12, where B's typical qal passive yulad is found; the second episode, the failed seduction of Joseph, is usually attributed to J (Driver, *Genesis*, 327-336).

17 Cf. Redford, *Joseph*, 177, who objects to the use of Pharaoh, and "King of Egypt" as indicators of distinct sources.

18 Concerning Joseph and the wife of Potiphar; thus Schmitt, *Joseph*, 32-35.

5.2.2 The Yahwistic Commentary

As noted above, the Yahwist inserts the wife of Potiphar episode into the E tapestry. Joseph's innocence in this matter demonstrates that, according to the Yahwist, Joseph is not entirely bad. His loyalty to his master is in direct contrast to Gen. 37, in which he was described as a teller of tales and a dreamer of pretentious dreams. Ironically, even when Joseph is loyal and good he gets into trouble and is thrown into another, deeper pit. The Yahwist partially models his story on Chapter 37: in both the stories Joseph's troubles are connected to love or trust. His desirability and the brothers' jealousy stem from his favoured status, the lies of the conspirators are both connected to Joseph's clothing, and finally, according to both narratives, Joseph ends up in a pit. Therefore, when the Yahwist emphasizes at the beginning of the Potiphar narrative and at its end (39:2-3, 21-23) that all of Joseph's troubles are elements of a divine plan, one can deduce that his first confrontation with his brothers as well as his future success stem from the Deity (cf. E's conclusion in Gen. 50:20). Now the yahwistic interpolations which allude to Joseph's prison sentence are even clearer. The Yahwist wants us to know that this episode and all the subsequent ordeal are part of the divine plan.[19]

5.3 Pharaoh's Dreams (Gen. 41)

1 After two whole years, Pharaoh dreamed that he was standing by the Nile, 2 and there came up out of the Nile seven sleek and fat cows, and they grazed in the reed grass. 3 Then seven other cows, ugly and thin, came up out of the Nile after them, and stood by the other cows on the bank of the Nile. 4 The ugly and thin cows ate up the seven sleek and fat cows. And Pharaoh awoke. 5 Then he fell asleep and dreamed a second time; seven ears of grain, plump and good, were growing on one stalk. 6 Then seven ears, thin and blighted by the east wind, sprouted after them. 7 The thin ears swallowed up the seven plump and full ears. Pharaoh awoke, and it was a dream. 8 In the morning his spirit was troubled; so he sent and called for all the magicians of Egypt and all its wise men. Pharaoh told them his dreams, but there was no

---

19 This exegetical method which derives insight from the comparison of parallel narratives is found in Miscall's work (P. D. Miscall, "The Jacob and Joseph Stories as Analogies", *JSOT* 6 (1978): 28-40), who compares chapters 37 and 38 – for an earlier permutation of this methodology, see R. Alter, A Literary Approach to the Bible, *Commentary* 60 (1975): 70-77.

one who could interpret them to Pharaoh. 9 Then the chief cupbearer said to Pharaoh, "I remember my faults today. 10 Once Pharaoh was angry with his servants, and put me and the chief baker in custody in the house of the captain of the guard. 11 We dreamed on the same night, he and I, each having a dream with its own meaning. 12 A young Hebrew was there with us, a servant of the captain of the guard. When we told him, he interpreted our dreams to us, giving an interpretation to each according to his dream. 13 As he interpreted to us, so it turned out; I was restored to my office, and the baker was hanged." 14 Then Pharaoh sent for Joseph, *and he was hurriedly brought out of the dungeon.* When he had shaved himself and changed his clothes, he came in before Pharaoh. 15 And Pharaoh said to Joseph, "I have had a dream, and there is no one who can interpret it. I have heard it said of you that when you hear a dream you can interpret it." 16 Joseph answered Pharaoh, "It is not I; God will give Pharaoh a favorable answer." 17 Then Pharaoh said to Joseph, "In my dream I was standing on the banks of the Nile; 18 and seven cows, fat and sleek, came up out of the Nile and fed in the reed grass. 19 Then seven other cows came up after them, poor, very ugly, and thin. Never had I seen such ugly ones in all the land of Egypt. 20 The thin and ugly cows ate up the first seven fat cows, 21 but when they had eaten them no one would have known that they had done so, for they were still as ugly as before. Then I awoke. 22 I fell asleep a second time and I saw in my dream seven ears of grain, full and good, growing on one stalk, 23 and seven ears, withered, thin, and blighted by the east wind, sprouting after them; 24 and the thin ears swallowed up the seven good ears. But when I told it to the magicians, there was no one who could explain it to me." 25 Then Joseph said to Pharaoh, "Pharaoh's dreams are one and the same; God has revealed to Pharaoh what he is about to do. 26 The seven good cows are seven years, and the seven good ears are seven years; the dreams are one. 27 The seven lean and ugly cows that came up after them are seven years, as are the seven empty ears blighted by the east wind. They are seven years of famine. 28 It is as I told Pharaoh; God has shown to Pharaoh what he is about to do. 29 There will come seven years of great plenty throughout all the land of Egypt. 30 After them there will arise seven years of famine, and all the plenty will be forgotten in the land of Egypt; the famine will consume the land. 31 The plenty will no longer be known in the land because of the famine that will follow, for it will be very grievous. 32 And the doubling of Pharaoh's dream means that the thing is fixed by God, and God will shortly bring it about. 33 Now therefore let Pharaoh select a man who is discerning and wise, and set him over the land of Egypt. 34 Let Pharaoh proceed to appoint overseers over the land, and take one-fifth of the produce of the land of Egypt during the seven plenteous years. 35 Let them gather all the food of these good years that are coming, and lay up grain under the authority of Pharaoh for food in the cities, and let them keep it. 36 That food shall be a reserve for the land against the seven years of famine that are to befall the land of Egypt, so that the land may not perish through the famine." 37 The proposal pleased Pharaoh and all his servants. 38 Pharaoh said to his servants, "Can we find anyone else like this—one in whom is the spirit of God?" 39 So Pharaoh said to Joseph, "Since God has shown you all this, there is no one so discerning and wise as you. 40 You shall be over my house, and all my people shall order themselves as you command; only with regard to the throne will I be greater than you." 41 And Pharaoh said to Joseph, "See, I have set you over all the land of Egypt." 42 Removing his signet ring from his hand, Pharaoh put it on Joseph's hand; he arrayed him in garments of fine linen, and put a gold chain around his neck. 43 He had him ride in the chariot of his second-in-command; and they cried out in front of him, "Bow the knee!" Thus he set him over all the land of Egypt. 44 Moreover Pharaoh said to Joseph, "I am Pharaoh, and without your consent no one shall lift up hand or foot in all the land of Egypt." 45 Pharaoh gave Joseph the name Zaphenath-paneah; and he gave him Asenath daughter of Potiphera, priest of On, as his wife. *Thus Joseph gained authority over the land of Egypt. 46 Joseph was thirty years old when he entered the service of Pharaoh King of Egypt.* And Joseph went out from the presence of Pharaoh, and went through all the land of Egypt. 47 During the seven plenteous years the earth produced abundantly. 48 He gathered up all the food of the seven years when there was plenty in the land of Egypt, and stored up food in the cities; he stored up in every city the food from the fields around it. *49 So Joseph stored up grain in such abundance—like the sand of the sea—that he stopped measuring it; it was beyond measure. 50 Before the years of famine came, Joseph had two sons, whom Asenath daughter of Potiphera, priest of On, bore to him. 51 Joseph named the firstborn Manasseh, "For," he said, "God has made me forget all my hardship and all my father's house." 52 The second he named Ephraim, "For God has made me fruitful in the land of my misfortunes." 53 The seven years of plenty that prevailed in the land of Egypt came to an end; 54 and the seven years of famine began to come, just as Joseph had said. There was famine in every country, but throughout the land of Egypt there was bread. 55 When all the land of Egypt was famished, the people cried to Pharaoh for bread. Pharaoh said to all the Egyptians, "Go to Joseph; what he says to you, do."* 56 And since the famine had spread over all the land, Joseph opened all that was in them [in the cities], and sold to the Egyptians, for the famine was severe in the land of Egypt. 57 Moreover, all the world came to Joseph in Egypt to buy grain, because the famine became severe throughout the world.

5.3.1 Source Division

Chapter 41, the longest elohistic episode, was preserved with barely any intervention of the later supplementary sources.[20] The Yahwist intervenes only once in the first forty-five verses and in accord with the editorial theme of the previous chapter he alludes to Joseph's prison sentence by the three words in 41:14: "and he was hurriedly brought out of the dungeon."[21] Verse 45b ("Thus Joseph gained authority over the land of Egypt") is probably an editorial glitch and is absent from the Septuagint.[22] Verse 46a adds priestly chronological data, i.e. Joseph's age at his ascension.[23] The second interpolation is broader (and more structured). The borders of the interpolation may be discerned if the explicit link between verse 48 and verse 56 is recognized: "[Joseph opened] *all that was in them*" ("כל אשר בהם") (verse 56) which refers to the cities in which Joseph stored food mentioned in verse 48.[24]

In verses 49-55 two sources are discernible[25]: verse 49, which uses the yahwistic expression "like the sand of the sea" as in Gen. 22:17 and is connected to verse 53,[26] which mentions the end of the years of plenty and then the beginning of the years of famine. Verses 50-52 further chronicle Joseph's life in Egypt and are attributed to B, based on the qal passive "יֻלַּד," typical of this source's genealogies; and *cf.* a reference to Ephraim and Menasseh's birth in B's gloss (46:27) to the priestly name list of Gen. 46.[27]

5.3.2 The Yahwistic Commentary

Since the Yahwist did not add much of his own color to this narrative, my comments will be brief. His second interpolation, verse 49 and verses 53-55, fill the narrative gap between the gathering of the produce and the years of hunger in verse 56. The verses mention the end of the years of plenty and the beginning of the years of famine, i.e. that all of

---

20   Cf. Driver, *Genesis*, 339-346, but note Gunkel's refusal to abandon documentary divisions even when the narrative is completely coherent (Gunkel, *Genesis*, 415-416).

21   Thus Schmitt, *Joseph*, 35, note 135.

22   Thus Westermann, *Genesis*, 1986, 96; but cf. Skinner, *Genesis*, 471.

23   Thus Driver, *Genesis*, 345, but cf. Van Seters' attribution of the verse to J who he claims was attempting to mimic historical text (Van Seters, *Prologue*, 320-321).

24   And is not a scribal error as previously maintained, e.g. Dillmann, *Genesis*, 417.

25   Usually identified in scholarship as J and E, and see Skinner, *Genesis*, 471.

26   Cf. C. J. Ball, *The Book of Genesis in Hebrew*, Leipzig, 1896, 36.

27   Westermann, *Genesis*, 1986, 97 also notes that vss. 50-52 interrupt the flow.

Joseph's prophecy came to pass. Verse 55: "When all the land of Egypt was famished, the people cried to Pharaoh for bread. Pharaoh said to all the Egyptians, 'Go to Joseph; what he says to you, do'" also connects us to the etiological story at the end of Gen. 47 (verses 13-27, which explain the Egyptian tax system).

5.4 Joseph's Brothers Beg (Gen. 42)

42:1 *When Jacob learned that there was grain in Egypt, he said to his sons, "Why do you keep looking at one another? 2 I have heard," he said, "that there is grain in Egypt; go down and buy grain for us there, that we may live and not die." 3 So ten of Joseph's brothers went down to buy grain in Egypt. 4 But Jacob did not send Joseph's brother Benjamin with his brothers, for he feared that harm might come to him.* 5 Thus the sons of Israel were among the other people who came to buy grain, for the famine had reached the land of Canaan. 6 Now Joseph was governor over the land; it was he who sold to all the people of the land. And Joseph's brothers came and bowed themselves before him with their faces to the ground. 7 When Joseph saw his brothers, he recognized them, but he treated them like strangers and spoke harshly to them. "Where do you come from?" he said. They said, "From the land of Canaan, to buy food." 8 *Although Joseph had recognized his brothers, they did not recognize him. 9 Joseph also remembered the dreams that he had dreamed about them.* He said to them, "You are spies; you have come to see the nakedness of the land!" 10 They said to him, "No, my lord; your servants have come to buy food. 11 We are all sons of one man; we are honest men; your servants have never been spies." 12 But he said to them, "No, you have come to see the nakedness of the land!" 13 They said, "We, *your servants,* are *twelve brothers,* the sons of a certain man in the land of Canaan; the youngest, however, is now with our father, and one is no more." 14 But Joseph said to them, "It is just as I have said to you; you are spies! 15 Here is how you shall be tested: as Pharaoh lives, you shall not leave this place unless your youngest brother comes here! 16 *Let one of you go and bring your brother, while the rest of you remain in prison, in order that your words may be tested, whether there is truth in you; or else, as Pharaoh lives, surely you are spies."* 17 And he put them all together in prison for three days. 18 On the third day Joseph said to them, "Do this and you will live, for I fear God: 19 if you are honest men, let one of your brothers stay here where you are imprisoned. The rest of you shall go and carry grain for the famine of your households, 20 and bring your youngest brother to me. Thus your words will be verified, and you shall not die." And they did so. 21 *They said to one another, "Alas, we are paying the penalty for what we did to our brother; we saw his anguish when he pleaded with us, but we would not listen. That is why this anguish has come upon us."* 22 *Then Reuben answered them, "Did I not tell you not to wrong the boy? But you would not listen. So now there comes a reckoning for his blood."* 23 *They did not know that Joseph understood them, since he spoke with them through an interpreter.* 24 *He turned away from them and wept; then he returned and spoke to them. And he picked out Simeon and had him bound before their eyes.* 25 *Joseph then gave orders to fill their bags with grain, to return every man's money to his sack, and to give them provisions for their journey. This was done for them.* 26 They loaded their donkeys with their grain, and departed. 27 *When one of them opened his sack to give his donkey fodder at the lodging place, he saw his money at the top of the sack.* 28 *He said to his brothers, "My money has been put back; here it is in my sack!" At this they lost heart and turned trembling to one another, saying, "What is this that God has done to us?"* 29 *When they came to their father Jacob in the land of Canaan, they told him all that had happened to them, saying,* 30 *"The man, the lord of the land, spoke harshly to us, and charged us with spying on the land.* 31 *But we said to him, 'We are honest men, we are not spies.* 32 *We are twelve brothers, sons of our father; one is no more, and the youngest is now with our father in the land of Canaan.'* 33 *Then the man, the lord of the land, said to us, 'By this I shall know that you are honest men: leave one of your brothers with me, take grain for the famine of your households, and go your way.* 34 *Bring your youngest brother to me, and I shall know that you are not spies but honest men. Then I will release your brother to you, and you may trade in the land.'"* 35 As they were emptying their sacks, there in each one's sack was his bag of money. When they *and their father* saw their bundles of money, they were dismayed.

5.4.1 Source Division

As stated, the elohistic narrative resumes in 41:56, which, together with verse 57 serves as an introduction to Joseph's brothers' journey to Egypt in search of food. Verses 1-4 in Chapter 42 were likely interpolated by J as suggested by the use of the name "Jacob" and the allusion to twelve brothers rather than seven.[28] The verses serve to inform us that even wealthy Jacob had to send emissaries to Egypt in search of food. Verse 4 is another case of proleptic editing (*cf.* Gen. 29:3; 35:1 etc.) letting the reader know that Benjamin stayed home, a fact which will be re-iterated in E's verse 13.

E's narrative, which begins in verses 5-7, relates how the *Children of Israel*[29] arrived in Egypt to find relief from the famine, their first meeting with Joseph, and their abasement before him. Verse 8 is a yahwistic interpolation, which repeats that Joseph recognised his brothers (verse

---

28 For this reason the verses are more commonly attributed to E (See Driver, *Genesis*, 348). Note Smend's assignment of these verses to his "J2" (Smend, *Hexateuch*, 105).

29 An Elohistic term in this context according to Wellhausen *Hexateuch*, 58, Schmitt, *Joseph*, 42.

7) and adds that they did not recognise Joseph.[30] Verse 9a is also yahwistic, since it mentions Joseph's dreams (in plural), while according to
the Elohist, Joseph had only one dream. The Yahwist wants to emphasize that Joseph's dreams were indeed fulfilled.[31] In the elohistic verses
9b-12, Joseph does not forgive his brothers, but accuses them of spying.
They counter his claims with the truth: "No, my lord; your servants
have come to buy food. We are all sons of one man; we are honest men;
your servants have never been spies." This claim is repeated in verse
13, together with the yahwistic insertion of the number of brothers –
twelve. (Compare verse 3: "So *ten of Joseph's brothers* went down to buy
grain in Egypt.") Joseph does not take pity on his brothers and commands them to bring Benjamin as proof of their innocence (verses 14-
15).

In verse 16 Joseph gives a confusing command—to arrest all the
brothers except for the one assigned to bring Benjamin. This command
is not implemented and Joseph releases all the brothers except for
Simeon (verse 19). Verse 16 is in all probability a yahwistic attempt to
explain why Joseph locked all the brothers up for three days, rather
than sending them immediately to bring Benjamin.[32] This interpolation
portrays Joseph as merciful: at first he was willing to release only one
brother, but finally he releases all save one.

Verse 20 ends with the remark "And they did so," namely they
went home.[33] Verse 26 briefly describes the brothers' journey and the
natural conclusion to verse 20 is their arrival in verse 35. Verses 21-22,
the dialogue between the brothers, followed by Joseph's tears in verse
23, interfere with the flow between verses 20, 26 and 35. Although Reuben is the main character in these verses, they are probably yahwistic.
They portray him as ineffectual, since he claims that the brothers did
not listen to him. Portraying Reuben as inept helps to emphasize Judah's effectiveness —a recurring editorial theme. In verse 24 Joseph
keeps his word and detains one of the brothers (verse 19). He chooses
Simeon, a brother who, according to the above analysis, is not known
to the elohistic source. Joseph arrests Simeon, the second most important brother, rather than Reuben, the eldest and most merciful, *cf.* 42:23:
"Then Reuben answered them, 'Did I not tell you not to wrong the
boy? But you would not listen. So now there comes a reckoning for his

---

30   The case for a parallel Yahwistic narrative is weak, but cf. Skinner, *Genesis*, 474.
31   Compare the Deuteronomistic editorial theme concerning prophecies and their
     fulfillment, e.g. I Kgs. 13:2 and II Kgs. 23:20.
32   Gunkel, *Genesis*, 423 *et al.* attribute this verse to E.
33   The contradiction between this verse and those that follow was identified by the
     Medieval commentator *Hizquni*, but see also Skinner, *Genesis*, 476.

blood.'" Verse 25, in which Joseph replaces his brothers' money, is another case of proleptic editing. The unnecessary information spoils the surprise of the brothers' discovery in verse 35: "As they were emptying their sacks, there in each one's sack was his bag of money. When they [and their father] saw their bundles of money, they were dismayed." The mention of "their father" in this verse is probably a bridge to the yahwistic addition of 42:29-34 and 42:36ff., which feature Joseph's father, who is otherwise absent from the tale until 45:28: "Israel said, 'Enough! My son Joseph is still alive. I must go and see him before I die.'" Indeed, even according to Documentary scholars, aside from the small section at the end of Chapter 42 (restricted in our division to vs. 35), Joseph's father plays an active role in this part of the Joseph cycle only according to J.[34]

    I tentatively attribute Verses 27-28 to B (the Bridger, the final redactor delineated in the introduction), both because of the use of "Elohim" by Joseph's brothers (which cannot be attributed to P, since the verses lack any characteristic markers of this source) and the contradiction with verse 35 (=E). In verse 28, the brothers find their money for the first time, and in verse 35 the "amnesiac" brothers find their money once more. The two verses (27-28) are usually attributed to J and not to a later source.[35] This is unlikely, however, since the brothers name their Deity "Elohim," while if the text were yahwistic the Israelite brothers would almost certainly use "Yhwh." An attribution to B is also unsubstantiated since characteristic themes and language are lacking, though it is clear that Verses 27-28 belong to a non-yahwistic source apparent throughout Chapters 42-44 distinguished by the use of the word "אמתחות" for packs (as opposed to "שק" in vs. 35). Discussion of this textual stratum will continue in the subsequent analysis of Chapters 43 and 44.

    Verses 29-34, on the other hand, may be attributed to J, because of the mention of Jacob (rather than Israel) and the allusion to *twelve* brothers. Verses 42:29-34, together with 42:36-43:5 (which use the name Jacob and the concept of "Sheol" [the underworld] in verse 38; *cf.* the use of this term in Gen. 37:35 [JJ]), constitute the report of the brothers' journey to Jacob and the ensuing discussion. Both Reuben and Judah volunteer to take care of Benjamin, but ultimately it is Judah who succeeds in convincing his father, thus once again proving Reuben's ineptitude. The verses explain how Jacob agreed to send Benjamin with his brothers despite the disappearance of Joseph and the arrest of Simeon.

---

34   The latter section is frequently assigned to J, e.g. Driver, *Genesis*, 352-353.

35   E.g Speiser, *Genesis*, 319-320.

This episode also adds an emotional dimension to the cycle by presenting Jacob with a new dilemma.

5.4.2 The Yahwistic Commentary

The majority of redactional themes have already been identified, but
one may add a final note regarding verses 21-24. Verse 24 is the first in
a set of three tearful episodes: 42:24, 43:30 (the reunion with Benjamin)
and 45:2 (the revelation of Joseph's identity). Joseph's last outburst
immediately precedes the revelation of his identity. While the second
and third cries are elohistic, J added Joseph's first outburst to create a
cycle of three.

5.5 Joseph's Brothers Return (Gen. 42-43)

42:36 *And their father Jacob said to them, "I am the one you have bereaved of children: Joseph is no
more, and Simeon is no more, and now you would take Benjamin. All this has happened to me!"
37 Then Reuben said to his father, "You may kill my two sons if I do not bring him back to you.
Put him in my hands, and I will bring him back to you." 38 But he said, "My son shall not go
down with you, for his brother is dead, and he alone is left. If harm should come to him on the
journey that you are to make, you would bring down my gray hairs with sorrow to Sheol." 43:1
Now the famine was severe in the land. 2 And when they had eaten up the grain that they had
brought from Egypt, their father said to them, "Go again, buy us a little more food." 3 But Judah
said to him, "The man solemnly warned us, saying, 'You shall not see my face unless your brother
is with you.' 4 If you will send our brother with us, we will go down and buy you food; 5 but if
you will not send him, we will not go down, for the man said to us, 'You shall not see my face,
unless your brother is with you.'" 6 Israel said, "Why did you treat me so badly as to tell the man
that you had another brother?" 7 They replied, "The man questioned us carefully about ourselves
and our kindred, saying, 'Is your father still alive? Have you another brother?' What we told him
was in answer to these questions. Could we in any way know that he would say, 'Bring your
brother down'?" 8 Then Judah said to his father Israel, "Send the boy with me, and let us be on
our way, so that we may live and not die—you and we and also our little ones. 9 I myself will be
surety for him; you can hold me accountable for him. If I do not bring him back to you and set him
before you, then let me bear the blame forever. 10 If we had not delayed, we would now have returned twice." 11 Then their father Israel said to them, "If it must be so, then do this: take some of
the choice fruits of the land in your bags, and carry them down as a present to the man—a little
balm and a little honey, gum, resin, pistachio nuts, and almonds. 12 Take double the money with
you. Carry back with you the money that was returned in the top of your sacks; perhaps it was an
oversight. 13 Take your brother also, and be on your way again to the man; 14 may El-Shaddai
grant you mercy before the man, so that he may send back your other brother and Benjamin. As for*

me, if I am bereaved of my children, I am bereaved." 15 So the men took a *(the)* present *and they took double the money with them* as well as Benjamin. Then they went on their way down to Egypt, and stood before Joseph. 16 When Joseph saw Benjamin with them, he said to the steward of his house, "Bring the men into the house, and slaughter an animal and make ready, for the men are to dine with me at noon." 17 The man did as Joseph said, and brought the men to Joseph's house. 18 *Now the men were afraid because they were brought to Joseph's house, and they said, "It is because of the money, replaced in our sacks the first time, that we have been brought in, so that he may have an opportunity to fall upon us, to make slaves of us and take our donkeys." 19 So they went up to the steward of Joseph's house and spoke with him at the entrance to the house. 20 They said, "Oh, my lord, we came down the first time to buy food; 21 and when we came to the lodging place we opened our sacks, and there was each one's money in the top of his sack, our money in full weight. So we have brought it back with us. 22 Moreover we have brought down with us additional money to buy food. We do not know who put our money in our sacks." 23 He replied, "Rest assured, do not be afraid; your God and the God of your father must have put treasure in your sacks for you; I received your money." Then he brought Simeon out to them. 24 When the steward had brought the men into Joseph's house, and given them water, and they had washed their feet, and when he had given their donkeys fodder, 25 they made the present ready for Joseph's coming at noon, for they had heard that they would dine there.* 26 When Joseph came home, they brought him the present that they had carried into the house, and bowed to the ground before him. 27 He inquired about their welfare, and said, "Is your father well, the old man of whom you spoke? Is he still alive?" 28 They said, "Your servant our father is well; he is still alive." And they bowed their heads and did obeisance. 29 Then he looked up and saw his brother Benjamin, his mother's son, and said, "Is this your youngest brother, of whom you spoke to me? God be gracious to you, my son!" 30 With that, Joseph hurried out, because he was overcome with affection for his brother, and he was about to weep. So he went into a private room and wept there. 31 Then he washed his face and came out; and controlling himself he said, "Serve the meal." 33 When they were seated before him, the firstborn according to his birthright and the youngest according to his youth, the men looked at one another in amazement. 34 Portions were taken to them from Joseph's table, but Benjamin's portion was five times as much as any of theirs. So they drank and were merry with him.

5.5.1 Source Division

Between the elohistic episodes of Chapter 42 and Chapter 43 there are two interpolations: 42:36-43:5 and 43:6-14. The yahwistic addition has been discussed above and in my opinion verses 6-14 are the Bridger's extension of this interpolation. This attribution is problematic since verses 6-14 (with virtually no exceptions) are attributed to J and even the priestly indicator "El Shadai" is attributed to E.[36]

Although dividing between J and later supplementers is not the primary goal of this book, it is necessary to digress and explain why I disagree with the majority of critical scholars. To begin with vss. 6-14, employ Israel, as Joseph's father's name with which J is uncomfortable, whereas 42:36 (the beginning of the dialogue) employs Jacob. Moreover, if the whole of the dialogue is attributed to J, Jacob/Israel's question or complaint in 43:6-7, is unclear. Jacob was told the entire story in 42:30-34 and he well understands why the brothers provided Joseph with information, his repeated question is extraneous. Based on these considerations, one should consider the possibility of more than one source in 42:36-43:14.[37]

According to all non-Northern authors (not only J), Judah is the preferred son: in Gen. 34 the priestly source has Simeon and Levi "transgress",[38] while in the subsequent chapter the same source recounts Reuben's transgression with Bilhah (Gen. 35:22 "While Israel lived in that land, Reuben went and lay with Bilhah his father's concubine; and Israel heard of it"). In this way Judah becomes the oldest unshamed son and is thus first in line to lead Israel. B (the late Bridger) or a late non-yahwistic source devotes an entire chapter to Judah in Gen. 38, highlighting his centrality.

The author of 43:6-14 is interested in emphasizing that it was specifically Judah, rather than Reuben, who convinced his father, Israel, to agree to send Benjamin. A division between 42:36-43:5 and 43:6-14 does not disrupt the integrity of the yahwistic interpolation (42:36-43:5). According to the (now) shorter yahwistic narrative, Jacob, who did not trust Reuben's melodramatic oath at the end of the chapter, is convinced by Judah's arguments and, most of all, by hunger, and does not argue with him. Similar literary complexity, namely J plus an expansion by a post-yahwistic source (again, probably B) is found in Judah's speech of Chapter 44 (44:32-34). Another possible connection to B material is this section's allusions to Chapter 38 which, following Redford, was assigned to B.[39] The affinity between Chapter 38 and this section is clear. Note the appearance of the following roots and themes: ערב [su-

---

36 Driver, *Genesis*, 354.

37 Instead of rearranging the text, and cf. Skinner, *Genesis*, 479-480.

38 If one accepts that the addition of Simon and Levi to Gen. 34 is Priestly, and cf. A. De Pury, Genèse XXXIV et l'histoire, *RB* 76 (1969): 5-49.

39 See also my own analyis in www.biblecriticism.com/com.genesis_38.

rety]; ש.ל.ח [to send] an innocent (Benjamin and the goat); ש.א.ל [to ask] about the origin of a person; ש.ו.ב [to return] to Judah/Jacob; י.ר.ד [to go down], to leave brothers or family, the theme of duality (two sons die, two sons are born; returning twice; begging Jacob twice); still having one remaining brother (Benjamin, Shela); losing children, etc. Note also the use of "אמתחות" for packs as in the redactional expansion of Gen. 42:27. Thus, in spite of the consensus to the contrary, I tend to attribute 43:6-14 to B.

In the analysis of previous cycles my divisions relied to a greater or lesser extent upon earlier scholarship, but in this cycle there is decreasing dependence on the divisions of predecessors. As early as Chapter 37, I emphasized that Documentary scholars wished to find two parallel versions of the Joseph cycle and thus divided the text mechanically. The obvious backlash was the complete rejection of the literary sources previously found by the Documentary scholars. Von Rad led the way and today many scholars accept the basic unity of the Joseph Cycle.[40] At this point in my analysis, my opinions most resemble Redford[41] and Dietrich,[42] who assume a basic source and one or more supplementers. In my opinion, according to E, Joseph's brethren meet with their lost brother three times before he reveals himself—the same number of meetings as in the canonical Joseph cycle, i.e. the first meeting (which begins with 43:15) and the majority of the goblet episode are elohistic in origin.

The next elohistic episode begins with verse 15 and the return of Israel's sons to Egypt. (Note the proleptic insertion of the command to come bearing gifts 43:14, which anticipates the E narrative in 43:15ff.). In verse 15, B (or the "אמתחות" source of 42:27) adds the words "and they took double the money with them." This interpolation alludes to verses 18-24, which are probably secondary. First of all, there is the resumptive repetition in 43:24: "When the steward had brought the men into Joseph's house..." which repeats verse 17. Moreover, the verses deal with money that was returned to the brothers' "אמתחות" (sacks) (cf. Gen. 42:27-28 and 43:6-14). According to the Elohist, the brothers do not attempt to return the money. The elohistic narrative resumes after the interruption in verse 24 or 25 (depending on which of the doublets, verse 17 or verse 24, is original) and proceeds to describe

40 E.g. G. W. Coats, Redactional Unity in Gen. 37-50, *JBL* 93 (1974): 15-21; G. A. Rendsburg, Redactional Structuring in the Joseph Stories, Gen. 37-50, in *Mappings of the Biblical Terrain* (V. L. Tollers and J. Maier eds.), Lewisburg, Philadelphia: 215-232.

41 In his 1970 commentary on the Joseph Cycle.

42 W. Dietrich, *Die Josepherzählung als Novelle und Geschichtschreibung* (BTS 14), Neukirchen-Vluyn, 1989.

the brothers' gift to Joseph. In verses 27-28 Joseph inquires whether his father is still alive and the brothers answer him in the affirmative. The repetition of his query in 45:3 ("Joseph said to his brothers, 'I am Joseph. Is my father still alive?'") probably has no critical significance and may be an indication of Joseph's excitement or concern.

In verses 29-31, Joseph meets Benjamin, weeps, and then the feast begins. Verse 32 is a yahwistic gloss, which attempts to explain how Joseph, who is second only to the king, eats with Hebrew wanderers. This verse is similar in content to the yahwistic distinction between Egyptians and Israelites in 46:34: "you shall say, 'Your servants have been keepers of livestock from our youth even until now, both we and our ancestors,' in order that you may settle in the land of Goshen, because all shepherds are abhorrent to the Egyptians," and is linked to the yahwistic Plague narrative: "But on that day I will set apart the land of Goshen, where my people live, so that no swarms of flies shall be there, that you may know that I the LORD am in this land" (Ex. 8:22). The elohistic episode concludes with lordly Joseph giving his brothers gifts (verses 33-34). The gift ratio (Benjamin vis-à-vis the rest of the brothers) is meaningful and is cited above as proof that according to E there were only seven brothers. As Joseph's full brother, Benjamin receives gifts equivalent to the sum of those given to the five half-brothers.

5.5.2 The Yahwistic Commentary

Since J did not significantly add to the composition of the episode, only a brief comment on the etiological gloss in verse 32 is in order. The verse is part of a yahwistic attempt to add some Egyptian flavour to the Joseph cycle (as in 46:34 ["Because all shepherds are abhorrent to the Egyptians]). The bureaucratic etiology concerning the Egyptian tax system (47:13-27), the yahwistic "סריס" [officer] (37:36; 40:2), which, while not Egyptian, is certainly language of a royal court, and the priestly name "Potiphera" (41:45), all serve to transport the reader to the Egyptian milieu.

5.6 The Silver Goblet (Gen. 44-45)

1 *Then he commanded the steward of his house, "Fill the men's sacks with food, as much as they can carry, and put each man's money in the top of his sack. 2 Put my cup, the silver cup, in the top of the sack of the youngest, with his money for the grain." And he did as Joseph told him.* 3 As soon as the morning was light, the men were sent away with their don-

keys. 4 When they had gone only a short distance from the city, Joseph said to his steward, "Go, follow after the men; and when you overtake them, say to them, 'Why have you returned evil for good? 5 Is it not from this that my lord drinks? Does he not indeed use it for divination? You have done wrong in doing this.'" 6 When he overtook them, he repeated these words to them. 7 They said to him, "Why does my lord speak such words as these? Far be it from your servants that they should do such a thing! 8 *Look, the money that we found at the top of our sacks, we brought back to you from the land of Canaan; why then would we steal silver or gold from your lord's house?* 9 Should it be found with any one of your servants, let him die; moreover the rest of us will become my lord's slaves." 10 He said, "Even so; in accordance with your words, let it be: he with whom it is found shall become my slave, but the rest of you shall go free." 11 *Then each one quickly lowered his sack to the ground, and each opened his sack.* 12 He searched, beginning with the eldest and ending with the youngest; and the cup was found *in Benjamin's sack.* 13 At this they tore their clothes. Then each one loaded his donkey, and they returned to the city. 14 *Judah and his brothers came to Joseph's house while he was still there; and they fell to the ground before him.* 15 Joseph said to them, "What deed is this that you have done? Do you not know that one such as I can practice divination?" 16 And (*Judah*) they said, "What can we say to my lord? What can we speak? How can we clear ourselves? God has found out the guilt of your servants; here we are then, my lord's slaves, both we and also the one in whose possession the cup has been found." 17 *But he said, "Far be it from me that I should do so! Only the one in whose possession the cup was found shall be my slave; but as for you, go up in peace to your father." 18 Then Judah stepped up to him and said, "O my lord, let your servant please speak a word in my lord's ears, and do not be angry with your servant; for you are like Pharaoh himself. 19 My lord asked his servants, saying, 'Have you a father or a brother?' 20 And we said to my lord, 'We have a father, an old man, and a young brother, the child of his old age. His brother is dead; he alone is left of his mother's children, and his father loves him.' 21 Then you said to your servants, 'Bring him down to me, so that I may set my eyes on him.' 22 We said to my lord, 'The boy cannot leave his father, for if he should leave his father, his father would die.' 23 Then you said to your servants, 'Unless your youngest brother comes down with you, you shall see my face no more.' 24 When we went back to your servant my father we told him the words of my lord. 25 And when our father said, 'Go again, buy us a little food,' 26 we said, 'We cannot go down. Only if our youngest brother goes with us, will we go down; for we cannot see the man's face unless our youngest brother is with us.' 27 Then your servant my father said to us, 'You know that my wife bore me two sons; 28 one left me, and I said, Surely he has been torn to pieces; and I have never seen him since. 29 If you take this one also from me, and harm comes to him, you will bring down my gray hairs in sorrow to Sheol.' 30 Now therefore, when I come to your servant my father and the boy is not with us, then, as his life is bound up in the boy's life, 31 when he sees that the boy is not with us, he will die; and your servants will bring down the gray hairs of your servant our father with sorrow to Sheol. 32 For your servant became surety for the boy to my father, saying, 'If I do not bring him back to you, then I will bear the blame in the sight of my father all my life.' 33 Now therefore, please let your servant remain as a slave to my lord in place of the boy; and let the boy go back with his brothers. 34 For how can I go back to my father if the boy is not with me? I fear to see the suffering that would come upon my father."* 45:1 Then Joseph could no longer control himself before all those who stood by him, and he cried out, "Send everyone away from me." So no one stayed with him when Joseph made himself known to his brothers. 2 And he wept so loudly that the Egyptians heard it, and the household of Pharaoh heard it. 3 Joseph said to his brothers, "I am Joseph. Is my father still alive?" But his brothers could not answer him, so dismayed were they at his presence.4 Then Joseph said to his brothers, "Come closer to me." And they came closer. *He said, "I am your brother, Joseph, whom you sold into Egypt. 5 And now do not be distressed, or angry with yourselves, because you sold me here; for God sent me before you to preserve life. 6 For the famine has been in the land these two years; and there are five more years in which there will be neither plowing nor harvest. 7 God sent me before you to preserve for you a remnant on earth, and to keep alive for you many survivors. 8 So it was not you who sent me here, but God; he has made me a father to Pharaoh, and lord of all his house and ruler over all the land of Egypt. 9 Hurry and go up to my father and say to him, 'Thus says your son Joseph, God has made me lord of all Egypt; come down to me, do not delay. 10 You shall settle in the land of Goshen, and you shall be near me, you and your children and your children's children, as well as your flocks, your herds, and all that you have. 11 I will provide for you there— since there are five more years of famine to come—so that you and your household, and all that you have, will not come to poverty.' 12 And now your eyes and the eyes of my brother Benjamin see that it is my own mouth that speaks to you. 13 You must tell my father how greatly I am honored in Egypt, and all that you have seen. Hurry and bring my father down here."* 14 Then he fell upon his brother Benjamin's neck and wept, while Benjamin wept upon his neck. 15 And he kissed all his brothers and wept upon them; and after that his brothers talked with him.

5.6.1 Source Division

Based on the term "אמתחה," the beginning of Chapter 44 (verses 1-2) is attributed to the Bridger and serves as this author's introduction.[43] These verses state that Joseph purposely placed his goblet in Benjamin's אמתחה (pack), an action which creates an entirely different narrative tension. Were these verses omitted, the reader would wonder whether the goblet was indeed stolen or whether this is a plot. If the

---

43   Many scholars recognize some secondary elements in these verses (*cf.* Westermann, *Genesis*, 1986, 131).

goblet was stolen, which of the brothers stole it? The elohistic story begins in verse 3, as the brothers leave the city and Joseph's servant gives chase (verses 4-7). Verse 8 is another B interpolation. The claim the brothers make: "Look, the money that we found at the top of our sacks (אמתחות), we brought back to you from the land of Canaan; why then would we steal silver or gold from your lord's house," alludes to the interpolation of 43:18-23. The term "אמתחה" is further indication that the verse is secondary. Verses 9-10 describe the elohistic negotiations regarding the severity of the potential punishment. Verse 11 is probably another B interpolation, since the term אמתחה appears again. The brothers do not need to repeat their assertion of innocence: "They said to him, 'Why does my lord speak such words as these? Far be it from your servants that they should do such a thing!'" (Verse 7). The words "in Benjamin's sack (אמתחת)" at the end of verse 12 are once more a B insertion. If Joseph's servant began by searching the eldest and *ended* by searching the youngest, it is obvious that the goblet was in Benjamin's sack. Although the case is weak here, one should probably attribute the term (אמתחה) to B in all places for the sake of consistency.

E continues in verse 13 but is cut off once again, this time by the Yahwist. Verse 14: "Judah and his brothers came to Joseph's house while he was still there; and they fell to the ground before him," is somewhat difficult. It is obvious that Joseph would be waiting for his brothers. In my opinion the function of this verse and the insertion of Judah as a subject in verse 16 are intended to prepare the readers for Judah's dominant role in verses 17-34.[44] Joseph's claim in verse 44:17 is a repetition of his servant's statements in 44:10 and introduces Judah's lengthy plea. Verses 17-31 are a long yahwistic text in which Judah eloquently begs Joseph to release Benjamin.[45] Verses 32-34, alluding to Judah's guarantee in 43:6-14, are very likely the Bridger's interpolation and indeed the yahwistic speech ends quite naturally in verse 31: "When he sees that the boy is not with us, he will die; and your servants will bring down the gray hairs of your servant our father with sorrow to Sheol." (Similar endings to yahwistic passages appear in 37:35, 42:38.) E resumes in 45:1: "Then Joseph could no longer control himself before all those who stood by him, and he cried out, 'Send everyone away from me.' So no one stayed with him when Joseph made himself known to his brothers." This is a natural response to the emo-

---

44 See Wellhausen, *Hexateuch*, 58, and cf. Redford (*Joseph*, 179) and Dietrich (*Josepherzählung*, 53-55) who posit similar "Judaic" insertions.
45 See Dietrich, *Josepherzählung*, 24, 68.

tional plea in 44:16. Joseph can no longer restrain himself and thus in 45:1 bursts into tears.

The elohistic text in Chapter 45 continues until verse 4a, when it is once again interrupted by a lengthy priestly interpolation (45:4b-13). Verse 4a is followed by verse 14 in which Joseph cries on Benjamin's shoulders and kisses his brothers. It is very unlikely that the emotional reunion is interrupted by a lengthy speech by Joseph. Moreover, verses 4b-13 contradict the Pharaonic command of verses 17-20 and place the request to bring Israel down to Egypt in Joseph's mouth. Likewise, the interpolation mentions Goshen (verse 10) as a likely dwelling place. According to the Elohist, however, Joseph settles his brethren in the land of Ramses.[46] The interpolation is attributed to P for a number of reasons. The Deity is named "Elohim" in verses 5, 7, 8 and 9. Moreover, verse 10: "You shall settle in the land of Goshen, and you shall be near me, you and your children and your children's children, as well as your flocks, your herds, and all that you have" is reminiscent of the priestly 46:7: "His sons, and his sons' sons with him, his daughters, and his sons' daughters; all his offspring he brought with him into Egypt." The preoccupation with chronology (both verse 6 and verse 11 specify that two out of the seven years of famine have passed) is a common feature of P texts. Many of the analyses of this section (verses 4-15) divide the text between J and E, dwelling on minutiae of little critical significance.[47] Though P is not primarily a narrative source, one should not "shortchange" him when there is evidence to the contrary.

5.6.2 The Yahwistic Commentary

I have claimed that in 44:16 the Yahwist added "Judah" to the verse instead of an unspecified plural subject which I posited was the original version. Is such an editorial procedure at all likely? In my opinion, the addition of specificity to the narrative is one of the Yahwist's primary objectives, especially since Judah plays such an important role in subsequent chapters.[48] This type of editing is very common and one of the best examples of it is the two editions of the book of Jeremiah and the differences between them. The Masoretic book of Jeremiah is significantly longer than the Septuagint's version of it and an important dif-

---

46   A locale which in our opinion is incorrectly assigned to the P rendition, e.g. Speiser, *Genesis*, 348.

47   Eg. Gunkel, *Genesis*, 435.

48   Dietrich, *Josepherzählung*, 24.

ference between them is specificity.[49] The later Masoretic text of Jeremiah transcribed fuller versions of many names, for instance, Jeremiah the son of Hilkiah instead of simply Jeremiah.

One may, of course, claim that the entire goblet episode, including verse 16, is yahwistic. However, attributing this episode to J would fragment the elohistic text. There would be no crisis and no reason for Joseph to reveal himself — a possibility which is difficult to accept since E has exhibited literary continuity up to this point. The insertion of Judah's name in verse 16 introduces Judah's lengthy plea. This interpolation is of utmost importance for the Yahwist, since it places Judah at the head of Jacob's sons and is a precursor to Judah's "blessing" (49:8): "Judah, your brothers shall praise you; your hand shall be on the neck of your enemies; your father's sons shall bow down before you."[50]

Judah's speech includes details not mentioned in previous narratives. For example, Joseph's brothers never informed him that if he compelled Benjamin to leave Jacob, it would cause his father grief (verse 22). Are we to assume a yahwisitic tradition in which this was part of the story? The answer is emphatically negative. Judah's deviations are solely a rhetorical ploy to convince Joseph and thus do not have to conform.[51] Although Judah's speech "deviates" somewhat, there are still numerous allusions to previous texts.[52] Jacob's statement regarding Joseph's fate, for instance: "One left me, and I said, Surely he has been torn to pieces; and I have never seen him since," (verse 28) is a repetition of the yahwistic interpolation in 37:33 and also of the brothers' excuse for Joseph's disappearance. Judah's masterly oration is of course connected with the dialogue between Jacob and his sons (Chapter 43) and with the role he plays in convincing his father to allow Benjamin's descent.

5.7 Pharaoh's Benevolence (Gen. 45)

16 When the report was heard in Pharaoh's house, "Joseph's brothers have come," Pharaoh and his servants were pleased. 17 Pharaoh said to Joseph, "Say to your brothers, 'Do this: load your animals and go back

---

49 Thus, E. Tov, *Textual Criticism of the Hebrew Bible* (Hebrew), Jerusalem, 1990, 243-249.

50 Note the myriad of studies dealing with the connections between Judah and David, e.g. G. A, Rendsburg, David and His Circle, *VT* 36 (1986): 438 –446; C. Y. S. Ho, The Stories of the Family Troubles of Judah and David: A Study of Their Literary Links, *VT* 49 (1999): 514-531.

51 Cf. Westermann, *Genesis*, 1986, 135 *et al.*

52 Dietrich, *Josepherzählung*, 24.

to the land of Canaan. 18 Take your father and your households and come to me, so that I may give you the best of the land of Egypt, and you may enjoy the fat of the land.' 19 You are further charged to say, 'Do this: take wagons from the land of Egypt for your little ones and for your wives, and bring your father, and come. 20 Give no thought to your possessions, for the best of all the land of Egypt is yours.'" 21 The sons of Israel did so. Joseph gave them wagons according to the instruction of Pharaoh, and he gave them provisions for the journey. 22 To each one of them he gave a set of garments; but to Benjamin he gave three hundred pieces of silver and five sets of garments. 23 To his father he sent the following: ten donkeys loaded with the good things of Egypt, and ten female donkeys loaded with grain, bread, and provision for his father on the journey. 24 Then he sent his brothers on their way, and as they were leaving he said to them, "Do not quarrel along the way."25 So they went up out of Egypt and came to their father *Jacob* in the land of Canaan. 26 And they told him, "Joseph is still alive! He is even ruler over all the land of Egypt." He was stunned; he could not believe them. 27 *But when they told him all the words of Joseph that he had said to them,* and when he saw the wagons that Joseph had sent to carry him, *the spirit of their father Jacob revived.* 28 Israel said, "Enough! My son Joseph is still alive. I must go and see him before I die."

5.7.1 Source Division

The elohistic text continues in 45:16-27a with the Pharaohnic command to transport Israel to Egypt, the return journey to Canaan and the report to Israel/Jacob.[53] I maintain that the yahwistic name "Jacob" was added to the original E-text in verse 25 "So they went up out of Egypt and came to their father *Jacob* in the land of Canaan." Evidence in support of this assumption is the Septuagint of verse 26, "Jacob was stunned; he could not believe them," as opposed to the unspecific Masoretic version "He was stunned; he could not believe them." Since there is indication of this type of addition in verse 26, Jacob's name may very well have been added in the preceding verse as well. If one assumes that the name Jacob is an editorial gloss, the consistency of elohistic terminology is preserved. The first part of verse 27: "But when they told him all the words of Joseph that he had said to them" is a priestly interpolation, which alludes to Joseph's earlier speech (verses 5-13, previously attributed to P). According to E, Joseph had not com-

---

53   Redford, *Joseph*, 185.

manded his brothers to tell their father anything: it was Pharaoh who
issued the command. Verse 27b: "the spirit of their father Jacob revived" is a yahwistic supplement, using the name Jacob, and compare
J's 44:22: "We said to my lord, 'The boy cannot leave his father, for if he
should leave his father, his father would die.'"[54] The elohistic episode
concludes with verse 27a-28. Israel sees the carriages and decides to see
his son before his imminent death.[55]

5.7.2 The Yahwistic Commentary

J additions to this episode consist of four or five words, hence the brevi-
ty of this section. (For the P's interpolation see immediately above). In a
bid to preserve consistency, I suggested that J or a later glossator added
"Jacob" to 45:25. If this is so, it was for one of two reasons: either the
glossator wanted to amend the text in order to make it clearer or he
wished to remind us of "Jacob's" true name, which has not appeared
since 42:36.

5.8 The Revelation at Beer-sheba (Gen. 46)

1 When Israel set out on his journey with all that he had and came to
Beer-sheba, he offered sacrifices to the God of his father *Isaac*. 2 God
spoke to Israel in visions of the night, and said, ("Jacob, Jacob." And he
said, "Here I am." 3 Then he said,)* I am God, the God of your father;
do not be afraid to go down to Egypt, for I will make of you a great
nation there. 4 I myself will go down with you to Egypt, and I will also
bring you up again; and Joseph's own hand shall close your eyes."

---

54 The tripartite division of this verse is suggested by Gunkel, *Genesis*, 438-439.
55 Verse 28 is usually attributed to J, and see Redford, *Genesis*, 185.

*I note here two possible readings of vs. 2, one including the name Jacob, the other without it, and see below in the Source Division for further comment.

5.8.1 Source Division

With good reason, the majority of scholars attribute the beginning of Chapter 46 to the Elohist.[56] The elohistic signature is very prominent: the terms "Israel"[57] and "Elohim," the revelation in the dream.[58] The sole yahwistic interpolation, in my opinion, is Isaac's name in the first verse (after "he offered sacrifices to the God of his father"). As has been repeatedly mentioned throughout this work, according to E, Isaac was not Jacob's father. Indeed, the appearance of Isaac's name at this juncture is highly problematic. According to the Elohist, Abraham and not Isaac founded Beersheba and it is more natural that Israel would sacrifice offerings to the Deity of the founder. Gunkel[59] assumes that there was an alternative elohistic tradition which connected between Beersheba and Isaac, but this claim is unsubstantiated. (However, note the yahwistic tradition connecting Isaac to this locale in Gen. 26:32-33.) As Römer hypothesizes, such insertion of names after "the God of your/his/their father" is common.[60]

Why does E use the name Jacob twice in verse 2? I maintain that this, the sole revelation of the Joseph cycle, which constitutes the mid-section of the E narrative and of the entire elohistic work, was central and very important to E. For this reason an exception was made and consistency sacrificed. In this verse Elohim reminds Israel/Jacob of the *past*: he identifies himself as "the God of your father" and identifies the object of the revelation as "Jacob" (Israel's previous name), thus alluding to the historical ties between Himself and the founding father. He speaks of the *present*: Israel's sons descending to Egypt; and hints to the *future*: Israel's death and the return of Israel (as a nation). Of course, it

---

56 Wellhausen, *Hexateuch*, 58-59.

57 Note the scrambling of Documentary scholars to explain this name's appearance in an elohistic text, for example, Gunkel, *Genesis*, 439-440.

58 Westermann's attempts to attribute this text to a late author, basing himself on the term "מראות" (dream), which is also used by Ezekiel (Westermann, *Genesis*, 153-155); and the dual call followed by "Here I am," which appears in two other elohistic revelations (to Abraham [Gen. 22:11] and Moses [Ex. 3:4]).

59 Gunkel, *Genesis*, 440.

60 T. Römer, *Israels Väter: Untersuchungen zur Väterthematik im Deuteronomium und in der deuteronomistischen Tradition* (OBO 99), Freiburg, 1990.

is entirely possible that the name "Jacob" in verse 2 is editorial and that the original version of the revelation was: "God spoke to Israel in visions of the night, and said, 'I am God, the God of your father.'"[61]

5.9 Joseph and Israel's First Encounter (Gen. 46-47)

46:5 Then Jacob set out from Beer-sheba; and the sons of Israel carried their father Jacob, their little ones, and their wives, in the wagons that Pharaoh had sent to carry him. 6 They also took their livestock and the goods that they had acquired in the land of Canaan, and they came into Egypt, Jacob and all his offspring with him, 7 his sons, and his sons' sons with him, his daughters, and his sons' daughters; all his offspring he brought with him into Egypt.

The Priestly Insertion of Jacob's Progeny with B additions 46:8-27

28 *Israel sent Judah ahead to Joseph to lead the way before him into Goshen. When they came to the land of Goshen,* 29 Joseph made ready his chariot and went up to meet his father Israel *in Goshen.* He presented himself to him, fell on his neck, and wept on his neck a good while. 30 Israel said to Joseph, "I can die now, having seen for myself that you are still alive." 31 *Joseph said to his brothers and to his father's household, "I will go up and tell Pharaoh, and will say to him, 'My brothers and my father's household, who were in the land of Canaan, have come to me. 32 The men are shepherds, for they have been keepers of livestock; and they have brought their flocks, and their herds, and all that they have.' 33 When Pharaoh calls you, and says, 'What is your occupation?' 34 you shall say, 'Your servants have been keepers of livestock from our youth even until now, both we and our ancestors'—in order that you may settle in the land of Goshen, because all shepherds are abhorrent to the Egyptians." 47:1 So Joseph went and told Pharaoh, "My father and my brothers, with their flocks and herds and all that they possess, have come from the land of Canaan; they are now in the land of Goshen." 2 From among his brothers he took five men and presented them to Pharaoh. 3 Pharaoh said to his brothers, "What is your occupation?" And they said to Pharaoh, "Your servants are shepherds, as our ancestors were." 4 They said to Pharaoh, "We have come to reside as aliens in the land; for there is no pasture for your servants' flocks because the famine is severe in the land of Canaan. Now, we ask you, let your servants settle in the land of Goshen."* 5 Then Pharaoh said to Joseph, "Your father and your brothers have come to you. 6 The land of Egypt is before you; settle your father and your brothers in the best part of the land; *let them live in the land of Goshen;* and if you know that there are capable men among them, put them in charge of my livestock." 7 *Then Joseph brought in his father Jacob, and presented him before Pharaoh, and Jacob blessed Pharaoh. 8 Pharaoh said to Jacob, "How many are the years of your life?" 9 Jacob said to Pharaoh, "The years of my earthly sojourn are one hundred*

---

61   According to Wellhausen, *Hexateuch*, 1899, 59, however, the text of vs. 2 is corrupt.

thirty; few and hard have been the years of my life. They do not compare with the years of the life of my ancestors during their long sojourn." 10 *Then Jacob blessed Pharaoh, and went out from the presence of Pharaoh.* 11 Joseph settled his father and his brothers, *and granted them a holding in the land of Egypt, in the best part of the land,* in the land of Rameses, as Pharaoh had instructed. 12 And Joseph provided his father, his brothers, and all his father's household with food, according to the number of their dependents.

Tax etiology: 47:13-26

5.9.1 Source Division

Prior to the first encounter between Israel and Joseph (46:29), there is a lengthy genealogical addition, which is difficult to attribute solely to P, due to the allusion to late non-priestly passages such as Gen. 38 (the deaths of Er and Onan); Ruth 4:12, 18 (Peretz's primacy), Deut. 10:22 (seventy as the number of Jacob's descendants).[62] These allusions are evidence of the Bridger's interpolation, an assertion bolstered by the appearance of the typical qal passive יֻלַּד in verses 23 and 27.[63]

The first elohistic encounter between Joseph and Israel is preceded by J's addition of verse 28: "He sent Judah ahead to Joseph to lead the way before him into Goshen...," which has Judah in a leadership role and emphasizes Goshen (twice) as the meeting place. The Yahwist adds "Goshen" a third time in verse 29. This emphasis upon Goshen is intended to trump the elohistic tradition of the land of Ramses as the dwelling place of the Israelites (47:11). Verse 29 is followed by Israel's reaction to the encounter (verse 30). Verses 46:31-47:4 were added by J and explain how Israel's sons settled in Goshen as shepherds. The supplementary nature of these verses is obvious. Chapter 46:34 comments upon the Egyptian revulsion to shepherds, which complements their general revulsion towards the Hebrews in 43:32. Distinguishing between Israel and Egypt is a common yahwistic theme throughout the plague narrative, e.g. Ex. 9:26; 10:23. In 47:2 Joseph chooses five representatives from among his brothers but, as I have repeatedly mentioned Joseph, had only six brothers according to E. Choosing five would have meant choosing all but one. Indeed in 47:5 (E) Pharaoh is not cognizant of the Israelite representatives from previous verses.

---

62   The calculations throughout the Genesis narrative (46:8-27) are probably a secondary effort to harmonize between the symbolic seventy and the actual list of names.

63   See a fuller analysis in www.biblecriticism.com/com_genesis_46.doc.

The elohistic account continues with Pharaoh's command to settle Joseph's brothers in the best part of the land (verses 5-6).[64] These verses are generally attributed to the priestly source, or to the Yahwist. Pharaoh's intervention, however, is entirely consistent with the previous elohistic episode and the command to bring Joseph's family to Egypt "so that they may eat the fat of the land" (45:18). The secondary gloss "let them live in the land of Goshen" (47:6) is yahwistic, since the beginning of the verse already states "settle your father and your brothers in the best part of the land" and the interpolation disrupts the syntax of the verse. (The land of Goshen is Israel's dwelling place according to J, and see Ex. 9:26.) Verses 7-11 are commonly attributed to P based on language criteria.[65] In my opinion, two sources are involved in this section: J (verses 7 and 10) and P (verses 8-9). Two factors point to this: first, the resumptive repetition in verse 10 ("Then Jacob blessed Pharaoh") and secondly, the dialogue between Jacob and Pharaoh (verses 8-9) instead of the promised blessing (verse 7). Verse 7 is the yahwistic signature for the previous unit —an expression of gratitude for Pharaoh's generous treatment of the Israelites. P adapted the signature in order to insert chronistic information (Jacob's age). The E text ends with the fulfillment of Pharaoh's command. Joseph settles his family in Egypt and sustains them throughout the famine (47:11-12). The clause "and granted them a holding in the land of Egypt," which stands between the verb (Joseph *settled* his father…) and its required object (in the best part of the land), is probably a priestly interpolation. (The term "אחזה" [holding] is priestly.) Finally the Yahwist adds a lengthy etiology on the origins of the Egyptian tax system (verses 13-26).[66]

5.9.2 The Yahwistic Commentary

In his main addition to this episode J emphasizes that the Israelites were for the most part shepherds, while, the Egyptians were mainly farmers, as the etiological account in Chapter 47 demonstrates. The conflict between shepherds and farmers is a sociological phenomenon

---

64 Dietrich, *Joseph*, 68, attributes vss. 1-6 to J (or the later Judean source), Driver, *Genesis*, 371, attributes vss. 5-6 to P.
65 Wellhausen, *Hexateuch*, 51, based on Priestly terminology such as אחזה in Gen. 23:4, 9, 20 *et passem*, and מגורים, Gen. 17:8. 28:4. 36:7, *et passem*.
66 The tax etiology is generally attributed to a relatively later source and not to J, compare Wellahausen, *Hexateuch*, 59. Gunkel, *Genesis*, 442-443, however, sees this as a parallel to the end of Gen. 41 (E), though in our opinion it is better viewed as a Yahwistic elaboration of the latter text.

and from the very beginning J lets his preference for shepherds be known (e.g. the preference of Abel over Cain). This difference between Israelite and Egyptian culture is assumed throughout the plague narrative. For example, when Yhwh devastates Egypt with locusts, Yhwh does not protect the Israelites as was promised in Ex. 8:19. There is indeed no need for such protection. While the locusts may have devastated the crops, the Israelite sheep herders had none and were thus unaffected. This distinction between Israelite and Egyptian culture is not elohistic. According to E, shepherding is an honourable Egyptian profession, as is evident from Pharaoh's commands in 47:6: "and if you know that there are capable men among them, put them in charge of my livestock."

Another matter worthy of note is the number of representatives chosen from among the brothers (47:2). Clearly the Yahwist is once again trying to blur the original elohistic number (the Hebrew "מקצה" [literally "from the edges, extremes" but translated by NRSV as "from among"] implies a large number), but why were five brothers chosen and not six, seven or more? By choosing five, J obfuscates the elohistic use of this number in 43:34 and 45:22 and implies that the choice of five in those cases was random (as opposed to the deliberate elohistic equation: Benjamin [his full brother] = the five [half] brothers).

5.10 The Second Meeting (Gen. 47)

47:27 Thus Israel settled in the land of Egypt, in the region of Goshen; and they gained possessions in it, and were fruitful and multiplied exceedingly. 28 Jacob lived in the land of Egypt seventeen years; so the days of Jacob, the years of his life, were one hundred forty-seven years. 29 When the time of Israel's death drew near, he called his son Joseph and said to him, "If I have found favor with you, put your hand under my thigh and promise to deal loyally and truly with me. Do not bury me in Egypt. 30 When I lie down with my ancestors, carry me out of Egypt and bury me in their burial place." He answered, "I will do as you have said." 31 And he said, "Swear to me"; and he swore to him. Then Israel bowed himself on the head of his bed.

5.10.1 Source Division

Following the bureaucratic etiology (47:13-26), the priestly source adds two verses of chronistic information. The first is a general description of Israel's prosperity, the second focuses upon "Jacob's fortune." The reason for the different terminology is clear. Verse 27 speaks of Israel's future as a nation, while verse 28 speaks of Jacob's past life. Jacob's life is an *inclusio* which revolves around Joseph: Joseph disappears as a seventeen-year-old in Gen. 37 and Jacob dies seventeen years after his reunion with Joseph. This chronology contrasts with the elohistic account which presents Jacob/Israel as dying very soon after his arrival in Egypt, 45:28: "Israel said, 'Enough! My son Joseph is still alive. I must go and see him before I die.'" (See also Gen. 48.) The meeting between Israel and his son is brief (verses 29-31) and without interpolations. Joseph's vow to bury Israel is clearly elohistic, since "Israel" is mentioned[67] and the verses are linked both to the elohistic revelation of Chapter 46 and to the fulfillment of Jacob's/Israel's request to be buried in Canaan in Chapter 50.

5.11 Israel's Blessing (Gen. 48)

1 After this Joseph was told, "Your father is ill." So he took with him his two sons, Manasseh and Ephraim. 2 *When Jacob was told, "Your son Joseph has come to you,"* Israel summoned his strength and sat up in bed. 3 *And Jacob said to Joseph, "God Almighty appeared to me at Luz in the land of Canaan, and he blessed me, 4 and said to me, 'I am going to make you fruitful and increase your numbers; I will make of you a company of peoples, and will give this land to your offspring after you for a perpetual holding.' 5 Therefore your two sons, who were born to you in the land of Egypt before I came to you in Egypt, are now mine; Ephraim and Manasseh shall be mine, just as Reuben and Simeon are. 6 As for the offspring born to you after them, they shall be yours. They shall be recorded under the names of their brothers with regard to their inheritance. 7 For when I came from Paddan, Rachel, alas, died in the land of Canaan on the way, while there was still some distance to go to Ephrath; and I buried her there on the way to Ephrath" (that is, Bethlehem).* 8 When Israel saw Joseph's sons, he said, "Who are these?" 9 Joseph said to his father, "They are my sons, whom God has given me here." And he said, "Bring them to me, please, that I may bless them." 10 Now the eyes of Israel were dim with age, and he could not see well. So Joseph brought them near him; and he kissed them and embraced them. 11 Israel said to Joseph, "I did not expect to see your face; and here God has let me see your children also." 12 Then Joseph removed them from his father's knees, and he bowed himself with his face to the earth. 13 Joseph took them both, Ephraim in his right hand toward Israel's left, and Manasseh in his left hand toward Israel's right, and brought them near him. 14 But Israel stretched out his right hand and laid it on the head of Ephraim,

---

67   For this reason it is often viewed as Yahwistic, and see Wellhausen, *Hexateuch*, 59.

who was the younger, and his left hand on the head of Manasseh, crossing his hands, for Manasseh was the firstborn. 15 *He blessed Joseph, and said, "The God before whom my ancestors Abraham and Isaac walked, the God who has been my shepherd all my life to this day, 16 the angel who has redeemed me from all harm, bless the boys; and in them let my name be perpetuated, and the name of my ancestors Abraham and Isaac; and let them grow into a multitude on the earth."* 17 When Joseph saw that his father laid his right hand on the head of Ephraim, it displeased him; so he took his father's hand, to remove it from Ephraim's head to Manasseh's head. 18 Joseph said to his father, "Not so, my father! Since this one is the firstborn, put your right hand on his head." 19 But his father refused, and said, "I know, my son, I know; he also shall become a people, and he also shall be great. Nevertheless his younger brother shall be greater than he, and his offspring shall become a multitude of nations." 20 So he blessed them that day, saying, "By you Israel will invoke blessings, saying, 'God make you like Ephraim and like Manasseh.'" So he put Ephraim ahead of Manasseh. 21 *Then Israel said to Joseph, "I am about to die, but God will be with you and will bring you again to the land of your ancestors. 22 I now give to you one portion more than to your brothers, the portion that I took from the hand of the Amorites with my sword and with my bow."*

49:1 *Then Jacob called his sons, and said: "Gather around, that I may tell you what will happen to you in days to come. 2 Assemble and hear, O sons of Jacob; listen to Israel your father. 3 Reuben, you are my firstborn, my might and the first fruits of my vigor, excelling in rank and excelling in power. 4 Unstable as water, you shall no longer excel because you went up onto your father's bed; then you defiled it—you went up onto my couch! 5 Simeon and Levi are brothers; weapons of violence are their swords. 6 May I never come into their council; may I not be joined to their company—for in their anger they killed men, and at their whim they hamstrung oxen. 7 Cursed be their anger, for it is fierce, and their wrath, for it is cruel! I will divide them in Jacob, and scatter them in Israel. 8 Judah, your brothers shall praise you; your hand shall be on the neck of your enemies; your father's sons shall bow down before you. 9 Judah is a lion's whelp; from the prey, my son, you have gone up. He crouches down, he stretches out like a lion, like a lioness— who dares rouse him up? 10 The scepter shall not depart from Judah, nor the ruler's staff from between his feet, until tribute comes to him; and the obedience of the peoples is his. 11 Binding his foal to the vine and his donkey's colt to the choice vine, he washes his garments in wine and his robe in the blood of grapes; 12 his eyes are darker than wine, and his teeth whiter than milk. 13 Zebulun shall settle at the shore of the sea; he shall be a haven for ships, and his border shall be at Sidon. 14 Issachar is a strong donkey, lying down between the sheepfolds; 15 he saw that a resting place was good, and that the land was pleasant; so he bowed his shoulder to the burden, and became a slave at forced labor. 16 Dan shall judge his people as one of the tribes of Israel. 17 Dan shall be a snake by the roadside, a viper along the path, that bites the horse's heels so that its rider falls backward. 18 I wait for your salvation, O LORD. 19 Gad shall be raided by raiders, but he shall raid at their heels. 20 Asher's food shall be rich, and he shall provide royal delicacies. 21 Naphtali is a doe let loose that bears lovely fawns. 22 Joseph is a fruitful bough, a fruitful bough by a spring; his branches run over the wall. 23 The archers fiercely attacked him; they shot at him and pressed him hard. 24 Yet his bow remained taut, and his arms were made agile by the hands of the Mighty One of Jacob, by the name of the Shepherd, the Rock of Israel, 25 by the God of your father, who will help you, by the Almighty who will bless you with blessings of heaven above, blessings of the deep that lies beneath, blessings of the breasts and of the womb. 26 The blessings of your father are stronger than the blessings of the eternal mountains, the bounties of the everlasting hills; may they be on the head of Joseph, on the brow of him who was set apart from his brothers. 27 Benjamin is a ravenous wolf, in the morning devouring the prey, and at evening dividing the spoil." 28 All these are the twelve tribes of Israel, and this is what their father said to them when he blessed them, blessing each one of them with a suitable blessing.*

5.11.1 Source Division

There is general consensus regarding the textual fractures of Chapter 48 which we accept.[68] Other aspects of the Documentary analysis are unconvincing, while attempts to isolate three parallel accounts are unsuccessful. P's account is fractured (47:8 does not connect with 48:3, the following priestly verse), and there does not seem to be an independent yahwistic tradition. Another "so-called" difficulty is the "conflicting" textual evidence. On the one hand, this chapter uses the name "Israel," which many scholars consider to be yahwistic; on the other hand, "Elohim" is used throughout the entire chapter.[69] This "conflicting evidence" is, of course, entirely consistent with my hypothesis. Israel is the Elohist's preferred name for Joseph's father.

According to many scholars, the opening verse of Chapter 48 is elohistic. The Yahwist adds a gloss in 2a: "Jacob was told, 'Your son Joseph has come to you,'" which seeks to explain why Israel suddenly sits on his bed in the second half of the verse. Verses 3-7 are a priestly interpolation which alludes to the priestly revelation in Gen. 35:9-15. Because he is quoting Gen. 35, the name P uses here is "Jacob" and not "Israel." The direct continuation of the elohistic account is Israel's question regarding the identity of Joseph's sons (verse 8). According to E, Jacob has just arrived in Egypt, since if he had already been there for seventeen years he would certainly have recognized Menasseh and

---

68   Since Budde (K. Budde, Genesis 48,7 und die Benachbarten Abschnitte, *ZAW* 3 (1883), 56-86) and see G. Von Rad, *Genesis: A Commentary* (J. H. Marks tr.) (Old Testament Library), Philadelphia. 1972, 413ff., but cf. H. Seebass, The Joseph Story, Gen. 48, and the Canonical Process, *JSOT* 35 (1986): 29-43 for an alternative division.

69   L. Ruppert, *Die Josepherzählung der Genesis: Ein Beitrag zur Theologie der Pentateuch*, München, 1965, 171 attributes this episode to E2 solely due to the use of Israel, which is quite difficult to accept.

Ephraim. The E text continues uninterrupted until the blessings in verses 15-16, which have been identified as secondary (priestly?) by Westermann and others.[70] The obvious continuation of verse 14 is verse 17, in which Joseph tries to correct his father's "mistake" by switching his hands. Menasseh and Ephraim are blessed in verse 20. This is the final meeting between Israel and his son and having blessed Joseph's children, Jacob can die peacefully.

5.12 Israel's Death and Burial (Gen. 49-50)

29 *Then he charged them, saying to them, "I am about to be gathered to my people. Bury me with my ancestors—in the cave in the field of Ephron the Hittite, 30 in the cave in the field at Machpelah, near Mamre, in the land of Canaan, in the field that Abraham bought from Ephron the Hittite as a burial site. 31There Abraham and his wife Sarah were buried; there Isaac and his wife Rebekah were buried; and there I buried Leah—32 the field and the cave that is in it were purchased from the Hittites." 33 When Jacob ended his charge to his sons,* he drew up his feet into the bed, breathed his last, and was gathered to his people. 50:1 Then Joseph threw himself on his father's face and wept over him and kissed him. 2 Joseph commanded the physicians in his service to embalm his father. So the physicians embalmed Israel; 3 they spent forty days in doing this, for that is the time required for embalming. And the Egyptians wept for him seventy days. 4 When the days of weeping for him were past, Joseph addressed the household of Pharaoh, "If now I have found favor with you, please speak to Pharaoh as follows: 5 My father made me swear an oath; he said, 'I am about to die. In the tomb that I hewed out for myself in the land of Canaan, there you shall bury me.' Now therefore let me go up, so that I may bury my father; then I will return." 6 Pharaoh answered, "Go up, and bury your father, as he made you swear to do."7 So Joseph went up to bury his father. With him went up all the servants of Pharaoh, the Elders of his household, and all the Elders of the land of Egypt, 8 as well as all the household of Joseph, his brothers, and his father's household, *only their children, their flocks, and their herds were left in the land of Goshen.* 9 Both chariots and charioteers went up with him. It was a very great company. 10 When they came to the threshing floor of Atad, which is beyond the Jordan, they held there a very great and sorrowful lamentation; and he observed a time of mourning for his father seven days. 11 *When the Canaanite inhabitants of the land saw the mourning on the threshing floor of Atad, they said, "This is a grievous mourning on the part of the Egyptians." Therefore the place was named Abel-mizraim; it is beyond the Jordan.* 12

---

70   Cf. Westermann, *Genesis*, 1986, 188-189.

Thus his sons did for him as he had instructed them. 13 *They carried him to the land of Canaan and buried him in the cave of the field at Machpelah, the field near Mamre, which Abraham bought as a burial site from Ephron the Hittite.* 14 After he had buried his father, Joseph returned to Egypt with his brothers and all who had gone up with him to bury his father.

5.12.1 Source Division

The elohistic account of Israel's death begins only at the end of Chapter 49 following lengthy interpolations. Verse 48:21 ("Then Israel said to Joseph, "'I am about to die, but God will be with you and will bring you again to the land of your ancestors'") is a priestly addition (note the terms "Israel" and "Elohim"). It hints that Israel's sons are not in Egypt of their own volition, and that they desire to return to the land of Canaan, a concept foreign to the elohistic narrative.[71] Chapter 48:22 is difficult to attribute to a specific source. (It refers to Shechem as part of Joseph's inheritance: "I now give to you one portion ["שכם"] more than to your brothers, the portion that I took from the hand of the Amorites with my sword and with my bow.") However, Israel's sons were the ones who attacked Shechem not Israel himself. Moreover, Shechem was not conquered but only sacked. As is made clear by the preference of Judah in vss. 8-12, the tribal blessings were added in 49:1-28 by a post-elohistic southern author who is hard to identify.[72] It is quite clearly not Yahwistic, since the text alludes to the sacking of Shechem by Shimon and Levi (vss. 5-7) which is a secondary addition to Gen. 34.[73] Chapter 49:29-33a is a priestly interpolation which alludes to Gen. 23 and the burial of the patriarchs and matriarchs in the Cave of Maḥpelah.[74] Jacob's command (49:29-33a) is an expansion of Israel's general request that he be buried outside Egypt in 47:29-31 (=E).

The elohistic account continues with 49:33b: "He drew up his feet into the bed, breathed his last, and was gathered to his people," which

---

71 Westermann, *Genesis*, 1986, 192; but cf. Driver, *Genesis*, 378, who considers this verse to be the conclusion of the E episode – this verse, however, hints that the Israelites are in Egypt against their will, a somewhat foreign idea to the Elohistic narrative at this juncture.

72 See G. Rendsburg, Israelian Hebrew Features in Gen. 49, *Maarav* 8 (1993): 161-170; J. D. Macchi, Die Stämmesprueche in Gen. 49, 3-27, *ZAW* 96 (1984): 333-350.

73 See www.biblecriticism.com/com_genesis_34.doc.

74 The presence of P in these verses is universally acknowledged, though the exact division is disputed, and see Wellhausen, *Hexateuch*, 52, Van Seters, *Prologue*, 322-323.

is consistent with Israel's confinement to the bed in 48:1-2. Joseph and Egypt grieve in verses 50:1-3 and the burial is described in verses 4-11. According to most scholars, who base themselves on the usage of the name Israel, the episode is yahwistic in its entirety,[75]　But if so, why would the delegation stop at גרן האטד, a trans-Jordanian location? A Northern elohistic attribution is thus more likely. In any case, the use of "Israel" as well as the conformity with the elohistic tradition of 47:29-31 indicates elohistic authorship. J does add that Jacob's sons left their children and property in the land of Goshen (verse 8b), as well as the etymology: "'This is a grievous mourning ("אבל") on the part of the Egyptians.' Therefore the place was named Abel-mizraim; it is beyond the Jordan." (Verse 11—and compare the yahwistic Mahanayim-etymology likely added to Gen. 32:2). Verses 12-13 describe the implementation of the priestly command that the brothers bury their father in his cave (49:29-33a).

5.12.2 The Yahwistic Commentary

Since yahwistic supplementation is again minimal, there is little to add. However, one should note the yahwistic gloss in 50:8b: "Only their children, their flocks, and their herds were left in the land of Goshen." In addition to the emphasis on Goshen as the Israelite dwelling place, the Yahwist wished to answer the following question: If Pharaoh had given the Israelites permission to leave Egypt (in order to bury their father), why did they not stay in the land of their forefathers? According to E, Israel died shortly after the journey to Egypt, perhaps during the last years of the famine, and therefore there was no reason his sons would want to return. J, whose timeline is unclear—did the famine end?—explains that the Israelites left their children and property in Egypt. More importantly, however, he adds that the "burial procession" had a military escort. Is this perhaps an ominous hint foreshadowing that the Israelites were going to stay in Egypt for a long time?

5.13 After Israel's Death (Gen. 50)

15 Realizing that their father was dead, Joseph's brothers said, "What if Joseph still bears a grudge against us and pays us back in full for all the wrong that we did to him?" 16 So they approached Joseph, saying,

---

75　E.g., Driver, *Genesis*, 395-397.

"Your father gave this instruction before he died, 17 'Say to Joseph: I beg you, forgive the crime of your brothers and the wrong they did in harming you.' Now therefore please forgive the crime of the servants of the God of your father." Joseph wept when they spoke to him. 18 Then his brothers also wept, fell down before him, and said, "We are here as your slaves." 19 But Joseph said to them, "Do not be afraid! Am I in the place of God? 20 Even though you intended to do harm to me, God intended it for good, in order to preserve a numerous people, as he is doing today. 21 So have no fear; I myself will provide for you and your little ones." In this way he reassured them, speaking kindly to them. 22 So Joseph remained in Egypt, he and his father's household; *and Joseph lived one hundred ten years. 23 Joseph saw Ephraim's children of the third generation; the children of Machir son of Manasseh were also born on Joseph's knees. 24 Then Joseph said to his brothers, "I am about to die; but God will surely come to you, and bring you up out of this land to the land that he swore to Abraham, to Isaac, and to Jacob." 25 So Joseph made the Israelites swear, saying, "When God comes to you, you shall carry up my bones from here."* 26 And Joseph died, *being one hundred and ten years old;* and he was embalmed and placed in a coffin in Egypt.

5.13.1 Source Division

The elohistic account begins in verse 15, continuing without interruption until verse 22a, closing E's cycle of sin and forgiveness, begun in Gen. 37. Verse 22b is an interpolation of age, which is usually a priestly concern.[76] Verse 23 should be assigned to B because of the qal passive of "יֻלְּדוּ." (See Gen. 4:26; 22:20, 23, 24 and, most importantly Ephraim and Menasseh's birth notice in 41:50), whereas the hiphil form of this verb is priestly (see the genealogical lists of Gen. 5, and Gen. 11). Verses 24-25 are also beyond the scope of the elohistic narrative (which knows of no promises to the patriarchs) and should also, like vs. 23, be attributed to the final redactor. The final verse of the Joseph cycle (50:26) is elohistic except for the chronistic addition of Joseph's age, which is probably priestly in view of its connection to 22b.

A few further remarks concerning 50:24-25 are in order: Prior to the Exodus account (Ex. 14) the following introduction is appended: Ex. 13:17-19: "When Pharaoh let the people go, God did not lead them by way of the land of the Philistines, although that was nearer; for God thought, 'If the people face war, they may change their minds and return to Egypt...'" Both sections (Gen. 50:24-25 and Ex. 13:17-19) have

---

76   Wellhausen, *Hexateuch*, 60.

much in common: a) Both use "Elohim" but are not elohistic. The use of this term in 13:17 contrasts with the non-elohistic term "Pharaoh," while the elohistic term is "the King of Egypt;" b) Both sections mention Elohim himself as taking the Israelites out of Egypt; c) Together, both sections, as well as parts of Gen. 46:6-27, connect the tradition cycles: Gen. 50:24-25 hints at the Exodus from Egypt before it occurs, and Ex. 13:18-19 quotes the oath of Gen. 50:24-25. Both sections are tied to Josh. 24:32, where the promise is actually fulfilled. Following Rendtorff,[77] I attribute these sections to the final redactor of the Pentateuch to whom I have, throughout this work, referred to as the Bridger.

5.14 Summary

5.14.1 E's Joseph Cycle

There is no need to demonstrate the unity and continuity of the elohistic Joseph cycle since it is not in contention. One must note, however, that the Joseph cycle, like the Jacob cycle, was constructed chiastically. The first and last episodes are parallel: in Gen. 37 Joseph's brothers throw him into a pit and in Chapter 50 they apologise. As a result of Pharaoh's dreams and the dreams of his servants Joseph becomes viceroy (Chapters 40-41). This ascent is recognized following his father's death, when all Pharaoh's servants and Elders accompany the burial procession and all Egypt mourns. In both sections Joseph turns to Pharaoh's servants before approaching the ruler. The three meetings between Joseph and his brothers are parallel to the three meetings between Joseph and his father: during the first meeting between Joseph and his brothers, Joseph's dream is realized, and during the last meeting between Joseph and his father, Israel informs Joseph of a new prophecy connected to Joseph's progeny (the dreams are equivalent to the prophecy). In both instances the brothers bow, and one of the sides is not able to identify the other. Both middle meetings are connected with Israel's death and a possible Exodus. In the meeting between Joseph and his brothers, Joseph asks: "Is your father well, the old man of whom you spoke? Is he still alive?" and his brothers answer in the affirmative (43:27-28). In contrast, the meeting between Joseph and his father is connected to Israel's death and burial. In his last meeting with his brothers and the first with his father, Joseph reveals himself and weeps. As in the Jacob cycle, the middle element is a divine revelation

---

77   Rendtorff, *Überlieferung*, 77.

—the only such in the Joseph cycle. This revelation alludes to the past, deals with the present and hints at the future Exodus. Although parallel sections share other unifying themes, I wanted only to demonstrate some of the connections, rather than embark upon a detailed analysis of the chiastic structure, which deserves a much fuller study of its own.

The Chiastic Structure

Joseph Contends with his Brothers (Gen. 37)

Joseph Forgives his Brothers (Gen. 50:1-14)

The Dreams of Pharaoh and his Ministers (Gen. 40-41)

Jacob's Burial by the Egyptian Entourage (Gen. 50:15-26)

Joseph and his Brothers' First Meeting (Gen. 42)

Joseph and his Father's Last Meeting (Gen. 48)

The Second Meeting (Gen. 43:15-34)

The Second Meeting (Gen. 47:29-31)

The Third Meeting (Gen. 44-45)

The First Meeting (Gen. 46:28-47:12)

Chiasmus: The Revelation at Beersheba (Gen. 46:1-4)

5.14.2 The Yahwistic Commentary: A Summary

The yahwistic supplementation of the Joseph cycle in comparison to J's involvement elsewhere is limited, and the editorial themes are quite clear. At every possible opportunity, the Yahwist emphasizes the "correct" number of Joseph's siblings (eleven) as opposed to the seven elohistic brothers. To this end, J added a second dream, which told of "the sun, the moon, and eleven stars" who bow down to Joseph (37:9), and stressed that ten brothers descended to Egypt (42:3). As was his wont in the Jacob cycle, the Yahwist "rounds off" his characters: thus the righteous Joseph becomes a teller of tales (37:2) (this verse fragment may, however, be attributed to P). It is, of course, noteworthy that Judah is portrayed as being righteous in comparison to the rest of the brothers: he is the brother who speaks up on behalf of Joseph when the other brothers want to kill him and he begs Joseph to spare Benjamin. This positive portrayal has a strong connection with the fact that the author is probably Judean. Judah's sexual transgression with Tamar in Gen. 38 belongs to the late Bridger.

Another yahwistic theme is the Egyptian contempt of the Hebrews' sheep herding. The Egyptians were farmers and hence are loath to share bread with the Hebrews (43:32). Finally, the Yahwist emphasizes Goshen as the Israelite dwelling place—a point which will be repeated in the book of Exodus. The emphasis on Goshen as an Israelite settlement is another example of the segregation between Egypt and Israel, between the shepherds and the farmers.

5.15 Appendix: "Jacob" and "Israel"

In the above analysis of the Joseph cycle I attempted to turn the tables and claimed that the elohistic name of the third Patriarch was "Israel" and not "Jacob," while the yahwistic name was "Jacob" and not "Israel." The reader must judge whether the argument and the proofs are convincing.

To summarize: According to my division the name Israel appears in all E texts. The sole anomaly is 46:2, part of a very special unit. Apart from being the chiasmus of the elohistic stories of Joseph, this unit is of utmost importance to the entire elohistic creation. It is the center of the elohistic work as a whole. However, if the reader prefers total consistency, the reference to Jacob may be excised without any damage to the integrity of the elohistic unit. In 45:25, I assumed that the name Jacob was added to the elohistic text, citing evidence in the Septuagint. In all yahwistic texts and additions, without exception, "Jacob" is the term for the third Patriarch. Gen. 43:6-14 (in which the name Israel appears three times) is usually attributed to the Yahwist, but as I have demonstrated this is not the only possibility and a number of factors point to different authorship. The hypothesis presented in the opening paragraph of this chapter is thus confirmed: The Elohist used the name Israel, while the Yahwist used Jacob.

6. The Elohistic Moses Cycle

6.1 The New King (Ex. 1)

1 *These are the names of the sons of Israel who came to Egypt with Jacob, each with his household:* 2 *Reuben, Simeon, Levi, and Judah,* 3 *Issachar, Zebulun, and Benjamin,* 4 *Dan and Naphtali, Gad and Asher.* 5 *The total number of people born to Jacob was seventy. Joseph was already in Egypt.* 6 *Then Joseph died, and all his brothers, and that whole generation. 7 But the Israelites were fruitful and prolific; they multiplied and grew exceedingly strong, so that the land was filled with them.* 8 Now a new king arose over Egypt, who did not know Joseph. 9 He said to his people, "Look, the Israelite people are mightier and more powerful than we. 10 Come, let us deal shrewdly with them, or they will increase and, in the event of war, join our enemies and fight against us and escape from the land." 11 *Therefore they set taskmasters over them to oppress them with forced labor. They built supply cities, Pithom and Rameses, for Pharaoh. 12 But the more they were oppressed, the more they multiplied and spread, so that the Egyptians came to dread the Israelites. 13 The Egyptians became ruthless in imposing tasks on the Israelites, 14 and made their lives bitter with hard service in mortar and brick and in every kind of field labor. They were ruthless in all the tasks that they imposed on them.* 15 The King of Egypt said to the Hebrew midwives, one of whom was named Shiphrah and the other Puah, 16 "When you act as midwives to the Hebrew women, and see them on the birthstool, if it is a boy, kill him; but if it is a girl, she shall live." 17 But the midwives feared God; they did not do as the King of Egypt commanded them, but they let the boys live. 18 So the King of Egypt summoned the midwives and said to them, "Why have you done this, and allowed the boys to live?" 19 The midwives said *to Pharaoh,* "Because the Hebrew women are not like the Egyptian women; for they are vigorous and give birth before the midwife comes to them." 20 *So God dealt well with the midwives; and the people multiplied and became very strong.* 21 And because the midwives feared God, he gave them families. 22 *Then Pharaoh commanded all his people, "Every boy that is born to the Hebrews you shall throw into the Nile, but you shall let every girl live."*

Ex. 2:1 *Now a man from the house of Levi went and married a Levite woman. 2 The woman conceived and bore a son; and when she saw that he was a fine baby, she hid him three months. 3 When she could hide him no longer she got a papyrus basket for him, and plastered it with bitumen and pitch; she put the child in it and placed it among the reeds on the bank of the river. 4 His sister stood at a distance, to see what would happen to him. 5 The daughter of Pharaoh came down to bathe at the river, while her attendants walked beside the river. She saw the basket among the reeds and sent her maid to bring it. 6 When she opened it, she saw the child. He was crying, and she took pity on him, "This must be one of the Hebrews' children," she said. 7 Then his sister said to Pharaoh's daughter, "Shall I go and get you a nurse from the Hebrew women to nurse the child for you?" 8 Pharaoh's daughter said to her, "Yes." So the girl went and called the child's mother. 9 Pharaoh's daughter said to her, "Take this child and nurse it for me, and I will give you your wages." So the woman took the child and nursed it. 10 When the child grew up, she brought him to Pharaoh's daughter, and she took him as her son. She named him Moses, "because," she said, "I drew him out of the water." 11 One day, after Moses had grown up, he went out to his people and saw their forced labor. He saw an Egyptian beating a Hebrew, one of his kinsfolk. 12 He looked this way and that, and seeing no one he killed the Egyptian and hid him in the sand. 13 When he went out the next day, he saw two Hebrews fighting; and he said to the one who was in the wrong, "Why do you strike your fellow Hebrew?" 14 He answered, "Who made you a ruler and judge over us? Do you mean to kill me as you killed the Egyptian?" Then Moses was afraid and thought, "Surely the thing is known." 15 When Pharaoh heard of it, he sought to kill Moses. But Moses fled from Pharaoh. He settled in the land of Midian, and sat down by a well. 16 The priest of Midian had seven daughters. They came to draw water, and filled the troughs to water their father's flock. 17 But some shepherds came and drove them away. Moses got up and came to their defense and watered their flock. 18 When they returned to their father Reuel, he said, "How is it that you have come back so soon today?" 19 They said, "An Egyptian helped us against the shepherds; he even drew water for us and watered the flock." 20 He said to his daughters, "Where is he? Why did you leave the man? Invite him to break bread." 21 Moses agreed to stay with the man, and he gave Moses his daughter Zipporah in marriage. 22 She bore a son, and he named him Gershom; for he said, "I have been an alien residing in a foreign land." 23 After a long time the King of Egypt died. The Israelites groaned under their slavery, and cried out. Out of the slavery their cry for help rose up to God. 24 God heard their groaning, and God remembered his covenant with Abraham, Isaac, and Jacob. 25 God looked upon the Israelites, and God took notice of them.*

6.1.2 Source Division

The three primary sources of the Tetrateuch are involved in the composition of Ex. 1. The beginning of the chapter (verses 1-7) is priestly and links the end of the book of Genesis to the beginning of the book of Exodus.[1] Such a connection existed in E even before this priestly insertion, "Now a new king arose over Egypt, who did not know Joseph" (verse 8): but the priestly source wished to bridge the temporal gap between Israel as a family and Israel's emergence as a nation, as we find in: "Look, the Israelite *people* are mightier and more powerful than we" (verse 9), and thus inserted verse 7: "But the Israelites were fruitful

---

1   M. Noth, *Exodus, A Commentary* (J. S. Bowden tr.) (OTL), Philadelphia, 1962, 2; Wellhausen, *Hexateuch*, 61, 68, attributes vs. 6 to J.

and prolific; they multiplied and grew exceedingly strong, so that the land was filled with them." Verses 8-10 should be assigned to E for the following reasons: a) The narrative link with verse 15ff, a section which is for the most part attributed to E (e.g. Propp 1998, 126, and see below). b) The parallel to the beginning of Num. 22 (an E narrative), which uses similar terms to describe a similar occurrence.[2] c) The words "king" and "Egypt" in verse 8 are separated, but nevertheless it appears that in the author's mind the title is the royal epithet "King of Egypt"), which is an Elohistic term,[3] cf. 1:15, 18, and below 3:18, 5:4, 14:5.

Verses 11-14, the first to imply that the Israelites were slaves, are linked to the J narrative of Ex. 5,[4] which also describes Israel's subjugation as intensive field work in 5:7: "You shall no longer give the people straw to make bricks, as before; let them go and gather straw for themselves." There is little argument regarding the assignment of (at least parts of) vss. 11-14 to a different/later source. The question is which source. Many scholars concur with Wellhausen who argues that the source in question is P.[5] If, however, E (rather than J) is identified as the base text, it is entirely possible to assign these verses to the J redactor.

Verse 10's link to verse 15 is self-evident: in verses 9-10 a problem is described ("He said to his people, 'Look, the Israelite people are mightier and more powerful than we...'") and in verse 15 the King of Egypt suggests a solution. The names of the midwives, Shifra and Puah, are in all likelihood original to the basic narrative, although we never hear of them again. The number of midwives matches the numbers of the Israelites according to the Elohist, that is, a small number, in contrast to the multitude in later sources. (According to P, Israel numbered 600,000 fighting men at the Exodus [Ex. 12:37 (P)]). According to E, the exodus from Egypt occurred only one or two generations after the death of Joseph, and not four hundred years (as in Gen. 15:13) or 430 years later (as in Ex. 12:40). Even if a miraculous multiplication of the People of Israel did occur in that period, there was no need for more than two midwives.[6]

---

2   Propp, *Exodus*, 126.
3   Carpenter, *Composition*, 384-398, did not record this term in his extensive vocabulary lists.
4   Wellhausen, *Hexateuch*, 72, but compare Propp, *Exodus*, 126, who assigns the entire chapter to E.
5   Wellhausen, *Hexateuch*, 61-62.
6   This problem was identified by the Rabbis, and a popular solution was the [very] de facto "appointment" of Shifrah and Puah as senior midwives, in charge of a veritable army of anonymous helpers (thus Ibn Ezra).

In verse 18 the King of Egypt asks a question, while in verse 19 the midwives answer Pharaoh, rather than the King of Egypt. In my opinion, the yahwistic (or priestly) editor added the words "(The midwives said) *to Pharaoh*" at this point in the narrative in order to emphasize that the elohistic King of Egypt and the yahwistic and priestly Pharaoh are one and the same. (An editorial preference for a certain term may lead to its addition even in places where it is not syntactically required.) Verse 20 is a Priestly expansion of E's vs. 21 (the midwives "fear of God" in vs. 21 is typical to E narrative), and details the outcome of the midwives subterfuge – note the linguistic affinity with vs. 7 (P), especially the use of the adverb "exceedingly" following the verbs of increase (מאד).[7]　　Finally, Pharaoh's command in verse 22 to kill all Israelite males sets the background for the yahwistic birth of Moses in the following chapter.[8]

Proponents of the fragmentary hypothesis or tradition cycle critics, most notably Konrad Schmid,[9] argue that the Exodus complex was independent of the Patriarchal complexes until a relatively late stage of redaction and that they represent two independent accounts of Israelite origins. At the crux of their analysis is Ex. 1, which clearly bridges between the two periods, and is thus largely attributed to late priestly redactors and other later sources. A good starting point for a dialogue with this school of thought is the attribution of Ex. 1:1-7 to (a) priestly editor/s, which source critics and proponents of the tradition cycle paradigm can agree upon (whether it was an early P redactor or late P redactor, and whether verses 1-7 were composed by more than one author is still debated). However, most tradition cycle critics (as I refer to them throughout this work) also attribute the narrative of verses 8-14 to a later redactional layer, relying on the linguistic affinity between the proliferation of the Israelites as described in verse. 7 and Pharaoh's proclamation, both of which employ the roots ר.ב.י and ע.צ.ם in reference to the Israelites. The verbs, however, have a different meaning in verse 9, where they are more aptly translated as referring to military might. Pharaoh states very clearly in verse 10 that he fears the Israelites will become numerous, indicating that they are clearly not yet numerous. This is supported by the account of verses 15-21, which is terminologically connected to verses 8-10 (מלך מצרים and see above), in which the Israelites are plainly only on their way to becoming numerous, since they only have two (!) midwives, which would hardly be equipped to

---

7　Many scholars regard 20 and 21 as doublets, e.g. Propp, *Exodus*, 138, Graupner *Elohist*, 410.
8　Noth, *Exodus*, 23.
9　K. Schmid, *Erzväter und Exodus*, 1999.

deal with a nation of the magnitude imagined by the Priestly author of vs. 7. The Egyptian monarch's strategy of killing all males also supports this reading since it is the military might of the Israelite males that worries the Egyptian king.

It is thus more expedient to understand verse 7 as a reinterpretive expansion to verse 9. Verses 1-7 summarize the liminal period between family and nation and rapidly arrive at Israel's pre-Exodus vastness, whereas verses 8-10, 15-21 describe a slower process. If verses 8-10 are not redactional, (and based on linguistic criteria there is virtually nothing that connects them to priestly, Deuteronomistic or other redactional layers), a firm non-redactional narrative link exists between Genesis and Exodus, which would put Schmid's theory into serious question.

Schmid claims that the arguments for the unity of Genesis and Exodus as presented by the Documentary Hypothesis and source criticism are remarkably weak. Nevertheless, the *a priori* assumption of source criticism that the books were literarily connected even at the earliest stages is justified, since the narratives of Genesis and Exodus fit together remarkably well despite the temporal gap: Israel's descent to Egypt (as the head of a family) is at the basis of the Joseph narratives and Israel's ascent from Egypt (as a nation) is at the basis of the Moses narratives. While it is true that each complex could be read independently as a coherent account, they do complement each other, so that positing independent literary existence for each of the two needlessly adds entities to the reconstruction of the literary process.

6.1.2 The Yahwistic Commentary

Since the main objective of this research is to isolate E and catalogue the yahwistic supplementation of the elohistic source, extensive discussion regarding the priestly supplementation is beyond its scope. Therefore, the priestly source will be referred to only when it is relevant to the main topics of the present work, namely, the yahwistic supplementation of the elohistic source and the isolation of the basic E narrative.

Although Ex. 1 is clearly linked to additional yahwistic narratives (especially the narrative of Ex. 5 detailing Israel's hard work), one may ask whether the identification of the links as yahwistic is correct. Many scholars identify these links as priestly and the verses in question (13-14) lack any "authentic" yahwistic indicators. Since there is no need to assume more than one author, and in view of the fact that editorial links to J narratives were identified throughout Genesis as an organic part of the J source, one may assume that when there is an allusion to a yahwistic narrative, that allusion is also yahwistic, unless there is good reason to suppose otherwise.

To return to Ex. 1: I believe that the yahwistic author was an aspiring historian who, like all historians, is interested in roots and origins. In the elohistic narrative of Chapter 3, Moses suddenly appears. The Elohist assumes that readers are familiar with the mythic national leader, but this is insufficient for the yahwistic historian, who needs to address Moses' origins. Hence the composition of Chapter 2, which narrates the story of the birth of Moses and his early years. The background for this story is provided in J's Ex. 1:22. Pharaoh's command to cast all new-born males into the Nile explains both why Moses' mother had to hide him and his subsequent childhood as a prince.[10]

Like the majority of critical scholars, I identify Chapter 2 as yahwistic (except for the final three verses, which are a priestly introduction to the revelation in Ex. 3) for reasons which will be detailed below: a) The elohistic source is unfamiliar with Levi the son of Jacob, who exists only in J and P interpolations; b) The chapter uses "Pharaoh" and not the equivalent elohistic sobriquet "The King of Egypt;" c) The name of Moses' father-in-law is "Reu El" and not Jethro, which we find in the elohistic narratives of Ex. 3 and 18. It is possible that the Yahwist calls Moses' father-in-law by this name as a result of his role: every priest is the friend (רע) of "El," especially Moses' father-in-law, who is a friend of Israel and shares in the glory of their successes;[11] d) Moses' son "Gershom" is mentioned in this chapter and the name is repeated in the yahwistic interpolation in Chapter 18. In reality, the only elohistic indicator is the word אמה (handmaiden), contrary to J's usual שפחה (also handmaiden). It is possible, however, that "אמתה" be vocalized differently (a short initial vowel followed by a doubled mem) and understood as "arm" since, as Zeligman and other Israeli scholars have shown,[12] "אמה" as "arm" exists in biblical Hebrew (the meaning of the term is not confined to "cubit").[13]

---

10 H. Gressmann, *Mose und Seine Zeit: Ein Kommentar zu den Mose Sagen*, Göttingen, 1913, 1ff, argues for an opposite evolution, i.e. that the midwife account is a literary expansion of Pharaoh's command in Ex 1:22.

11 *Cf.* the Yahwistic additions to Ex. 18 which emphasize Jethro's support of Moses and Israel - Driver, *Exodus*, 163, attributes these verses to the Redactor, we concur – since this "Redactor" is in our eyes none other than J himself.

12 Y. A. Zeligman, Inquiries into the Biblical Text (Hebrew), *Tarbiz* 25 (1956): 118-139.

13 H. P. Stähli, "Da schickte sie ihre Magd..." (Ex. 2,5); zur Vokalisation eines hebräischen Wortes, ein Beispiel des Ringens um das richtige Textverständnis, *Wort und Dienst* (17): 1983, 27-54, maps out the extra-biblical evidence for this understanding, but his conclusions regarding the authenticity of the Masoretic vocalization ignore Zeligman's observations.

Chapter 2 again presents a yahwistic theme already expanded upon in earlier discussion regarding J's additions to the Abraham cycle, i.e. "the exploits of fathers repeated by progeny" — an expansion technique which lightens the task of the yahwistic editor, who can thus recycle old material without needing to compose new stories or search for other old traditions. In Ex. 3:1 Moses is presented as the sheep herder of his father-in-law, similar to his ancestor Jacob. In Chapter 2 the Yahwist expands upon this comparison between Moses and Jacob, at the same time emphasizing the differences between Laban and Jethro. Like Jacob, Moses met his wife by the well as she was coming to water the sheep and, like Jacob, demonstrated his strength before the shepherds. While Moses, unlike Jacob, is not a relative of his father-in-law, he too resides with his wife's family for many years. Laban pursues his son-in-law, but does not harm him because of Elohim's mediation, while Jethro comes to Moses in peace and admits to the greatness of Yhwh (below, Ex. 18). Laban pursues Jacob in order to take back his daughters, while Jethro returns Moses' wife and sons without being asked to do so.[14]

6.2 Moses' Mission (Ex. 3)

1 Moses was keeping the flock of his father-in-law Jethro, the priest of Midian; he led his flock beyond the wilderness, to the mountain of God, *to Horeb.* 2 *There the angel of the LORD appeared to him in a flame of fire out of a bush.* He looked, and *a* bush was blazing, yet it was not consumed. 3 Then Moses said, "I must turn aside and look at this great sight, and see why the bush is not burned up." 4 *When the LORD saw that he had turned aside to see,* God called to him out of the bush, "Moses, Moses!" And he said, "Here I am." 5 Then he said, "Come no closer! Remove the sandals from your feet, for the place on which you are standing is holy ground." 6 He said further, "I am the God of your father, *the God of Abraham, the God of Isaac, and the God of Jacob,"* and Moses hid his face, for he was afraid to look at God. 7 *Then the LORD said, "I have observed the misery of my people who are in Egypt; I have heard their cry on account of their taskmasters. Indeed, I know their sufferings, 8 and I have come down to deliver them from the Egyptians, and to bring them up out of that land to a good and broad land, a land flowing with milk and honey, to the country of the Canaanites, the Hittites, the Amorites, the Perizzites, the Hivites, and the Jebusites.* 9 (And He said) Behold, the cry of the Israelites has now come to me; I have also seen how the Egyptians oppress them. 10 So come, I will send you to the King of Egypt to bring

14   For a fuller comparison between the two figures, see Propp, *Exodus,* 241-242.

my people, the Israelites, out of Egypt." 11But Moses said to God, "Who am I that I should go to the King of Egypt, and bring the Israelites out of Egypt?" 12 He said, "I will be with you; and this shall be the sign for you that it is I who sent you: when you have brought the people out of Egypt, you shall worship God on this mountain."13 But Moses said to God, "If I come to the Israelites and say to them, 'The God of your ancestors has sent me to you,' and they ask me, 'What is his name?' what shall I say to them?" 14 God said to Moses, "I AM WHO I AM." He said further, "Thus you shall say to the Israelites, 'I AM has sent me to you.'" 15 *God also said to Moses, "Thus you shall say to the Israelites, 'The LORD, the God of your ancestors, the God of Abraham, the God of Isaac, and the God of Jacob, has sent me to you': This is my name forever, and this my title for all generations. 16 Go and assemble the Elders of Israel, and say to them, The LORD, the God of your ancestors, the God of Abraham, of Isaac, and of Jacob, has appeared to me, saying: I have given heed to you and to what has been done to you in Egypt. 17 I declare that I will bring you up out of the misery of Egypt, to the land of the Canaanites, the Hittites, the Amorites, the Perizzites, the Hivites, and the Jebusites, a land flowing with milk and honey.'* 18 They will listen to your voice; and you and the Elders of Israel shall go to the King of Egypt and say to him, '*The* LORD the God of the Hebrews, has met with us; let us now go a three days' journey into the wilderness, so that we may sacrifice to *The LORD* our God.' 19 I know, however, that the King of Egypt will not let you go even if compelled by a mighty hand. *20 So I will stretch out my hand and strike Egypt with all my wonders that I will perform in it; after that he will let you go. 21 I will bring this people into such favor with the Egyptians that, when you go, you will not go empty-handed; 22 each woman shall ask her neighbor and any woman living in the neighbor's house for jewelry of silver and of gold, and clothing, and you shall put them on your sons and on your daughters; and so you shall plunder the Egyptians."*

4 Then Moses answered, "But suppose they do not believe me or listen to me, but say, 'The LORD did not appear to you.' " 2 The LORD said to him, "What is that in your hand?" He said, "A staff." 3 And he said, "Throw it on the ground." So he threw the staff on the ground, and it became a snake; and Moses drew back from it. 4 Then the LORD said to Moses, "Reach out your hand, and seize it by the tail"—so he reached out his hand and grasped it, and it became a staff in his hand—5 "so that they may believe that the LORD, the God of their ancestors, the God of Abraham, the God of Isaac, and the God of Jacob, has appeared to you."6 Again, the LORD said to him, "Put your hand inside your cloak." He put his hand into his cloak; and when he took it out, his hand was leprous, as white as snow. 7 Then God said, "Put your hand back into your cloak"—so he put his hand back into his cloak, and when he took it out, it was restored like the rest of his body—8 "If they will not believe you or heed the first sign, they may believe the second sign. 9 If they will not believe even these two signs or heed you, you shall take some water from the Nile and pour it on the dry ground; and the water that you shall take from the Nile will become blood on the dry ground." 10 But Moses said to the LORD, "O my Lord, I have never been eloquent, neither in the past nor even now that you have spoken to your servant; but I am slow of speech and slow of tongue." 11 *Then the LORD said to him, "Who gives speech to mortals? Who makes them mute or deaf, seeing or blind? Is it not I, the LORD?* 12 *Now go, and I will be with your mouth and teach you what you are to speak."* 13 *But he said, "O my Lord, please send someone else."* 14 *Then the anger of the LORD was kindled against Moses and he said, "What of your brother Aaron, the Levite? I know that he can speak fluently; even now he is coming out to meet you, and when he sees you his heart will be glad.* 15 *You shall speak to him and put the words in his mouth; and I will be with your mouth and with his mouth, and will teach you what you shall do.* 16 *He indeed shall speak for you to the people; he shall serve as a mouth for you, and you shall serve as God for him.* 17 *Take in your hand this staff, with which you shall perform the signs."*

(Two textual notes: The Septuagint in verses 10, 11 reads: "Pharaoh, King of Egypt" in lieu of the Masoretic text's "Pharaoh." This may indicate conflation and a possible original reading of "King of Egypt," [See below in my comments.] Also, the Septuagint's shorter readings in verse 18: "The God of the Hebrews" and "Our God" are preferred over the Masoretic text's "The LORD, God of the Hebrews," and "The LORD our God," and see below in my commentary.)

6.2.1 Source Division

For traditional "Documentarians," Chapter 3 is one of the most important chapters of the Pentateuch. According to the classic Documentary Hypothesis, the Elohist began using Yhwh in conjunction with Elohim[15] With this in mind, it is interesting to note that many researchers continued (and continue) to divide the sources according to the differing names of the Deity even after Ex. 3. Indeed, both McNeile[16] and later Kohata[17] divide Ex. 3 into two independent sources fracturing along the lines of the name of God criterion. However, neither arrive at the desired conclusion, namely that the Yahwist is a relatively late source which edited and supplemented the elohistic narrative of Ex. 3. As Ska argues,[18] it is very difficult to accept the Documentary Hypothesis in Ex. 3, since (as usual) it is impossible to isolate two complete indepen-

---

15 Although according to some of the researchers, the Elohist used the name Yhwh even before Ex. 3, cf. for example, the various documentary analyses of Gen. 15 recorded in J. Ha, *Genesis 15: A Theological Compendium of Pentateuchal History* (BZAW 181), Berlin, 1989.

16 McNeile, *Exodus*, 16-22.

17 Kohata, *Jahwist und Priestershrift.*

18 J. L. Ska, Récit et Récit Métadiégétique en Ex. 1-15, Remarques Critique et Essai d'Interprétation de Ex. 3:16-22, in *Le Pentateuque: Débats et Recherches* (P. Haudbert ed.), Paris, 1992, 135-171.

dent narratives. This conclusion led researchers such as Blum[19] to seek unity and attribute the chapter largely to one source. However, such an analysis is a complete rejection of divine names as a distinguishing criterion and flies in the face of the evidence so far gathered. I accept Schmitt's proposed solution of a basic narrative and editorial supplementation,[20] with the proviso that the Elohist uses only "Elohim."

6.2.2 My Division

My division of Ex. 3 is as follows. "Horev" in 3:1, the Deuteronomic name for Mount Sinai, is a secondary gloss[21] and is an attempt to identify the holy mountain in a more precise manner. The elohistic name for Mount Sinai is "the mountain of Elohim." The beginning of verse 2: "There the angel of the LORD appeared to him in a flame of fire out of a bush," is also an editorial interpolation. Since the Deity reveals his presence only in verse 4, this interpolation perhaps emphasizes that only an angel, and not the "Deity" in all his glory, revealed himself to Moses, and that every other mention of the Deity in this chapter should be understood in this light. (Compare this to the two calls of the Angel of Yhwh to Abraham in Gen. 22, as opposed to the first revelation of Elohim.) The verse fragment "When the LORD saw that he had turned aside to see" (verse 4) is secondary; the narrative assumption is that the Deity led Moses to the burning bush. Hence, there is no need to describe Yhwh as Moses' tempter. This verse fragment was inserted to serve as a bridge between the appearance of Moses and the beginning of his speech with the Deity.

"The God of Abraham, the God of Isaac, and the God of Jacob" in verse 6 (a God of multiple personages) contradicts the beginning of the verse: "I am the God of your father," (one father), and therefore appears to be an editorial interpolation.[22] I have already shown that the Elohist does not identify Isaac as a Patriarch and I believe that this phrase is part of the Yahwist's preoccupation with familial connections which was evident in the Jacob and Joseph cycles. Verses 9 and 10 are parallel to verses 7 and 8. Verse 7 appears to be yahwistic for two rea-

---

19   E. Blum, *Studien zur Komposition des Pentateuch* (BZAW 189), Berlin, 1990, 22-28.

20   H. C. Schmitt, Das sogenannte vorprophetisch Berufungsschema, *ZAW* 104 (1992): 202-216, notes 63 and 64.

21   Noth, *Exodus*, 28.

22   The expression – "The God of your father/s" appears by itself in a number of places throughout Genesis e.g. Gen. 31:29; 46:3, for the addition of the names of the patriarchs as an editorial theme, see Römer, *Israels Väter*.

sons: a) The name of Yhwh at the beginning of the verse; b) The word "נגש" (taskmaster) is used a number of times in the yahwistic narrative of Chapter 5. Verse 8, poetically connected to verse 7, may also be yahwistic because of the mention of the six nations and the phrase "a land flowing with milk and honey."[23] According to E, the ultimate objective—the land of Canaan—is never promised to Israel. Since verse 9 does not begin a new divine utterance but occurs in the middle of one in the canonical text, I added "and He said" ("ויאמר") which was, in my opinion, deleted from the original text, so that the J's addition of vss. 7-8 would read more smoothly. Note the appearance of: "And [the LORD] said" = "ויאמר" at the beginning of verse 7, i.e. the beginning of the divine speech. I excised the superfluous word "ועתה" ("so" or "now") at the beginning of verse 9. There are two temporal adverbs ("ועתה" and "הנה") at the beginning of the verse where only one ("Behold") is needed. Possibly "ועתה" in verse 9 was affected by the same expression at the beginning of verse 10, making "הנה" the better choice.

Contrary to most scholars,[24] I regard the Septuagint's "Pharaoh the King of Egypt" in verses 10 and 11 as evidence for an original unspecific version "King of Egypt." In my opinion, the Septuagint adds "Pharaoh" to this hypothetical original version in order to clarify the rarer expression. According to this reconstruction, the Masoretic text preferred the more common "Pharaoh" over the rarer "King of Egypt" and thus either substituted the more common title or, alternatively, omitted "the King of Egypt" as superfluous (Indeed, the Septuagint's reading is preferable in verses 18 and 19 as well, see below.) Only in Chapter 3 does the Septuagint "deviate" from the Masoretic text and use the more specific title "Pharaoh, King of Egypt" (cf. the Masoretic text's "King of Egypt" in verse 19 as opposed to the Septuagint's "Pharaoh King of Egypt"). Since the phenomenon is restricted to Chapter 3, it is difficult to accept that the Septuagint was simply trying to be more specific and thus it is entirely possible that the longer version is evidence of conflation.

The sign of vs. 12, presents a logical conundrum: how can the revelation of God upon the mountain and his worship function as a sign proving that Moses was sent by God? Ostensibly Moses needs proof much sooner in order to be effective. This type of sign is indeed nigh incomprehensible in the canonical text of Exodus, but it makes good sense as part of the anthropocentric elohistic narrative. As we shall soon see, God does not make any further appearances in the E narrative

---

23   For further mention of this expression, and of the nations see Ex 23:23; 33:2-3.

24   E.g. Propp, *Exodus*, 184-185.

until the revelation at God's mountain. Moses is left to his own devices and successfully delivers Israel. However, he must still prove that his prowess and leadership were divinely sanctioned. Hence God promises him a revelation when he arrives at the final destination (God's mountain) with Israel in tow.

Verses 15-17 are a yahwistic interpolation and a classic statement of J's theology (the aggrandizement of Yhwh and His name, and see the introduction). Verses 18-20a describe the way in which Moses is to carry out his mission. Since the title "King of Egypt" appears in verses 18 and 19, I attribute them to the Elohist. While the divine name Yhwh appears twice in the Masoretic text in verse 18 (The LORD, the God of the Hebrews, has met with us; let us now go a three days' journey into the wilderness, so that we may sacrifice to the LORD our God.), in my opinion these are secondary glosses. (See the Septuagint's shorter non-yahwistic "The God of the Hebrews, has met with us; let us now go a three days' journey into the wilderness, so that we may sacrifice to our God") . The same verse is repeated in E's 5:3, and this time the Masoretic text also does not include the name Yhwh.[25]

Verse 20: "So I will stretch out my hand and strike Egypt with all my wonders that I will perform in it; after that he will let you go," is once again a yahwistic interpolation and contradicts what is said in the previous verse: "The King of Egypt shall not let you go even if compelled by a mighty hand." Many scholars, however (including the NRSV translators), seek to alter the plain meaning of the negative "ולא" in verse 19 ("even if," "not even"), since the canonical text clearly indicates that Pharaoh sent the Israelites off.[26] In E's version of the Exodus, the Israelites simply escaped from Egypt as is partially indicated here.[27] Verses 21-22, maintain that the Israelites left peacefully and were even provided with silver and gold. This tradition appears in two other places in Exodus (11:2, and 12:34-35), as well as in Gen. 15:14, which are generally considered late.[28]

25　The expression: "the God of the Hebrews" was appropriated by J and appears four further times, in 7:16; 9:2, 13; 10:3, always with the addition of "the Lord."

26　J. L. Ska, Notes sur la Traduction de "welo'" en Exode III 19b, *VT* 44 (1994): 60-65; P. Addinal, "Exodus III 19B and the Interpretation of Biblical Narrative", *VT* 49 (1999): 289-300.

27　As we shall see below in our analysis of Ex. 14, and cf. G. W. Coats, Despoiling the Egyptians, *VT* 18 (1968): 450-457; N. L. Collins, Evidence in the Septuagint of a Tradition in Which the Israelites Left without Pharoah's Consent, *CBQ* 56 (1994): 442-448.

28　See Driver *Exodus*, 26, and Coats, *Despoiling*. Cf. B. Ziemer, *Abram – Abraham kompositionsgeschichtliche Untersuchungen zu Genesis 14, 15 und 17*, Berlin, 2005, for the most recent discussion regarding Gen. 15 and its connection to the composition of

6.2.3 The Yahwistic Commentary

According to E, the Deity reveals Himself to Moses by means of a burning bush, but the Yahwist, who maintains that "no one shall see the
divine and live" (Ex. 33:20), tries to blur this explicit revelation. Thus
the figure revealed in verse 2 according to J is "the angel of Yhwh," not
"Elohim." The angel's revelation functions as a kind of bait to draw
Moses towards it, but the moment Moses arrives at the bush the dialogue with the unseen Deity begins without the mediation of the angel:
3:4: "When the LORD saw that he had turned aside to see, God called
to him out of the bush, 'Moses, Moses!' And he said, 'Here I am.'"
Verse 6 refers to the "familiar" familial links (the God of Abraham,
Isaac and Jacob), a threesome mentioned again in verses 15 and 16.
Verses 7 and 8 expand the historical scope of the narrative by mentioning Israel's final destination. E, the basic source, is interested only in the
Exodus from Egypt and does not mention a final destination here or
anywhere else. The name "ehyeh asher ehyeh" (I AM WHAT I AM) in
verse 13 is understood by many commentators as the biblical etymology for Yhwh. (For an overview of some of the considerable bibliography see Childs 1974, 60-70). In my opinion it is just a word play with
the promise of verse 12 "כי אהיה עמך" ("He said, 'I will be with you'"), or,
as Propp (225-226) suggests, a manoeuvre on the Deity's part in order
to evade specificity. J, not E, is interested in glorifying Yhwh's name in
Chapter 3 (3:15-17). Indeed, this is one of the more prominent themes
of the yahwistic Moses cycle.[29]

Chapter 4:1-17 is yahwistic and builds upon the elohistic theme of
questioning the Divine, thus answering an important question arising
from the elohistic narrative.[30] The Elohist in 3:18 clearly states: "They
will listen to your voice." One may ask why the Elders and the rest of
the Israelites should believe Moses. He needs to prove himself as a true
messenger of Elohim. To achieve this, the Yahwist arms Moses with
two miraculous signs. Moses' questions fulfill two additional functions:
a) As a result of Moses' last comment/question, 4:13: "But he said, 'O
my Lord, please send someone else,'" Yhwh suggests (or commands)
that Aaron be Moses' spokesperson. It is important for the text to intro-

---

the Pentateuch. I attribute these passage to B, and see www.biblecriticism.
com/com.genesis_15 and www.biblecriticism.com/com.exodus_3. For an overview of
the considerable bibliography see B. Childs 1974, *The Book of Exodus, A Critical and
Theological Commentary* (OTL), Philadelphia, 60-70.

29 J. I. Durham, *Exodus* (World Biblical Commentary) Waco Texas, 1987, submits that
the whole book of Exodus may be viewed as an ode to Yhwh.

30 Thus Wellhausen, *Hexateuch*, 70, excepting vs. 17.

duce Aaron, since he plays a key role in the subsequent narratives and is not directly identified in the elohistic source. b) I have already mentioned that the Yahwist likes to "humanize" his characters. Thus Moses, who until this point was quite righteous in his conduct (according to J as well. *cf.* his rescue at the well in Ex. 2) is now portrayed as a coward and a skeptic, like his ancestor Jacob.

6.3 Moses Returns to Egypt (Ex. 4-5)

18 Moses went back to his father-in-law Jether and said to him, "Please let me go back to my kindred in Egypt and see whether they are still living." And Jethro said to Moses, "Go in peace." 19 *The LORD said to Moses in Midian, "Go back to Egypt; for all those who were seeking your life are dead."* 20 So Moses took his wife and his sons, put them on a donkey *and went back to the land of Egypt;* and Moses carried the staff of God in his hand. 21 *And the LORD said to Moses, "When you go back to Egypt, see that you perform before Pharaoh all the wonders that I have put in your power; but I will harden his heart, so that he will not let the people go. 22 Then you shall say to Pharaoh, 'Thus says the LORD: Israel is my firstborn son. 23 I said to you, "Let my son go that he may worship me." But you refused to let him go; now I will kill your firstborn son.'" 24 On the way, at a place where they spent the night, the LORD met him and tried to kill him. 25 But Zipporah took a flint and cut off her son's foreskin, and touched Moses' feet with it, and said, "Truly you are a bridegroom of blood to me!" 26 So he let him alone. It was then she said, "A bridegroom of blood by circumcision." 27 The LORD said to Aaron, "Go into the wilderness to meet Moses."* And *Aaron* set out; and met him at the mountain of God and kissed him. 28 *Moses told Aaron all the words of the LORD with which he had sent him, and all the signs with which he had charged him.* 29 Then Moses and Aaron went and assembled all the Elders of the Israelites. 30 *Aaron spoke all the words that the LORD had spoken to Moses, and performed the signs in the sight of the people. 31 The people believed; and when they heard that the LORD had given heed to the Israelites and that he had seen their misery, they bowed down and worshiped. 5:1 Afterward Moses and Aaron went to Pharaoh and said, "Thus says the LORD, the God of Israel, 'Let my people go, so that they may celebrate a festival to me in the wilderness.' " 2 But Pharaoh said, "Who is the LORD, that I should heed him and let Israel go? I do not know the LORD, and I will not let Israel go."* 3 They said *to the King of Egypt,* "The God of the Hebrews has revealed himself to us; let us go a three days' journey into the wilderness to sacrifice to our God, or he will fall upon us with pestilence or sword." 4 But the King of Egypt said to them, "Moses and Aaron, why are you taking the people away from their work? Get to your labors!" 5 *Pharaoh continued, "Now they are more numerous than the people of the land and yet you want them to stop working!" 6 That same day Pharaoh commanded the taskmasters of the people, as well as their supervisors, 7"You shall no longer give the people straw to make bricks, as before; let them go and gather straw for themselves.*

8 *But you shall require of them the same quantity of bricks as they have made previously; do not diminish it, for they are lazy; that is why they cry, 'Let us go and offer sacrifice to our God.' 9 Let heavier work be laid on them; then they will labor at it and pay no attention to deceptive words. " 10 So the taskmasters and the supervisors of the people went out and said to the people, "Thus says Pharaoh, 'I will not give you straw. 11 Go and get straw yourselves, wherever you can find it; but your work will not be lessened in the least.' " 12 So the people scattered throughout the land of Egypt, to gather stubble for straw. 13 The taskmasters were urgent, saying, "Complete your work, the same daily assignment as when you were given straw." 14 And the supervisors of the Israelites, whom Pharaoh's taskmasters had set over them, were beaten, and were asked, "Why did you not finish the required quantity of bricks yesterday and today, as you did before?"15 Then the Israelite supervisors came to Pharaoh and cried, "Why do you treat your servants like this? 16 No straw is given to your servants, yet they say to us, 'Make bricks!' Look how your servants are beaten! You are unjust to your own people." 17 He said, "You are lazy, lazy; that is why you say, 'Let us go and sacrifice to the LORD.' 18 Go now, and work; for no straw shall be given you, but you shall still deliver the same number of bricks." 19 The Israelite supervisors saw that they were in trouble when they were told, "You shall not lessen your daily number of bricks." 20 As they left Pharaoh, they came upon Moses and Aaron who were waiting to meet them. 21 They said to them, "The LORD look upon you and judge! You have brought us into bad odor with Pharaoh and his officials, and have put a sword in their hand to kill us."22 Then Moses turned again to the LORD and said, "O LORD, why have you mistreated this people? Why did you ever send me? 23 Since I first came to Pharaoh to speak in your name, he has mistreated this people, and you have done nothing at all to deliver your people."*

(A textual note: I prefer the Septuagint in 5:3: "Our God" over the Masoretic text, which writes: "The LORD our God")

6.3.1 Source Division

Until this point, the elohistic narrative was usually found in recognizable sections throughout the canonical text. In the Plague and Exodus narratives the elohistic material is more sporadic, due to the extensive supplementation of the later sources. Thus the E material is scattered piecemeal throughout, at times in sections of no more than two verses, while the gaps between them are much longer. Nonetheless, when these sections are combined, a short but continuous elohistic narrative is revealed.

Subsequent to the yahwistic signs, Moses returns to Egypt. E is found again in verse 18 and can be identified as such by the appearance of the "elohistic" "Jethro," of which "Jether" is apparently a minor variation, whereas in J narratives Moses' father-in-law is called Reuel. Verse 19: "The LORD said to Moses in Midian, 'Go back to Egypt; for all those who were seeking your life are dead,'" is a yahwistic interpolation, which links this narrative to the yahwistic narrative in Ex. 2, specifically 2:15, where Pharaoh attempts to have Moses killed, and contradicts the elohistic reason for Moses' departure from Midian and Jethro given in chapter 3, and see also 4:18: "Moses went back to his father-in-law Jethro and said to him, 'Please let me go back to my kindred in Egypt and see whether they are still living.'"[31] The E narrative resumes in verse 20 and is identified as such by the "the staff of God," which is used by the elohistic Moses on other occasions.[32]

Verses 4:21-23 are in my opinion a late priestly summary of the plagues[33] which together with 11:9-10 create a priestly inclusio encompassing the plague cycle.[34] I attribute this text to a priestly author due to the distinction between the smiting of the first born and the remainder of the plagues which is similar to the distinction made by P in Chapter 12.[35] Another sign of priestly authorship is the term "מופת" (sign), used by P on other occasions (as in Ex. 7:8-14). Note also the appearance of the root ח.ז.ק (to harden), which, following Greenberg,[36] is evidence of priestly authorship. The three verses (4:21-23) are attributed to a late priestly author despite the unconventional use of Yhwh before Ex. 6 (P switches from Elohim to Yhwh only in Ex. 6:2,). In my opinion, the later priestly editor of the Pentateuch did not pay particular attention to divine names.

Verses 4:24-26 are enigmatic and their attribution to any of the usual sources/redactors is doubtful. To quote Childs:[37] "Few texts contain more problems for the interpreter than these few verses which have continued to baffle throughout the centuries." The passage is certainly not elohistic, since it mentions Moses' spouse by name, thus alluding to Ex. 2 (a yahwistic chapter).[38] The elohistic narrative continues with verse 27b with the reference to "Elohim's mountain."[39] I inserted Aaron's name in the second half of verse 27, since in my opinion it was taken out by the J redactor in order to avoid repeating the name twice in the same verse. The elimination of redundant sentence fragments is

31 Thus McNeile, *Exodus*, 26.
32 Driver, *Exodus*, 30.
33 Following Israel Knohl in an oral communication.
34 The attribution of 11:9-10 follows Wellhausen, *Hexateuch*, 68.
35 *Cf.* the divine involvement in the plague as opposed to Moses and Aaron's, the Israelite preparation, the Egyptian response. *cf.* Propp 1998, 310-317.
36 M. Greenberg, *Understanding Exodus*, New York, 1969.
37 Childs, *Exodus*, 95.
38 For a review of scholarship on this passage, see Propp *Exodus*, 233-238.
39 Thus McNeile, *Exodus*, 28, *et al.*

a common editorial technique which has been assumed elsewhere. According to E, the meeting between Aaron and Moses is miraculous and fulfils a literary purpose: Aaron is one of the brothers of verse 18 whom Moses wishes to see. This meeting should be compared to the miraculous meeting between Jacob and Esau in the E narrative of Gen. 33. Because an explanation of this sort does not satisfy the Yahwist, he adds verse 27a and explains that the meeting was not accidental. His desire to insert Yhwh and Yahwism at every juncture causes tension within J itself. In 4:14 the meeting is described as a surprise "and when he sees you his heart will be glad." Aaron, however, is not surprised, because he too received a command in verse 27a. In verse 28, Aaron, who will participate in the yahwistic plagues as Moses' spokesman and aide (4:15), is informed of their joint mission by Moses.

The existence of E material at the end of Chapter 4 and at the beginning of Chapter 5 is controversial. Many assume that there is no need whatsoever to divide the text, and that the end of Chapter 4 and all of Chapter 5 belong to the same source.[40] Moses' two demands of Pharaoh, as well as the different terms ("Pharaoh" and "the King of Egypt"), are, however, evidence of different sources,[41] especially since one of the pleas repeats the elohistic command of Ex. 3:18 ("The God of the Hebrews has met with us; let us now go a three days' journey into the wilderness, so that we may sacrifice to our God.").[42] The elohistic narrative thus resumes in verse 29 (following the insertion of vs. 28) and tells of the gathering of the Elders (cf. 3:18). Verse 5:3 describes the fulfillment of the next section of the divine command, i.e. the plea to leave Egypt.[43]

J in turn records the fulfillment of the yahwistic command to tell the People of Israel and the Elders about the mission (3:15-17) and to perform the miraculous signs (4:1-10). In Ex. 5:1, the Yahwist adds his usual prophetic formula "Thus says the LORD, the God of Israel" and in verse 2 Pharaoh responds to Moses' explanation that Yhwh has

---

40   Thus Wellhausen, *Hexateuch*, 72; and recently, Propp, *Exodus*, 249-251.

41   Thus Driver, *Exodus*, 33-36; McNeile, *Exodus*, 28-31, G. Fohrer, *Überlieferung und Geschichte des Exodus* (BZAW 91), Berlin, 1964, 43, adds his Nomadic source "N" to the equation.

42   U. Cassuto, *A Commentary on the Book of Exodus* (I. Abrahams tr.), Jerusalem, 65-66 explains that the two pleas form a natural progression, at first Moses approaches Pharaoh full of brash confidence, when he is rebuffed he quotes God's words verbatim.

43   Contra Noth, *Exodus*, 53, this is not a short Elohistic fragment, rather it is part of a short but complete episode.

commanded worship and sacrifice in the wilderness.[44] The elohistic
narrative continues with 5:3. I find it necessary to add the words "to
the King of Egypt" after "Then they said" because I believe they were
taken out due to J's mention of Pharaoh in 5:2. It is clear that the speech
is directed towards the king. J deleted the redundant reference "to the
King of Egypt," since if the King of Egypt answered Moses, it is probable that he (the "King" rather than "Pharaoh") was the character to
whom the question was addressed. The rest of the chapter is a yahwistic expansion of the King of Egypt's response and an elaboration of the
suffering of the Israelites and the type of work they did for the Egyptians. Both themes are found in the yahwistic additions to Chapters 1
and 3. Moreover, the yahwistic term "נגש" (taskmaster) (*cf.* J's Ex. 3:7)
appears here a number of times (5:5, 10, 12, 14).

6.3.2 The Yahwistic Commentary

In Ex. 4:19 the elohistic narrative states that Moses returned to Egypt
with his wife and sons. The terse Elohist, however, does not expand on
minor details and Moses' wife and sons remain anonymous. In Ex. 2:21
the Yahwist already mentioned Moses' wife "*Zipporah*," and the name
of one of his sons, "*Gershom*." The elohistic verse, however, explicitly
states "sons" in the plural: Where is Moses' second son? The difficult
episode concerning the attack on Moses and his family, beginning in vs.
4:24, may (advertently or inadvertently) provide a partial answer to this
question. While the episode is incomprehensible, the fact that Moses
has an "elder son" is narrative corroboration of at least one more child.
We learn the name of Moses' second son, Eliezer, in Ex. 18:3, which is
another yahwistic interpolation. (Compare the interest in family
throughout the previous narrative cycles.)

In vs. 20, the Elohist adds that Moses took the "staff of Elohim"
with him to Egypt. The Elohist does not feel it is necessary to explain
where and how Moses got this special staff. According to E, Moses
conducts the plagues with this staff and performs other miracles. In
contrast, the yahwistic historian feels it necessary to explain the source
of the staff and thus Ex. 4:2 opens with the question: "The LORD said
to him, 'What is that in your hand?'" According to J, Moses' staff is thus
merely a shepherd's staff lacking special powers. The ultimate power to
perform miracles comes from Yhwh. Ex. 4 emphasizes that Yhwh, not

---

44   McNeile and Driver's attribution of this verse to E is questionable since Moses'
     demand: "Let My people go" occurs throughout the Yahwistic plague narrative.

Moses, is the initiator of the miraculous signs. In fact, Moses is so afraid
that he even runs away from the snake in verse 3. According to J (but
not E), Moses' staff is no more than concretization of Yhwh's power.
Thus the Yahwist emphasizes in Ex. 4:17: "Take in your hand this staff,
with which you shall perform the signs," which is yet another case of a
proleptic insertion of a command, as we also see in 4:27a.

J's standard prophetic formula in 5:1: "Thus says the LORD, the
God of Israel," introduces Yhwh's true name to Pharaoh as opposed to
the anonymous elohistic entity, "The God of the Hebrews." According
to the Yahwist, the plagues emphasize the uniqueness of Yhwh, and it
is therefore important that Pharaoh know that Yhwh is the power behind them. These verses also add an element of negotiation to the text.
The first yahwistic request is forceful and very general: Ex. 5:1: "Thus
says the LORD, the God of Israel, 'Let my people go, so that they may
celebrate a festival to me in the wilderness.'" After Pharaoh's refusal,
the second request, which is elohistic, is more realistic.[45] Thus, Ex. 5:3:
"Let us go a three days' journey into the wilderness to sacrifice to our
God, or he will fall upon us with pestilence or sword."

The yahwistic verses at the end of Chapter 5 supplement E's
straightforward characterization. This time, instead of making the characters themselves more human, the Yahwist elaborates upon the relationship between characters. At the end of Chapter 4 (verses 30-31) the
Elders and the People of Israel listened to Moses and believed his signs.
The narrative in Chapter 5, however, alters their positive opinion of
Moses and Aaron. The Elders now turn to the brothers and in Ex. 5:21
say: "The LORD look upon you and judge! You have brought us into
bad odor with Pharaoh and his officials, and have put a sword in their
hand to kill us."

6.4 The Three Plagues (Ex. 9-10)

[[7:1 *The LORD said to Moses, "See, I have made you like God to Pharaoh, and your brother*
Aaron shall be your prophet. 2 You shall speak all that I command you, and your brother Aaron
shall tell Pharaoh to let the Israelites go out of his land. 3 But I will harden Pharaoh's heart, and I
will multiply my signs and wonders in the land of Egypt. 4 When Pharaoh does not listen to you, I
will lay my hand upon Egypt and bring my people the Israelites, company by company, out of the
land of Egypt by great acts of judgment. 5 The Egyptians shall know that I am the LORD, when I
stretch out my hand against Egypt and bring the Israelites out from among them." 6 Moses and
Aaron did so; they did just as the LORD commanded them. 7 Moses was eighty years old and

---

45   See comment 42.

Aaron eighty-three when they spoke to Pharaoh. 8 The LORD said to Moses and Aaron, 9 "When Pharaoh says to you, 'Perform a wonder,' then you shall say to Aaron, 'Take your staff and throw it down before Pharaoh, and it will become a snake.'" 10 So Moses and Aaron went to Pharaoh and did as the LORD had commanded; Aaron threw down his staff before Pharaoh and his officials, and it became a snake. 11Then Pharaoh summoned the wise men and the sorcerers; and they also, the magicians of Egypt, did the same by their secret arts. 12 Each one threw down his staff, and they became snakes; but Aaron's staff swallowed up theirs. 13 Still Pharaoh's heart was hardened, and he would not listen to them, as the LORD had said. 14 Then the LORD said to Moses, "Pharaoh's heart is hardened; he refuses to let the people go. 15 Go to Pharaoh in the morning, as he is going out to the water; stand by at the river bank to meet him, and take in your hand the staff that was turned into a snake. 16 Say to him, 'The LORD, the God of the Hebrews, sent me to you to say, "Let my people go, so that they may worship me in the wilderness." But until now you have not listened.' 17 Thus says the LORD, "By this you shall know that I am the LORD." See, with the staff that is in my hand I will strike the water that is in the Nile, and it shall be turned to blood. 18 The fish in the river shall die, the river itself shall stink, and the Egyptians shall be unable to drink water from the Nile.'" 19 The LORD said to Moses, "Say to Aaron, 'Take your staff and stretch out your hand over the waters of Egypt—over its rivers, its canals, and its ponds, and all its pools of water—so that they may become blood; and there shall be blood throughout the whole land of Egypt, even in vessels of wood and in vessels of stone.'" 20 Moses and Aaron did just as the LORD commanded. In the sight of Pharaoh and of his officials he lifted up the staff and struck the water in the river, and all the water in the river was turned into blood, 21 and the fish in the river died. The river stank so that the Egyptians could not drink its water, and there was blood throughout the whole land of Egypt. 22 But the magicians of Egypt did the same by their secret arts; so Pharaoh's heart remained hardened, and he would not listen to them; as the LORD had said. 23 Pharaoh turned and went into his house, and he did not take even this to heart. 24 And all the Egyptians had to dig along the Nile for water to drink, for they could not drink the water of the river. 25 Seven days passed after the LORD had struck the Nile. 8:1 Then the LORD said to Moses, "Go to Pharaoh and say to him, 'Thus says the LORD: Let my people go, so that they may worship me. 2 If you refuse to let them go, I will plague your whole country with frogs. 3 The river shall swarm with frogs; they shall come up into your palace, into your bedchamber and your bed, and into the houses of your officials and of your people, and into your ovens and your kneading bowls. 4 The frogs shall come up on you and on your people and on all your officials.'" 5 And the LORD said to Moses, "Say to Aaron, 'Stretch out your hand with your staff over the rivers, the canals, and the pools, and make frogs come up on the land of Egypt.'" 6 So Aaron stretched out his hand over the waters of Egypt; and the frogs came up and covered the land of Egypt. 7 But the magicians did the same by their secret arts, and brought frogs up on the land of Egypt. 8 Then Pharaoh called Moses and Aaron, and said, "Pray to the LORD to take away the frogs from me and my people, and I will let the people go to sacrifice to the LORD." 9 Moses said to Pharaoh, "Kindly tell me when I am to pray for you and for your officials and for your people, that the frogs may be removed from you and your houses and be left only in the Nile." 10 And he said, "Tomorrow." Moses said, "As you say! So that you may know that there is no one like the LORD our God, 11 the frogs shall leave you and your houses and your officials and your people;

they shall be left only in the Nile." 12 *Then Moses and Aaron went out from Pharaoh; and Moses cried out to the LORD concerning the frogs that he had brought upon Pharaoh.* 13 *And the LORD did as Moses requested: the frogs died in the houses, the courtyards, and the fields.* 14 *And they gathered them together in heaps, and the land stank.* 15 *But when Pharaoh saw that there was a respite, he hardened his heart, and would not listen to them, just as the LORD had said.* 16 *Then the LORD said to Moses, "Say to Aaron, 'Stretch out your staff and strike the dust of the earth, so that it may become gnats throughout the whole land of Egypt.'"* 17 *And they did so; Aaron stretched out his hand with his staff and struck the dust of the earth, and gnats came on humans and animals alike; all the dust of the earth turned into gnats throughout the whole land of Egypt.* 18 *The magicians tried to produce gnats by their secret arts, but they could not. There were gnats on both humans and animals.* 19 *And the magicians said to Pharaoh, "This is the finger of God!" But Pharaoh's heart was hardened, and he would not listen to them, just as the LORD had said.* 20 *Then the LORD said to Moses, "Rise early in the morning and present yourself before Pharaoh, as he goes out to the water, and say to him, 'Thus says the LORD: Let my people go, so that they may worship me.* 21 *For if you will not let my people go, I will send swarms of flies on you, your officials, and your people, and into your houses; and the houses of the Egyptians shall be filled with swarms of flies; so also the land where they live.* 22 *But on that day I will set apart the land of Goshen, where my people live, so that no swarms of flies shall be there, that you may know that I the LORD am in this land.* 23 *Thus I will make a distinction between my people and your people. This sign shall appear tomorrow.'"* 24 *The LORD did so, and great swarms of flies came into the house of Pharaoh and into his officials' houses; in all of Egypt the land was ruined because of the flies.* 25 *Then Pharaoh summoned Moses and Aaron, and said, "Go, sacrifice to your God within the land."* 26 *But Moses said, "It would not be right to do so; for the sacrifices that we offer to the LORD our God are offensive to the Egyptians. If we offer in the sight of the Egyptians sacrifices that are offensive to them, will they not stone us?* 27 *We must go a three days' journey into the wilderness and sacrifice to the LORD our God as he commands us."* 28 *So Pharaoh said, "I will let you go to sacrifice to the LORD your God in the wilderness, provided you do not go very far away. Pray for me."* 29 *Then Moses said, "As soon as I leave you, I will pray to the LORD that the swarms of flies may depart tomorrow from Pharaoh, from his officials, and from his people; only do not let Pharaoh again deal falsely by not letting the people go to sacrifice to the LORD."* 30 *So Moses went out from Pharaoh and prayed to the LORD.* 31 *And the LORD did as Moses asked: he removed the swarms of flies from Pharaoh, from his officials, and from his people; not one remained.* 32 *But Pharaoh hardened his heart this time also, and would not let the people go.* 9:1*Then the LORD said to Moses, "Go to Pharaoh, and say to him, 'Thus says the LORD, the God of the Hebrews: Let my people go, so that they may worship me.* 2 *For if you refuse to let them go and still hold them,* 3 *the hand of the LORD will strike with a deadly pestilence your livestock in the field: the horses, the donkeys, the camels, the herds, and the flocks.* 4 *But the LORD will make a distinction between the livestock of Israel and the livestock of Egypt, so that nothing shall die of all that belongs to the Israelites.'"* 5 *The LORD set a time, saying, "Tomorrow the LORD will do this thing in the land."* 6 *And on the next day the LORD did so; all the livestock of the Egyptians died, but of the livestock of the Israelites not one died.* 7 *Pharaoh inquired and found that not one of the livestock of the Israelites was dead. But the heart of Pharaoh was hardened, and he would not* *let the people go. 8 Then the LORD said to Moses and Aaron, "Take handfuls of soot from the kiln, and let Moses throw it in the air in the sight of Pharaoh. 9 It shall become fine dust all over the land of Egypt, and shall cause festering boils on humans and animals throughout the whole land of Egypt." 10 So they took soot from the kiln, and stood before Pharaoh, and Moses threw it in the air, and it caused festering boils on humans and animals. 11 The magicians could not stand before Moses because of the boils, for the boils afflicted the magicians as well as all the Egyptians. 12 But the LORD hardened the heart of Pharaoh, and he would not listen to them, just as the LORD had spoken to Moses.]]*

The Plague of Hail (Ex. 9)

13 *Then the LORD said to Moses, "Rise up early in the morning and present yourself before Pharaoh, and say to him, 'Thus says the LORD, the God of the Hebrews: Let my people go, so that they may worship me. 14 For this time I will send all my plagues upon you yourself, and upon your officials, and upon your people, so that you may know that there is no one like me in all the earth. 15 For by now I could have stretched out my hand and struck you and your people with pestilence, and you would have been cut off from the earth. 16 But this is why I have let you live: to show you my power, and to make my name resound through all the earth. 17 You are still exalting yourself against my people, and will not let them go. 18 Tomorrow at this time I will cause the heaviest hail to fall that has ever fallen in Egypt from the day it was founded until now. 19 Send, therefore, and have your livestock and everything that you have in the open field brought to a secure place; every human or animal that is in the open field and is not brought under shelter will die when the hail comes down upon them.'" 20 Those officials of Pharaoh who feared the word of the LORD hurried their slaves and livestock off to a secure place. 21 Those who did not regard the word of the LORD left their slaves and livestock in the open field. 22 The LORD said to Moses, "Stretch out your hand toward heaven so that hail may fall on the whole land of Egypt, on humans and animals and all the plants of the field in the land of Egypt."* 23 Then Moses stretched out his staff toward heaven; *and the LORD sent thunder and hail, and fire came down on the earth. And the LORD rained hail on the land of Egypt;* 24 there was hail with fire flashing continually in the midst of it, such heavy hail as had never fallen in all the land of Egypt since it became a nation. 25 The hail struck down everything that was in the open field throughout all the land of Egypt, both human and animal; the hail also struck down all the plants of the field, and shattered every tree in the field. 26 *Only in the land of Goshen, where the Israelites were, there was no hail. 27 Then Pharaoh summoned Moses and Aaron, and said to them, "This time I have sinned; the LORD is in the right, and I and my people are in the wrong. 28 Pray to the LORD! Enough of God's thunder and hail! I will let you go; you need stay no longer." 29 Moses said to him, "As soon as I have gone out of the city, I will stretch out my hands to the LORD; the thunder will cease, and there will be no more hail, so that you may know that the earth is the LORD's. 30 But as for you and your officials, I know that you do not yet fear the LORD God." 31(Now the flax and the barley were ruined, for the barley was in*

the ear and the flax was in bud. 32 But the wheat and the spelt were not ruined, for they are late in
coming up.) 33 So Moses left Pharaoh, went out of the city, and stretched out his hands to the
LORD; then the thunder and the hail ceased, and the rain no longer poured down on the earth. 34
But when Pharaoh saw that the rain and the hail and the thunder had ceased, he sinned once more
and hardened his heart, he and his officials.

The Plague of Locusts (Ex. 10)

10:1 *Then the LORD said to Moses, "Go to Pharaoh; for I have hardened his heart and the heart of*
his officials, in order that I may show these signs of mine among them, 2 and that you may tell
your children and grandchildren how I have made fools of the Egyptians and what signs I have
done among them—so that you may know that I am the LORD." 3 So Moses and Aaron went to
Pharaoh, and said to him, "Thus says the LORD, the God of the Hebrews, 'How long will you
refuse to humble yourself before me? Let my people go, so that they may worship me. 4 For if you
refuse to let my people go, tomorrow I will bring locusts into your country. 5 They shall cover the
surface of the land, so that no one will be able to see the land. They shall devour the last remnant
left you after the hail, and they shall devour every tree of yours that grows in the field. 6 They shall
fill your houses, and the houses of all your officials and of all the Egyptians—something that
neither your parents nor your grandparents have seen, from the day they came on earth to this
day.'" Then he turned and went out from Pharaoh. 7 Pharaoh's officials said to him, "How long
shall this fellow be a snare to us? Let the people go, so that they may worship the LORD their God;
do you not yet understand that Egypt is ruined?" 8 So Moses and Aaron were brought back to
Pharaoh, and he said to them, "Go, worship the LORD your God! But which ones are to go?" 9
Moses said, "We will go with our young and our old; we will go with our sons and daughters and
with our flocks and herds, because we have the LORD's festival to celebrate." 10 He said to them,
"The LORD indeed will be with you, if ever I let your little ones go with you! Plainly, you have
some evil purpose in mind. 11 No, never! Your men may go and worship the LORD, for that is
what you are asking." And they were driven out from Pharaoh's presence. 12 Then the LORD said
to Moses, "Stretch out your hand over the land of Egypt, so that the locusts may come upon it and
eat every plant in the land, all that the hail has left." 13 So Moses stretched out his
staff over the land of Egypt, *and the LORD brought an east wind upon the land all that*
day and all that night; and when morning came, the east wind had brought
the locusts. 14 The locusts came upon all the land of Egypt and settled
on the whole country of Egypt, such a dense swarm of locusts as had
never been before, nor ever shall be again. 15 They covered the surface
of the whole land, so that the land was black; and they ate all the plants
in the land and all the fruit of the trees that the hail had left; nothing
green was left, no tree, no plant in the field, in all the land of Egypt. 16
Pharaoh hurriedly summoned Moses and Aaron and said, "I have sinned against the LORD your
God, and against you. 17 Do forgive my sin just this once, and pray to the LORD your God that
at the least he remove this deadly thing from me." 18 So he went out from Pharaoh and prayed to

the LORD. 19 *The LORD changed the wind into a very strong west wind, which lifted the locusts and drove them into the Red Sea; not a single locust was left in all the country of Egypt.* 20 *But the LORD hardened Pharaoh's heart, and he would not let the Israelites go.*

The Plague of Darkness (Ex. 10)

21 *Then the LORD said to Moses, "Stretch out your hand toward heaven so that there may be darkness over the land of Egypt, a darkness that can be felt."* 22 So Moses stretched out his hand toward heaven, and there was dense darkness in all the land of Egypt for three days. 23 People could not see one another, and for three days they could not move from where they were; *but all the Israelites had light where they lived.* 24 *Then Pharaoh summoned Moses, and said, "Go, worship the LORD. Only your flocks and your herds shall remain behind. Even your children may go with you."* 25 *But Moses said, "You must also let us have sacrifices and burnt offerings to sacrifice to the LORD our God.* 26 *Our livestock also must go with us; not a hoof shall be left behind, for we must choose some of them for the worship of the LORD our God, and we will not know what to use to worship the LORD until we arrive there."* 27 *But the LORD hardened Pharaoh's heart, and he was unwilling to let them go.* 28 *Then Pharaoh said to him, "Get away from me! Take care that you do not see my face again, for on the day you see my face you shall die."* 29 *Moses said, "Just as you say! I will never see your face again."*

6.4.1 Source Division

Since I do not wish to embark on a long discussion of the non-elohistic plague narrative, I shall provide only a short description of the general themes which will help distinguish the elohistic text from J and P.[46] The Yahwist added five plagues to the basic E narrative, (blood, frogs, wild beasts, livestock epidemic and the death of the firstborn and extensively supplemented the original E plagues (hail, locusts and darkness). There are many scholars who find J, P, and E in the narration of the first plague of blood.[47] But as Greenberg[48] and Noth[49] convincingly demonstrate, two sources (J and P) are sufficient. (One should note that the final plague, the death of the firstborn, should not be counted as an actual plague, but rather as a prelude to the Exodus. Thus the tally of yahwistic plagues is actually seven.) Generally speaking (and for now,

---

46   This overview echoes Childs, *Exodus*, 133-141.
47   E.g. Driver, *Exodus*, 59-61, Childs, *Exodus*, 62.
48   Greenberg, *Understanding Exodus*, 85.
49   Noth, *Exodus*, 62.

not taking the E material into consideration) the yahwistic plagues follow the following plan: a) Before each plague Moses warns Pharaoh
regarding the nature and severity of the plague; b) Yhwh is the one
striking Egypt. The one exception is in the plague of blood, where
Yhwh uses Moses' staff as a medium (Ex. 7:17-20). The reason for this
may be that the first plague is actually an expansion of Moses' third
sign ("If they will not believe even these two signs or heed you, you
shall take some water from the Nile and pour it on the dry ground; and
the water that you shall take from the Nile will become blood on the
dry ground.") Ex. 4 makes it clear that while Moses is acting merely as
the messenger, he nevertheless "is obligated," to conduct the sign himself in order that the People of Israel believe in him. Perhaps this more
active role in the first plague is intended to have the same effect on
Pharaoh; c) Each plague is accompanied by negotiations between Pharaoh and Moses regarding the Exodus. This element also exists in the
preamble to the first plague (in Ex. 5), but the two parts are severed due
to the priestly interpolations (of Chapter 6 and the beginning of Chapter 7); d) The Yahwist emphasizes throughout his narrative that the
ultimate objective of the plagues is to prove Yhwh's dominance. Thus,
for example, Ex. 9:14-16: "For this time I will send all my plagues upon
you yourself, and upon your officials, and upon your people, so that
you may know that there is no one like me in all the earth... But this is
why I have let you live: to show you my power, and to make my name
resound through all the earth;" e) The plagues are highly formulaic:
Moses comes or appears before Pharaoh in Ex. 9:1 and states "Thus
says the LORD, the God of the Hebrews: Let my people go, so that they
may worship me." Following Moses' prayer and the plague's conclusion, Pharaoh hardens his heart; f) Beginning with the plague of wild
beasts, the Yahwist is careful to emphasize that Yhwh distinguishes
between Egypt and Israel and only the Egyptians are ravaged. The
themes enumerated above are for the most part expansions of, or answers to, questions arising from the terse elohistic narrative.[50]

The priestly redactor added the snake miracle (Ex. 7:1-13), and two
plagues of his own – lice and boils (8:16-19; 9:8-12). He is also involved
in the other plagues, most prominently in the plagues of blood and
frogs.[51] The following is a brief description of the priestly plague narra-

---

50   Cf. Van Seters ("The Plagues of Egypt, Ancient Tradition or Literary Invention",
     ZAW 98, (1986): 31-39.), who argues that the J plagues are a literary expansion of
     general Deuteronomic formulae such as "But the LORD brought us out of Egypt
     with a mighty hand" (Deut. 6:21).

51   According to Greenberg, *Understanding Exodus*, 187, and Noth, *Exodus*, 67 the plague
     of Darkness should also be attributed to P. Childs, *Exodus*, 131, counters and argues

tive: a) Contrary to the yahwistic plagues, Moses and Aaron conduct the plagues with no prior warning;[52] b) "The Magicians of Egypt" compete with Moses and Aaron until their ultimate defeat after the plague of boils; c) P emphasizes Aaron as a participant at every possible opportunity in accord with his prominent position as high priest; d) The Lord hardens (ק.ז.ח) Pharaoh's heart as opposed to Pharaoh's independent intransience in the J text. Some of the other "so called" priestly themes noted by scholars, such as paying no heed to time (the isolated P narrative makes no reference to the passing of time), depend upon the independence of the source according to the Documentary model and thus are not referred to.[53]

The traditional Documentary division identifies elohistic material in the plagues of blood, hail, locusts and darkness. However, many analyses attempt to show that the first plague is probably composed of only two sources – J and P. In general I agree with the Documentary division of the remaining plagues, but not with the conclusions.[54] Although the elohistic material is scarce, it is without a doubt the earliest layer, as the following analysis will attempt to show.

According to Driver's division of the plague of hailstones between J and E, Yhwh's command to Moses to wave his staff and the performance of the plague by Yhwh (9:22-23) are part of E.[55] This division, however, is difficult: If Yhwh commands Moses to point his staff skywards and Yhwh performs the plague, why does Moses need to wave this staff? There is no reason to suppose that Moses' act is in anyway theatrical or ostentatious. It is abundantly clear that according to these verses Yhwh is in total control, but if this is the case why does Moses even have a role? Why does the Deity not perform the plague on His own, as in the plagues of wild beasts and pestilence in Ex. 8:24 and 9:6? It is clear that either Moses or Yhwh was the original performer, but not

---

that: "by including much of the E material under P, Noth in effect, blurs the clear Priestly schema."

52   The deliberate intertwining of the Priestly and Yahwistic plagues produces a literary structure of two plagues with a warning followed by one without repeated three times – noted by Rashbam, Abravanel, and Greenberg, *Understanding Exodus*, 172ff.

53   In the case of P's purported timelessness (Propp, *Exodus*, 310). If P (as we posit) knows of J and E then there is no need for "time" since P followed the J chronology.

54   Graupner, *Elohist*, following the recent trend of modern documentary scholars, argues that there is no true Elohistic plague narrative – it may be true that the name Elohim is not present in these chapters, but the "staff of Elohim" brought in by E in 4:20 is, and see our arguments below for an Elohistic plague cycle as indicated by the tension between Moses' role and Yhwh's role in the plagues of Hail, Locusts, and Darkness.

55   Driver, *Exodus*, 74.

both. Since it is difficult to conceive of a later author emphasizing Moses, as the later sources (J, P, D) are more rather than less theocentric, I conclude that Yhwh's role is secondary here as well as in the plague of locusts.[56] Since the Yahwist's quest throughout the plague narrative is to stress Yhwh's superiority, he could not have Moses stealing the limelight. J subscribed to a conservative editorial methodology, whereby he made only the most minimal changes to the E corpus, and thus did not delete Moses; rather, he repeatedly emphasized Yhwh's responsibility for the plagues through his additions, at the expense of textual logic.

Here as in many other places, it is of course possible, to assume a third source that mediated between the anthropocentric elohistic tradition and the theocentric yahwistic tradition. My method (the Yahwist as the supplementary editor) is simpler since it assumes less and is therefore more likely.

Though short, the elohistic narrative is easy to identify. According to the Elohist, there were three plagues: hail, locusts and darkness. In all three plagues Moses strikes without warning. He is the sole initiator and uses his staff or his arm. The elohistic plagues are especially severe and their scope is emphasized in the text.

The plague of hail begins in 9:13 with the characteristic yahwistic introduction: "Then the LORD said to Moses, 'Rise up early in the morning and present yourself before Pharaoh, and say to him, "Thus says the LORD, the God of the Hebrews: Let my people go, so that they may worship me.'"" It continues with the reason for the plagues in general, namely, proving Yhwh's greatness (verses 15-16) and is followed by a characteristic warning in verses 17-21. The Yahwist then inserts a divine command to Moses (verse 22). The Elohist, on the other hand, begins his plagues with verse 9:23a, as Moses points his arms towards the heavens. Since the Yahwist wishes to emphasize that Yhwh and not Moses was responsible for the plagues he adds verse 9:23b: "And the LORD sent thunder and hail, and fire came down on the earth. And the LORD rained hail on the land of Egypt" as a precursor to the elohistic description in verses 24-25, which deal with the unique aspects of the plague. Verse 26 is another example of a yahwistic theme already delineated i.e. the distinction between Israel and Egypt. Verses 27-35 are a typical J conclusion, with the following elements: Pharaoh negotiates with Moses, Moses prays to Yhwh and stops the plague, but Pharaoh hardens his heart.

---

56 Cf. Childs, *Exodus*, 131, Gressmann, *Moses*, 85, argues that the Moseo-centric plague tradition is the more ancient, and see Loewenstamm, *Evolution*, 128-134.

The plague of locusts also begins with a yahwistic warning (10:1-6). However, here the negotiation takes place before the plague itself (verses 7-11), at the behest of Pharaoh's servants. As in the plague of hailstones, the Yahwist inserts a divine command (10:12) prior to the (original) performance of the plague by Moses. The Yahwist once again emphasizes that even though Moses waved his staff, Yhwh was the power behind the plague. The elohistic narrative resumes with two verses (14-15) describing the severity of the plague. A second yahwistic negotiation was added after the plague (verses 16-19) and possibly these additional negotiations further emphasize the severity of this plague. As always, Pharaoh hardens his heart (verse 20) and since the root "ח.ז.ק" (to make strong or hard) is used rather than the yahwistic "כ.ב.ד," this reference is probably priestly.

There is no warning prior to the plague of darkness, (*Contra* the yahwistic paradigm), but this is not surprising, since the plague of darkness is effective only because the populace had no time to prepare for it. Again, the Yahwist inserts a divine command prior to the elohistic plague. Moses performs this plague without his staff (10:22), which may be a variation. However, it is possible to understand this as a simple metonymy, since waving one's arm is understood by E as waving one's staff (14:16). In accordance with the paradigm, J adds that Israel continued to have light (10:23), while the Egyptians languished in darkness. In conclusion, the Yahwist adds the final negotiation between Pharaoh and Moses in verses 24-29.

My main disagreement with the standard Documentary analyses of the elohistic narratives of Exodus relates to their state of preservation. Contrary to Documentarians, my analysis shows that the elohistic narrative is brief, but nonetheless continuous. According to the Elohist, Moses is commanded to take the People of Israel out of Egypt; the manner in which this will take place is left to Moses. Moses arrives in Egypt and requests permission to leave from the King of Egypt. When the King of Egypt denies this request, Moses immediately retaliates by striking Egypt with three devastating plagues. Neither warning nor negotiations precede the plagues, thus rendering them all the more effective. The consternation which ensues causes the Egyptians to dispatch the Israelites without asking their king. After a hot pursuit, the king dies at sea.

6.4.2 The Yahwistic Commentary

It is quite possible that the yahwistic plague tradition is genuinely early rather than a literary invention à la Van Seters. Note the plague lists in Psalms 78, Psalms 105 and elsewhere which demonstrate the wide scope of the plague tradition.[57] The manner in which the Yahwist describes the plagues is, however, dependent upon the earlier elohistic narrative. Hence the yahwistic expansions address questions and difficulties that arise from the terse basic narrative. The most "disturbing" aspect of the elohistic plagues is their anthropocentrism. The Elohist portrays Moses as a magician. The more "advanced" Yahwist is uncomfortable with "magicians" and humans with supernatural powers, since this approach places at least some humans on the same plane as God and thus reduces divine prowess. J intercedes and laces the E narrative with divine commands, divine acts, and divine intercession. The Yahwist also adds five plagues of his own (or four plagues and the death of the firstborn). In the yahwistic plague narrative Moses is relegated to prophesying and warning, while the plagues are carried out by Yhwh. (According to the Yahwist, Moses does not excel even in those functions to which he is relegated, because he stutters.) Moses' "secondary" role is made all the more clear by the addition of the lengthy negotiations between him and Pharaoh, in which he is no more than God's mouthpiece.

The yahwistic warnings address the difficult theological conundrum: How can one man, let alone an entire nation, be punished so heavily, without adequate warning? The warnings are especially relevant after the addition of five yahwistic plagues. When Pharaoh hardens his heart, even after being warned, the responsibility for the ensuing plagues falls upon him. (According to J, Pharaoh hardens his heart, whereas according to P, the Lord hardens Pharaoh's heart.) Pharaoh's stubbornness helps the Yahwist explain why so many plagues were necessary. The warnings also continue to emphasize Yhwh's supremacy. His ability is further accentuated when he demonstrates that he can distinguish between Egypt and Israel. This last expansion also addresses the obvious question: What happened to the Israelites when Yhwh was striking Egypt?

The Yahwist had the option of inserting his plagues at any place he wished relative to the elohistic plagues. The severity of the E plagues is the reason for their appearance towards the end of the yahwistic narra-

---

57   For the relationship between the Psalmic traditions and the Pentateuchal plague narrative, see Loewenstamm, *Exodus*, 71.

tive, rather than at its beginning. The Yahwist emphasizes that these plagues in particular have the function of proving the primacy of Yhwh (9:14-16: "For this time I will send all my plagues upon you your-self...so that you may know that there is no one like me in all the earth....But this is why I have let you live: to show you my power, and to make my name resound through all the earth"). Yhwh can inflict severe plagues, yet continues to distinguish between Egypt and Israel, as promised in 8:22.

Due to the severity of the hail in Ex. 9:25: "The hail struck down everything that was in the open field throughout all the land of Egypt, both human and animal; the hail also struck down all the plants of the field, and shattered every tree in the field," the Yahwist finds it neces-sary to explain what is left for the locusts in Ex. 9:31-32: "Now the flax and the barley were ruined, for the barley was in the ear and the flax was in bud. But the wheat and the spelt were not ruined, for they are late in coming up." A description of the extent of the damage continues in 10:15: "And they ate all the plants in the land and all the fruit of the trees that the hail had left." After the plague of locusts, there is no way in which to damage the livelihood of the Egyptians further, since most of the livestock died in the plagues of disease and hail, while all the produce of two crop seasons was destroyed by the plagues of hail and locusts. Hence darkness, the subsequent plague, constitutes a change in tactics involving severe psychological warfare. The fear of darkness (which is a frontal attack against the Egyptian sun god) is what finally causes the inhabitants of Egypt (according to E), but not their king, to expel the Israelites from their country.[58]

6.5 The Exodus (Ex. 12-14)

11:1 *The LORD said to Moses, "I will bring one more plague upon Pharaoh and upon Egypt; afterwards he will let you go from here; indeed, when he lets you go, he will drive you away. 2 Tell the people that every man is to ask his neighbor and every woman is to ask her neighbor for objects of silver and gold." 3 The LORD gave the people favor in the sight of the Egyptians. Moreover, Moses himself was a man of great importance in the land of Egypt, in the sight of Pharaoh's officials and in the sight of the people. 4 Moses said, "Thus says the LORD: About midnight I will go out through Egypt. 5 Every firstborn in the land of Egypt shall die, from the firstborn of Pha-raoh who sits on his throne to the firstborn of the female slave who is behind the handmill, and all the firstborn of the livestock. 6 Then there will be a loud cry throughout the whole land of Egypt,*

---

58   For the importance of the sun god in the Egyptian Pantheon, see J. B. Pritchard (ed.),
     Ancient Near Eastern Texts Relating to the Old Testament, Princeton, 1955, 3-4.

such as has never been or will ever be again. 7 But not a dog shall growl at any of the Israelites—
not at people, not at animals—so that you may know that the LORD makes a distinction between
Egypt and Israel. 8 Then all these officials of yours shall come down to me, and bow low to me,
saying, 'Leave us, you and all the people who follow you.' After that I will leave." And in hot
anger he left Pharaoh. 9 The LORD said to Moses, "Pharaoh will not listen to you, in order that
my wonders may be multiplied in the land of Egypt." 10 Moses and Aaron performed all these
wonders before Pharaoh; but the LORD hardened Pharaoh's heart, and he did not let the People of
Israel go out of his land.

Legal Section (12:1-28) (not included)

12:29 *At midnight the LORD struck down all the firstborn in the land of Egypt, from the firstborn*
of Pharaoh who sat on his throne to the firstborn of the prisoner who was in the dungeon, and all
the firstborn of the livestock. 30 Pharaoh arose in the night, he and all his officials and all the
Egyptians; and there was a loud cry in Egypt, for there was not a house without someone dead. 31
Then he summoned Moses and Aaron in the night, and said, "Rise up, go away from my people,
both you and the Israelites! Go, worship the LORD, as you said. 32 Take your flocks and your
herds, as you said, and be gone. And bring a blessing on me too!" 33 The Egyptians urged
the people to hasten their departure from the land, for they said, "We
shall all be dead."34 So the people took their dough before it was leavened, with their kneading bowls wrapped up in their cloaks on their
shoulders. 35 *The Israelites had done as Moses told them; they had asked the Egyptians for*
jewelry of silver and gold, and for clothing, 36 and the LORD had given the people favor in the
sight of the Egyptians, so that they let them have what they asked. And so they plundered the
Egyptians. 37 The Israelites journeyed from Rameses to Succoth, about six hundred thousand men
on foot, besides children. 38 A mixed crowd also went up with them, and livestock in great num-
bers, both flocks and herds. 39 They baked unleavened cakes of the dough that they had brought out
of Egypt; it was not leavened, because they were driven out of Egypt and could not wait, nor had
they prepared any provisions for themselves. 40 The time that the Israelites had lived in Egypt was
four hundred thirty years. 41 At the end of four hundred thirty years, on that very day, all the
companies of the LORD went out from the land of Egypt. 42 That was for the LORD a night of
vigil, to bring them out of the land of Egypt. That same night is a vigil to be kept for the LORD by
all the Israelites throughout their generations.

Legal Section (12:43-13:16) (not included)

13:17 *When Pharaoh let the people go, God did not lead them by way of the land of the Philistines,*
although that was nearer; for God thought, "If the people face war, they may change their minds
and return to Egypt." 18 So God led the people by the roundabout way of the wilderness toward
the Red Sea. The Israelites went up out of the land of Egypt prepared for battle. 19 And Moses took
with him the bones of Joseph who had required a solemn oath of the Israelites, saying, "God will
surely take notice of you, and then you must carry my bones with you from here." 20 They set out

from Succoth, and camped at Etham, on the edge of the wilderness. 21 *The LORD went in front of them in a pillar of cloud by day, to lead them along the way, and in a pillar of fire by night, to give them light, so that they might travel by day and by night.* 22 *Neither the pillar of cloud by day nor the pillar of fire by night left its place in front of the people.* 14:1 *Then the LORD said to Moses:* 2 *Tell the Israelites to turn back and camp in front of Pi-hahiroth, between Migdol and the sea, in front of Baal-zephon; you shall camp opposite it, by the sea.* 3 *Pharaoh will say of the Israelites, "They are wandering aimlessly in the land; the wilderness has closed in on them."* 4 *I will harden Pharaoh's heart, and he will pursue them, so that I will gain glory for myself over Pharaoh and all his army; and the Egyptians shall know that I am the LORD. And they did so.* 5 When the King of Egypt was told that the people had fled; *the minds of Pharaoh and his officials were changed toward the people, and they said, "What have we done, letting Israel leave our service?"* 6 *So he had his chariot made ready, and took his army with him;* 7 he took six hundred picked chariots and all the other chariots of Egypt with officers over all of them. 8 *The LORD hardened the heart of Pharaoh King of Egypt and he pursued the Israelites, who were going out boldly.* 9 The Egyptians pursued them, *all Pharaoh's horses and chariots, his chariot drivers and his army;* and they overtook them camped by the sea, *by Pi-hahiroth, in front of Baal-zephon.* 10 *As Pharaoh drew near, the Israelites looked back, and there were the Egyptians advancing on them. In great fear the Israelites cried out to the LORD.* 11 *They said to Moses, "Was it because there were no graves in Egypt that you have taken us away to die in the wilderness? What have you done to us, bringing us out of Egypt?* 12 *Is this not the very thing we told you in Egypt, 'Let us alone and let us serve the Egyptians'? For it would have been better for us to serve the Egyptians than to die in the wilderness."* 13 *But Moses said to the people, "Do not be afraid, stand firm, and see the deliverance that the LORD will accomplish for you today; for the Egyptians whom you see today you shall never see again.* 14 *The LORD will fight for you, and you have only to keep still."* 15 *Then the LORD said to Moses, "Why do you cry out to me? Tell the Israelites to go forward.* 16 *But you lift up your staff, and stretch out your hand over the sea and divide it, that the Israelites may go into the sea on dry ground.* 17 *Then I will harden the hearts of the Egyptians so that they will go in after them; and so I will gain glory for myself over Pharaoh and all his army, his chariots, and his chariot drivers.* 18 *And the Egyptians shall know that I am the LORD, when I have gained glory for myself over Pharaoh, his chariots, and his chariot drivers."* 19 The angel of God who was going before the Israelite army moved and went behind them; *and the pillar of cloud moved from in front of them and took its place behind them.* 20 and came between the army of Egypt and the army of Israel; *And so the cloud was there with the darkness, and it lit up the night;* one did not come near the other all night. 21 Then Moses stretched out his hand over the sea. *The LORD drove the sea back by a strong east wind all night,* and turned the sea into dry land; and the waters were divided. 22 The Israelites went into the sea on dry ground, the waters forming a wall for them on their right and on their left. 23 The Egyptians pursued, and went into the sea after them, *all of Pharaoh's horses, chariots, and chariot drivers.* 24 *At the morning watch the LORD in the pillar of fire and cloud looked down upon the Egyptian army, and threw the Egyptian army into panic. 25 He clogged their chariot wheels so that they turned with difficulty. The Egyptians said, "Let us flee from the Israelites, for the LORD is fighting for them against Egypt." 26 Then the LORD said to Moses, "Stretch out your hand over the sea, so that the water may come back upon the Egyptians, upon their chariots and chariot drivers."* 27 So Moses stretched out his hand over the sea, and at dawn the sea returned to its normal depth. *As the Egyptians fled before it, the LORD tossed the Egyptians into the sea.* 28 The waters returned and covered the chariots and the chariot drivers, *the entire army of Pharaoh that had followed them into the sea;* not one of them remained. *29 But the Israelites walked on dry ground through the sea, the waters forming a wall for them on their right and on their left. 30 Thus the LORD saved Israel that day from the Egyptians; and Israel saw the Egyptians dead on the seashore. 31 Israel saw the great work that the LORD did against the Egyptians. So the people feared the LORD and believed in the LORD and in his servant Moses.*

6.5.1 Source Division

While the elohistic account of Israel's Exodus from Egypt is undoubtedly the most diffuse of any elohistic account, I believe that it is nevertheless possible to isolate it. According to J and P, the reason that Pharaoh finally lets Israel leave is the ultimate devastation following the death of every firstborn. The shock is so profound that instead of Moses and Aaron coming to Pharaoh, he comes to them and demands that they leave Egypt; Ex. 12:31-32: "Then he summoned Moses and Aaron in the night, and said, 'Rise up, go away from my people, both you and the Israelites! Go, worship the LORD, as you said. Take your flocks and your herds, as you said, and be gone. And bring a blessing on me too!'" These verses and this idea, however, contradict Ex. 14:5: "The King of Egypt was told that the people had fled...". While this contradiction is tempered somewhat by the yahwistic addition to the verse: "The minds of Pharaoh and his officials were changed toward the people, and they said, 'What have we done, letting Israel leave our service?'", there is no escaping the linguistic and thematic parallel to Jacob's flight, reported to Laban after the fact: "So he fled with all that he had; starting out he crossed the Euphrates. On the third day Laban was told that Jacob had fled." (Gen. 31:21-22). Verse 14:5a is thus at odds with much of the canonical account and no amount of editorial obfuscation can cover this up. This verse and the tradition that Israel escaped Egypt are almost certainly elohistic. (Note also the use of the expression "King of Egypt,", as opposed to "Pharaoh"). But where does the story begin?

In my opinion, the beginning of the elohistic account is found in 12:33: "The Egyptians urged the people to hasten their departure from the land, for they said, 'We shall all be dead.'" This verse is an anomaly. It is the only verse in the entire plague narrative which relates to the desires of the commoners. Pharaoh sends his slave nation to worship their God, but the Egyptians expel them altogether. Since Pharaoh was warned, in 11:4-8, the Egyptian fear of total annihilation contradicts the yahwistic tradition that Pharaoh (and hence Egypt) knew of the impending ultimate plague.

On the other hand, 12:33 is comprehensible when taken as part of the elohistic account. According to the Elohist, the King of Egypt consulted with his people before enslaving Israel, Ex. 1:9-10: "He said to his people, 'Look, the Israelite people are mightier and more powerful than we. Come, let us deal shrewdly with them, or they will increase and, in the event of war, join our enemies and fight against us and escape from the land.'" In Ex. 12:33 the Egyptians, realizing that their "conniving" king is responsible for their dire predicament, take matters into their own hands and decide to banish Israel. The king's prediction that they will escape from the land (Ex. 1:10) is realised. In an ironic twist, the steps the king takes to prevent this eventuality ultimately bring about Israel's salvation and his downfall.

The Israelites are expelled by the Egyptians following the plague of darkness; Ex. 10:23: "People could not see one another, and for three days they could not move from where they were." The fear of darkness, one of the most basic fears, affected all Egyptians. Their immediate reaction was to banish the cause of all their troubles. When the king hears that the People of Israel have left without his consent—"an escape," in his view—he gives chase.[59]

One and a half chapters separate this fragment of the story from the rest of the elohistic tradition and the intervening material is certainly diverse. The first insertion is the "borrower" tradition, which appears for the third and last time in Ex. 12:35-36, and we are inclined to tie it to the late Gen. 15:14 ("But I will bring judgment on the nation that they serve, and afterward they shall come out with great possessions"). The priestly source then adds his usual chronistic details, namely the number of Israelites and the years they spent in Egypt (12:37-42). Ex. 12:43-51 sum up the laws of the priestly Passover and 13:1-2 add the laws of the firstborn (also P).[60] Chapter 13:3-16, the second cluster of such laws, again the laws of primogeniture, is usually attributed to Deuteronomis-

---

59 According to Kohata, *Jahwist und Priesterschrift*, 280, who has a much shorter E source, the escape is a natural progression following the revelation to Moses in ch. 3.
60 Propp, *Exodus*, 373ff, et al.

tic redaction though its divergence from mainstream Deuteronomistic language should be noted.[61]

A short summary of previous scholarship is in order prior to presenting my own analysis of 13:17-14:31. Opinions regarding the division of this account may be divided into two groups: The first "school of thought," beginning with Wellhausen [62] claims that P's participation is at best sporadic and that verses attributed to P by other scholars are usually elohistic. Other scholars go further and claim that P does not take part in this account at all and that the Exodus narrative should be divided between the pre-priestly sources.[63] Subscribers to the second school of thought assume that P participated in the Exodus account in a significant way, but are divided as to P's precise role. There are those who assume that at least in this instance P is a supplementary redactor,[64] but other scholars claim that P is independent.[65] One of the main points of contention is the source of Moses' staff (14:21, 27).[66] Those who claim that E participated in this account believe that Moses' use of the staff is an elohistic indicator, basing themselves upon its appearance in E's plagues. If, however, one does not find E in the plague narrative, attributing Moses' staff to P is natural, since P emphasizes the human role more than J and Aaron does perform miracles with his staff. Even those who maintain that E did participate in this narrative assume that the Exodus account is fragmented. Yet, if the parting of the Red Sea (by means of Moses' staff) is attributed to E, a continuous account can be isolated.

---

61 And thus some scholars attribute the section to J. (Thus Driver *Exodus*, 106-110; Clements 1972, 78), which accords with the blurring of boundaries between J and D in scholarship, and see H. H. Schmid, *Der Sogenannte Jahwist, Beobactungen und Fragen zur Pentateuch Forschung*, Zürich, 1976, and M. Rose, *Deuteronomist und Jahwist: Untersuchungen zu den Beruehrungspunkten beider Literatur*, Zürich.

62 Wellhausen, *Hexateuch*, 75-77.

63 Smend, *Hexateuch*, 137-144; O. Eissfeldt, *Hexateuch Synopse*, Leipzig, 35-37; G. Fohrer, *Überlieferung und Geschichte des Exodus* (BZAW 91), Berlin, 1964, 98.

64 J. Van Seters, *The Life of Moses, The Yahwist as Historian in Exodus – Numbers*, Kampen, 1994, 128-139.

65 Blum, *Studien*, 256-262; H. C. Schmitt, "Priesterliches" und "prophetisches" Geschichts-verständnis in der Meerwundererzählung Ex. 13,17-14,31, in *Textgemäss* (A. H. J. Gunneweg and O. Kaiser eds.), Göttingen: 139-155.

66 Cf. Childs, *Exodus*, 219.

6.5.2 My Division

At first glance, the elohistic account continues/begins in 13:17-19.[67] The evidence is, however, ambiguous. Verse 17 states "When Pharaoh let the people go, God did not lead them by way of the land of the Philistines, although that was nearer; for God thought, 'If the people face war, they may change their minds and return to Egypt.'" However, as mentioned above, "the King of Egypt" does not expel the Israelites from his kingdom; rather, the Israelites escape (14:5). Moreover, according to verse 17, not "Pharaoh" but the elohistic "King of Egypt" sends them off. The continuation of the verse, however, uses the term "Elohim" — an E term par excellence — at this point, since P stopped using this general appellation in Ex. 6:2 ("God also spoke to Moses and said to him: 'I am the LORD.'"). This mélange of elements from various sources can also be found in other texts (Gen. 46:5-27 and Ex. 4:21-23) and was attributed above to the post-P redactor B.[68]

The priestly chronicle of the Israelite's journey continues in verse 20.[69] Verses 21-22, which describe how Yhwh led the Israelites, is either a priestly expansion of verse 20 or a yahwistic expansion of the E introduction to the Exodus account which ended in 12:34. The attribution of these verses to the J account would mean that *none* of the intervening legal sections are yahwistic (since the verses would interrupt the flow). The idea of God appearing in a cloud is found in J (Ex. 34:5: "The LORD descended in the cloud and stood with him there, and proclaimed the name, 'The LORD.'"), but especially in P. (*cf.* the Sinai periscope, Ex. 19:9: "Then the LORD said to Moses, 'I am going to come to you in a dense cloud, in order that the people may hear when I speak with you and so trust you ever after.'")

The first verses of Chapter 14 are priestly (note the typical priestly introduction of verse 1 and the root "ח.ז.ק" (to make hard) which is the priestly equivalent of "כ.ב.ד"). They perform two functions: one is to have God command the Israelites to go (*cf.* the proleptic insertions in other episodes, such as, Gen. 29:3; 31:2-3; 35:1; Ex. 4:27, etc.); the second is to describe God as all-powerful and omniscient, (*cf.* Ex. 14:4: "'I will harden Pharaoh's heart, and he will pursue them, so that I will gain glory for myself over Pharaoh and all his army; and the Egyptians shall

---

67   Thus Wellhausen, *Hexateuch*, 77; Propp, *Exodus*, 461; Graupner, *Elohist*, 411.

68   Rendtorff, *Überlieferung*, 77; T. Krüger, Erwägungen zur Redaktion der Meerwundererzählung (Ex 13,17-14,31), *ZAW* 108 (1996): 519-533; and cf. Gressmann, *Moses*, 110, who argues that the Israel's first and primary destination was "Elohim's mount" – and thus attributes these verses to a later tradition.

69   Wellhausen, *Hexateuch*, 76.

know that I am the LORD.' And they did so.") God is privy to Pharaoh's thoughts and desires and influences them. The theme of omnipotence is found twice more in this section: once in 14:8 ("The LORD hardened the heart of Pharaoh King of Egypt and he pursued the Israelites, who were going out boldly"), while the chase is in progress, and a second time before the Deity causes Pharaoh and his army to enter the sea (14:17).

The E narrative resumes in Ex. 14:5a (The King of Egypt was told that the people had fled). This verse (without the yahwistic interpolation at its end) uses the same language as E's Gen. 31:22: "On the third day Laban was told that Jacob had fled," which also belongs to the elohistic source. Verses 6 and 7 are also elohistic, since any other attribution would pose difficulties. The King of Egypt pursues Israel with a mere six hundred chariots (verse 7)—a minute number compared to the six-hundred thousand men on the Israelite side according to P (12:37) and J (cf. 18:21a). The Israelites would easily have overcome so small an Egyptian contingent. According to E, the Israelite population is so small that "twelve springs of water and seventy palm trees" (Ex. 15:27) are enough to sustain them and small enough for Moses to judge them all (Ex. 18). Hence even a small Egyptian force would suffice to frighten the Israelites into submission. In order to solve this problem, the Yahwist inflates the number of Egyptians (in 14:9, 28 as glosses to the E verses and in 14:18, 23 as part of more extensive additions) and emphasizes that Pharaoh pursued the Israelites with his entire army, with all his chariots and cavalry.

A further yahwistic expansion (14:10-14) describes what the People of Israel felt when they saw Pharaoh pursuing them and when they heard Moses' promise to redeem them. Ex. 14:15-18, which are also yahwistic, introduce the Elohistic parting of the Red Sea with the customary proleptic insertion of the divine command. The E account continues in verses 19-20 with a short statement regarding the protection afforded by the angel of Elohim.[70] The way in which this protection is achieved (19b-20a) is a yahwistic or priestly addition[71] which seeks to limit the anthropomorphic revelation of God and his angels and thus describes the angel's protective presence as a screen of clouds. This same pillar of clouds attacks the Egyptians in verse 23-25: "The Egyptians pursued, and went into the sea after them, all of Pharaoh's horses, chariots, and chariot drivers. At the morning watch the LORD in the pillar of fire and cloud looked down upon the Egyptian army, and

---

70   Driver, *Exodus*, 118.
71   Driver, *Exodus*, 118.

threw the Egyptian army into panic." Part of verse 21: "The LORD drove the sea back by a strong east wind all night, and turned the sea into dry land," and the end of verse 27: "As the Egyptians fled before it, the LORD tossed the Egyptians into the sea," are yahwistic interpolations in the same vein as this author's plague narrative and emphasize Yhwh's ultimate responsibility for the miracles preformed by Moses. Ex. 14:29-31 are the yahwistic introduction to Israel's song of praise (Chapter 15).

To summarize: The E episode begins with Israel's expulsion by the commoners (Ex. 12:33-34), the King of Egypt then gives chase (Ex. 14:5-7), but the Israelites are protected by Elohim's angel (14:19a, 20a). Finally Israel passes through the Reed Sea, which Moses had parted with his staff (14:21-23, 27). Moses then fuses the divided Reed Sea together and the Egyptians drown (14:28).

6.5.3 The Yahwistic Commentary

According to J, the impetus for the expulsion of the Israelites from Egypt was the plague of the firstborn. This is probably an ancient tradition rather than a literary construct, since it is corroborated by other biblical texts (e.g. Ps. 78 and Ps. 105). Ancient tradition or not, the plague contributes to textual coherence. The last elohistic plague was the plague of darkness which, regardless of its psychological influence, would not convince someone as obstinate as Pharaoh is in the J narrative. Only a plague that strikes at the heart of the nation can convince this stubborn king to let the Israelites go.

In my division, I noted that the yahwistic supplement to this account does not differ from his extensive additions to previous narratives (especially the plague chapters). Thus, almost all yahwistic additions to this account emphasize Yhwh's power. Another redactional theme is the emphasis on numbers. According to the Priestly author (and to a lesser extent J), the Israelites were in Egypt for many years and multiplied exponentially. According to E, the People of Israel did indeed multiply, but they were not in Egypt for such a long time. The impression at the beginning of the elohistic narrative is of no more than one or two generations at most after the death of Joseph, as we see in Ex. 1:8. Thus despite their fertility, their numbers are much smaller. The Yahwist thus emphasizes the size of Pharaoh's army in an attempt to deal with this discrepancy. Finally, the yahwistic interpolation that describes the reaction of the nation when they see Egypt pursuing them adds an emotional dimension to the narrative. Their fear at the begin-

ning of the account neatly contrasts with the praise of the Song of the
Sea in Chapter 15.

6.6 Water Shortages (Ex. 15 [Ex. 17])

22 Then Moses ordered Israel to set out from the Red Sea, and they
went into the wilderness of Shur. They went three days in the wilderness and found no water. 23 When they came to Marah, they could not
drink the water of Marah because it was bitter. *That is why it was called Marah.*
24 And the people complained against Moses, saying, "What shall we
drink?" 25 *He cried out to the LORD; and the LORD showed him a piece of wood; he threw it
into the water, and the water became sweet. There the LORD made for them a statute and an
ordinance and there he put them to the test. 26 He said, "If you will listen carefully to the voice of
the LORD your God, and do what is right in his sight, and give heed to his commandments and
keep all his statutes, I will not bring upon you any of the diseases that I brought upon the Egyptians; for I am the LORD who heals you."* 27 Then they came to Elim, where there
were twelve springs of water and seventy palm trees; and they camped
there by the water.
    *17:1From the wilderness of Sin the whole congregation of the Israelites journeyed by stages,
as the LORD commanded. They camped at Rephidim, but there was no water for the people to
drink. 2 The people quarreled with Moses, and said, "Give us water to drink." Moses said to them,
"Why do you quarrel with me? Why do you test the LORD?" 3 But the people thirsted there for
water; and the people complained against Moses and said, "Why did you bring us out of Egypt, to
kill us and our children and livestock with thirst?" 4 So Moses cried out to the LORD, "What
shall I do with this people? They are almost ready to stone me." 5 The LORD said to Moses, "Go
on ahead of the people, and take some of the Elders of Israel with you; take in your hand the staff
with which you struck the Nile, and go. 6 I will be standing there in front of you on the rock at
Horeb. Strike the rock, and water will come out of it, so that the people may drink." Moses did so,
in the sight of the Elders of Israel. 7 He called the place Massah and Meribah, because the Israelites
quarreled and tested the LORD, saying, "Is the LORD among us or not?"*

6.6.1 Source Division

It is difficult to attribute Ex. 15:22-27 to a specific source. Verses 22, 23
and 27 describe Israel's desert journey and although chronistic verses
are usually attributed to P,[72] these verses are an integral part of the

---

72   W. Johnstone, From the Sea to The Mountain, Ex. 15:22-19:2, a Case Study in
    Editorial Techniques, in *Studies in the Book of Exodus* (M. Vervenne ed.), Leuven, 1996,
    245-263, divides the section between P and a Deuteronomistic redactor.

narrative (as opposed to other P chronicles). As Wellhausen shows,[73] the verses do not employ priestly language or phraseology.[74] Indeed, verses 24-25a are often assigned to the original (elohistic) account.[75] Although the obvious indicators are absent, I concur with Driver that E is probably the author of much of this passage.[76]

The core narrative begins in verse 22, in which Moses "transports Israel" (in Hebrew, "ויסע" (the hifil of נ.ס.ע)). This verbal form is not found in other places in the Pentateuch and contrasts with the usual priestly terms ("ויסעו" "ויחנו" "they set out," "they camped"). "Israel" (ישראל) is the older term (as opposed to P's "בני ישראל," "the Children of Israel") and common in E texts, and to a lesser extent in J texts (e.g. Ex. 18:1, 9; Num. 21:1-3).[77] The theme of this short narrative is lack of water. The first station, Marah, does not solve the water shortage since the water there is bitter (verse 24) and unpotable. The canonical narrative provides two solutions: first Moses drops a piece of wood into the water (verse 25a), then, in verse. 27, Israel arrives at the desert oasis of Elim. The second solution is probably the original and authentic one. Elim could conceivably accommodate the small elohistic nation, but not the inflated numbers posited by J and P (in Ex. 12:37 and 18:21). Chapter 16 gives P's explanation of how God fed the huge Israelite nation by raining manna upon them. The solution in verse 25a is typically yahwistic: Moses acts as Yhwh's representative and does not initiate any independent action except for prayer.

6.6.2 The Yahwistic Commentary

The Yahwist adds his own solution to the Israelites' water shortage (15:25-26), expanding the narrative for two reasons. To walk three days in the desert without water is torture, and one could conceivably ask why Yhwh did not address this need immediately. Why must the nation be left to their own devices? The Yahwist[78] answers both these questions in his interpolation. According to J, the desert march was a

---

73   Wellhausen, *Hexateuch*, 77-78.

74   Cf. Van Seters, *Moses*, 155ff. who assigns the episode in its entirety to J, and Propp, *Exodus*, 573, 582 who attributes the verses to a non Priestly redactor.

75   Cf. Noth, *Exodus*, 127.

76   Driver, *Exodus*, 141-144.

77   See A. Besters, "Israel" et "fils d'Israel" dans les Livres Historiques: Genèse–II Rois, *RB* 74 (1967): 5-23.

78   Or the Deuteronomistic redactor according to Childs, *Exodus*, 266; E. Aurelius, *Der Fürbitter Israel: Eine Studie Zum Mosebild im Alten Testament*, Stockholm, 1988.

trial of faith; Ex. 15:25: "And there he put them to the test," which is similar to the yahwistic test in Ex. 17:7 (another narrative dealing with the water shortage): "He called the place Massa and Meribah, because the Israelites quarreled and tested the LORD, saying, 'Is the LORD among us or not?'" When the need became dire, Yhwh was indeed able to provide. He sweetened the bitter water in the same manner He conducted the plagues, with Moses' mediation. The sweetening of the water is parallel to the yahwistic plague of blood:[79] Blood is the first Yahwisitc plague, while the sweetening of the water is the first miracle Yhwh performs in the desert. In one, Yhwh befouls the water, while in the other he purifies it. The means in both cases is a piece of wood. The Yahwist alludes to this connection in verse Ex. 15:26 by referring to "Egyptian diseases."

6.7 The War with Amalek (Ex. 17)

8 Then Amalek came and fought with Israel at Rephidim. 9 Moses said to Joshua, "Choose some men for us and go out, fight with Amalek. Tomorrow I will stand on the top of the hill with the staff of God in my hand." 10 So Joshua did as Moses told him, and fought with Amalek, while Moses, Aaron, and Hur went up to the top of the hill. 11 Whenever Moses held up his hand, Israel prevailed; and whenever he lowered his hand, Amalek prevailed. 12 But Moses' hands grew weary; so they took a stone and put it under him, and he sat on it. Aaron and Hur held up his hands, one on one side, and the other on the other side; so his hands were steady until the sun set. 13 And Joshua defeated Amalek and his people with the sword. 14 *Then the LORD said to Moses, "Write this as a reminder in a book and recite it in the hearing of Joshua: I will utterly blot out the remembrance of Amalek from under heaven." 15 And Moses built an altar and called it, The LORD is my banner. 16 He said, "A hand upon the banner of the LORD The LORD will have war with Amalek from generation to generation."*

6.7.1 Source Division

Chapter 16 is a late priestly etiology explaining the Manna and the origin of the Sabbath. The beginning of Chapter 17 is essentially another

---

79   See B. P. Robinson, Symbolism in Ex. 15:22-27 Marah and Elim, *RB* 94 (1987): 376-388.

yahwistic miracle account, with some priestly interpolation.[80] The elo-
histic narrative begins in verse 8 and continues without interruption
until verse 13.[81] Evidence of elohistic authorship is abundant: "Elohim,"
"Hur" (who appears in the E's Ex. 24:13), Moses' staff and "Israel."
Verses 14-16 are a short yahwistic appendix to this episode,[82] in which
Yhwh commands Moses to remind Joshua to totally annihilate Amalek,
thus connecting this narrative to the broader biblical context. (See
Saul's war against Amalek in I Sam. 15.)

6.7.2 The Yahwistic Commentary

The yahwistic interpolation at the end of Chapter 17 is difficult. Why
should Amalek be singled out and other troublesome nations be "let off
easy"?[83] In order to understand the divine command one must compare
this yahwistic addendum with the Deuteronomic tradition. In Deut.
25:17-19 the war with Amalek is portrayed as a despicable and coward-
ly ambush: "Remember what Amalek did to you on your journey out
of Egypt, how he attacked you on the way, when you were faint and
weary, and struck down all who lagged behind you; he did not fear
God. Therefore… you shall blot out the remembrance of Amalek from
under heaven; do not forget.". While this is not the appropriate context
for a full discussion regarding the J-D relationship, one thing is clear: J
would not have added a divine injunction of such a nature without a
tradition or (more likely) an understanding of E's account close to the
one found in the book of Deuteronomy.[84] For this reason, many scholars consider the verses here a Deuteronomistic addition.[85] Amalek's
fate is not unique: According to J, when a nation initiates a war against
Israel without reason its fate is total destruction, as we see when the
Canaanites dwelling in Arad are killed and their city razed following
their unprovoked attack on Israel (Num. 21:1-3). According to E, Og

---

80   Wellhausen, *Hexateuch*, 79; Childs, *Exodus*, 306.
81   Thus McNeile, *Exodus*, 102-103; Driver, *Exodus*, 158; Noth, *Exodus*, 141 attribute this
     passage to J – consistent with Noth's doubts regarding the presence of Elohistic
     passages in the book of Exodus in general.
82   Cf. Noth, *Exodus*, 143-144, who also divides between 17:8-13 and 17:14-16.
83   J. Grønbaek, Juda und Amalek – Überlieferungsgeschichtliche Erwägungen zu
     Exodus 17, 8 –16, *Studia Theologica* 18 (1964): 26-45, conjectures that these final verses
     were added at a time when Amalek and Israel were once more at war.
84   Van Seters, *Moses*, 202-207, argues that this episode in its entirety is an expansion of
     the shorter Deuteronomistic tradition.
85   Cf. Childs, *Exodus*, 313.

and his nation were annihilated for initiating hostilities in Num. 21:33-35. In Num. 21:34, J lets us understand that this was also the fate of the Amorite king Sihon. (According to Num. 21:21-25 [E], the Israelites defeated the Amorites, but annihilation is not mentioned.) Moses ensures that the divine injunction is remembered by building the "Yhwh Nisi" altar (Ex. 17:14-16). Perhaps this hints that Yhwh was the real source of Israel's victory.[86]

6.8 Jethro Aids Moses (Ex. 18)

1 Jethro, the priest of Midian, Moses' father-in-law, heard of all that God had done for Moses and for his people Israel, *how the LORD had brought Israel out of Egypt.* 2 *After Moses had sent away his wife Zipporah, his father-in-law Jethro took her back,* 3 *along with her two sons. The name of the one was Gershom for he said, "I have been an alien in a foreign land,"* 4 *and the name of the other, Eliezer for he said, "The God of my father was my help, and delivered me from the sword of Pharaoh".* 5 Jethro, Moses' father-in-law, came into the wilderness where Moses was encamped at the mountain of God, *bringing Moses' sons and wife to him.* 6 He sent word to Moses, "I, your father-in-law Jethro, am coming to you, *with your wife and her two sons."* 7 Moses went out to meet his father-in-law; he bowed down and kissed him; each asked after the other's welfare, *and they went into the tent.* 8 *Then Moses told his father-in-law all that the LORD had done to Pharaoh and to the Egyptians for Israel's sake, all the hardship that had beset them on the way, and how the LORD had delivered them.* 9 *Jethro rejoiced for all the good that the LORD had done to Israel, in delivering them from the Egyptians.* 10 *Jethro said, "Blessed be the LORD, who has delivered you from the Egyptians and from Pharaoh.* 11 *Now I know that the LORD is greater than all gods, because he delivered the people from the Egyptians, when they dealt arrogantly with them."* 12 And Jethro, Moses' father-in-law, brought a burnt offering and sacrifices to God; and Aaron came with all the Elders of Israel to eat bread with Moses' father-in-law in the presence of God. 13 The next day Moses sat as judge for the people, while the people stood around him from morning until evening. 14 When Moses' father-in-law saw all that he was doing for the people, he said, "What is this that you are doing for the people? Why do you sit alone, while all the people stand around you from morning until evening?" 15 Moses said to his father-in-law, "Because the people come to me to inquire of God. 16 When they have a dispute, they come to me and I decide between one person and another, and I

---

86   Gressmann, *Mose,* 155-161, argues that the rock or altar were the original catalyst for this episode – and not a secondary addition; Noth, *Exodus,* 143-144, connects this altar and the Rock of Refidim at the beginning of the chapter, for further discussion regarding the function of this altar, see our Appendix on Centralization of Cult.

make known to them the statutes and instructions of God." 17 Moses'
father-in-law said to him, "What you are doing is not good. 18 You will
surely wear yourself out, both you and these people with you. For the
task is too heavy for you; you cannot do it alone. 19 Now listen to me. I
will give you counsel, and God be with you! You should represent the
people before God, and you should bring their cases before God; 20
teach them the statutes and instructions and make known to them the
way they are to go and the things they are to do. 21 You should also
look for able men among all the people, men who fear God, are trustworthy, and hate dishonest gain and set such men over them *as officers
over thousands, hundreds, fifties and tens.* 22 Let them sit as judges for the people
at all times; let them bring every important case to you, but decide
every minor case themselves. So it will be easier for you, and they will
bear the burden with you. 23 If you do this, and God so commands
you, then you will be able to endure, and all these people will go to
their home in peace." 24 So Moses listened to his father-in-law and did
all that he had said. 25 *Moses chose able men from all Israel and appointed them as heads
over the people, as officers over thousands, hundreds, fifties, and tens. 26 And they judged the
people at all times; hard cases they brought to Moses, but any minor case they decided themselves.*
27 Then Moses let his father-in-law depart, and he went off to his own
country.

6.8.1 Source Division

The elohistic Jethro narrative begins in 18:1, as does the yahwistic supplementation. The first half of the verse is elohistic: "Jethro, the priest of
Midian, Moses' father-in-law, heard of all that God had done for Moses
and for his people Israel," while the second half of the verse: "How the
LORD had brought Israel out of Egypt," is yahwistic.[87] The second half
of the verse explains what brought Jethro all the way to God's mountain. Like other Canaanite nations he had heard of the miraculous Exodus from Egypt (Ex. 15:14), and was awed by this demonstration of
God's power. The yahwistic interpolation then continues in verses 2-4,
explaining exactly who came on this visit. "Zipporah," "Gershom" and
"Pharaoh" appear in previous yahwistic narratives (e.g. Ex. 2). According to E, Moses' wife and sons came with him to Egypt, but J separates
Moses from the members of his family (Ex. 18:2: "After Moses had sent
away his wife Zipporah, his father-in-law Jethro took her back").
Verses 5 and 6 feature Moses' family and here, too, the words "bringing

---

87   Driver, *Exodus*, 162.

Moses' sons and wife to him" and subsequently "with your wife and her two sons" are yahwistic additions.[88] The bulk of verses 5-7, however, are part of the original elohistic account. Verses 8-11 are once more attributed to the yahwistic redactor. According to these verses, Moses gives an account of his journeys to Jethro: "Then Moses told his father-in-law all that the LORD had done to Pharaoh and to the Egyptians for Israel's sake, all the hardship that had beset them on the way, and how the LORD had delivered them." According to E (and also J, who, as is his wont, emphasizes the miracles once more), Jethro has already heard about the miracles (Ex. 18:1) and his natural reaction is one of thanksgiving, found in 18:12: "And Jethro, Moses' father-in-law, brought a burnt offering and sacrifices to God; and Aaron came with all the Elders of Israel to eat bread with Moses' father-in-law in the presence of God."

The bulk of the elohistic account begins in verse 13: Jethro, the experienced priest of Midyan, explains the intricacies of leadership to his son-in-law Moses.[89] This basic account continues until verse 21a: "You should also look for able men among all the people, men who fear God, are trustworthy, and hate dishonest gain; set such men over them," which is supplemented by J's "inflationary" gloss: "over thousands, hundreds, fifties and tens" (repeated in verse 25). It is out of the question that the original narrative would have assumed that Moses could accommodate the legal needs of a nation in need of "officers over thousands." Once again, my assumption of a low population figure in E's Exodus account is corroborated. It is possible that verse 26: "And they judged the people at all times; hard cases they brought to Moses, but any minor case they decided themselves" is also secondary, since it is an unnecessary repetition of Jethro's instructions (perhaps to emphasize that they were fulfilled to the letter). The narrative concludes with Jethro's departure.

---

88   Driver, *Exodus*, 162, attributes the first appearance of Moses' wife and sons in vss. 2-4 to the redactor, but arbitrarily attributes the whole of vss. 5 and 6 which also mention family members, to E.

89   Gressmann, *Mose*, 161ff in a division which many find unconvincing (Childs, *Exodus*, 321), argues for two parallel accounts the second of which begins here; there is some truth to Gressmann's division however, the Yahwistic additions are for the most part confined to the first part of the chapter.

6.8.2 The Yahwistic Commentary

In 18:1, J explains exactly what Jethro heard and what drove him to visit Moses, emphasizing once again that Yhwh rather than Moses was responsible for the Exodus. In verse 2 the names of Moses' sons and wife are provided, expanding upon Chapter 2's genealogical information. One should note the parallel to Joseph, who also married the daughter of a priest and fathered two sons. This interpolation adds another very interesting fact: "...after Moses had sent away his wife Zipporah" (verse 2). Why did the Yahwist choose to expand the narrative in this specific manner? Is it possible that this is an attempt to portray Moses as an ascetic individual who abstained from the pleasures of this world? In Ex. 19, according to the basic narrative, Moses instructs the entire nation to "Prepare for the third day; do not go near a woman" in readiness for the divine revelation. Perhaps the Yahwist sought to emphasize Moses' ascetic righteousness. While the Israelites abstained from sexual relations for three days, Moses, who was in frequent contact with God, gave up marriage altogether. (This is, however, contradicted by Num. 12:1 [J], which alludes to Moses' marriage to a Cushite woman). In verses 9-11 Jethro praises Yhwh's miracles. Jethro's statement is part of the semi-conversion to Yahwism of Moses' father-in-law, an attitude one expects of an individual related to Moses. It is possible that this positive portrayal of Jethro is based upon the wisdom he demonstrates according to E.

6.9 Preparing for Revelation (Ex. 19)

1 *On the third new moon after the Israelites had gone out of the land of Egypt, on that very day, they came into the wilderness of Sinai.* 2 *They had journeyed from Rephidim, entered the wilderness of Sinai, and camped in the wilderness; Israel camped there in front of the mountain.* 3 Then Moses went up to God; [who] / *and the LORD* called to him *from the mountain,* saying, *"Thus you shall say to the house of Jacob, and tell the Israelites:* 4 *You have seen what I did to the Egyptians, and how I bore you on eagles' wings and brought you to myself.* 5 *Now therefore, if you obey my voice and keep my covenant, you shall be my treasured possession out of all the peoples. Indeed, the whole earth is mine,* 6 *but you shall be for me a priestly kingdom and a holy nation. These are the words that you shall speak to the Israelites."* 7 *So Moses came, summoned the Elders of the people, and set before them all these words that the LORD had commanded him.* 8 *The people all answered as one: "Everything that the LORD has spoken we will do." Moses reported the words of the people to the LORD.* 9 *Then the LORD said to Moses, "I am going to come to you in a dense cloud, in order that the people may hear when I speak with you and so trust you ever after." Moses told the words of the people to the LORD,* 10 And *the Lord*

said: "Go to the people and consecrate them today and tomorrow. Have them wash their clothes 11 and prepare for the third day, *because on the third day the LORD will come down upon Mount Sinai in the sight of all the people.* 12 *You shall set limits for the people all around, saying, 'Be careful not to go up the mountain or to touch the edge of it. Any who touch the mountain shall be put to death.* 13 *No hand shall touch them, but they shall be stoned or shot with arrows; whether animal or human being, they shall not live.' When the trumpet sounds a long blast, they may go up on the mountain."* 14 So Moses went down from the mountain to the people. He consecrated the people, and they washed their clothes. 15 And he said to the people, "Prepare for the third day; do not go near a woman."16 On the morning of the third day there was thunder and lightning, as well as a thick cloud on the mountain, and a blast of a trumpet so loud that all the people who were in the camp trembled. 17 Moses brought the people out of the camp to meet God. They took their stand at the foot of the mountain. 18 *Now Mount Sinai was wrapped in smoke, because the LORD had descended upon it in fire; the smoke went up like the smoke of a kiln, while the whole mountain shook violently.* 19 As the blast of the trumpet grew louder and louder, Moses would speak and God would answer him in thunder. 20 *When the LORD descended upon Mount Sinai, to the top of the mountain, the LORD summoned Moses to the top of the mountain, and Moses went up.* 21 *Then the LORD said to Moses, "Go down and warn the people not to break through to the LORD to look; otherwise many of them will perish.* 22 *Even the priests who approach the LORD must consecrate themselves or the LORD will break out against them."* 23 *Moses said to the LORD, "The people are not permitted to come up to Mount Sinai; for you yourself warned us, saying, 'Set limits around the mountain and keep it holy.'"* 24 *The LORD said to him, "Go down, and come up bringing Aaron with you; but do not let either the priests or the people break through to come up to the LORD; otherwise he will break out against them."* 25 *So Moses went down to the people and told them.*

6.9.1 Source Division

This chapter is a difficult one for traditional Documentary scholars. It is full of repetitions and textual difficulties, and the divine names alternate for no apparent reason. No Documentary scholar has succeeded in dividing the chapter in a convincing manner.[90] One of the reasons for this failure is the assumption that the documents were independent and that each document therefore had its own story. Scholars who attempted to isolate two or even three independent narratives in Ex. 19 invariably failed. Dozeman suggests a supplementary model for Ex. 19

---

90   Cf. Childs, *Exodus*, 344.

and for the Sinai narratives.[91] He does not attempt to isolate two or
three whole narratives, but rather one "pre-exilic" narrative supplemented by two editors—D and P. I agree with his methodology in Ex.
19 and identify the same basic source, but not the same editors (J replaces D). Dozeman's division is further corroborated by the distribution
of the divine names, though this criterion is conspicuously absent from
Dozeman's division: Elohim appears only in elohistic material, whereas
Yhwh appears in the two editorial strata (Dozeman's D and P, my J and
P).

There is a consensus among scholars in attributing the itinerary
notes of verses 1-2 to the priestly editor.[92] Ex. 19:3a is usually attributed
to E on the basis of the Deity's name ("Elohim"). Verse 3b begins a
Deuteronomistic-like interpolation which ends in verse 8.[93] These
verses are indeed secondary (but not necessarily Deuteronomistic) and
together with Ex. 24:3-8 (the Covenant ceremony) frame the Covenant
Code and the Sinai narratives of Ex. 19-24.[94] Following Driver,[95] I identify this interpolation as a rare yahwistic legal passage. The so-called
Deuteronomistic language (none of the most prominent Dtr markers
are in evidence) may be no more than legal phraseology common to the
period.[96] The real question here is where E's interrupted narrative continues. "Elohim" is not mentioned again until verse 17.

Prior to identifying the borders of the elohistic exchange, however,
other textual problems must be addressed. In verse 7 Moses summons
the Elders and the people and relates God's covenantal offer. In 8a the
Elders and the people accept the conditions of the covenant and in 8b
Moses ascends once more and informs God of the people's acceptance
("Moses reported the words of the people to the LORD.") In verse 9 the
manner of the upcoming revelation is "revealed," and in 9b Moses once
again reports the people's response to God. This is highly problematic,
since Moses received no new information concerning the Israelite response in the interim. In fact, this is a resumptive repetition (verse 8b =
verse 9b), which often indicates the presence of an insertion. Indeed,
verse 9 is out of place. In verse 8 the nation answers "Everything that
the LORD has spoken we will do," and this message is faithfully deli-

---

91   T. Dozeman, *God on the Mountain* (The Society of Biblical Literature Monograph
     Series), Atlanta, 1989.
92   E. Kautzsch, *Die Heilige Schrift des Alten Testament (I Band)*, Tübingen, 1922, 124, but
     cf. Levin, *Jahwist*, 78, who attributes vs. 2 to J.
93   Thus Noth, *Exodus*, 157.
94   Cf. Blum, *Komposition*, 92.
95   Driver, *Exodus*, 170-171.
96   For J's composition date. see the Appendix on Centralization of Cult in J.

vered. God's reaction is not forthcoming; instead, God describes the nature of the public revelation which is mentioned again only in verse 11b. The way in which God proposes to reveal himself is also anomalous, His revelation "in a dense cloud" (verse 9) contrasts with his fiery descent according to J (verse 18). This holy "cloud" is most characteristic of priestly revelations (as we see in Ex. 24:15b and throughout the books of Leviticus and Numbers). Thus in all likelihood verse 9 is a priestly insertion.[97]

Verses 10ff, God's instructions to Israel prior to the revelation, seem out of place. After the People of Israel agree to Yhwh's demands of verses 3b-6, we expect a reaction from Elohim acknowledging the agreement, but such a reaction does not appear in the chapter. This type of break in continuity usually indicates a plurality of sources, but to which source should verses 10ff. be attributed? Verses 3b-8 are yahwistic (as I claimed above) and verse 9 is priestly (the cloud as opposed to the fire), but verse 10 is the continuation of neither. What about E? On the face of it, this verse is hard to attribute to the Elohist since it uses Yhwh. The solution to this problem is simple: the original elohistic verse consisted of 3a and most of verse 10: "Then Moses went up to God; who called him and said 'Go to the people and consecrate them today and tomorrow. Have them wash their clothes,'" Since the interpolation separated the two parts of the verse, J as a matter of course added a subject ("the Lord") to the truncated verse.[98]

Verse 11b-13—the promise of a public revelation and the restrictions concerning the mountain—are usually attributed to J based on the "yahwistic signature" in 11b and in light of the thematic link to verses 20-25, a section which Schwartz has argued convincingly must be attributed to J.[99] (Verses 20-25 tell of the negotiations concerning the proximity of various groups to the mountain and since they mention priests prior to Aaron's consecration by the priestly source (Ex. 28), an attribution to J is likely.) In verses 14-17 Moses repeats the elohistic instructions of 19:10-11a, and finally the people approach the mountain.[100]

---

97 Cf. Mcneile, *Exodus*, 111; Van Seters, *Moses*, 249, solves the problem by reading: "Moses returned to the LORD" in vs. 8, in lieu of the Masoretic text: "Moses reported the words of the people to the LORD."

98 Cf. Driver's (*Exodus*, 162) and McNeile's (*Exodus*, 111) attribution of vs. 10 to E.

99 B. Schwartz, The Priestly Account of the Theophany and Lawgiving at Sinai, in *Text Temples and Tradition – A Tribute to Menachem Haran* (M. V. Fox ed.), Winona Lake, 1996, 103-134; Van Seters, *Moses*, 249-251 and Dozeman, *Mountain*, 103-106, however, attribute vss. 20-25 to P, which is highly unlikely considering that the priesthood doesn't exist yet.

100 Compare Jacob's orders to his family prior to his return to Beit El in another E text, Gen. 35:2-3: " So Jacob said to his household and to all who were with him, 'Put

Verse 18, recounting Yhwh's descent, is yet another yahwistic addition (based on the terms Yhwh, Mount Sinai, and the theme of descent, as in 11b). The E narrative continues, concluding in verse 19: "As the blast of the trumpet grew louder and louder, Moses would speak and God would answer him in thunder." (Note the symmetry in this passage: God speaks with Moses, Moses is given instructions, Moses repeats those instructions, God speaks with Moses once again.)

In summary: the yahwistic interpolations/additions to Chapter 19 are verses 3b-8—the "poetic" covenant; verses 12-13—the restrictions concerning proximity to the mountain; verses 11b,18—the nature of the revelation, and verses 20-25—the proximity issue in greater detail. The priestly interpolations include the chronistic details of verses 1-2, and verse 9 (God's "cloudy" revelation).

Driver arrives at a similar division of Chapter 19 in his commentary, significantly differing only in attributing verse 9 to J. The real difference lies in the way one interprets these results. Instead of Driver's three fragmented accounts, I have isolated one full account, supplemented by two "creative redactors" whose goals are clear.

6.9.2 Yahwistic Commentary

The addition of verses 3b-8 alters our understanding of the Sinai narrative. The elohistic account is a simple revelation of God's laws to the Israelites. The laws are very general and imply neither a unique bond between Israel and God, nor a special status. However, verses 3b-8 emphasize, that a special relationship does exist: With little help from Moses or other parties, Yhwh engineered the exodus of his people and is now prepared to bind them to him as a "holy nation." The central idea of these verses, the forging of the covenant, is repeated in Ex. 24, also edited by J.[101] The two sections, Ex. 19:3b-8 and Ex. 24:1-11, frame the Ten Commandments and the book of the covenant. The other yahwistic interpolations deal with the proximity of the various groups to the mountain.[102] On the one hand, the Yahwist wants to emphasize the power of Yhwh and his awesome revelation, while on the other hand

---

away the foreign gods that are among you, and purify yourselves, and change your clothes; then come, let us go up to Bethel, that I may make an altar there to the God who answered me in the day of my distress and has been with me wherever I have gone'."

101 L. Perlitt, *Bundes Theologie im Alten Testament* (WMANT 36), Neukirchen-Vluyn, 1969 argues for the relatively late date of the covenant formulae here and in Ex. 24.
102 And see our analysis of Ex. 24 in the Appendix.

he cannot allow the nation to see God in all his glory. Hence the addition of verses 11b-13 and 20-25.

6.10 The Seven Commandments (Ex. 20)

1 Then God spoke all these words: 2 *I am the LORD your God, who brought you out of the land of Egypt, out of the house of slavery* 3 You shall have no other gods before me. 4 You shall not make for yourself an idol of any form *that is in heaven above, or that is on the earth beneath, or that is in the water under the earth.* 5 *You shall not bow down to them or worship them; for I the LORD your God am a jealous God, punishing children for the iniquity of parents, to the third and the fourth generation of those who reject me, 6 but showing steadfast love to the thousandth generation of those who love me and keep my commandments. 7 You shall not make wrongful use of the name of the LORD your God, for the LORD will not acquit anyone who misuses his name. 8 Remember the sabbath day, and keep it holy. 9 Six days you shall labor and do all your work. 10 But the seventh day is a sabbath to the LORD your God; you shall not do any work—you, your son or your daughter, your male or female slave, your livestock, or the alien resident in your towns. 11 For in six days the LORD made heaven and earth, the sea, and all that is in them, but rested the seventh day; therefore the LORD blessed the sabbath day and consecrated it. 12 Honor your father and your mother, so that your days may be long in the land that the LORD your God is giving you.* 13 You shall not murder. 14 You shall not commit adultery. 15 You shall not steal. 16 You shall not bear false witness against your neighbor. 17 You shall not covet your neighbor's house; *you shall not covet your neighbor's wife, or male or female slave, or ox, or donkey, or anything that belongs to your neighbor.* 18 When all the people witnessed the thunder and lightning, the sound of the trumpet, and the mountain smoking, they were afraid and trembled and stood at a distance, 19 and said to Moses, "You speak to us, and we will listen; but do not let God speak to us, or we will die." 20 Moses said to the people, "Do not be afraid; for God has come only to test you and to put the fear of him upon you so that you do not sin." 21 Then the people stood at a distance, while Moses drew near to the thick darkness where God was.

6.10.1 Source Division

The elohistic commandments are short and to the point. Ex. 20:1 introduces the speaker, Elohim, who is immediately reintroduced (20:2) by J as Yhwh, the God of the Exodus.[103] The first elohistic commandment

---

103 Compare Ex. 3:14 and 3:15; for Yhwh and Elohim as names of the same deity cf. Gen. 2's composite "Yhwh Elohim" which in our eyes is an equation, Yhwh = Elohim. For

appears in verse 3 "You shall have no other gods before me," followed immediately by verse 4a. The specification of types of idols (verse 4b) and the promise of reward/punishment (verses 5-6) are most probably secondary, as are similar elaborations of other commandments. Verses 4b-7 are more in the spirit of lengthy legal compositions such as the Covenant Code and do not accord with the terse style of the subsequent prohibitions. Indeed, it seems likely that the key to this pericope's analysis is the distinction between the general prohibitions (E) and everything else, namely minute specification, reward, punishment, and legal explanations.[104] Verses 8-11 (the Sabbath) are a priestly interpolation (the allusion to P's six-day creation in Gen. 1), as are other commands/admonishments concerning the Sabbath (the etiology of Ex. 16, 31:12-17 and 35:2-3). Another possibility is that P simply added the creation etiology to J's short commandment. (cf. Deut. 5:15, which develops this commandment in a Deuteronomistic manner.) Ex. 20:12 "Honor your father and your mother, so that your days may be long in the land that the LORD your God is giving you" is, like verse 8, a positive injunction which promises the faithful the inheritance of the land (a yahwistic theme). The lengthy interpolations of these first commandments, which seek to define the human relationship to the divine, "weigh down" this part of the pericope. The second part of the commandment pericope—the short negative injunctions, beginning with vs. 13: "You shall not murder"—was left untouched except for 17b "You shall not covet your neighbour's wife, or male or female slave, or ox, or donkey, or anything that belongs to your neighbour," which specifies the objects one is forbidden to covet.[105] Following the septalogue, E explains the reason for the revelation: "Do not be afraid; for God has come only to test you and to put the fear of him upon you so that you do not sin." (note E's familiar "fear of God" theme) But what "trial" was there? The people evinced no lack of faith. Perhaps according to E all God's miracles are understood as "trials," trying experiences intended to bolster people's faith.

One should note that the isolated E commandments are organized chiastically: The first two commandments relate to the interactions

---

more on this Yahwistic introduction see W. Zimmerli, Ich bin Jahwe, in *Geschichte und Altes Testament* (W. F. Albright ed.), Tübingen, 1953, 179-209.

104 See J. J. Stamm and M. E. Andrews, *The Ten Commandments in Recent Research* (Studies in Biblical Theology Second Series), London, 1967, and more minutely, E. Nielsen, *The Ten Commandments in New Perspective* (Studies in Bible: the Second Series 7), London, 1968.

105 Perhaps a Yahwistic interpolation, and compare J's elaboration of E's general prohibition against idols in Ex. 19:4b, see Driver, *Exodus*, 200.

between humans and the Diety, the three middle ones are short commandments, each composed of two words, and the last two are interpersonal injunctions. The first and the last commandments are parallel: One deals with the coveting of foreign gods, the other with the coveting of one's neighbour's property. The second and the sixth commandments are also parallel: One prohibits idols, which are "false witnesses" of the divine presence, the other prohibits bearing false witness against a fellow human being.

6.10.2 The Yahwistic Commentary

The elohistic septalogue is straightforward and to the point. The yahwistic decalogue is entirely different. The yahwistic "Ten Commandments" (Ex. 34:28, Deut. 10:4) are, in fact, difficult to enumerate and some scholars speak of a dodecalogue.[106] The number ten was chosen because it was considered a "perfect" number. In the above analysis I mentioned that the yahwistic interpolations emphasize the power of Yhwh, especially His power to punish (but also to reward). Rules are impractical and unhelpful unless the legislator has the ability to implement them, and this power is emphasized by J.

6.11 The Golden Calf (Ex. 24 and 32)

[[24:13 Moses set out with his assistant Joshua, and Moses went up into the mountain of God. 14 To the Elders he had said, "Wait here for us, until we come to you again; for Aaron and Hur are with you; whoever has a dispute may go to them." 15 Then Moses went up on the mountain.]] *and the cloud covered the mountain. 16 The glory of the LORD settled on Mount Sinai, and the cloud covered it for six days; on the seventh day he called to Moses out of the cloud. 17 Now the appearance of the glory of the LORD was like a devouring fire on the top of the mountain in the sight of the People of Israel. 18 Moses entered the cloud, and went up on the mountain. Moses was on the mountain for forty days and forty nights.*

Legal Section: Ch. 25:1-31:16 (omitted)

---

106 K. Rabast, *Das Apodiktische Recht im Deuteronomium und im Heiligkeitgesetz*, Berlin, 1949, 35.

31:17 *When God finished speaking with Moses on Mount Sinai, he gave him the two tablets of the covenant, tablets of stone, written with the finger of God* 32:1 When the people saw that Moses delayed to come down from the mountain, the people gathered around Aaron, and said to him, "Come, make gods for us, who shall go before us; as for this Moses, the man who brought us up out of the land of Egypt, we do not know what has become of him." 2 Aaron said to them, "Take off the gold rings that are on the ears of your wives, your sons, and your daughters, and bring them to me." 3 So all the people took off the gold rings from their ears, and brought them to Aaron. 4 He took the gold from them, formed it in a mold, and cast an image of a calf; and they said, "These are your gods, O Israel, who brought you up out of the land of Egypt!" 5 *When Aaron saw this, he built an altar before it; and Aaron made proclamation and said, "Tomorrow shall be a festival to the LORD."* 6 They rose early the next day, and offered burnt offerings and brought sacrifices of well-being; and the people sat down to eat and drink, and rose up to revel. 7 *The LORD said to Moses, "Go down at once! Your people, whom you brought up out of the land of Egypt, have acted perversely; 8 they have been quick to turn aside from the way that I commanded them; they have cast for themselves an image of a calf, and have worshiped it and sacrificed to it, and said, 'These are your gods, O Israel, who brought you up out of the land of Egypt!'"* 9 *The LORD said to Moses, "I have seen this people, how stiff-necked they are. 10 Now let me alone, so that my wrath may burn hot against them and I may consume them; and of you I will make a great nation."* 11 *But Moses implored the LORD his God, and said, "O LORD, why does your wrath burn hot against your people, whom you brought out of the land of Egypt with great power and with a mighty hand? 12 Why should the Egyptians say, 'It was with evil intent that he brought them out to kill them in the mountains, and to consume them from the face of the earth'? Turn from your fierce wrath; change your mind and do not bring disaster on your people. 13 Remember Abraham, Isaac, and Israel, your servants, how you swore to them by your own self, saying to them, 'I will multiply your descendants like the stars of heaven, and all this land that I have promised I will give to your descendants, and they shall inherit it forever.'"* 14 *And the LORD changed his mind about the disaster that he planned to bring on his people.* 15 Then Moses turned and went down from the mountain, carrying the two tablets *of the covenant* in his hands, tablets that were written on both sides, written on the front and on the back. 16 The tablets were the work of God, and the writing was the writing of God, engraved upon the tablets. 17 When Joshua heard the noise of the people as they shouted, he said to Moses, "There is a noise of war in the camp." 18 But he said, "It is not the sound made by victors, or the sound made by losers ;it is the sound of revelers that I hear."19 As soon as he came near the camp and saw the calf and the dancing, Moses' anger burned hot, and he threw the tablets from his hands and broke them at the foot of the mountain. 20 He took the calf that they had made, burned it with fire, ground it to powder, scattered it on the water, and made the Israelites drink it. 21 *Moses said to Aaron, "What did this people do to you that you have brought so great a sin upon them?" 22 And Aaron said, "Do not let the anger of my lord burn hot; you know the people, that they are bent on evil. 23 They said to me, 'Make us gods, who shall go before us; as for this Moses, the man who brought us up out of the land of Egypt, we do not know what has become of him.' 24 So I said to them, 'Whoever has gold, take it off'; so they gave it to me, and I threw it into the fire, and out came this calf!" 25 When Moses saw that the people were running wild (for Aaron had let them run wild, to the derision of their enemies), 26 then Moses stood in the gate of the camp, and said, "Who is on the LORD's side? Come to me!" And all the sons of Levi gathered around him. 27 He said to them, "Thus says the LORD, the God of Israel, 'Put your sword on your side, each of you! Go back and forth from gate to gate throughout the camp, and each of you kill your brother, your friend, and your neighbor.'" 28 The sons of Levi did as Moses commanded, and about three thousand of the people fell on that day. 29 Moses said, "Today you have ordained yourselves for the service of the LORD, each one at the cost of a son or a brother, and so have brought a blessing on yourselves this day." 30 On the next day Moses said to the people, "You have sinned a great sin. But now I will go up to the LORD; perhaps I can make atonement for your sin." 31 So Moses returned to the LORD and said, "Alas, this people has sinned a great sin; they have made for themselves gods of gold. 32 But now, if you will only forgive their sin—but if not, blot me out of the book that you have written." 33 But the LORD said to Moses, "Whoever has sinned against me I will blot out of my book. 34 But now go, lead the people to the place about which I have spoken to you; see, my angel shall go in front of you. Nevertheless, when the day comes for punishment, I will punish them for their sin." 35 Then the LORD sent a plague on the people, because they made the calf—the one that Aaron made. 33:1 The LORD said to Moses, "Go, leave this place, you and the people whom you have brought up out of the land of Egypt, and go to the land of which I swore to Abraham, Isaac, and Jacob, saying, 'To your descendants I will give it.' 2 I will send an angel before you, and I will drive out the Canaanites, the Amorites, the Hittites, the Perizzites, the Hivites, and the Jebusites. 3 Go up to a land flowing with milk and honey; but I will not go up among you, or I would consume you on the way, for you are a stiff-necked people." 4 When the people heard these harsh words, they mourned, and no one put on ornaments. 5 For the LORD had said to Moses, "Say to the Israelites, 'You are a stiff-necked people; if for a single moment I should go up among you, I would consume you. So now take off your ornaments, and I will decide what to do to you.'" 6 Therefore the Israelites stripped themselves of their ornaments, from Mount Horeb onward.*

6.11.1 Source Division

The Golden Calf episode, which begins in Ex. 24, is interrupted by a lengthy priestly interpolation dealing with the construction of the tabernacle and the appointment of Aaron (Ex. 25-31). Many exegetes attribute the covenant ceremony (24:3-8) or part of it to E.[107] However, this assignment is highly unlikely. 24:4: "He rose early in the morning, and built an altar at the foot of the mountain, and set up twelve pillars, corresponding to the twelve tribes of Israel" refers to twelve tribes, whereas according to E, Jacob had only seven sons. The beginning of Chapter 24:1-12 is an amalgam of the Covenant Code's final ceremony and yahwistic editing (See below in the Appendix on Centralization of Cult). E begins his account in 24:13 and is cut off after verse 15a.[108] One should note the rare repetitiveness in E: 24:13 and 24:14 impart the same information as 20:21 "Then the people stood at a distance, while Moses drew near to the thick darkness where God was." As my division emphasizes, the elohistic narrative cycles were divided into chapters or episodes. Ex. 20 concluded with a general statement concerning Moses' ascent, but since this ascent is at the basis of the Golden Calf episode it is hardly surprising that this detail is reiterated together with Moses' instructions to his deputies. Another option is to view this section (or the revelation at Mount Sinai) as a secondary elohistic refinement. My preference throughout this work, however, has been to posit as few authors as possible. Following the lengthy priestly interpolation, the E narrative resumes in Ex. 32:1-6,[109] with the exception of verse 5, which I believe is a secondary gloss. In 32:1-4, 6 Aaron is passive, but in verse 5 he is an active initiator and declares "Tomorrow shall be a festival to the LORD." Compare verse 25: "When Moses saw that the people were running wild for Aaron had caused them to run wild, to the derision of their enemies...," which serves to paint Aaron in the same active colors, and note the use of Yhwh in verse 5, an indicator of yahwistic supplementation. The E account ends in verse 20 with the shattering of the tablets, the immolation of the Calf and the forced consumption of its remnants.

Verses 21-24, which delineate Aaron's responsibility (or irresponsibility), are difficult to attribute to E, since this section is obviously inadequate as a conclusion. (The E account most certainly does not continue beyond verse 24, which features the Levites, a group not recognized by E.) On the other hand, this section functions very well as an introduction to the Yahwist's more lethal punishment in verses 25ff. Except for verses 21-24 (and verse 5), my division accords with the Documentary analysis which for the most part views the E account (or the

---

107 Driver, *Exodus*, 252-254; M. Weinfeld, *Deuteronomy and the Deuteronomistic School*, Oxford, 1972, 63, but compare Perlitt, *Bundes*, who argues for a later date for these covenantal elements.

108 Thus Driver, *Exodus*, 256.

109 Thus Driver, *Exodus*, 349-350.

verses I regard as the E account) as original, and the rest of Chapters 32-34 as interpolations.[110]

Three sections identified by many as elohistic separate this account and the E episode of Num. 20 (the lack of water at Qadesh): 1) Ex. 33:7-11 (the origin of the tent of meeting), 2) Num. 11 (the conferring of God's spirit upon the Elders, and the quail episode), 3) Num. 12 (Miriam and Aaron's jealousy of Moses and the confrontation with the Lord). These so called "prophetic" sections, which I attribute to J, are dealt with in a separate chapter.

6.11.2 The Yahwistic Commentary

Aaron's activism is part and parcel of J's character enhancement. According to J, Aaron's role is not restricted to serving Moses. In E he accedes to the nation's demands and builds an idol, but in J he takes it a step farther and declares a holiday celebrating the construction of the idol. Further development of Aaron's role is found in P, where he becomes the high priest. The Yahwist is also interested in enhancing Yhwh's role in the story. The nation of Israel transgressed against their divine protector and E's symbolic punishment, the forced consumption of the Golden Calf's remnants, is certainly not severe enough for such grave iniquity. The yahwistic commandment in Ex. 20:4: "You shall not make for yourself an idol, whether in the form of anything that is in heaven above, or that is on the earth beneath, or that is in the water under the earth," specifically prohibits any kind of idol. The severity of the sin warrants further and more exacting punishment. Moses begins by calling the faithful Levites to his banner and commanding them to kill the sinners, thus distinguishing this tribe as the Lord's servants.

The Lord is wroth enough to annihilate the entire Israelite nation, and it is only Moses' intercession (32:7-14) that stays the Lord's vengeful hand. Appealing to the Lord's "ego," Moses asks him to save Israel for the sake of the Lord's "good name". But there are limits to what Moses can do. His second prayer (32:31-34) is not as effective, for Yhwh answers him in 32:34: "Nevertheless, when the day comes for punishment, I will punish them for their sin," and he indeed smites Israel with a general plague, and refuses to lead them into the promised land.[111]

---

110 Childs, *Exodus*, 558.

111 See Cassuto's (U. Cassuto, *A Commentary on the Book of Exodus* [I. Abrahams tr.], Jerusalem, 1967, 411-451), argument for literary unity.

The subsequent J episode (33:17-23) resumes the important theme of God's visibility or invisibility. According to J, even Moses, the holiest of men, is not permitted to see God face to face. J then addresses the problematic status of the breached covenant, the tangible evidence of which is "unavailable." The lack of clarity as to whether the covenant still stands, is untenable for the Yahwist, who therefore adds a second covenant ceremony, basically an updated version of the cultic .laws of Ex. 23.[112]

6.12 The Waters of Meribah (Num. 20)

1 *The Israelites, the whole congregation, came into the wilderness of Zin in the first month, [and]* the people stayed in Qadesh. *Miriam died there, and was buried there* 2 and there was no water *for the congregation; so they gathered together against Moses and against Aaron.* 3 So the people quarreled with Moses and said, *"Would that we had died when our kindred died before the LORD! 4 Why have you brought the assembly of the LORD into this wilderness for us and our livestock to die here?* 5 Why have you [singular] brought us up out of Egypt, to bring us to this wretched place? It is no place for grain, or figs, or vines, or pomegranates; and there is no water to drink." 6 *Then Moses and Aaron went away from the assembly to the entrance of the tent of meeting; they fell on their faces, and the glory of the LORD appeared to them. 7 The LORD spoke to Moses, saying: 8 Take the staff, and assemble the congregation, you and your brother Aaron, and command the rock before their eyes to yield its water. Thus you shall bring water out of the rock for them; thus you shall provide drink for the congregation and their livestock. 9 So Moses took the staff from before the LORD, as he had commanded him.* 10 *Moses and Aaron gathered the assembly together before the rock, and* he said to them, "Listen, you rebels, shall we bring water for you out of this rock?" 11 Then Moses lifted up his hand and struck the rock twice with his staff; water came out abundantly, *and the congregation and their livestock drank.* 12 *But the LORD said to Moses and Aaron, "Because you did not trust in me, to show my holiness before the eyes of the Israelites, therefore you shall not bring this assembly into the land that I have given them." 13 These are the waters of Meribah, where the People of Israel quarreled with the LORD, and by which he showed his holiness.*

---

112 See Bar-On's doctorate (S. Bar-On, *The Festival Laws in the Pentateuch* (Hebrew), Doctorate, Hebrew University of Jerusalem, 2000) regarding the relationship between the laws of Ex 23 and Ex 34.

6.12.1 Source Division

After Ex. 32 the E narrative and yahwistic supplementation are interrupted by the priestly book of Leviticus and the first part of Numbers. Only in Num. 10 does J resurface. According to many exegetes, E disappears completely after Ex. 32, never to resurface.[113] One should, however, consider Num. 20:1-13 as a diluted E episode.[114] Although no "true" elohistic indicators appear in this chapter (except perhaps Moses' staff), E is identified by a process of elimination. In Ex. 17:1-7 the yahwistic Massa-wonder is recounted: The nation complains to Moses and demands water, Moses in turn asks for divine aid, and Yhwh tells him to take his staff and strike the rock. Moses does not carry out the miracle alone, but with the inevitable aid of Yhwh in Ex. 17:6: "I will be standing there in front of you on the rock in the dryness. Strike the rock, and water will come out of it, so that the people may drink." In Num. 20 the same basic story is repeated. Although, as in the yahwistic account, Yhwh commands Moses to take his staff (verse 7), the staff has no discernible function, since Moses is supposed to talk to the rock. Why therefore did God initially ask Moses to take his staff?

Other inconsistencies are apparent: a) The *community* ("העדה") gathers as if to address both Moses and Aaron (Num. 20:2), but the *nation* ("העם") accuses only Moses (verse 3); b) Verse 5: "'Why have you brought us up out of Egypt, to bring us to this wretched place? It is no place for grain, or figs, or vines, or pomegranates; and there is no water to drink.'" adds no new information and essentially reiterates the complaint of verse 4: "Why have you brought the assembly of the LORD into this wilderness for us and our livestock to die here?"; c) Both Moses and Aaron were supposed to participate in the miracle (according to verses 7-8), but only Moses addresses the nation, and only Moses strikes the rock. Yet, according to verse 12, both are punished; d) Verse 13, "These are the waters of Meribah, where the People of Israel quarreled with the LORD, and by which he showed his holiness," indicates that the nation had tested and tried God. This is inaccurate, since the Israelite confrontation is with Moses, not with God.

These inconsistencies suggest the following: P, whose mark is readily apparent throughout (עדה, קהל, the chronicle, the emphasis on Aaron etc.), adapted an earlier non-P narrative and rewrote it. This earlier account is not yahwistic since Moses performs the miracle by himself—

113 M. Noth, *Numbers, A Commentary* (OTL), London, 1968.
114 Compare, A. Dillmann, *Numeri, Deuteronmium, und Josua*, (Kurzgefasstes Exegetisches Handbuch), Leipzig, 1886, 110-117.

too independent an act to be consistent with J. Moreover, J's parallel account is already preserved in Ex. 17. It is therefore entirely possible that the core of the P account is elohistic.

I shall now attempt a division into sources.[115] Chapter 20:1a is P's typical itinerary note; *cf.* Ex. 19:1: "On the third new moon after the Israelites had gone out of the land of Egypt, on that very day, they came into the wilderness of Sinai." The original introduction was perhaps the terse: "And the people stayed in Qadesh." Miriam's death must also be assigned to P, since E never mentions Moses' sister. After this background information comes the crisis, Num. 20:2: "Now there was no water for the congregation; so they gathered together against Moses and against Aaron." While the first part of this verse is correctly attributed to the basic narrative stratum, the words "to the community" and the joint participation of Moses and Aaron (2b) indicate priestly authorship. The original "verse" was probably no more than "And there was no water." Verses 2b and 3a are doublets, and since no P vocabulary or motifs exist in 3a ("So the people quarreled with Moses and said"), it is likely also part of the original stratum. The use of "עם" (the people) in verse 1a and verse 3a, rather than "עדה" (community) in verse 2, should be noted. The second half of verse 3 "Would that we had died when our kindred died before the LORD!" alludes to the priestly Korah narrative (Num. 15). The whining complaint of vs. 4 is suffused with priestly language: "Why have you brought the assembly of the LORD into this wilderness for us and our livestock to die here?" In verse 5 the people's complaint is restated, this time in non-priestly language. It is also Moseo–centric since Moses rather than God is the redeemer (if one reads "העליתנו" [singular], as opposed to the Masoretic text's plural which would imply both Aaron and Moses as the subjects). There follows a divine response to national complaints that is typical of P: "Then Moses and Aaron went away from the assembly to the entrance of the tent of meeting; they fell on their faces, and the glory of the LORD appeared to them" (verse 6). In verse 7 Moses is, for no discernible reason, commanded to take his staff and, together with Aaron, to speak to the rock. Verses 9-10a portray Moses complying with the first part of the divine injunction by taking the staff. Verse 10b's introduction to the miracle ("He said to them, 'Listen, you rebels, shall we bring water for you out of this rock?'".) is probably original, although the plural verb "נוציא" does pose difficulties, since as it stands it refers

---

115 For various divisions of this episode between P and E, see Holzinger's tables at the end of his 1893 *Hexateuch* – a documentary division is, however, highly unlikely since as Gressmann (Mose, 153) correctly notes the P sections of this episode cannot stand alone.

to plural subjects, i.e. Moses and Aaron. This plural may imply generality or may simply be an alteration. In verse 11, Moses defies Yhwh and
instead of speaking to the rock, strikes it. Verse 11 is clearly a part of
the basic narrative because of the problems it causes for the priestly
source, which concludes with "and the congregation and their livestock
drank." On the one hand, P considered Moses' independent initiative
as decidedly negative, but on the other hand, he did not want to depict
Moses as wielding the staff without an express command, since that
would be to admit to Moses' magical prowess. When presented with
verse 11, P decided to command Moses to take the staff, even though it
had no discernible function. Perhaps the priestly author believed that
the readers would perceive the divine command to take the staff as a
personal trial for Moses, a trial which he then fails. In my opinion, if P
had had any choice in the matter, he would have excised the staff from
the story altogether, but since it was already there it became the vehicle
by which Moses and Aaron were punished. This allowed for Joshua's
ascension (in verses 12 -13).

In summary, the basic narrative—a simple report of a water shortage rectified without divine mediation—becomes an etiological narrative concerning Moses' transgression and the reason God denies him
entry into the Promised Land.

6.12.2 J and P Commentary

The E narrative is supplemented twice in two different ways—J's "parallel" account in Ex. 17 and the more invasive P redaction (above).
While a lengthier analysis of P supplementation is beyond the scope of
this work, one should note P's familiarity with J's account, "These are
the waters of Meribah, where the People of Israel quarreled with the
LORD, and by which he showed his holiness" (Num. 20:13) (Compare
Ex. 17:7: "He called the place Massah and Meribah, because the Israelites quarreled and tested the LORD, saying, 'Is the LORD among us or
not?'") Since there is no confrontation with the divine in this episode,
P's etiology must be an allusion to Ex. 17:2: "The people quarreled
("וירב" – from the same root as Meribah) with Moses, and said, 'Give us
water to drink.' Moses said to them, 'Why do you quarrel ("תריבון" –
also related to Meribah) with me? Why do you test the LORD?'" Moses'
miracle is dealt with in Ex. 17 in the same manner in which it is always
dealt with in J; the Lord tells Moses exactly what to do. This pattern—a
complaint to Moses, a call for help to Yhwh, and finally a divinely sup-

ported solution—is found twice more in J: in Ex. 15:24-26, the sweetening of water at Marah, and in Num. 11, the quail episode.

6.13 The Bronze Snake (Num. 21)

21:4: *From Mount Hor they set out by the way to the Red Sea, to go around the land of Edom; but*
the people became impatient on the way. 5 The people spoke against
God and against Moses, "Why have you brought us up out of Egypt to
die in the wilderness? For there is no food and no water, *and we detest this*
miserable food." 6 Then *the LORD sent* poisonous serpents *among the people, and they*
bit the people, so that many Israelites died. 7 The people came to Moses and said, "We have sinned *by speaking against the LORD and against you; pray to*
the LORD to take away the serpents from us." So Moses prayed for the people. 8 And the LORD
said to Moses, "Make a poisonous serpent, and set it on a pole; and everyone who is bitten shall
look at it and live." 9 So Moses made a serpent of bronze, and put it upon a
pole; and whenever a serpent bit someone, that person would look at
the serpent of bronze and live.

6.13.1 Source Division

Since the divine name "Elohim" appears in this account for the first
time since Ex. 32 (in narrative material), the presence of E material is
likely. The episode begins with P's itinerary note in verse 4a.[116] The E
narrative begins in verse 5 with a typical Israelite complaint—lack of
sustenance—similar to the complaints in Ex. 15:24 and Num. 20:2 regarding the lack of potable water. The last part of verse 5, "and we
detest this miserable food," is P's attempt to harmonize Israel's pro-
fessed lack of food with the sustaining manna which, according to P,
falls from the sky every day (Ex. 16). While in E's complaint narratives
in Ex. 15 and Num. 20 God kept himself aloof, this time the nation's ire
is directed towards God himself: Num. 21:5: "The people spoke against
God and against Moses, 'Why have you brought us up out of Egypt to
die in the wilderness?'" Divine retribution is, of course, imminent. In
verse 6, the Lord sends a plague of poisonous snakes. His direct involvement in this narrative is, however, problematic. If the Lord sent
the snakes, he can simply remove them and heal Israel. Why did Moses
need to go through the lengthier process of hammering out an idol-like

---

116 Note that most scholars do not divide this episode between two sources, but see,
   Gressmann, *Mose*, 285, who attributes the divine intercession to a later tradition.

copper snake? The J redactor was very uncomfortable with Moses' magic snake (as was the Deuteronomistic redactor, who described its destruction in the days of Hezekiah, according to II Kgs. 18:4: "He broke in pieces the bronze serpent that Moses had made, for until those days the People of Israel had made offerings to it; it was called Nehush-tan"). Thus J inserted Yhwh at every juncture: Yhwh sends the snakes; the people ask forgiveness from Moses and Yhwh; Moses prays to Yhwh; Yhwh commands him to build a copper snake. The original verse 6 was therefore "And poisonous serpents bit the people, so that many Israelites died." Here there is no divine participation (the snakes are now the subject of the verb instead of the direct object). In verse 7a the nation pleads for forgiveness for speaking against Moses and Yhwh. The restating of the sin is superfluous, and perhaps one of the reasons for its addition ("by speaking against the LORD and against you") is to induce Moses to "pray to the LORD to take away the ser-pents from us," and indeed Moses hears the people's plea. Verses 7b-8, Moses' prayer and the divine response, are further yahwistic interpola-tions (verse 8 is a proleptic insertion of command such as found in Gen. 35:1, Ex. 4:27 and elsewhere). According to E, the snake was built by Moses in verse 9 of his own volition and without God's command or intercession.

6.13.2 The Yahwistic Commentary

The Yahwist, extremely insistent upon divine intervention, adds the Deity at four points in this short narrative (verses 6, 7[2X], 8). Yhwh's command to make the copper snake is in fact critical, since without it, Moses is transformed into a magician whose actions border on idolatry.

6.14 The Conquest (Num. 20-21)

20:14 *Moses sent messengers from Qadesh to the King of Edom, "Thus says your brother Israel: You know all the adversity that has befallen us: 15 how our ancestors went down to Egypt, and we lived in Egypt a long time; and the Egyptians oppressed us and our ancestors; 16 and when we cried to the LORD, he heard our voice, and sent an angel and brought us out of Egypt; and here we are in Qadesh, a town on the edge of your territory. 17 Now let us pass through your land. We will not pass through field or vineyard, or drink water from any well; we will go along the King's Highway, not turning aside to the right hand or to the left until we have passed through your territory." 18 But Edom said to him, "You shall not pass through, or we will come out with the sword against you." 19 The Israelites said to him, "We will stay on the highway; and if we drink of your water, we and our livestock, then we will pay for it. It is only a small matter; just let us pass through on foot."* 20 But he said, "You shall not pass through." And Edom came out against them with a large force, heavily armed. 21 *Thus Edom refused to give Israel passage through their territory; so Israel turned away from them.*

(The Divestment of Aaron, Num. 20:23-29)

21:1 *When the Canaanite, the King of Arad, who lived in the Negeb, heard that Israel was coming by the way of Atharim, he fought against Israel and took some of them captive. 2 Then Israel made a vow to the LORD and said, "If you will indeed give this people into our hands, then we will utterly destroy their towns." 3 The LORD listened to the voice of Israel, and handed over the Canaanites; and they utterly destroyed them and their towns; so the place was called Hormah.*

(The Copper Snake 21:4-9; Itinerary verses 21:10-20)

21:21 Then Israel sent messengers to King Sihon of the Amorites, saying, 22 "Let me pass through your land; we will not turn aside into field or vineyard; we will not drink the water of any well; we will go by the King's Highway until we have passed through your territory." 23 But Sihon would not allow Israel to pass through his territory. Sihon gathered all his people together, and went out against Israel to the wilderness; he came to Jahaz, and fought against Israel. 24 Israel put him to the sword, and took possession of his land from the Arnon to the Jabbok, as far as to the Ammonites; for the boundary of the Ammonites was strong. 25 Israel took all these towns, and Israel settled in all the towns of the Amorites, in Heshbon, and in all its villages. 26 *For Heshbon was the city of King Sihon of the Amorites, who had fought against the former King of Moab and captured all his land as far as the Arnon. 27 Therefore the ballad singers say, "Come to Heshbon, let it be built; let the city of Sihon be established. 28 For fire came out from Heshbon, flame from the city of Sihon. It devoured Ar of Moab, and swallowed up the heights of the Arnon. 29 Woe to you, O Moab! You are undone, O people of Chemosh! He has made his sons fugitives, and his daughters captives, to an Amorite king, Sihon. 30 So their posterity perished from Heshbon to Dibon, and we laid waste until fire spread to Medeba." 31 Thus Israel settled in the land of the Amorites.* 32 Moses sent to spy out Jazer; and they captured its villages, and dispossessed the Amorites who were there. 33 Then they turned and went up the road to Bashan; and King Og of Bashan came out against them, he and all his people, to battle at Edrei. 34 *But the LORD said to Moses, "Do not be afraid of him; for I have given him into your hand, with all his people, and all his land. You shall do to him as you did to King Sihon of the Amorites, who ruled in Heshbon."* 35 So they killed him, his sons, and all his people, until there was no survivor left; and they took possession of his land.

6.14.1 Source Division

There are no special elohistic markers in Num. 21:21-35 (except perhaps for the Emori in verses 21, 32). Why, then, must this series of conquests be attributed to E? As in Num. 20, it is through a process of elimination. In typical J and P conquests divine participation is critical; without divine approval there is no possibility that such an initiative would meet with success. Thus, in the first verses of Chapter 21, when Arad attacks Israel, the nation pleads with Yhwh for victory, which is granted.[117] A number of additional details in this account explicitly contradict J and P and therefore preclude their involvement in this passage. a) Israel *dwells* in the Emorite cities they conquer. In other words, this chapter is in essence a full-fledged occupation narrative.[118] According to Num. 13 (J) however, the Israelites were promised a land of vastly different contours, their inheritance including Hebron, the Negev and the South (which were also promised to Abraham in Gen. 13). The emphasis here is upon the Trans Jordanian North (part of the Northern Kingdom where the elohistic narrative originated); b) According to Deut. 31:14 (J), and Num. 21:13 (P), Moses was not supposed to participate in the conquest of Canaan. This was left to Joshua, Moses' young and vigorous protégé (as we see in Ex. 17:14: "Write this as a reminder in a book and recite it in the hearing of Joshua: I will utterly blot out the remembrance of Amalek from under heaven"). In Num. 21, however, Moses, not Joshua, sends scouts and conquers Yazer; c) Bashan was not among the six Canaanite nations Israel was supposed to battle and annihilate according to Ex. 3:8 (J) (but perhaps Bashanites were considered Emorite, compare Deut. 3:8: "So at that time we took from the two kings of the Amorites the land beyond the Jordan, from the Wadi Arnon to Mount Hermon"); d) Finally, according to J, in Num. 14:20-25 the Israelites are commanded by God to wander the desert until the Egyptian generation dies of old age.[119] There is no indication that this has indeed come to pass, and that it is now time for Israel to occupy and inherit.

Since this account explicitly contradicts J and P more than once, I prefer to assign it to the third tetrateuchal source (E), instead of engaging in eisegetical harmonization. The E conquest narrative begins in Num. 21:21 and continues uninterrupted until verse 25. Verses 26–31

---

117 This episode is generally attributed to J, and cf. Dillmann, Numeri, 117.

118 Cf. Van Seters, *Moses*, 363, who speaks of scholarship's inattention to the widespread evidence of a conquest tradition in the book of Numbers.

119 The passage is attributed to JE by many scholars, e.g., A. H. McNeile, *The Book of Numbers* (Cambridge Bible), Cambridge, 1911, 75-76.

are a poetic interlude or expansion explaining how the Emorite monarch conquered Moabite territory.[120] The E narrative resumes in verse
32 with the conquest of Yaazer and with Og's threatening manoeuvres
in verse 33. Verse 34 is a typical proleptic insertion of command which
gives Israel's bellicosity a yahwistic stamp of approval and implies that
the Lord is responsible for the success of the military campaign. Indeed,
the insertion of this verse just before the final conquest implies divine
approval of all Israelite conquests in Num. 21 (compare the Deuteronomistic command to engage Sihon in Deut. 2:31). The E narrative ends
with the conquest of the Bashan in verse 35.[121]

Although the account in verses 33-35 is very similar to Deut. 3:1-6
(the D parallel), there is little reason to attribute the verses to D[122] or to
a late J.[123] Apart from the proleptic insertion of command, the war plays
out in the same manner as the war with Sihon (the complete annihilation of Og is also parallel to the mass death of the Egyptians in Ex.
14:28). The late frame of Deuteronomy, and especially Deut. 2-3, expands and reworks a number of ancient traditions (e.g. the conquests of
Yair and Mahir, the sons of Menasseh) and there is no reason to assume
the conquest of the Bashan is any different.[124]

6.14.2 The Yahwistic Commentary

E is a northern source and indeed this elohistic conquest is restricted to
the North. The land occupied in this chapter was a significant segment
of the Northern Kingdom, especially towards the end of the eighth
century B.C.E..[125] According to the southern sources (J and P), however,
these conquests are secondary to the main Israelite goals which are
achieved in the books of Joshua–Samuel. According to E, the occupation of these territories is accidental. Israel initially wanted only to pass
through Sihon's land, but when the opportunity presented itself they

---

120 Cf. Gressmann, *Mose*, 306.
121 Vss., 33-35 are attributed by K. H. Cornill (*Einleitung in das Alte Testament*, Freiburg),
     to a later Elohistic stratum.
122 Thus McNeile, *Numbers*, 122-123.
123 Cf. Van Seters, *Moses*, 383-404; "The Conquest of Sihon's Kingdom: A Literary Re-
     examination", *JBL* 91 (1972): 182 – 187.
124 Cf. B. A. Levine *Num. 21-36, A New Translation with Introduction and Commentary*,
     New York, 2000, 128: "On the whole it would appear that Deuteronomy 2-3 drew
     upon the JE {especially E} historiography of Numbers" [the words in parentheses are
     an excerpt from Levine's subsequent discussion].
125 Cf. M. Cogan and H. Tadmor, *II Kings, A New Translation with Introduction and
     Commentary (Anchor Bible)*, New York, 1988, 178.

occupied the territory and settled it. Though this may have been the land of their forefathers, they were never promised it. According to J, the occupation of the ancestral land promised to Israel time and again, is deliberate. Israel has a definite territory in mind and it is not the Emorite lands of Num. 21. Thus, when the Canaanite King of Arad attacks Israel (Num. 21:1-3) they annihilate him but do not occupy his territory. The yahwistic dispatch of messengers to the King of Edom (Num. 20:14-21) fills a similar function in that it emphasizes that Israel has no hostile intentions towards the nations surrounding their ancestral home and only when provoked will they respond. The conquest of Sihon and the Bashan is considered as extraterritorial by J, conquered only because of these nations' bellicosity toward Israel. P expands upon this "accident" and gives these lands to Reuben, Gad and half the tribe of Menasheh (in Num. 32), on condition they help with Israel's intended target, Canaan.

6.15 Addendum: Balaq's fear (Num. 22)

22:2 Now Balaq son of Zippor saw all that Israel had done to the Amorites. 3 Moab was in great dread of the people, *because they were so numerous;* (indeed) Moab was overcome with fear of the People of Israel. 4 *And Moab said to the Elders of Midian, "This horde will now lick up all that is around us, as an ox licks up the grass of the field." Now Balaq son of Zippor was King of Moab at that time* 5 He sent messengers to Balaam son of Beor at Pethor, which is on the Euphrates, in the land of Amaw, to summon him, saying, "A people has come out of Egypt; *they have spread over the face of the earth,* and they have settled next to me. 6 Come now, curse this people for me, since they are stronger than I; perhaps I shall be able to defeat them and drive them from the land; for I know that whomever you bless is blessed, and whomever you curse is cursed." 7 *So the Elders of Moab and the Elders of Midian departed with the fees for divination in their hand; and they came to Balaam, and gave him Balaq's message. 8 He said to them, "Stay here tonight, and I will bring back word to you, just as the LORD speaks to me"; so the officials of Moab stayed with Balaam.* 9 God came to Balaam and said, "Who are these men with you?" 10 Balaam said to God, "King Balaq son of Zippor of Moab, has sent me this message: 11'A people has come out of Egypt and has spread over the face of the earth; now come, curse them for me; perhaps I shall be able to fight against them and drive them out.' " 12 God said to Balaam, "You shall not go with them; you shall not curse the people, for they are blessed." 13 So Balaam rose in the morning, and said to the officials of Balaq, "Go to your own land *for the*

LORD *has refused to let me go with you.*" 14 So the officials of Moab rose and went to Balaq, and said, "Balaam refuses to come with us."

6.15.1 Explanation

This elohistic narrative is properly part of the Balaam cycle and will be discussed further in the following chapter. I include it here as the obvious parallel to the first episode in Ex. 1, thus forming an *inclusio*. Both speak of the monarchical fear of Israel and of a failed attempt to counter the threat. In both accounts, Israel has demonstrated no bellicosity towards the kingdom in question; neither episode mentions Moses, who features prominently in every other elohistic narrative of this cycle.

6.16 Summary

6.16.1 The Elohistic Narrative: A Summary

The isolation and analysis of the elohistic Moses cycle is particularly difficult. A modicum of continuity is apparent in E's Abraham cycle, as well as in E's account of Joseph's sojourn in Egypt. Even in the elohistic Jacob cycle, the "gaps" in narrative continuity are relatively minor and are usually an indication of the terse elohistic style. The Moses cycle is quite different. Documentarians have always contended that the elohistic Moses cycle was at best fragmented and, according to some, non-existent. In this chapter I hope to have proved not only the existence of the elohistic Moses cycle but also its narrative continuity. The main distinguishing criteria between E and his supplementary redactors are linguistic and ideological. Some of the better examples are, of course, the exclusive use of "Elohim" as opposed to Yhwh, "the King of Egypt" as opposed to Pharaoh, and "Israel" as opposed to "the People of Israel." According to E, Moses is a miracle worker whose power is independent of God's power. Elohim commands Moses to take Israel out of Egypt but he leaves the *modus operandi* to Moses' discretion. According to E, Israel's sojourn in Egypt lasted a few generations at most, resulting in a small population at the Exodus in contrast to the large numbers posited by J and P (Ex. 12:37; 18:21; Num. 11:21).

The E narrative begins with the decrees of the new King of Egypt, who enslaves the People of Israel and attempts to kill all the new-born males. From Egypt, the narrative moves to Midian and to Elohim's revelation to Moses, the shepherd, who was chosen by Elohim to lead the Israelites out of Egypt. Moses takes leave of his father-in-law and arrives in Egypt, meeting his brother Aaron on the way. Together with the Elders they stand before the King of Egypt and request permission to worship God in the desert. When the King of Egypt refuses, 'Moses retaliates by inflicting three plagues upon Egypt (hailstones, locusts, and darkness). The final plague of darkness causes the Egyptians (but not the King of Egypt) to expel the Israelites. When the King of Egypt hears of the so-called escape, he pursues them until the Sea of Reeds. Moses splits the sea and Israel walks across the sea on dry land. The pursuing Egyptians drown at sea. When the Israelites reach the desert they are faced with three problems: the first is the water shortage, which is solved when the nation arrives at Elim; the second is the attack of Amalekite marauders, which is thwarted by Joshua and Moses' staff; the third is the logistics of leading the nation and judging them, which is solved by Jethro, Moses' wise father-in-law. Finally, at Elohim's mountain, after three days of preparation on the part of Israel, Elohim informs the nation of his seven commandments. Moses stays on Elohim's mountain in order to receive additional instructions and leaves the leadership in the hands of Aaron and Hur. Moses delays his descent and in the absence of a capable leader the people seek an alternative; hence the construction of the Golden Calf. This is the first of a second series three "problems" after the revelation at Elohim's mountain. When Moses hears that Aaron has built a golden calf he breaks the tablets that he received on Elohim's mountain, melts the calf, grinds it to dust and compels the nation to drink the remnants. The second problem is again a lack of water, which Moses solves with his magical staff by striking a rock from which water flows forth. Israel's third encounter with adversity is their rebellion against Elohim, in response to which Elohim (or Moses) sends venomous snakes that cause the death of many Israelites. The nation asks for forgiveness and Moses builds a copper snake which magically heals the stricken Israelites. At this point the Israelites arrive at the border of Canaan and ask permission to pass through the land of Sihon, King of the Emori. Sihon rejects their request and attacks them. The Israelites annihilate Sihon and settle in his land. They then continue, conquer Yaazer and are in turn attacked by Og, whose people they annihilate. The E narrative ends with the Moabite fear of Israel in Chapter 24:2-6, which is parallel the first elohistic episode in Ex. 1 and forms an *inclusio*.

The Elohist does not develop his characters' personalities or create detailed situations as J does. The elohistic narrative is characterized by terse reports which usually present only the minimal necessary information. Like all other E narrative cycles, the elohistic Moses cycle is arranged in a chiastic structure.

The Chiastic Structure

The Egyptian Fear of Israel (Ex. 1:8-20)	The Moabite Fear of Israel (Num. 24:2-15)
The Exodus from Egypt (Ex. 3-14)	The Conquest of the Land (Num. 21:21-35)
I. The Desert Shortages: a) The Water Shortage (Ex. 15:22-27) b) The Amalekite Marauders (Ex. 17:8-13) c) The Appointment of Judges (Ex. 18)	II. The Desert Shortages: c) The Snakes (Num. 21:4-9) b) The Miracle at Qadesh (Num. 20:1-11) a) The Golden Calf (Ex. 24:13-15; 32:1-20)

Chiasmus: The Revelation at Elohim's Mountain (Ex. 19-20)

A.   The Egyptian subjugation of Israel (the first narrative of E's Moses cycle) is parallel to the Moabite fear in 24:2-15 (the final E narrative). Both monarchs (the King of Egypt and Balaq) are terrified of Israel's great vitality and the threat it poses to their regimes. The statements of the two kings regarding Israel are similar: Ex. 1:9-10: "He said to his people, 'Look, the Israelite people are more vital and more powerful than we. Come, let us deal shrewdly with them, or they will increase and, in the event of war, join our enemies and fight against us and escape from the land,'" and Num. 24:6: "Come now, curse this people for me, since they are stronger than I; perhaps I shall be able to defeat them and drive them from the land" (24:6). In both episodes the king attempts to deal with the problem through emissaries, the midwives and Balaam respectively. The attempt ultimately fails because the emissaries are uncompliant, hence the outcome is diametrically opposed to the monarch's wishes: Israel leaves Egypt in one case and is ultimately blessed in the other.

B. Although the Exodus narrative is approximately thirty-five verses long and the entrance to the land is but eight verses, the "entrance narrative" is packed with action and therefore the difference in their relative lengths does not preclude a relationship between the two. Thematically, the connection between these episodes is obvious (exodus and eisodos) but there are more specific signs of the parallelism. Before fleeing, the Israelites ask their Egyptian overlords for permission to sacrifice to their God, and before entering the land Moses asks Sihon for permission to pass through. Both modest requests are refused and aggression is initiated by the nations refusing the right of passage. Israel, however, successfully overcomes these obstacles and succeeds beyond all expectations: the aggressors are drowned or killed. In both accounts, E adds historical details not directly connected to the People of Israel: he states that the Egyptians had never experienced hail or locusts in such force (Ex. 9:24; 10:14), and in Num. 21 he mentions that the border of Amon was difficult to breach. Finally, the three plagues of Egypt (hailstones, locusts and darkness) correspond to the three wars that the Israelites fought in Canaan (against the Emorite king, Sihon, against Yaazer and against Og, the King of the Bashan).

C. The first three problems with which the Israelites are confronted in the desert are parallel to the last three:

1. The first problem of the first series—the water shortage at Shur— is identical with the final problem of the second set (the copper snake narrative). In both cases Israel complains and in both cases the problem is not immediately solved. They continue without water until they reach more fertile lands.

2. The second problem of the first series—the war with Amalek—is parallel to the second problem of the second series, the water shortage at Qadesh. In both cases Moses uses his magic staff and a rock: at Refidim Moses lifts his staff and Israel wins the war, but when Moses tires, he sits on a rock; at Qadesh Moses causes water to flow by striking the rock. Similarly, the construction "להרים יד" (to lift one's hand) introduces the miracle in both short texts.

3. The third problem of the first series—Moses as leader sitting in judgment—is parallel in nature to the first problem of the second series, the Golden Calf. In both cases the *locus in quo* is Elohim's mountain and the problem is connected with Mosaic leadership: in the first instance the cause is his constant presence (from dawn to dusk) and in the second the cause is his prolonged absence. Moses'

task in both cases is identical: to bring God's laws to the masses. In these episodes there is a celebration dedicated to "God," with sacrifices in which Aaron participates. The solution or conclusion in both cases is connected to "spreading the word of God" to the public: Jethro suggests that Moses appoint judges, while as a punishment for building the Golden Calf, the Israelites drink water polluted with its remnants.

Chiasmus: In the middle (the chiasmus) is the most important event in ancient Israelite history—Elohim's revelation of the seven commandments, which are themselves organized chiastically. A divine revelation is also at the center of the Jacob and Joseph cycles.

In addition to the chaistic structures, the numbers three and seven recur several times throughout the narrative. In addition to the seven commandments, there are also the seven stations Israel traversed on their way to Canaan—Shur, Marah, Elim, Refidim, Elohim's mountain, Qadesh, Yahatz—and seven desert episodes: the first series of problems (three), the second series of problems (three) and the revelation at Elohim's mountain. The prominence of the number three is emphasized by the three plagues, the three nations Israel fought, the two triads of desert shortages.

6.16.2 The Yahwistic Commentary: A Summary

The Yahwist fills the gaps in the terse elohistic narrative and addresses some of the many questions that arise. While the editorial themes are similar to those found in the previous narrative cycles, there is a distinct shift in emphasis. Above all else, J emphasizes Yhwh's ascendancy: Yhwh is responsible for the plagues, for the Exodus and for the desert miracles. According to E, Moses is an independent operative. Elohim commands Moses to lead Israel out of Egypt, but the *modus operandi* is left to Moses' discretion. By means of his supplementary interpolation, J succeeds in transforming Moses into a divine vessel with little will of his own, who does nothing without the explicit command or consent of Yhwh. This reaches its height when Yhwh, after the command to strike the rock (Ex. 17), needs to be present during the miracle. The Yahwist also adds a moral dimension to the basic narrative. Before every yahwistic plague, Moses warns Pharaoh of the consequences and gives him a chance to repent. J emphasizes that Yhwh struck only Egypt and not the Israelites dwelling in Goshen. When the

Israelites displease God by building the Golden Calf (idolatry, according to J), J adds three punishments of his own (the Levite's massacre of the sinners [Ex. 32:26-29], the plague [Ex. 32:35] and the replacement of divine leadership with that of an angel [Ex. 33:1-6]). As always, the Yahwist is concerned with Yhwh's status: the plagues are carried out in order to prove Yhwh's supremacy; the miracles in the desert emphasize His power, and even Jethro, a foreigner, states that Yhwh is "is greater than all gods" (Ex. 18:11). A unique element of Yhwh is His awesome countenance. According to J, Yhwh cannot be seen, and therefore a long negotiation concerning boundaries is required prior to the Sinai revelation. Even Moses, the arch-prophet, is permitted to see only Yhwh's back.

J also fills in narrative gaps. He elaborates upon Moses' origins (according to E, Moses appears on the scene only in Midian) and his mostly anonymous family members are given names. E notes that the Israelites were subjects of Pharoah, but J adds that they became his slaves and describes the type of labour the Israelites were forced to perform. As noted previously, erasure was not an option for J. When he disagreed with his elohistic predecessor, he expressed his opinion through repeated interpolations. According to E, the Israelites left Egypt only a few generations after Joseph's death and were therefore not very numerous. According to the Yahwist (and P), the People of Israel left Egypt after many, many years and numbered in the hundreds of thousands (Ex. 18:21). J and P emphasize this opinion/tradition in various ways: a) The original Egyptian army consisting of 600 is enhanced in size so they can pursue such a numerous nation; b) According to J, Moses appointed "officers over the thousands," a bureaucratic necessity in the governance of a large population; c) It is inconceivable that the fragile desert ecology could support the needs of so many people— hence the quails and the manna (Ex. 16[P]).

According to E, the territories which the Israelites inherit are the "Emorite lands" east of the Jordan (Num. 21). According to the Yahwist, however, the majority of the Israelite inheritance is west of the Jordan, especially the Judean territories in the south. The Yahwist highlights the secondary nature of the elohistic conquests in a number of ways: a) The episode which tells of the Edomites' refusal to allow Israel to pass through their land is parallel to E's conquest of Sihon and was added to the Moses cycle in order to bolster the impression that the only reason those lands were occupied was the Emorite aggression and was not due to any promise. "The promised land" is the land of the six nations west of the Jordan; b) In Num. 13, J describes the spies' journey to the promised land, concentrating the narrative on Judean sites (Hebron, Eshkol) and does not mention any territories east of the Jordan; c) According to J, Joshua conquers the promised land, while in Num. 21 the conquest has not yet begun.

7. The Elohistic Balaam Cycle

7.1 Introduction

In an essay reminiscent of Redford's revolutionary analysis of the Joseph cycle, Rofe attempts to demonstrate that the assumption of parallel and independent documents in this part of the Pentateuch is erroneous.[1] Of special note is his analysis of the donkey episode and his suggestion that it should not be attributed to one of the "known" sources.[2] Rofe, also rejects both the supplementary method[3] and the use of the divine names as a distinguishing tool without seriously engaging these positions. As I have stated repeatedly throughout this work, divine names are an important tool of the critical exegete, especially in this unit of the Pentateuch.[4] Yhwh is the Israelite God and it is difficult to assume that he would agree that his people be cursed. After Balaam declares that he is a follower of the Israelite God (Num. 22:18), how could anyone envision that he would curse Israel in favour of Moab? On the other hand, if Balaam is a follower of "Elohim," who represents a more universal Deity than Yhwh, the premise behind the story is believable and Balak's request appears more logical. If this is the case, Yhwh is a foreign element in this cycle and my supplementary

---

1   A. Rofe, *"The Book of Bilaam"* (Numbers 22:2-24:25), *An Inquiry employing the Critical Method and Transmission & Religion History with an Appendix: Bilam in the Deir Alla Inscription* (Hebrew), Jerusalem, 1980.
2   See also J. Van Seters, *Moses*, 405ff. and 19th century precursors M. M. Kalisch, *Bible Studies, Part I: The Prophecies of Balaam (Num. xxii-xxiv) or the Hebrew and the Heathen*, London, 1877; A. Kuenen, "Bileam", *Theologisch Tijdschrift* 18 (1880): 497-540. For a completely different supplementary analysis of this episode see H. C. Schmitt, "Der heidnische Mantiker als Eschatoligischer Jahweprophet, zum Verständnis Bileams in der Endgestalt von Num. 22-24", in *Studien zur Theologie und Religiongeschichte Israels für Otto Kaiser zum 70 Geburtstag* (I. Kottsieper ed.), Göttingen: 1994, 180-198.
3   Rofe, *Balaam*, 12.
4   Rofe claims that there is some logic underlying the use of divine names in ch. 22, but that it cannot be used to distinguish sources; G. B. Gray, *Numbers, A Critical and Exegetical Commentary* (ICC), Edinburgh, 1963, 311, claims that "No conclusive and complete explanation of this usage can be given".

paradigm (E as original, J as the redactor) seems entirely plausible[5]
Even prior to the critical analysis of this cycle one can see that the
verses in which Yhwh is mentioned present an entirely different picture of Balaam and his relationship with God from that in the E verses.

> 1. "He said to them, 'Stay here tonight, and I will bring back
> word to you, just as the LORD speaks to me.'" (22:8).
> 2. "So Balaam rose in the morning, and said to the officials of
> Balak, 'Go to your own land, for the LORD has refused to let
> me go with you.'" (22:13).
> 3. "But Balaam replied to the servants of Balak, 'Although
> Balak were to give me his house full of silver and gold, I could
> not go beyond the command of the LORD my God, to do less
> or more.'" (22:18).
> 4. "You remain here, as the others did, so that I may learn what
> more the LORD may say to me" (22:19).
> 5. The LORD'S [6] anger was kindled because he was going, and
> the angel of the LORD took his stand in the road as his adver-
> sary. Now he was riding on the donkey, and his two servants
> were with him"(22:22).
> 6. "Then Balaam said to Balak, 'Stay here beside your burnt of-
> ferings while I go aside. Perhaps the LORD will come to meet
> me. Whatever he shows me I will tell you.'" (23:3).[7]
> 7. "The LORD put a word in Balaam's mouth, and said, 'Return
> to Balak, and this is what you must say.'" (23:5).
> 8. "How can I curse whom El has not cursed? How can I de-
> nounce those whom the LORD has not denounced?" (23:16).
> 9. "When he came to him, he was standing beside his burnt of-
> ferings with the officials of Moab. Balak said to him, 'What has
> the LORD said?'" (23:17).
> 10. "But Balaam answered Balak, 'Did I not tell you, "Whatever
> the LORD says, that is what I must do?"'" (23:26)

---

5   Compare H. Seebass, Zur literarischen Gestalt der Bileam-Perikope, *ZAW* 107 (1995):
     409-419, who isolates a basic Elohistic document as well, although his divisions
     differ considerably from our own.
6   According to the Septuagint and Samaritan translation, the name of the deity here is
     Yhwh, this is contra the Masoretic text which has Elohim, we accept Yhwh as the
     original with Rudolph, 1938, 103.
     Yahweh also appears throughout the entire donkey episode.
7   *Contra* Gray, *Numbers*, 311, who follows the Syriac translation's "Elohim."

11. "Now Balaam saw that it pleased the LORD to bless Israel, so he did not go, as at other times, to look for omens, but set his face toward the wilderness." (24:1)

12. "Now be off with you! Go home! I said, 'I will reward you richly,' but the LORD has denied you any reward." (24:11)

13. "If Balak should give me his house full of silver and gold, I would not be able to go beyond the word of the LORD, to do either good or bad of my own will; what the LORD says, that is what I will say." (24:13)

It is at once apparent that almost all divine participation in dialogue is "yahwistic." There are two anomalies: "Balaam said to Balak, 'I have come to you now, but do I have power to say just anything? The word God (Elohim) puts in my mouth, that is what I must say.'" (22:38), and, "So Balak said to Balaam, 'Come now, I will take you to another place; perhaps it will please God that you may curse them for me from there.'" (23:27). Following *BHS* (255), I regard the version in 22:38 as dittographic: The original probably read "My God" ("אלהי") *cf.* 22:18: "I could not go beyond the command of the LORD my God, to do less or more." Yhwh's participation in dialogue indicates the following: a) According to the Yahwist, Balaam is a prophet who can speak with Yhwh at any time; hence his promise to the messengers that Yhwh will speak with him during the night. Without these verses, *Elohim* appears to Balaam on his own initiative; b) Balaam promises to speak *Yhwh's* words, whereas *Elohim* commands Balaam to do as he says; c) *Yhwh* puts words into Balaam's mouth, but *Elohim* "encounters Balaam," and the spirit of Elohim descends upon him; d) Balaam claims that Yhwh is his God ("I could not go beyond the command of the LORD my God, to do less or more" [22:18]) and that for this reason he must follow his directives. Elohim, however, must command Balaam not to transgress.

These yahwistic verses paint a picture of Balaam that does not exist in the basic E source.[8] According to E's depiction, Balaam is a magician who was hired by Balak to curse Israel. Elohim, however, prevents this and causes Balaam to bless Israel. The Yahwist portrays Balaam in an entirely different manner. In the yahwistic version, Balaam the sorcerer becomes Balaam the prophet – a favoured prophet at that, with direct access to the Lord. Balaam is presented as a devout believer unwilling to act without Yhwh's express consent. In his role as a prophet, Balaam

---

8   For a third portrayal of Balaam's relationship to the divine cf. Rofe, *Balaam*, and his analysis of the donkey episode in Num. 22:23ff.

is a loyal conveyer of Yhwh's words, and the blessings are thus presented as originating with Yhwh.[9] According to E, however, the words
may be inspired by God, but Balaam is their author. The way in which
Balaam is portrayed in the elohstic text as opposed to the yahwistic
verses listed above is remarkably similar to J's transformation of Moses.
It seems likely that both Balaam and Moses were independent magicians, transformed by J into Yhwh's willing slaves.[10] This preliminary
analysis indicates the likelihood of my supplementary paradigm. The
following pages will be devoted to a lengthier proof.

7.2 The Summons (Num. 22)

2 Now Balak son of Zippor saw all that Israel had done to the Amorites.
3 Moab was in great dread of the people, *because they were so numerous;* (indeed) Moab was overcome with fear of the People of Israel. 4 *And Moab
said to the Elders of Midian, "This horde will now lick up all that is around us, as an ox licks up
the grass of the field." Now Balak son of Zippor was King of Moab at that time.* 5 He sent
messengers to Balaam son of Beor at Pethor, which is on the Euphrates,
in the land of Amaw, to summon him, saying, "A people has come out
of Egypt; *they have spread over the face of the earth,* and they have settled next to
me. 6 Come now, curse this people for me, since they are stronger than
I; perhaps I shall be able to defeat them and drive them from the land;
for I know that whomever you bless is blessed, and whomever you
curse is cursed." 7 *So the Elders of Moab and the Elders of Midian departed with the fees for
divination in their hand; and they came to Balaam, and gave him Balak's message.* 8 *He said to
them, "Stay here tonight, and I will bring back word to you, just as the LORD speaks to me"; so
the officials of Moab stayed with Balaam.* 9 God came to Balaam and said, "Who
are these men with you?" 10 Balaam said to God, "King Balak son of
Zippor of Moab, has sent me this message: 11 'A people has come out
of Egypt and has spread over the face of the earth; now come, curse
them for me; perhaps I shall be able to fight against them and drive
them out.' " 12 God said to Balaam, "You shall not go with them; you
shall not curse the people, for they are blessed." 13 So Balaam rose in

---

9   J. W. Wevers, The Balaam Narrative according to the Septuagint, in *Lectures et
     Relectures* (J. M. Avwers and A. Wenin eds.), Leuven, 1999, 133-144, explains the
     Septuagint's tendency to substitute Elohim in lieu of almost every occurrence of
     Yhwh, as the translator's reticence to attribute true "yahwistic" prophecy to Balaam.

10   G. W. Coats, Balaam, Sinner or Saint in Num. 24?, *Biblical Research* 18 (1973): 21-29,
     and J. Van Seters, From Faithful Prophet to Villian; Observations on the Tradition
     History of the Bilaam Story, in *A Biblical Itinerary, JSOTS* 240 (1997): 126-132, omit
     this stage of character development.

the morning, and said to the officials of Balak, "Go to your own land, *for the LORD has refused to let me go with you."* 14 So the officials of Moab rose and went to Balak, and said, "Balaam refuses to come with us."15 Once again Balak sent officials, more numerous and more distinguished than these. 16 They came to Balaam and said to him, "Thus says Balak son of Zippor: 'Do not let anything hinder you from coming to me; 17 for I will surely do you great honor, and whatever you say to me I will do; come, curse this people for me.' " 18 *But Balaam replied to the servants of Balak, "Although Balak were to give me his house full of silver and gold, I could not go beyond the command of the LORD my God, to do less or more. 19 You remain here, as the others did, so that I may learn what more the LORD may say to me."* 20 That night God came to Balaam and said to him, "If the men have come to summon you, get up and go with them; but do only what I tell you to do." 21 So Balaam got up in the morning, saddled his donkey, and went with the officials of Moab.

The Donkey Episode 22:22-35

7.2.1 Source Division

Wellhausen[11] speaks of verses 2-5 as being a complicated amalgam of material and Rofe,[12] maintains that the first verses reflect the parallelism of ancient Canaanite-Israelite poesy. To my mind, however, there are no real complications in the opening verses of the chapter and the material may be safely assigned to the usual Pentateuchal sources capable of both poesy and prose. According to Rofe (36), verse 2 ["Now Balak son of Zippor saw all that Israel had done to the Amorites"] is a secondary addition connecting the Balaam cycle with the preceding narrative. However, I maintain that this pericope is organic to the E source and there is little reason to assume an independent tradition history. Moreover "Amorites" is the term used to describe the inhabitants of the land in the E narrative of the preceding chapter (Num. 21). Verses 2-6 are partially attributed to E, the later insertions include "because they were so numerous" in verse 3, and "they have spread over the face of the earth" in verse 5 which in all likelihood should be attributed to J, who has emphasized Israel's large population in past narratives; and the priestly insertion of verse 4, which features the Elders of

---

11   Wellhausen, *Hexateuch*, 109-111.

12   Rofe, *Balaam*, 35, following E. J. Sutcliffe, "De Unitate Litteraria Num xxii", *Biblica* 7 (1926): 3-9.

Midian, thus alluding to the sin of Baal Peor in Num. 25.[13] The Moabite
king of these verses is parallel to E's "King of Egypt," as noted above in
the Moses cycle.

Verse 7 (P) alludes once more to the sin of Baal Peor.[14] Verse 8 is
yahwistic ("He said to them, 'Stay here tonight, and I will bring back
word to you, just as the LORD speaks to me'; so the officials of Moab
stayed with Balaam").[15] One need not necessarily resort to the divine
name criterion, as there are other reasons to attribute verse 8 to a secondary source, as I shall proceed explain. In verse 14, Balak's messengers inform him of Balaam's refusal: "So the officials of Moab rose and
went to Balak, and said, 'Balaam refuses to come with us.'" According
to verse 13b, however, Yhwh caused Balaam to refuse Balak's messengers: "Go to your own land, for the LORD has refused to let me go with
you." One may claim that the difference between the two quotations is
insignificant and that verse 14 is merely an interpretation or restating of
Balaam's response. In 24:11, however, Balak himself declares "Now be
off with you! Go home! I said, 'I will reward you richly,' but the LORD
has denied you any reward," Why then should his messengers refrain
from mentioning the deity's role? Thus verse 8, as well as verses 18-19,
which all feature Yhwh, should be attributed to a secondary source.

7.3 The First Blessing (Num. 22-23)

36 When Balak heard that Balaam had come, he went out to meet him
at Ir-moab, on the boundary formed by the Arnon, at the farthest point
of the boundary. 37 Balak said to Balaam, "Did I not send to summon
you? Why did you not come to me? Am I not able to honor you?" 38
*Balaam said to Balak, "I have come to you now, but do I have power to say just anything? The
word my God puts in my mouth, that is what I must say."* 39 Then Balaam went with
Balak, and they came to Kiriath-huzoth. 40 Balak sacrificed oxen and
sheep, and sent them to Balaam and to the officials who were with him.

---

13 *Contra* Rofe, *Balaam*, 35 who only attributes the expression "the Elders of Midian" to
    P. P should not, however, be discounted as the author of the more poetic "This
    horde will now lick up all that is around us, as an ox licks up the grass of the field."

14 Dillmann, *Numeri*, 143 assigns the verse to J, but Wellhausen's assignment to P is
    more judicious.

15 Cf. the above analysis of verses featuring Yahweh. Very interestingly, the German
    scholar Steuernagel (C. Steuernagel, *Lehrbuch der Einleitung in das Alte Testament mit
    einem Anhang ueber die Apokryphen und Pseudepigraphen*, Tübingen, 1912, 171),
    attributes all appearances of Yhwh (including verse 8, see also verses 13, 18-19) to a
    later expansion of E ("E2") – an early parallel, to my methodology.

41 *On the next day Balak took Balaam and brought him up to Bamoth-baal; and from there he could see part of the People of Israel.* 23:1 Then Balaam said to Balak, "Build me seven altars here, and prepare seven bulls and seven rams for me." 2 Balak did as Balaam had said; and Balak and Balaam offered a bull and a ram on each altar. 3 *Then Balaam said to Balak, "Stay here beside your burnt offerings while I go aside. Perhaps the LORD will come to meet me. Whatever he shows me I will tell you." And he went to a bare height.* 4 God met Balaam; *and Balaam said to him, "I have arranged the seven altars, and have offered a bull and a ram on each altar."; 5 The LORD put a word in Balaam's mouth, and said, "Return to Balak, and this is what you must say." 6 So he returned to Balak, who was standing beside his burnt offerings with all the officials of Moab. 7 Then Balaam uttered his oracle, saying: "Balak has brought me from Aram, the King of Moab from the eastern mountains: 'Come, curse Jacob for me; Come, denounce Israel!' 8 How can I curse whom God has not cursed? How can I denounce those whom the LORD has not denounced? 9 For from the top of the crags I see him, from the hills I behold him; Here is a people living alone, and not reckoning itself among the nations! 10 Who can count the dust of Jacob, or number the dust-cloud of Israel? Let me die the death of the upright, and let my end be like his!" 11 Then Balak said to Balaam, "What have you done to me? I brought you to curse my enemies, but now you have done nothing but bless them." 12 He answered, "Must I not take care to say what the LORD puts into my mouth?" 13 So Balak said to him, "Come with me to another place from which you may see them; you shall see only part of them, and shall not see them all; then curse them for me from there." 14 So he took him to the field of Zophim, to the top of Pisgah. He built seven altars, and offered a bull and a ram on each altar. 15 Balaam said to Balak, "Stand here beside your burnt offerings, while I meet the LORD over there." 16 The LORD met Balaam, put a word into his mouth, and said, "Return to Balak, and this is what you shall say." 17 When he came to him, he was standing beside his burnt offerings with the officials of Moab. Balak said to him, "What has the LORD said?"* 18 Then Balaam uttered his oracle, saying: "Rise, Balak, and hear; listen to me, O son of Zippor: 19 God is not a human being, that he should lie, or a mortal, that he should change his mind. Has he promised, and will he not do it? Has he spoken, and will he not fulfill it? 20 *See, I received a command to bless; he has blessed, and I cannot revoke it. 21 He has not beheld misfortune in Jacob; nor has he seen trouble in Israel. The LORD their God is with them, acclaimed as a king among them.* 22 God, who brings them out of Egypt, is like the horns of a wild ox for them. 23 Surely there is no enchantment in Jacob, no divination in Israel; now it shall be said of Jacob and Israel, 'See what God has done!' 24 Look, a people rising up like a lioness, and rousing itself like a lion! It does not lie down until it has eaten the prey and drunk the blood of the slain." 25 *Then Balak said to Balaam, "You do not curse them at all, and do not bless them at all." 26 But Balaam answered Balak, "Did I not tell you, 'Whatever the LORD says, that is what I must do'?"*

7.3.1 Source Division

Num. 22:22-37 (the donkey episode) belongs to a non-yahwistic secondary source. This episode's portrayal of the divine differs markedly
from J's or E's descriptions. According to J, Yhwh is not angry at Balaam; after all, Balaam embarks upon his journey only after being explicitly instructed by the Lord to do so. However, according to Num.
22:22-37, Yhwh *is* angry with Balaam, who in this episode is portrayed
as cruel and easily annoyed. Outside these verses Balaam is a positive
character who blesses Israel and "converts" (or is converted) to Yahwism.[16]

The basic E narrative resumes in 22:36-37 with the meeting between
Balak and Balaam. Following BHS, I hypothesized that verse 38 was
yahwistic and that it originally read "אלהי" (in lieu of "Elohim"). Although I consider this likely in light of the idea expressed in the verse,
it is hypothetical, and there is no textual corroboration for this slight
emendation. Verse 41 is secondary (Israel's large population): According to this verse Balaam sees only a small part of a large nation, but
according to E, Israel is not so numerous, *cf.* vs. 23:13 (another yahwistic elaboration in the same vein). The E narrative continues in verse
23:1-2 with the construction of the altars and the prepatory ceremony.
Verse 3: "Then Balaam said to Balak, 'Stay here beside your burnt offerings while I go aside. Perhaps the LORD will come to meet me. Whatever he shows me I will tell you.' And he went to a bare height" reiterates Balaam's promise to faithfully convey Yhwh's message.[17]
According to E, Balaam makes no such commitment. This is clearly a
yahwistic addition which reflects J's conversion of Balaam. E continues
in 4a: "God met Balaam:"—Elohim encounters Balaam who then delivers his first blessing. Verses 4b-6 are yahwistic and imply that this prepatory ceremony met with Yhwh's approval; without this insertion, the
text could imply that the sacrifices were responsible for Elohim's re-
sponsiveness.[18]

In Num. 23:7-24:25 Balaam blesses Israel four times, thus thwarting
Balak's plans to use him to curse Israel. Following Dillmann,[19] Documentary scholars attributed the first two blessings to E and the final
two blessings to J. Correctly observing that the first two compositions

---

16   For the *Sitz im Leben* of the episode *cf.* Rofe, *Balaam*, and my own analysis in www.
     biblecriticism.com/com.numbers_22.doc.

17   Although according to Gray, *Numbers*, 310, Steuernagel also attributes this verse to
     his E2, I was unable to locate this particular assignment in Steuernagel's work.

18   Note Steuernagel's assignment of 4b and 5a to his E2, *Lehrbuch*, 171.

19   Dillmann, *Numeri*, 149.

are blessings while the final two are poetic prophecy, Dillmann attributed each pair to a different source. However, his division does not do justice to the internal connections between the second and the third compositions.[20] My division of the blessings—the first blessing as yahwistic, while the second, third and fourth are attributed to E—is closer to Wellhausen's original assignment of the final two blessings to the elohistic corpus.[21] The first blessing begins in verse 7 with the summons "Come, curse Jacob for me; Come, denounce Israel!" which is answered in verse 8: "How can I curse whom God has not cursed? How can I denounce those whom the LORD has not denounced?" In other words, "Yahweh" is integral to the first part of this blessing. In verse 10, Israel's great size is emphasized: "Who can count the dust of Jacob, or number the dust-cloud of Israel?," a theme which I have throughout attributed to J (or to P). Finally, at the conclusion of Balaam's oration (10b), he expresses a sincere desire: "Let me die the death of the upright, and let my end be like his!" Balaam is presented as a philo-Israelite, an idea consistent with Balaam's Yahwism throughout the Balaam cycle.

The second blessing is primarily elohistic, with the exception of verses 20-21: "See, I received a command to bless; he has blessed, and I cannot revoke it. He has not beheld misfortune in Jacob; nor has he seen trouble in Israel. The LORD their God is with them, acclaimed as a king among them" – an allusion to the previous yahwistic oration.[22] Verse 23:19 claims that "God is not a human being, that he should lie, or a mortal, that he should change his mind. Has he uttered, and will he not do it? Has he spoken, and will he not fulfill it?" But what promise did God carry out? God's only "word" to Israel according to E, is the facilitation of their deliverance from Egypt through Moses, which is indeed alluded to in verse 22: "God, who brings them out of Egypt, is like the horns of a wild ox for them." One may object and claim that according to E, Moses delivered Israel (as in Ex. 32:1: "Moses, the man who brought us up out of the land of Egypt"), but, as in the case of Joseph's ascendancy to the throne, the text makes it clear (in Gen. 50:20: "Even though you intended to do harm to me, God intended it for good, in order to preserve a numerous people, as he is doing today") that Elohim/God is ultimately responsible for the deliverance. (And

---

20 The internal connections will be elaborated upon in my analysis of those units, see Levine, *Numbers*, 211.

21 Wellhausen, *Hexateuch*, 349; note however that Wellhausen eventually concurred with Dillmann's opinion and assigned Chapter 24 to J.

22 Compare L. E. Binns, *The Book of Numbers*, Westminster, 1927, 164-165, who also identified Yahwistic additions.

note the appearance of his angel in Ex. 14:"The angel of God...moved and went behind them.") Furthermore, it should be noted that biblical poetry is often drawn from outside non-narrative sources and, should therefore not be expected to conform entirely to the worldview or storyline of the compiler (in this case E). Verse 23, which may be safely assigned to E, since it coheres well with the previous verse ("See what God has done") is probably a further reference to the Exodus. The crouching lion of Verse 24 appears once more in the following oracle/blessing.

7.3.2 The first in a series of three

This blessing is the first in a series of three.[23] I reject the previous Documentary division of Balaam's blessings.[24] Despite the fact that Balaam's first orations are ones of praise and Balaam's final orations are prophetic, the compositions are interconnected and should not be arbitrarily assigned to different sources. Indeed, as Balak himself says, the first elohistic composition is neither a blessing nor a curse (verse 25) but rather speaks of the fulfilment of divine promises and is thus a fitting introduction to the two prophetic compositions.

Since the first blessing was assigned to J, it follows that E's prepatory ceremony in 23:1-2,4a functioned as the introduction to the second blessing (23:18 ff.). The dialogue between Balaam and Balak which follows the first blessing (23:11-13), as well as the introduction to the second blessing (23:14-17), are yahwistic interpolations which were added for the sake of continuity and cohesiveness and the name Yahweh indeed appears three times in this section (23:12, 16, 17). Since there are no textual fractures in the verses under discussion (23:11-17), there is also no reason to assume a plurality of sources and the entire section can be safely attributed to J.[25] A similar dialogue is recorded in 23:25-26, following the second blessing, and this too can be attributed to J. As I mentioned above in my discussion of yahwistic verses compared to elohistic verses, the J dialogues strip Balaam of any independence and present him as no more than Yahweh's mouthpiece.

---

23 And compare Levine *Numbers*, 212, who spoke of the sequential dynamic of all four blessings.

24 Modern documentary divisions such as Graupner, *Elohist*, 413, offer little improvement.

25 Indeed Gray, *Numbers*, 313 and others consider some of the frames to the blessings to be secondary, anticipating our supplementary methodology.

7.4 The Second Blessing (Num. 23-24)

23:27 So Balak said to Balaam, "Come now, I will take you to another place; perhaps it will please God that you may curse them for me from there." 28 So Balak took Balaam to the top of Peor, *(which overlooks the wasteland.)* 29 Balaam said to Balak, "Build me seven altars here, and prepare seven bulls and seven rams for me." 30 So Balak did as Balaam had said, and offered a bull and a ram on each altar. 24:1 *Now Balaam saw that it pleased the LORD to bless Israel, so he did not go, as at other times, to look for omens, but set his face toward the wilderness.* 2 Balaam looked up and saw Israel camping tribe by tribe. Then the spirit of God came upon him, 3 and he uttered his oracle, saying: "The oracle of Balaam son of Beor, the oracle of the man whose eye is clear, 4 the oracle of one who hears the words of God, who sees the vision of the Almighty, who falls down, but with eyes uncovered: 5 How fair are your tents, O Jacob, your encampments, O Israel! 6 Like palm groves that stretch far away, like gardens beside a river, *like aloes that the Lord has planted,* like cedar trees beside the waters.7 Water shall flow from his buckets, and his seed shall have abundant water, his king shall be higher than Agag, and his kingdom shall be exalted. 8 God who brings him out of Egypt, is like the horns of a wild ox for him; he shall devour the nations that are his foes and break their bones. He shall strike with his arrows. 9 He crouched, he lay down like a lion, and like a lioness; who will rouse him up? Blessed is everyone who blesses you, and cursed is everyone who curses you."

7.4.1 Source Division

J supplements E's second blessing only minimally. Num. 24:1: "Now Balaam saw that it pleased the LORD to bless Israel, so he did not go, as at other times, to look for omens, but set his face toward the wilderness" is attributed to J on the basis of the name Yahweh.[26] Its addition to the text achieves two goals. The verse transforms Balaam into an "Israelite" prophet of sorts rather than a powerful sorcerer and induces prophecy by "legitimate means" rather than sorcery or incantations, as Balaam himself remarks in the first (elohistic) blessing: "Surely there is no enchantment in Jacob, no divination in Israel".[27] The verse also reflects a different standpoint concerning the conquest of the land: Ba-

---

26 Compare Steuernagel's assignment to "E2", *Lehrbuch*, 171.

27 And cf. Y. Licht, *A Commentary on the Book of Numbers* (Hebrew), Jerusalem, 1995, 33, on this verse.

laam faces the desert and sees the People of Israel (note also the last
words of 23:28: "Which overlooks the wasteland," which are in the
yahwistic vein). According to E, however, the Israelites have just finished their occupation and settlement of the Emorite land; their desert
wandering has ended. This verse is in agreement, therefore, with the
later yahwistic tradition which maintains that the land was conquered
by Joshua. The elohistic verse 2 originally stood on its own. Balaam did
not face the desert; rather, he faced the recently conquered Emorite
lands. Aside from this verse, the Yahwist intervened only once more in
the blessing, in verse 6b "like aloes that the LORD has planted." This
yahwistic fragment adds a theological dimension to the agricultural
image in verse 6 by alluding to Yhwh's munificence: "Like palm groves
that stretch far away, like gardens beside a river, like cedar trees beside
the waters."

7.5 The Third Blessing (Num. 24)

10 Then Balak's anger was kindled against Balaam, and he struck his
hands together. Balak said to Balaam, "I summoned you to curse my
enemies, but instead you have blessed them *these three times.* 11 Now be off
with you! Go home! *I said, 'I will reward you richly,' but the LORD has denied you any
reward.*" 12 And Balaam said to Balak, *"Did I not tell your messengers whom you sent
to me,* 13 *'If Balak should give me his house full of silver and gold, I would not be able to go beyond the word of the LORD, to do either good or bad of my own will; what the LORD says, that is
what I will say'?* 14 I am going to my people; let me advise you what this
people will do to your people in days to come. 15 So he uttered his
oracle, saying: "The oracle of Balaam son of Beor, the oracle of the man
whose eye is clear, 16 the oracle of one who hears the words of God,
and knows the knowledge of the Most High, who sees the vision of the
Almighty, who falls down, but with his eyes uncovered: 17 I see him,
but not now; I behold him, but not near—a star shall come out of Jacob,
and a scepter shall rise out of Israel; it shall crush the borderlands of
Moab, and the territory of all the Shethites.18 Edom will become a possession, Seir a possession of its enemies, while Israel does valiantly.19
One out of Jacob shall rule, and destroy the survivors of Ir."20 Then he
looked on Amalek, and uttered his oracle, saying: "First among the
nations was Amalek, but its end is to perish forever." 21 Then he
looked on the Kenite, and uttered his oracle, saying: "Enduring is your
dwelling place, and your nest is set in the rock; 22 yet Kain is destined
for burning. How long shall Asshur take you away captive?" 23 Again
he uttered his oracle, saying: "Alas, who shall live when God does this?

24 But ships shall come from Kittim and shall afflict Asshur and Eber; and he also shall perish forever."25 Then Balaam got up and went back to his place, and Balak also went his way.

7.5.1 Source Division

In this third and final prophetic blessing, J's supplementation is re-stricted to the introduction. Balak is, of course, angry with Balaam, because Balaam has reneged on their "bargain" and blessed Israel in-stead of cursing them: "I summoned you to curse my enemies, but in-stead you have blessed them" (24:10). I attribute this verse to E, aside from the addition at the end of the verse "these three times," which is secondary and consistent with J's addition of numbers to Gen. 29-30's list of Jacob's sons.[28] Verses 11b and 12b-13 are theological additions emphasizing Balaam's conversion to "abject" Yahwism.[29] Levine claims that the final verses of the chapter are a secondary expansion of the prophecy / blessing, since they discuss occurrences beyond the limited Israelite scope; [30] this, however, is the final Elohistic episode and thus a concluding statement of this nature is not unexpected. Poetic prophecy or blessing is a common way of concluding narrative complexes, and compare the ending of the book of Genesis, Deuteronomy, and II Sam-uel.

7.6 Summary

The unity and integrity of the elohistic Balaam cycle is apparent. This cycle is the story of how Balaam, a non-Israelite sorcerer, converted to the elohistic "religion" of fear of God and was granted true prophecy (The yahwistic conversion is confined to the manner in which Balaam induces the prophetic state; while at first he requires "props" [נחשים], beginning with the third blessing (24:1) the Lord confers his spirit di-rectly upon Balaam.) At the beginning of the story cycle Balaam was willing to curse Israel and only Elohim's express warning prevented him from doing so. At the end of the story (24:14), Balaam blesses Is-rael without being asked to do so: "I am going to my people; let me advise you what this people will do to your people in days to come."

---

28   Compare, Gray, *Numbers*, 313, and many others.
29   Compare Steuernagel's assignment to "E2", *Lehrbuch*, 171.
30   Levine, *Numbers*, 237-238.

At the beginning of the story, Balaam "calls on God" by means of altars and sacrifices, perhaps in order to try to influence the divine will, whereas at the end of the story he does not attempt to influence the divine will and is granted true prophecy. The Yahwist, on the other hand, converts Balaam to Yahwism from the outset. Thus Balaam expects divine communication, already in the introduction to the story and is unwilling to transgress against Yhwh for any reason whatsoever. The Yahwist thus succeeds in obfuscating the spiritual revolution depicted in the E story.

Structural Analysis:
The first part of the Balaam cycle (Num. 22:2-14) belongs structurally and linguistically to the Moses cycle and is parallel to the first elohistic episode in Ex. 1. Thematically, it belongs to the Balaam narratives and for this reason it was analysed here. The structural analysis of the cycle must therefore begin with 22:15-21 (Balak's second attempt to convince Balaam to come and curse Israel). As in all previous "cycles," the Balaam narratives are organized chiastically.

> 1. The introduction to the blessings (22:15-21) is parallel to the final blessing/prophecy: Balak is frightened of Israel and hires Balaam's services (22:20). This fear is entirely justified, since Balaam predicts Moab's annihilation in 24:17: "a star shall come out of Jacob, and a scepter shall rise out of Israel; it shall crush the borderlands of Moab, and the territory of all the Shethites." When Balak sent for Balaam he came and when Balak commanded him to leave, he left. Balak's expectation regarding Balaam's power to curse at the beginning of the cycle—"Come, curse this people for me"—is crushed at its end: (22:17): "Balak said to Balaam, 'I summoned you to curse my enemies, but instead you have blessed them'" (24:10); Balaam is promised "I will surely do you great honor, and whatever you say to me I will do" (22:17), but ultimately he spurns it all. At the beginning Balaam "got up in the morning, saddled his donkey, and went with the officials of Moab" (22:21); in the end "Balaam got up and went back to his place" (24:25).
> 2. The first two blessings share two sets of similar verses: a) 23:24: "Look, a people rising up like a lioness, and rousing itself like a lion! It does not lie down until it has eaten the prey and drunk the blood of the slain," and 24:9: "He crouched, he lay down like a lion, and like a lioness; who will rouse him up?" (For the subjugation of enemies in the second blessing, see

24:8b: "He shall devour the nations that are his foes and break their bones"); b) 23:22: "God, who brings them out of Egypt, is like the horns of a wild ox for them," and 24:8: "God who brings him out of Egypt, is like the horns of a wild ox for him." The obvious parallels between the two blessings should not be interpreted as evidence of two independent sources but rather as part of the chiastic structure.

8. Angels and the Tent of Meeting in the J and E Corpuses

8.1 The Angel

In Ex. 33:1-7, Yhwh punishes the Israelites for the construction of the Golden Calf. Instead of unmediated divine leadership, an angel is appointed by Yhwh to lead them the rest of the way, since Yhwh's anger would probably overwhelm him if he were to lead them and might well "consume them on their way" (33:3). Many exegetes, especially the more conservative Documentary scholars (thus Kautzsch, 151), claim that this passage is part of the E document and that Yhwh's angel is parallel to the guardian angel who protected Israel during their Exodus from Egypt.[1] The assignment of this section to E is, however, untenable, for the following reasons: a) The angel's leadership role is portrayed in these verses as a punishment; according to 33:1-7 *Yhwh* led Israel before their sin. Divine leadership is a yahwistic concept, whereas according to the elohistic document Moses led Israel out of Egypt and brought them to the land of the Emori (e.g. Ex. 32:2: "As for this Moses, the man who brought us up out of the land of Egypt, we do not know what has become of him."); b) Ex. 33:1-3 cites a promise made to the patriarchs. According to the Elohist, however, God never promised Canaan to the patriarchs. The promise stratum is a yahwistic novelty, as demonstrated throughout my work; c) The language and themes in this section are yahwistic (the promise, the Canaanite nations, a land of milk and honey);[2] d) Last, but certainly not least, is the consistent use of "Yhwh" and the complete absence of "Elohim."[3]

Why, according to J, would Yhwh choose to punish Israel in this way? The answer to this question is straightforward if one accepts these verses as Supplementary redaction. In the Covenant Code (Ex. 23:20-21), God announces the appointment of an emissary or angel to lead the People of Israel into Canaan. This appointment, however, is not presented as a punishment as it is in Ex. 33:1-7. The Yahwist, who

---

1   Thus E. Kautzsch, *Heilige Schrift*, 151.

2   For Mount Horev or Horev (verse 6) *cf.* above, Ex. 3:1.

3   Indeed neither Zimmer, *Elohist*, nor Graupner, *Elohist*, in their very different treatments of the Elohistic corpus, assign this passage to E.

was familiar with the Covenant Code and edited it (*cf.* below, Appendix A, Ex. 24:1-11), was faced with a problem: according to his theocentric world view, Yhwh and not his angel was supposed to lead the Israelites to their promised land (see Ex. 3:8: "I have come down to deliver them from the Egyptians, and to bring them up out of that land to a good and broad land"). In order to integrate his viewpoint with the Covenant Code, the Yahwist presented the angel's leadership as the unsavoury but necessary alternative. Indeed, in other J verses Yhwh is once again established as leader (Ex. 34:11).

Supplementation of the same nature is also found in Num. 20:14-21—Israel's failed attempt to reach Canaan via Edom—also identified as elohistic by many Documentary scholars who ignore the use of Yhwh in this passage.[4] Israel's petition to Edom includes an historical preamble: "and when we cried to the LORD, he heard our voice, and sent an angel and brought us out of Egypt; and here we are in Kadesh, a town on the edge of your territory...let us pass through your land" (20:16). According to J, however, Yhwh, and not a mere angel or messenger, was the sole redeemer. Even according to E, the angel's role in the Exodus was minor and Moses was the true facilitator. Was there perhaps a third position, according to which an angel or divine emissary delivered the Israelites from their oppressors (in accordance with Josh. 2:1-4: "Now the angel of the LORD went up from Gilgal to Bochim, and said, 'I brought you up from Egypt, and brought you into the land that I had promised to your ancestors'")? The unidentified subject of the verb "[He] brought us out of Egypt" could refer to the Lord's messenger, but also to the Lord himself (as in the first part of the verse—"He [the Lord] heard our voice.") This ambiguity may be deliberate and perhaps represents a subtle attempt to harmonise between E's tradition of an angel and J's theocentricism.

8.2 The Tent of Meeting

In the Pentateuch there are two traditions concerning the Tent of Meeting.[5] The first and more widespread tradition is priestly, describing the Tent of Meeting as Yhwh's residence at the center of the camp. The other "Tent Tradition" appears in three Pentateuchal episodes—Ex.

---

4   E.g. Binns, *Numbers*, 133-134.
5   For a longer discussion on this subject, see I. Knohl, Two Aspects of the Tent of Meeting, in *Tehillah le-Moshe: Biblical and Judaic Studies in Honour of M. Greenberg*, Winona Lake, 73-80.

33:7-11, Num. 11:16-17, 24b-30,[6] and Num. 12—and describes the Tent as a secluded retreat outside the camp where people search for Yhwh. These three sections are often assigned to the elohistic composition because of their connection to prophetic narrative. Such an assignment is, however, completely untenable for many reasons, including the following: a) The Pentateuchal corpus with the most affinity to prophecy is the yahwistic plague narrative rather than E, which is characterised by the relative absence of the divine and the dominance of human initiative;[7] b) In Ex. 18 (a predominantly elohistic chapter), Moses appoints judges and leaders who are to aid him with their inquiries regarding God's word and make known "the statutes and instructions of God" to the nation. In Ex. 33:7 everyone who needed to know Yhwh's word was to seek it at the tent; c) Num. 11 speaks of "the seventy Elders" who are mentioned earlier only in the yahwistic supplementation of Ex. 24. Instead of seventy Elders, E has judges; d) Num. 12 features Miriam, Moses' sister, who is absent in the elohistic Moses cycle. Miriam does appear, however, in the yahwistic addendum to Israel's thanksgiving song in Ex. 14 and may also be the unidentified sister of Ex. 2; e) In Ex. 33 and in Num. 11 Joshua is referred to as "Moses' aide" and supposedly never leaves Moses or the tent of meeting. According to the Elohist (Ex. 17:8-13), however, Joshua is a war-chief; f) The sobriquet "עבד" (slave, servant) to describe the relationship between a prophet and God (Num. 12:7: "Not so with my servant Moses; he is entrusted with all my house") appears only in later strata of narrative material such as Deuteronomy 34 and throughout Joshua[8] g) Moses' humility in Num. 12 is reminiscent of his evasion of God's mission in Ex. 4 (which is a yahwistic narrative); h) God reveals himself above the tent of meeting in a cloud, a yahwistic and priestly mode of revelation; God never appears in a cloud according to the Elohist; i) Most importantly, the absence of the elohistic "Elohim" and the exclusive use of Yhwh throughout these passages are very telling.

---

6 Binns division in *Numbers*, 65-72; and cf. Sommer's superior treatment of the chapter in B. D. Sommer, Reflecting on Moses – The Redaction of Num. 11, *JBL* (118): 1999, 601-624.

7 Compare Childs, *Exodus*, 146-147.

8 This sobriquet leads some scholars to assign Num. 12 to a late editorial stratum, cf. T. Römer, Nombre 11-12 et la Question d'une Redaction Deuteronomique dans le Pentateuque, in *Deuteronomy and Deuteronomistic Literature* (M. Vervenne and J. Lust eds.), Leuven: 481-498; , A. H. Gunneweg, Das Gesetz und die Propheten: Eine Auslegung von Ex. 33,7-11, Num.11,4-12,8, Dtn 31,14ff, *ZAW* 102 (1990): 169-180; L. Schmidt, Mose, die 70 Ältesten und die Propheten in Num. 11 und 12, in *Gesammelte Aufsätze zum Pentateuch* (BZAW 263), Berlin, 1998, 251-279.

In fact, there is only one reason not to assign these sections to J. According to Num. 12:7 Yhwh speaks to Moses: "face to face, clearly, not in riddles; and he beholds the form of the LORD." These verses seemingly contradict the divine prohibition "you cannot see my face; for no one shall see me and live" (Ex. 33:20). Even Moses (the holiest of men, according to J) is able to see only God's back. One must, however, distinguish between speaking to Yhwh face to face in Num. 12:7 and "setting eyes upon his presence" in Ex. 33:18-23. They are different types of contact: Ex. 34:5 states that "the Lord descended in a cloud." The image or form which Moses beheld in his "face to face" dialogues with Yhwh is a pillar of cloud, (P makes this very clear in Ex. 33:9-11: "When Moses entered the tent, the pillar of cloud would descend and stand at the entrance of the tent, and the LORD would speak with Moses".) The difference between Moses and other prophets, according to Num. 12, is that while "most" prophets' revelatory experience consists of a dream or a riddle, Moses speaks to God directly, via a cloud. Even Moses, however, is unable to behold Yhwh in his glory.[9]

A few more words concerning the function of the above passages are perhaps in order. In Ex. 3-4, Moses was portrayed as a coward and based upon these chapters one may question his qualifications for the task of leading Israel out of Egypt and through the desert. Ex. 33 and Num. 12 describe Moses' uniqueness as the only prophet privileged to speak to God "face to face." Num. 11 emphasizes Moses' humility; he did not desire leadership and shared his (spirit) with the seventy Elders.[10] When two of these Elders, Eldad and Meidad, prophesy without his permission he does not chastise them. His siblings, Aaron and Miriam, prophets in their own right according to Num. 12, could not have replaced Moses. Their petty jealousies and slanderous tongues ("Miriam and Aaron spoke against Moses..." [Num. 12:1]) make them unworthy. Moses, however, does not hold a grudge and when jealous Yhwh lashes out and smites Miriam, unpretentious Moses prays on her behalf.

---

9   Thus Levine, *Numbers*, 342: "The idiom 'face to face' does not mean...that one sees the face of the other [it is] merely a way of expressing communication with nothing intervening between the speakers.

10 Contra J. Milgrom, The Strucutres of Numbers 11-12 and 13-14 and their Redaction, Preliminary Gropings, in *Judaic Perspectives on Ancient Israel* (J. Neusner ed.), Philadelphia, 1987, 49-61; and Chizkuni on Num. 11:17 who view this as a punishment.

9. Summary

9.1 The Elohistic Narrative

The goal of this work—the isolation of the elohistic source—has, I hope, been achieved. E is undoubtedly the first source of the Pentateuch and the Yahwist was E's first supplementary redactor. There is not even one case in the Pentateuch of E as an editor or as a chronologically "late" source. There is no need to assume an RJE redactor; the Yahwist himself was the first editor of E. The J narrative can be divided into three categories: a) Direct supplementation of E texts; b) The addition of narratives connected to the E framework; c) Independent narratives connected to the new yahwistic framework. The present book deals only with the first two categories.

The elohistic source as it is preserved in the Pentateuch is an unfragmented unity. Since E was not an historian, he did not find it necessary to relate origins, sources or beginnings. The Elohist's assumption that his readers knew who the characters were is a valid one, since they were the progenitors and heroes of the Israelite nation. E texts are short and concise. The source usually provides the minimal information necessary to understand the story, but no more. E's skeletal narratives provided fertile ground for J's editorial supplementation and the later author was able to mould the E material pretty much to his heart's content.

The greatest difficulty with the identification and isolation of E is the propensity for circular reasoning: A text is elohistic if it exhibits certain characteristics, characteristics we found by attributing other texts to E. The only way around this problem is consistency of method and accretion of evidence as the study progresses. This enabled the isolation of thematically linked texts and finally the entire E corpus. The proof that this methodology is justified lies in the thematic integrity and structure of the isolated texts.

The elohistic corpus is made up of three main parts: the Jacob cycle, the Joseph cycle and the Moses cycle, with two shorter appendices: the Abraham cycle, which serves as an introduction, and the Balaam account, which serves as a conclusion. The structure of each of these sections is chiastic. The ingeniousness of the Elohist truly comes to light when one examines the master plan of the source in its entirety. Each section is independently chiastic, while the elohistic corpus as a whole, including the appendices, forms a more general chiastic structure. The introduction and conclusion are parallel: in both narratives a king on the borders of Canaan (Abimelech, King of Gerar and Balak, King of Moab) attempts to find a way to live with the foreign element in or adjacent to his country. (Abimelech encounters Abraham; the King of Moab confronts the Israelite presence). In order to solve their problems, they solicit the help of a prophet or sorcerer. (Abimelech sues for peace between himself and Abraham, the prophet, and Balak tries to hire Balaam, the sorcerer, to curse Israel.) In both cases Elohim appears in dreams and influences the course of the events. Ultimately both the prophet and the sorcerer learn to fear Elohim. In both these cycles the Israelite God is not remote and speaks to and through the prophets more than once. The Moses cycle clearly parallels the Jacob cycle. In both corpuses the protagonists pass through seven stations; Jacob wanders from Beersheva to Beit-El and back and the Israelites wander the desert; Jacob's final stop (not in the Jacob cycle) is Egypt, which is also Moses' starting point. The chiasmus in both cases is a divine revelation (at Bethel and God's mountain). The protagonists, Moses and Jacob, are surprisingly similar. They were both employed as sheep herders and worked for their fathers-in-law. Elohim revealed Himself while they were at work—a revelation which caused them to end their servitude and embark upon a perilous journey. Their enemies ultimately caught up with them (Laban overtakes Jacob and Egypt overtakes Israel at the Red Sea), but through Elohim's intervention they were saved. After their escape they struggle against a foe (the Angel and Amalek) and in both cases their physical strength saves them. Along the way they encounter a family member who is happy to see them (Esau and Aaron). Finally, Moses and Jacob return to the place of the first revelation following a ritual of purification. The chiasmus of the overall structure is the Joseph cycle and the Egyptian exile, the centre of which is the revelation to Jacob in Gen. 46:1-4 prior to his descent to Egypt, which alludes to the past, to the present and to the future and, as always, Elohim is in the centre. The chiastic structure of each section as well as of the overall structure supports my division of the text. I feel privileged to have discovered the answer to the "elohistic riddle." Von Rad has correctly claimed that the Yahwist was a genius. My research has enabled the identification of the genius who preceded him and who began the long process of the Pentateuch's compilation.

9.2 The Yahwistic Supplementation

Having identified the diverse themes and editorial techniques of J's supplementation throughout this work, a short summary will suffice. Much of the yahwistic participation may be summarized under the title "The Role of the Divine in Israelite History." The elohistic narrative, on the other hand, is anthropocentric. J's aim is to demonstrate the theocentricism of Israelite history: Yhwh brought Abraham to the Land of Canaan and protected him throughout his journeys; Yhwh chose the right woman for Isaac and cured her barrenness; Yhwh brought Joseph to Egypt and made him viceroy. Yhwh (and not Moses, as in the elohistic text) smote Egypt and performed the miracles in the desert. At most, Moses was a mediator. Yhwh requires mediators because, according to the Yahwist, a human cannot look upon God and live. According to the Elohist, however, both Jacob and Moses see "Elohim." In short, J inserts Yhwh into the story wherever possible. The yahwistic theology (as was emphasized in the Abraham cycle) is one of excessive mercy and thus Yhwh saves every major Israelite figure at least once, even if the Isrealite figure in question deserved death (like Adam, who was warned of death if he ate from the tree, or the sons of Jacob, who pillaged Shechem but were not punished). In this way Israel's unworthiness and their dependence upon God's good will are emphasized.

Another yahwistic trend is "rounding out" the one dimensional elohistic characters, and amplifying the story. According to E, Abraham was a righteous prophet, but J adds that he exploited his wife for monetary benefit. Jacob is described as strong and trustworthy by E, but J adds that he was a cheater, a thief and a coward. Esau is a loving brother according to the Elohist, while according to the Yahwist he hated his brother and sought to kill him. Laban is described by the Elohist as an extortionist, but J asserts that he loved his "sons and daughters" and cared for their welfare. The elohistic account describes Joseph as an innocent interpreter of dreams whose generosity was prolific, but J (or possibly P) adds that he was a tale-teller. According to E, Moses was a powerful miracle worker and the leader of a nation, but according to J he was a coward, a shirker and merely a divine vessel. Aaron was Moses' aide according to E, but J hastens to add that he was responsible for the Golden Calf.

In his capacity as an historian, the Yahwist is interested in reasons and origins of people and events. Thus he specifies who Abraham was and by furnishing us with stories of Abraham's family and place of origin. The Yahwist resurrects Isaac and connects him to Jacob, the father of the nation; he also expounds on the familial connection between Jacob and his wives. According to J, Laban had good reason to pursue his thieving son-in-law. The Yahwist explains the Egyptian hate of the Hebrews by referring to the general antagonism between shepherds and farmers. The Yahwist informs his readers of Moses' origin and supplies the names of his wife and sons (Zipporah, Gershom, Eliezer).

In order to append these themes to the basic E narrative, the Yahwist used an array of editorial techniques, of which I will mention two. When J disagreed with E, he did not delete parts of the document. If the detail was important, the Yahwist simply emphasized it repeatedly, giving his version of events precedence in the minds of his readers. We see this in the frequent repetition of the Israelite genealogy through Isaac, the number of the tribes (twelve as opposed to seven) and Israel's dwelling place while in Egypt (Goshen as opposed to Ramses).

Sometimes J did not insert original stories of his own, but rather relied upon his predecessor's paradigms. Thus both of J's "ancestor in danger" narratives (Abraham's descent to Egypt in Gen. 12:10-20 and Isaac's residence in Gerar in Gen. 26:6-12) are dependent upon Gen. 20 (Abraham's residence in Gerar). Similarly, both the meeting at the well of Abraham's servant and Rebecca and that of Moses and Zipporah are dependent upon the elohistic meeting between Jacob and Rachel in Gen. 29.

In conclusion, the Yahwist supplemented the elohist narrative only when he thought necessary, but since he was writing a text for a different audience, with different sensibilities (Judean), in a different time period, his supplementation was thorough. It was also successful. The tale he tells is the one we remember.

10. Appendix : Did J Believe or Accept the Centralization of Cult?

10.1 Introduction

According to the classic Documentary Hypothesis, the centralization of cult in Jerusalem is the main differentiating criterion for determining the relative chronology of the Pentateuchal sources. This criterion is based upon De Wette's equation between "the place that the Lord will choose," an expression most often found in the book of Deuteronomy (D), with Jerusalem, which became the central and the only legitimate center of cult at the end of the eighth century B.C.E. following Hezekiah's cultic reform as recounted in II Kings 18. De Wette's hypothesis, based upon the recurrence of the expression "the place that Lord will choose" in Deuteronomy, was that Deuteronomy advocated centralization and thus was composed at the same period as Hezekiah's reform (or at least some time between Hezekiah's reform and his grandson Josiah's reform [II Kgs. 22]). J and E do not subscribe to centralization of cult and they are therefore "early." Since D and H subscribe to centralization of cult, they are, according to this chronological scheme, "later." In the late 1960s, as the consensus concerning the Documentary Hypothesis began to crumble, the issue of the centralization of cult and its importance for relative dating resurfaced. Winnet, one of the first challengers of the Documentary method, noted the absence of sacrifices on the patriarchal altars.[1] He interpreted this absence as evidence for his division of the corpus into two—an early Yahwist and a later Yahwist who accepted D's centralization of cult.[2] Elaborating upon his teacher's idea and on the basis of a comparison between the Genesis altars and the altar of Josh. 22, Van Seters claims that all the patriarchal altars were testimonial.[3]

These claims were dismissed in a few sentences by Nicholson,[4] who argued that since the substantive "מזבח" (altar) is derived from the root

---

1   E. V. Winnet, Re-examining the Foundations, *JBL* (84), 1965, 1-19.
2   Levin (*Jahwist*, 432) cautions, however, that awareness of the reform does not necessarily mean that it was accepted by all the authors.
3   J. Van Seters, The Religion of the Patriarchs in Genesis, *Biblica* (61), 1980, 220-233.
4   E. Nicholson, *The Pentateuch in the Twentieth Century*, Oxford, 1975, 165-166.

"ז.ב.ח" (to sacrifice), it is highly unlikely that an altar had any other unspecified functions. (Indeed, following this line of reasoning, the post-biblical Book of Jubilees [e.g. Jubilees 13:4, 9] added sacrifices following the construction of patriarchal altars.) One may add that a comparison with Josh. 22 provides no adequate proof. Rather, it is the exception that proves the rule: The account proves that the erection of altars is perceived by all as an indication that sacrifice is about to ensue. The People of Israel, led by Phineas, certainly thought so. Due to the absence of a statement to this effect in Genesis, Nicholson's criticism seems to be accurate. The discussion would end here were it not for the statistical evidence: In Genesis the connection between altars and sacrifice is not conclusive and in fact the majority of altars are not sacrificed upon. In the rest of Scripture, however, the opposite is the rule and it is exceedingly *rare* that altars are mentioned other than in sacrificial contexts. To find a satisfactory answer for this anomaly, I herewith contribute my own observations to the scholarly debate on the subject.

A list of the relevant verses follows:

1. "And Abel for his part brought of the firstlings of his flock, their fat portions. And the LORD had regard for Abel and his offering." Gen. 4:4 (J).

2. "Then Noah built an altar to the LORD, and took of every clean animal and of every clean bird, and offered burnt offerings on the altar." Gen. 8:20 (J).

3. "Then the LORD appeared to Abram, and said, 'To your offspring I will give this land.' So he built there an altar to the LORD, who had appeared to him." Gen. 12:7 (J).

4. "From there he moved on to the hill country on the east of Bethel, and pitched his tent, with Bethel on the west and Ai on the east; and there he built an altar to the LORD and invoked the name of the LORD." Gen. 12:8 (J).

5. "To the place where he had made an altar at the first; and there Abram called on the name of the LORD." Gen. 13:4 (J).

6. "So Abram moved his tent, and came and settled by the oaks of Mamre, which are at Hebron; and there he built an altar to the LORD." Gen. 13:18 (J).

7. "And King Melchizedek of Salem brought out bread and wine; he was priest of God Most High. He blessed him and said, 'Blessed be Abram by God Most High, maker of heaven and earth; and blessed be God Most High, who has delivered your enemies into your hand!' And Abram gave him one tenth of everything." Gen. 14:18-20 (B or an unknown source).

8. "Abraham planted a tamarisk tree in Beersheba, and called there on the name of the LORD, the Everlasting God." Gen. 21:33 (J).

9. "And Abraham looked up and saw a ram, caught in a thicket by its horns. Abraham went and took the ram and offered it up as a burnt offering instead of his son." Gen. 22:13 (J).

10. "So he built an altar there, called on the name of the LORD, and pitched his tent there. And there Isaac's servants dug a well." Gen. 26:25 (J).

11. "So Jacob rose early in the morning, and he took the stone that he had put under his head and set it up for a pillar and poured oil on the top of it." Gen. 28:18 (E).

12. "And Jacob offered a sacrifice on the height and called his kins-folk to eat bread; and they ate bread and tarried all night in the hill country." Gen. 31:54 (E).

13. "There he erected an altar and called it El-Elohe-Israel." Gen. 33:20 (J).

14. "God said to Jacob, 'Arise, go up to Bethel, and settle there. Make an altar there to the God who appeared to you when you fled from your brother Esau.'" Gen. 35:1 (P).

15. "And there he built an altar and called the place El-Bethel." Gen. 35:7 (E)

16. "Jacob set up a pillar in the place where he had spoken with him, a pillar of stone; and he poured out a drink offering on it, and poured oil on it." Gen. 35:14 (P).

17. "When Israel set out on his journey with all that he had and came to Beersheba, he offered sacrifices to the God of his father (*Isaac*)." Gen. 46:1 (E).

Despite Van Seters's injudicious use of Josh. 22, his general thrust is correct and his observation will therefore provide the basis of my dis-cussion. One must closely examine Scripture to determine whether altars were used elsewhere for objectives other than sacrifice, and if so, for what objective. At least two altars warrant a closer examination. The first is the altar mentioned in Ex. 17:14-16 (attributed to J). Follow-ing the war with Amalek, Moses erects an altar but does not sacrifice upon it: "Then the LORD said to Moses, 'Write this as a reminder in a book and recite it in the hearing of Joshua: I will utterly blot out the remembrance of Amalek from under heaven.' And Moses built an altar and called it, The LORD is my banner. He said, 'A hand upon the ban-ner of the LORD, The LORD will have war with Amalek from genera-tion to generation.'" The function of this altar is clearly mimetic or commemorative. Moses is commanded by Yhwh to "Write this as a reminder in a book and recite it in the hearing of Joshua" and his first act is the erection of the altar.

The second example is Gideon's altar "Yhwh Shalom" in Jud. 6:24. In this narrative, Yhwh or his angel appears before Gideon in Ofrah. When Gideon discovers the identity of his visitor he fears for his life, but Yhwh (or his angel) tells him "But the LORD said to him, 'Peace be to you; do not fear, you shall not die.'" (verse 23). To memorialize this revelation Gideon erects an altar which is clearly meant to commemorate the event. No sacrifice is mentioned and the account ends with the following verse (verse 24) "Then Gideon built an altar there to the LORD, and called it, The LORD is peace. To this day it still stands at Ophrah, which belongs to the Abiezrites," i.e. the altar served its purpose: it reminded the author of the event/story. Finally, in the following unit Gideon is commanded to build a second altar—for sacrificial purposes, in contrast to the first commemorative altar.[5]

While an altar can clearly be commemorative, why should we suppose that this is its role in Genesis? To answer this question, one must first refer to "pillars" (מצבות) in general and the pillars of Genesis in particular. It is abundantly clear that, unlike altars, pillars fill a commemorative purpose, e.g. the pillar on Mount Grizim in Deut. 27 or the pillar by the Jordan River in Josh. 3. Documentary scholars observed that "pillar" was often used by E in lieu of J's "altar" and listed the two as parallel terms. On the face of it, this is mystifying, considering that the two structures are essentially different and not parallel. Nevertheless, the Documentary assertion is correct. Similarly, the two parallel accounts of Gen. 35: in the first Jacob erects an altar (35:7) (and does not sacrifice upon it) and in the second a pillar (35:14). Outside of Genesis the parallelism is explicit, e.g. "Break down their altars, smash their pillars" (Deut 12:3); "Without sacrifice (זבה) or pillar, without ephod or teraphim" (Hos. 3:4). At the root of this confusion in Genesis are the secondary functions of the two structures. Although pillars are not used as altars, they, too, have cultic significance (e.g. Gen. 35:8-14), while altars are occasionally commemorative. Based upon the confusion between the two, their overlapping functions and the commemorative role altars fill elsewhere, it is entirely possible that the anomalous altars of Genesis are indeed commemorative.

Two questions remain: 1. Why does the yahwistic source prefer the term "altar" to pillar? 2. What are these altars commemorating? The answer to the first question is connected, in my opinion, to the date of

---

5   Cf. G. F. Moore, *A Critical and Exegetical Commentary on Judges* (ICC), Edinburgh, 1895, 182.

J's composition. On this matter I agree with contemporary scholars and their equation between J and D (at least with regard to the dates of composition) and date J to the time between the reigns Hezekiah and Josiah.[6] Deuteronomic law explicitly prohibits erecting pillars: "Nor shall you set up a stone pillar—things that the LORD your God hates" (Deut. 16:22). Presumably this prohibition was known to the Yahwist, and thus he preferred to use the altar instead of the pillar for acts of commemoration.[7]

10.2 The Altars of Genesis

The relevant verses, listed above, may be subdivided into two groups. The first group (#1, 2, 7, 9 of the above list) consists of acts prohibited by Deuteronomy. The second group (#3-6, 8, 10, 13, 14/15 of the list) consists of instances in which altars are constructed but no sacrifice ensues. The first group includes Abel's offering of his first sheep, Noah's sacrifice as he leaves the Ark, Abram's tithe in Gen. 14, and the ram Abraham sacrifices instead of his son. The second group includes the construction of altars in Shechem, next to Beth-El and in Elonei Mamreh; the planting of the tamarisk in Beersheba, and the building of the altar in Beersheba by Isaac.

In four of the seven instances listed in the second group above (12:7, 8; 13:18; 26:25), the building of the altar comes after God promises the land to Abraham (or to Isaac) and the erection of the altar commemorates this important occasion. The fifth verse listed, Gen. 13:3-4: "He journeyed on by stages from the Negeb as far as Bethel, to the place where his tent had been at the beginning, between Bethel and Ai, To the place where he had made an altar at the first; and there Abram called on the name of the LORD," alludes to previously constructed altars (Gen. 12:7) and hence also to the promises attached to these altars.[8] Number 8 on our list, the planting of a tamarisk in Beersheba, follows a treaty with Abimelech concerning the land. The planting of this tamarisk is parallel to Isaac's construction of an altar following the renewal of this same alliance with Abimelech (#10). The planting of the tamarisk is therefore not a prelude to the worship of the Canaanite

---

6   T. Yoreh, *The Time of J's Composition and Its Relationship to E* (Hebrew), Masters' Thesis, Hebrew University of Jerusalem, 2001.

7   Skinner, *Genesis*, 378, notes J's early aversion to altars.

8   This geographical reference is used by W. Zwickel, Der Alterbau Abrahams Zwischen Bethel und Ai, Gen 12f: Ein Beitrag zur Datierung der Jahwisten, *BZ* 36 (1995): 207-219, as proof for an earlier chronology.

goddess Asherah: rather, like the altar in the parallel account, it is a symbol commemorating the treaty forged between Abimelech and Abraham. This is supported by the chronological addendum to God's name—"עולם" (everlasting), i.e. Abraham's ownership of the land will endure for evermore. The "erection" [from the root נ.צ.ב] of an altar by Jacob adjacent to the city of Shechem (#13 on the list) is evidence of the confusion between altars and pillars and their overlapping functions. In this case the altar fills a commemorative function and is "a monument" to Jacob's connection to the place. Indeed, Jacob perpetuates his ownership over the place by buying the field (where Joseph was buried, according to Josh. 24:32). In summary, it appears that the yahwistic altars listed commemorate God's promise to the patriarchs concerning their inheritance of the land.[9]

There remains the first group of verses, the so-called transgressions against the Deuteronomic laws. Clearly the first two instances on the list do not contradict the Deuteronomic rule concerning the construction of altars outside of Jerusalem since they deal with a time when neither Jerusalem nor the People of Israel existed. The other two verses on the list are more interesting. The first is the tithe given to Melchizedek the King of Salem, a priest of El Elyon. Abram subsequently identifies El Elyon with Yhwh ("I have sworn to the LORD [Yhwh], God Most High [El Elyon], maker of heaven and earth"). Salem is one of Jerusalem's many names, according to Psalms 76:2 ("His abode has been established in Salem, his dwelling place in Zion"). Hence, when Abram gives a tenth of his property to Melchizedek, he is giving it in the right place (Jerusalem) and to the proper authorities (the high priest). Similarly, when Abraham sacrifices a ram instead of his son Isaac in the land of Moriah, he is sacrificing at a site which, according to later traditions (II Chr. 2:3), is Jerusalem. The equation between " ה' יראה" (Yhwh shall see or choose) (Gen. 22:14) and "ה' יבחר"(Yhwh shall choose – a Deuteronomic allusion to Jerusalem) pointed out by scholars[10] is indication that the equation between Moriah and Jerusalem was in all likelihood known to the J editor of this chapter as well.

---

9   Thus the medieval commentator Rashi on Gen 12:7: "So he built there an altar: commemorating the promise of progeny and the promise of the land."

10   E.g. A. Saviv, המקום אשר יבחר = ה' יראה (Hebrew), *Beit Miqra* (26): 1981, 279-281; K. Baltzer, Jerusalem in den Erzväter-Geschichten der Genesis? Traditionsgeschichtliche Erwägungen zu Gen 14 und 22, in *Die Hebräische Bibel und ihre zweifache Nachgeschichte, Festschrift für R. Rendtorff* (E. Blum, C. Macholz, E. W. Stegeman eds.), Neukirchen-Vluyn, 1990, 3-12; Y. Kalimi, The Land of Moriah, the Mountain of Moriah, and the Site of Solomon's Temple (Hebrew), in *Shnaton LeMiqra* 11 (1997): 180-194.

10.2.1 The Centralization of Cult and E

The majority of verses in the second half of the list (11-17) are attributed to E according to our divisions above. *Contra* Van Seters (who argues against an elohistic source and thus attributes these verses to the late yahwistic author who accepted D's centralization of cult), E clearly does not accept centralization of cult. There is no way to harmonize "Bethel's holy stone" (#11 on our list) with D's laws. The pillar that Laban and Jacob erect in Gen. 31 (#12) is for the most part commemorative, but the cultic elements worried J and thus his redaction. Num. 14 and 15 on the list are the divine command to build an altar at Bethel (attributed to P) and the fulfillment of this command (E). For E the construction of this altar is a fulfillment of Jacob's vow (Gen. 28:22) and thus in opposition to D's centralization of cult (since Bethel is now the site of a temple). P reinterprets this event and views it as a monument to divine salvation (35:1), i.e. commemorative. Number 17 on our list mentions sacrifices in Beersheba and not in Jerusalem, once again contradicting D's edicts. Number 16 on the list (the erection of a pillar in Bethel) is priestly. (See the above analysis of this section.) The E verses are clear evidence of an earlier stage of worship, i.e. multiple sanctuaries, pillars and the divine connection to specific sites. This made J uncomfortable and he therefore attempts to harmonize E with his viewpoint. (See the analyses of Gen. 28 and 31 for more detail.)

10.2.2 Conclusion

My conclusion is straightforward: E, the earlier source, did not know of D's centralization of cult, but his supplementary redactor certainly did. J could not ignore E's abrogation of D's cultic laws and the following is a summary of his harmonistic activities: a) Instead of E's "hateful pillars" (Deut. 16) J substitutes/inserts altars/trees (Gen. 12:7,8; 21:33); b) The altars or trees are constructed in places where according to E the patriarchs engaged in what J would refer to as "forbidden cultic locations," namely in Bethel and Beersheba. Following J's interventions, the monuments in these places are now interpreted as commemorative rather than cultic and exist in order to remind onlookers of God's promise; c) Finally, J attempts to blur E's account of forbidden cult with a variety of insertions.[11]

---

11   See my above divisions, especially of Gen. 28 and 31.

10.3 Centralization of Cult in Exodus

In the book of Exodus there also exist "undesirable" cultic acts which must be examined. Genesis and Exodus are discussed separately, since they differ in scope: in Genesis we were within the narrow confines of family, while in Exodus we are dealing with the Israelite nation, whose modes of worship are quite different.

10.3.1 The Worship of God in the Desert

Beginning in Ex. 5:1, Moses repeatedly asks Pharaoh's permission for a mass Exodus in order to sacrifice to God. Following the death of the firstborn, Pharaoh releases the nation and they do indeed worship God at Mount Sinai in a covenantal ceremony described in Chapter 24.[12] Many scholars attribute the covenant to J. The issue at hand is whether this ceremony conforms with D's cultic laws. At a glance, it appears that the ceremony is diametrically opposed to Deut. 12 and 16 (the laws against sacrifice outside of Jerusalem and the erection of pillars). Moses constructs an altar at the foot of Mount Sinai and sacrifices upon it. He also erects twelve pillars, thus transgressing against "Nor shall you set up a stone pillar— things that the LORD your God hates" (Deut. 16:22). The following is my analysis of these problematic verses.

10.3.2 A Source Division of Ex. 24

Ex. 24 remains a baffling chapter despite many analyses.[13] The following is the most common Documentary division of Ex. 24. Moses' ascension to Mount Sinai (Verses 1-2, and 9) is attributed to the chapter's basic source. The Covenant ceremony in verses 3-8 is attributed to a later interpolator (sometimes J). Verses 13-15 are generally attributed to E and are usually seen as a prelude to the sin of the Golden Calf in Ex. 32. The rest of Chapter 24 unanimously assigned to P, continues without any interruptions until Ex. 32.

This division, however, is problematic, or in Childs's words:[14] "The arbitrariness of much of this reasoning does not increase confidence in the suggested source analysis." Firstly, it fails to account for the lack of

---

12 See J. L. Ska, Le Repas de Ex. 24: 11, *Biblica* 74 (1993): 305–327.

13 For a survery see Childs, *Exodus*, 499-502.

14 *Exodus*, 500.

continuity between the end of Chapter 23 and the beginning of Chapter 24. According to Chapters 20-23, Moses has been continuously on the mountain ("Then the people stood at a distance, while Moses drew near to the thick darkness where God was," 20:21) and has not yet descended, whereas in Chapter 24:1-2 Moses is commanded to ascend, which indicates that he is not on the mountain. Secondly, the above division ignores textual fractures: in verse 3 Moses delivers a body of laws to Israel, who accept it: "Moses came and told the people all the words of the LORD and all the ordinances; and all the people answered with one voice, and said, 'All the words that the LORD has spoken we will do,'" while in verse 7 Moses reads the words of the covenant and once again the nation answers, "Then he took the book of the covenant, and read it in the hearing of the people; and they said, 'All that the LORD has spoken we will do, and we will be obedient.'" Furthermore, it is also totally unclear who was granted the privilege of seeing the divine. In verses 1 and 2, Moses and Aaron, Nadav and Avihu and the seventy Elders ascended the mountain, but only Moses approached God. In verse 11, however, an unspecified group of "nobles" saw God, and finally verse 10 may indicate that *the entire nation* saw God: "And they saw the God of Israel. Under his feet there was something like a pavement of sapphire stone, like the very heaven for clearness."

These problems and others lead me to offer my own analysis of the chapter. I submit that the legal treatise of Chapters 20-23 continues in 24:4 with the writing of the laws delineated in the previous chapters (an account in which Moses descends only in verse 4), making verses 1-3 secondary.[15] This division solves the problematic repetition in verses 3 and 7 ("All that the LORD has spoken we will do"), since they are now attributed to different sources. A problem not yet mentioned, since it is not textual, is the very explicit anthropomorphism in verses 10-11, which is also an issue since according to Ex. 33:20 (J), "No one shall see me and live." It follows that later authors/editors would attempt to cloud the problematic revelation of 24:10-11. Hence verse 9, "Then Moses and Aaron, Nadab, and Abihu, and seventy of the Elders of Israel went up," which was inserted prior to verses 10-11 ("And they saw the God of Israel...") in order to create the impression that the people seeing the divine countenance are the same group described in verse 1 and then in verse 9. Prior to the "ten" commandments, J dedicates five verses to negotiations with the divine regarding who is allowed onto the mountain (Ex. 19:21-25). This occasion, of similar importance, also

---

15   Compare Noth (*Numbers*, 198) who connects between the ceremony beginning in vs. 3 and the narrative of Ex. 23.

requires divine injunctions limiting the participants (especially since verses 10-11 imply that the revelation is so widespread). Hence verses 1 and 9 are added. Verse 2 further limits the contact between God and humans and creates the impression that Moses alone truly saw God, while the other "onlookers" only bowed from afar.

One must also address the tension between verses 10 and 11: in verse 10 the subject of "ויראו" (and they saw) is unidentified, thus implying a general revelation. Verse 11 seemingly "retracts" and states that only "אצילי בני ישראל" (chief men of the People of Israel) saw God. The understanding of "אצילים" as a group of nobles (thus Onkelos) is solely contextual, however. The substantive "אציל" as a description of a human being is a hapax and other appearances of the root as a verb do not lend themselves to such a definition.[16] In my opinion, based on Num. 11:25: "Then the LORD came down in the cloud and spoke to him, and took (ויאצל) some of the spirit that was on him and put it on the seventy Elders; and when the spirit rested upon them, they prophesied," the root indicates inclusion rather than exclusion (and see Midrash Tanhuma 184-5 on Num. 11:25). I consider the correct interpretation of the verse to be that "even the furthest among them" saw God, that is it conforms with verse 10[17] (compare Is 41:9: "I took from the ends of the earth, and called from its farthest corners" ["אצילי"]). Verse 3, "Moses came and told the people all the words of the LORD and all the ordinances..." is resumptive: in other words it helps smooth over the abrupt break in context caused by the insertion of verses 1 and 2.

It appears that the editorial insertions (verses 1-3 and 9) should be attributed to J, who in Ex. 19 is concerned about the proximity of various groups to Mount Sinai. In fact, 24:3 virtually quotes 19:7-8: "So Moses came, summoned the Elders of the people, and set before them all these words that the LORD had commanded him. The people all answered as one: 'Everything that the LORD has spoken we will do.'" (J).

What about the covenant ceremony? As implied above, it is part of the early Covenant Code and thus its explicit anthropomorphism is not problematic.[18] Verse 12: "The LORD said to Moses, 'Come up to me on the mountain, and wait there; and I will give you the tablets of stone, with the law and the commandment, which I have written for their instruction'" is also attributed to J and constitutes this source's link

---

16 And see *BDB*, 69.

17 "Even" is one of the many translations of the waw conjunction, and see *KB*, 245.

18 Ex. 20-23; *cf.* Noth, *Numbers*, 198ff.

between the covenant ceremony and the sin of the Golden Calf in Ex. 32. Otherwise our division follows previous analyses.

If this analysis is correct, the "twelve pillars" are not yahwistic, but are to be attributed to the Covenant Code. The early Covenant Code most certainly does not know of D's cultic innovation. The following is the original covenantal ceremony as conceived by the author of the Covenant Code. (The additions are added in a smaller font and italics.)

The Covenant Ceremony (Ex. 24)

1*Then he said to Moses, "Come up to the LORD, you and Aaron, Nadab, and Abihu, and seventy of the Elders of Israel, and worship at a distance. 2 Moses alone shall come near the LORD; but the others shall not come near, and the people shall not come up with him." 3 Moses came and told the people all the words of the LORD and all the ordinances; and all the people answered with one voice, and said, "All the words that the LORD has spoken we will do."* 4 And Moses wrote down all the words of the LORD. He rose early in the morning, and built an altar at the foot of the mountain, and set up twelve pillars, corresponding to the twelve tribes of Israel. 5 He sent young men of the People of Israel, who offered burnt offerings and sacrificed oxen as offerings of well-being to the LORD. 6 Moses took half of the blood and put it in basins, and half of the blood he dashed against the altar. 7 Then he took the book of the covenant, and read it in the hearing of the people; and they said, "All that the LORD has spoken we will do, and we will be obedient." 8 Moses took the blood and dashed it on the people, and said, "See the blood of the covenant that the LORD has made with you in accordance with all these words." *9 Then Moses and Aaron, Nadab, and Abihu, and seventy of the Elders of Israel went up,* 10 and they saw the God of Israel. Under his feet there was something like a pavement of sapphire stone, like the very heaven for clearness. 11 God did not lay his hand on the furthest reaches of the People of Israel; also they beheld God, and they ate and drank.

10.3.4 Three Additional Sources

Ex. 20:24-25: "You need make for me only an altar of earth and sacrifice on it your burnt offerings and your offerings of well-being, your sheep and your oxen; in every place where I cause my name to be remembered I will come to you and bless you. But if you make for me an altar of stone, do not build it of hewn stones; for if you use a chisel upon it you profane it."

Ex. 23:17-18: "Three times in the year all your males shall appear before the Lord GOD. You shall not offer the blood of my sacrifice with anything leavened, or let the fat of my festival remain until the morning."

Ex. 34:23-26: "Three times in the year all your males shall appear before the LORD God, the God of Israel. For I will cast out nations before you, and enlarge your borders; no one shall covet your land when you go up to appear before the LORD your God three times in the year. You shall not offer the blood of my sacrifice with leaven, and the sacrifice of the festival of the passover shall not be left until the morning."

According to most scholars, the first of the above verses (Ex. 20:24-25) belongs to the early Covenant Code,[19] a collection of laws (Ex. 20:20–23:32) independent of J. The injunction stated in this verse is diametrically opposed to D's centralization of cult (Deut. 12:11: "Then you shall bring everything that I command you to the place that the LORD your God will choose as a dwelling for his name" versus Ex 20:24 "… and sacrifice on it your burnt offerings and your offerings of well-being, your sheep and your oxen; in every place where I/you cause my name to be remembered I will come to you and bless you.") The law also contradicts the Deuteronomic injunction to build an altar from unhewn stones (Deut. 27:5). This was apparently excessive for the Yahwist (or the Deuteronomistic editor), who emended the Law by appending the Deuteronomic option in the following verse (20:25). Number 2 on the list also belongs to the non-yahwistic Covenant Code. It does not explicitly contradict D's laws, but it is unspecific (it does not speak of a specific locale for seeking God). The second covenant in Ex. 34 (the "minor" Covenant Code) is a yahwistic revision of the problematic or unspecific laws of the original code and *cf.* Bar-On's comparative analysis of the two codes.[20] Thus number 3 "For I will cast out nations before you, and enlarge your borders; no one shall covet your land when you go up to appear before the LORD your God three times in the year" (34:24) emends number 2 and does conform with D's centralization of cult. The verse implies one specific locale that may be far from one's abode (*cf.* the Deuteronomic parallel in Deut. 19:8 "If the LORD your God enlarges your territory, as he swore to your ancestors— and he will give you all the land that he promised your ancestors to give you").

---

19   Kautszch, *Heilige Schrift*, 127-128.

20   S. Bar-On, *The Festival Laws in the Pentateuch* (Hebrew), Doctorate, Hebrew University of Jerusalem, 2000.

10.3.5 Summary

My conclusions may be summarized in one sentence: the predeuter-onomic Covenant Code does not know of the Deuteronomic innova-tion. J, however, does and attempts to harmonize the earlier source's deviations with the Deuteronomic laws.

Bibliography

P. Addinal, Exodus III 19B and the Interpretation of Biblical Narrative, *VT* 49 (1999): 289-300.

R. Aharoni, Concerning Three Similar Narratives in the Book of Genesis (Hebrew), *Beit Mikra* 24 (1979): 213-222.

J. D. Alexander, The Hagar Traditions in Gen. XVI and XXI, in *Studies in the Pentateuch* (J. A. Emerton ed.), Leiden, 1990, 131-148.

A. Alt, *Der Gott der Vater - Ein Beitrag zur Vorgeschichte der Israelitischen Religion*, Stuttgart, 1929.

R. Alter, A Literary Approach to the Bible, *Commentary* 60 (1975), 70-77.

M. Anbar, La Reprise, *VT* 38 (1988): 385-398.

F. I. Andersen, Note on Geneis 30, *JBL* 88 (1969), 200.

E. Auerbach, The Scar of Odyseus, in *Mimesis: The Representation of Reality in Western Literature* (W. Trask tr.), New York, 1946, 1-20.

E. Aurelius, *Der Fürbitter Israel: Eine Studie Zum Mosebild im Alten Testament*, Stockholm, 1988.

Y. Avishur, The Sacrifice of Isaac (Gen. 22); the Structure of the Narrative, its Link to Gen. 12 and its Canaanite Background, in *Studies in Biblical Narrative* (Y. Avishur ed.), Tel Aviv, 1999, 75-103.

C. J. Ball, *The Book of Genesis in Hebrew*, Leipzig, 1896.

J. R. Barlett, The Conquest of Sihon's Kingdom; A Literary Re-examination, *JBL* 97 (1978): 347-351.

S. Bar-on, Zur Literarkritischen Analyse von Ex 12, 21 – 27, *ZAW* 107 (1995): 18 –30.

—, The Festival Calendars in Ex. XXIII 14-19, and XXXIV 18-26, *VT* 48 (1998): 161-195.

—, *The Festival Laws in the Pentateuch* (Hebrew), Doctorate, The Hebrew University of Jerusalem, 2000.

J. Barr, Story and History in Biblical Theology, *JR* 56 (1976): 1-17.

L. M. Bechtel, What if Dinah is not Raped (Gen. 34), *JSOT* 62 (1994): 19-36.

W. H. Bennett, *Genesis: Introduction* (Century Bible), Edinburgh, 1904.

A. Besters, "Israel" et "fils d'Israel" dans les Livres Historiques: Genèse -II Rois, *RB* 74 (1967): 5-23.

L. E. Binns, *The Book of Numbers*, Westminster.

K. Baltzer, Jerusalem in den Erzväter-Geschichten der Genesis? Traditions-geschichtliche Erwägungen zu Gen 14 und 22, in *Die Hebräische Bibel und ihre zweifache Nachgeschichte, Festschrift fur R. Rendtorff* (E. Blum, C. Macholz, E. W. Stegeman eds.), Neukirchen-Vluyn, 1990, 3-12.

H. Bloom, *The Book of J translated from the Hebrew by D. Rosenberg, Interpreted by H. Bloom*, New York, 1990.

E. Blum, *Die Komposition der Vätergeschichte*, (Wissenschaftliche Monographe zum Alten und Neuen Testament Vol. 57), Neukirchen –Vluyn, 1984.

—, *Studien zur Komposition des Pentateuch* (BZAW 189), Berlin, 1990.

—, Noch Einmal; Jakobs Traum in Bethel Gen. 28, 10-22, in *Rethinking the Foundations: Historiography in the Ancient World and in the Bible, Essays in Honor of John Van Seters* (S. L. McKenzie, T. Römer and H. H. Schmid eds.), 2000, 33-54.

O. Boehm, The Binding of Isaac: An Inner Biblical Polemic on the Question of "Disobeying" a Manifestly Illegal Order, *VT* 52 (2002): 1-12.

R. G. Boling (with Introduction by E. Wright), *Joshua: A New Translation with Notes and Commentary*, New-York, 1982.

S. Boorer, *The Promise of the Land as Oath* (BZAW 205), Berlin, 1992.

M. Breuer, On Bible Criticism (Hebrew), *Megadim* 30, (1999): 97-107.

H. C. Brichto, *The Names of God: Poetic Readings in Biblical Beginnings*, New York, 1998.

J. Bright, *Jeremiah: A New Translation with Introduction and Commentary*, New York, 1984.

W. Brueggemann and H. W. Wolff, *The Vitality of Old Testament Traditions*, Atlanta, 1975.

E. Bubitz, Ruben, Issakar und Zebulon in den Israelitischen Genealogien, *ZAW* 33 (1913): 241-250.

K. Budde, Genesis 48,7 und die Benachbarten Abschnitte, *ZAW* 3 (1883): 56-86.

J. E. Carpenter, *The Composition of the Hexateuch: An Introduction with a Select List of Words and Phrases*, London, 1902.

D. M. Carr, *Reading the Fractures of Genesis*, Louisville, Kentucky, 1996.

D. M. Carr, No Return to Wellhausen, *Biblica* 86, 107-114, 2005.

A. M. Cartun, "Who Knows Ten"? The Structural and Symbolic Use of Numbers in the Ten Plagues - Ex. 7:14-13:16, *USQR* 45 (1992): 65-119.

M. Cassiner, The Date of the Elohist in the Light of Gen. XXXVII 9, *JThS* 50 (1949): 173ff.

U. Cassuto, *From Noah to Abraham* (I. Abrahams tr.), Jerusalem, 1964.

—, *The Documentary Hypothesis and the Order of the Books of the Bible: Eight Lessons* (Hebrew), Jerusalem, 1965.

—, *A Commentary on the Book of Exodus* (I. Abrahams tr.), Jerusalem, 1967.

—, *The Book of Genesis and its Structure* (Hebrew), 1990.

B. S. Childs, A Study of the Formula "Until this Day", *JBL* 82 (1963): 179-192.

—, Deuteronomic Formulae of the Exodus Tradition, *SVT* 16 (1967): 30-39.

—, *The Book of Exodus, A Critical and Theological Commentary* (OTL), Philadelphia, 1974.

—, *Introduction to the Old Testament as Scripture*, Philadelphia, 1979.

W. M. Clark, *The Origin and Development of the Land Promise Theme in the Old Testament*, Ann Arbor, Michigan (Doctorate), 1964.

R. E. Clements, *Exodus* (Cambridge Bible Commentary), Cambridge University, 1972.

D. J. A. Clines (ed.), *The Dictionary of Classical Hebrew, Vol. 4*, Sheffield, 1998.

G. W. Coats, Despoiling the Egyptians, *VT* 18 (1968): 450-457.

—, Balaam, Sinner or Saint in Num. 24?, *Biblical Research* 18 (1973): 21-29.

—, Redactional Unity in Gen. 37-50, *JBL* 93 (1974): 15-21.

—, *From Canaan to Egypt*, Washington Catholic Biblical Association, 1976.

—, *Genesis with Introduction to Narrative Literature*, Grand Rapids, Michigan, 1983.

M. Cogan and H. Tadmor, *II Kings, A New Translation with Introduction and Commentary (Anchor Bible)*, New York, 1988.

Y. Cohen, למילדות העבריות, *Leshonneinu* 55 (1995): 295-297.

N. L. Collins, Evidence in the Septuagint of a Tradition in Which the Israelites Left without Pharoah's Consent, *CBQ* 56 (1994): 442-448.

R. C. Coote, *In Defense of Revolution: The Elohist History*, Minneapolis, 1991.

R. Couffingal, Le Songe de Jacob; Approches Nouvelles de Genèse 28: 10-22, *Biblica*, 58 (1977): 582-597.

K. H. Cornill, *Einleitung in das Alte Testament*, Freiburg, 1892.

J. C. Crenshaw, *A Whirlpool of Torment: Israelite Traditions about God as an Oppressive Presence*, Philadelphia, 1984.

F. M. Cross, Reuben, First Born of Jacob, *ZAW* 100 Supplement (1988): 46-65.

M. J. Dahood, Abraham's Reply in Gen. 20,11, *Biblica* 61 (1990): 90-99.

M. David, Zabal (Gen. XXX 20), *VT* 1 (1951): 69 –70.

E. W. Davies, A Mathematical Conundrum: The Problem of the Large Numbers in Num. I and XXVI, *VT* 45 (1995): 449-469.

G. I. Davies, The Wilderness Iteneraries: A Comparitive Study, *TynB* 25 (1974): 46-81.

A. De Pury, Genèse XXXIV et l'Histoire, *RB* 76 (1969): 5-49.

J. Derby, Why Did God Want to Kill Moses? *JBQ* 18 (1990): 222-229.

K. A. Deurloo, Beerseba; Genesis 21, 22-34, *Amsterdamse Cahiers* 11 (1992): 7-13.

B. J. Diebner, Deborah's Tod, Gen. 35,8; "Schwierig" und "Unverständlich"?, *DBAT* 25 (1988): 173-84.

W. Dietrich, *Die Josepherzählung als Novelle und Geschichtsschreibung* (BTS 14), Neukirchen-Vluyn, 1989.

M. Dijkstra, Is Balaam also among the Prophets?, *JBL* 114 (1995): 43-64.

A. Dillmann, *Numeri, Deuteronmium, und Josua*, (Kurzgefasstes Exegetisches Handbuch), Leipzig, 1886.

—, *Die Genesis* (Handbuch zum Alten Testament), Leipzig, 1892.

H. Donner, *Die literarische Gestalt der alttestamentlichen Josephgeschichte*, Heidelberg, 1976.

T. Dozeman, *God on the Mountain* (The Society of Biblical Literature Monograph Series), Atlanta, 1989.

T. Dozeman and K. Schmid (eds.), *A Farewell to the Yahwist*, Leiden and Boston, 2006.

S. R. Driver, *A Critical and Exegetical Commentary on Deuteronomy*, Edinburgh, 1895.

—, *The Book of Genesis with Introduction and Notes* (Westminster Commentaries), London, 1904.

—, *The Book of Exodus with Introduction and Notes* (The Cambridge Bible for Schools and Colleges), Cambridge, 1953.

J. I. Durham, *Exodus* (World Biblical Commentary) Waco Texas, 1987.

O. Eissfeldt, *Hexateuch Synopse*, Leipzig, 1922.

—, *Einleitung in das Alte Testament*, Tübingen, 1964.

—, *The Old Testament: An Introduction* (D. Ackroyd tr.), Evanston, New York, 1965.

J. A. Emerton, The Origin of The Promises to the Patriarchs in the Older Sources, *VT* 32 (1982): 14-32.

M. Fishbane, Composition and Structure in the Jacob Cycle Gen. 25:19-35:22, *Journal of Jewish Studies* 26 (1975): 15-38.

G. Fleischer, Jakob traümt - eine Auseinandersetzung mit E. Blum Methodischen Ansatz am Beispiel von Gen. 28, 10-22, *BN* 76 (1995): 82-102.

J. Fleishman, Why did Simeon and Levi Rebuke their Father in Gen. 34,31, *JNSL* 26 (2000): 101-116.

G. Fohrer, *Überlieferung und Geschichte des Exodus* (BZAW 91), Berlin, 1964.

—, *Introduction to the Old Testament* (D. E. Green tr.), Nashville, 1968.

J. P. Fokkelman, Time and the Structure of the Abraham cycle, *Oudtestamentische Studien* 25 (1989): 96-109.

M. V. Fox, Wisdom in the Joseph Story, *VT* 51 (2001): 26-41.

R. E. Friedman, Deception for Deception, *Brev* 2 (1986): 22-31.

—, *The History of Biblical Studies, The Hebrew Scriptures*, Atlanta, 1987.

—, *Who Wrote the Bible?*, New-York, 1987.

J. Ch. Gertz, K. Schmid and M. Witte, *Abschied vom Jahwisten: Die Komposition des Hexateuch in der jüngsten Diskussion* (BZAW 315), Berlin, 2002.

J. Ch. Gertz, *Tradition und Redaktion in der Exoduserzählung: Untersuchungen zur Endredaktion des Pentateuch* (FRLANT 186), Göttingen, 2000.

S. Gevirtz, Of Patriarchs and Puns: Joseph at the Fountain, Jacob at the Ford, *HUCA* 46 (1975): 33-54.

R. K. Gnuse, Redefining the Elohist, *JBL* 119 (2000): 201-220.

J. Goldin, The Youngest Son or Where does Gen. 38 Belong?, *JBL* 96 (1977): 27-44.

B. Gosse, Les Premiers Chapitres du Livre d'Exode et l'Unification de la Redaction du Pentateuch, *BN* 86 (1997): 31-35.

A. Graupner, *Der Elohist: Gegenwart und Wirksamkeit des transzendenten Gottes in der Geschichte* (WMANT 97), Neukirchen-Vluyn, 2002.

G. B. Gray, *Numbers, A Critical and Exegetical Commentary* (ICC), Edinburgh, 1963.

M. Greenberg, *Understanding Exodus*, New York, 1969.

H. Gressmann, *Mose und Seine Zeit: Ein Kommentar zu den Mose Sagen*, Göttingen, 1913.

—, Ursprung und Entwicklung der Joseph-Sage, in *Eucharisterion: Studien zur Religion und Literatur des Alten und Neuen Testaments* (H. Schmidt ed.), Göttingen, 1923, 1-55.

J. Grönbäk, Juda und Amalek – Überlieferungsgeschichtliche Erwägungen zu Exodus 17, 8 –16, *Studia Theologica* 18 (1964): 26-45.

H. Gunkel, *The Legends of Genesis: The Biblical Saga and History* (W. H. Carruth tr.), New York, 1970.

—, *Genesis* (M. D. Rutter tr.), Macon, Georgia, translation of *Genesis, Übersetzt und Erklärt*, 1917.

—, *The Stories of Genesis* (J. J. Scullion tr.), Vallejo, California, 1994.

A. H. Gunneweg, Das Gesetz und die Propheten: Eine Auslegung von Ex. 33,7-11, Num.11,4-12,8, Dtn 31,14f, *ZAW* 102 (1990): 169-180.

J. Ha, *Genesis 15: A Theological Compendium of Pentateuchal History* (BZAW 181), Berlin, 1989.

P. Heger, Comparison and Contrast Between the 2 Laws of the Altar, Ex. 20:22 "ki charbeka heinafta" and Deut. 27,5, "lo tanif aleihem barzel"; in Consideration of their Historical Setting, *WCJS* 12 A (1999): 95-106.

M. Haran, *Introduction to Bible* (compiled on the basis of lectures, A. Shinan) (Hebrew), Jerusalem, 1968.

C. Y. S. Ho, The Stories of the Family Troubles of Judah and David: A Study of Their Literary Links, *VT* 49 (1999): 514-531.

G. Holscher, *Das Buch der Könige, seine Quellen und seine Redaktion* (FRLANT 36), Göttingen, 1923.

H. Holzinger, *Einleitung in den Hexateuch: Mit Tabellen über die Quellenscheidung*, Freiburg and Leipzig, 1893.

—, *Genesis* (KHAT), Freiburg, 1898.

—, Nachprüfung von B. D. Eerdmans, Die Komposition der Genesis, *ZAW* 31 (1911): 44-68.

C. J. Humphreys, The Number of People in the Exodus in Num. I and XXVI, *VT* 48 (1998): 196-213.

A. G. Hunter, Father Abraham: A Structural and Theological Study of the Yahwists Presentation of the Abraham Material, *JSOT* 35 (1986): 3-27.

H. Hupfeld, *Die Quellen der Genesis und die Art ihrer Zusammenhang*, Berlin, 1853.

A. Hurvitz, Early and Late in Biblical Hebrew: The Characteristics of Late Biblical Hebrew *in Chapters on Hebrew* (Hebrew) (ed. M. Bar-Asher), Jerusalem, 1997. 15-28.

J. M. Husser, Les Metamorphoses d'un Songe: Critque Littéraire de Genèse 28,10-22, *RB* 98 (1991): 321-342.

J. P. Hyatt, *Exodus* (New Century Bible Commentary), London, 1971.

K. Jaros, *Die Stellung des Elohisten zur Kannäischen Religion* (OBO 4), Freiburg, Schweiz, 1974.

A. W. Jenks, *The Elohist and North Israelite Traditions* (SBLMS 22), Missoula, 1977.

W. Johnstone, From the Sea to The Mountain, Ex. 15,22-19,2, a Case Study in Editorial Techniques, in *Studies in the Book of Exodus* (M. Vervenne ed.), Leuven, 1996, 245-263.

O. Kaiser, *Einleitung in das Alte Testament: Eine Einführung in ihre Ergebnisse und Probleme*, Gütersloh, 1969.

W. C. Kaiser, Balaam Son of Beor in Light of Deir Alla and Scripture; Saint or Soothsayer?, in *Go to the Land I Will Show You* (J. E. Coleson and V. H. Matthews eds.), Winona Lake, 1996, 95-100.

M. M. Kalisch, *Bible Studies, Part I: The Prophecies of Balaam (Num. xxii-xxiv) or the Hebrew and the Heathen*, London, 1877.

J. Kaminsky, Review of R. Rendtorff, The Covenant Formula: An Exegetical and Theological Investigation, *Journal of Religion* 80 (2000): 485-486.

E. Kautzsch, *Die Heilige Schrift des Alten Testament (I Band)*, Tübingen, 1922.

M. Kasher, *Torah Shlemah Pentateuch: VaYerah* (Hebrew), Jerusalem, 1938.

—, *Torah Shlemah Pentateuch: Mishpatim* (Hebrew), New-York, 1960.

—, *Torah Shlemah Pentateuch: BeHaalotechah* (Hebrew), Jerusalem, 1983.

O. Keel, Der Vergraben der "Fremden Götter" in Gen. 35,4, *VT* 23 (1973): 305-336.

P. Keuer, "Les Fils de Jacob" a Sichem, in *Pentateuchal and Deuteronomic Studies* (C. Breklemans and J. Lust eds.), Leuven, 1990, 41-46.

R. Killian, *Dir Vorpriesterlichen Abrahams-Überlieferungen*, Bonn, 1966.

G. A. Klingbeil, The Finger of God in the O.T., *ZAW* 112 (2000): 409-415.

I. Knohl, *The Temple of Silence* (Hebrew), Jerusalem, 1992.

—, Two Aspects of the Tent of Meeting, in *Tehillah le-Moshe: Biblical and Judaic Studies in Honour of M. Greenberg*, Winona Lake, 1997, 73-80.

—, In the Face of Death: Mortality and Religious Life in the Bible, in Rabbinic Literature, and in the Pauline Letters, in *Self, Soul, and Body in Religious Experience* (Studies in the History of Religion 78), Boston, 1998, 87-95.

—, Cain the Father of Humanity, in *Festschrift Weinfeld*, 2004, 63-67.

K. Koch, Auf der Suche nach der Geschichte, *Biblica* 67 (1986): 109-117.

J. Kodell, Jacob Wrestles with Esau Gen. 32,23-32, *BTB* 10 (1980): 65-70.

F. Kohata, *Jahwist und Priesterschrift in Ex. 3-14* (BZAW 166), Berlin, 1986.

L. Köhler and W. Baumgartner, *Lexicon in Veteris Testamenti Libros*, Leiden, 1953.

R. G. Kratz, *The Composition of the Narrative Books of the Old Testament*, London, 2005.

T. Krüger, Erwägungen zur Redaktion der Meerwundererzählung (Ex 13,17-14,31), *ZAW* 108 (1996): 519-533.

A. Kuenen, Dina en Shechem, *Theologisch Tijdscrhift* 14 (1880): 257-281.

—, Bileam, *Theologisch Tijdschrift* 18 (1884): 497-540.

—, *Historisch-Kritische Einleitung in die Bücher des A.T. Hinsichtlich ihrer Enstehung und Sammlung*, Leipzig, 1887.

L. Kundert, *Die Opferung/Bindung Isaaks*, Neukirchen-Vluyn, 1998.

S. T. Kunin, The Death of Isaac; Structuralist Analysis of Gen. 22, *JSOT* 64 (1994): 57-81.

A. J. Lambe, Judah's Development; the Pattern of Departure-Return-Transition, *JSOT* 83 (1999): 53-68.

A. M. Langrer, The Ninth Plague, *JBQ* 29 (2001): 48-55.

S. Lehming, Zur Überlieferugsgeschichte von Gen. 34, *ZAW* 70 (1958): 228-250.

—, Geburt der Jakobsöhne, *VT* 13 (1963): 74-81.

N. Leiter, The Translator's Hand in Transpositions? Notes on the LXX of Genesis 31, *Textus* 14 (1988): 105-130.

B. Lemmelijn, As Many Texts as Plagues: A Preliminary Report of the Main Results of the Text-Critical Evaluation of Ex. 7:14-11:10, *JNSL* 24 (1998): 111-125.

—, The Phrase ובעצים ובאבנים in Ex. 7:19, *Biblica* 80 (1999): 264-268.

C. Leviant, Ishmael and Hagar in the Wilderness; a Parallel Akedah, *Midstream* 43 (1997): 17-19.

Ch. Levin, *Der Jahwist* (FRLANT 157), Göttingen, 1993.

B. A. Levine, *Num. 1 – 20, A New Translation with Introduction and Commentary*, New York, 1993.

—, *Num. 21 –36, A New Translation with Introduction and Commentary*, New York, 2000.

Y. Licht, *A Commentary on the Book of Numbers (Hebrew)*, Jerusalem, 1995.

N. Lohfink, *Die Väter Israels im Deuteronomium* mit einer Stellungnahme von Thomas Römer (OBO 111), Freiburg, 1991.

S. E. Loewenstamm, *Evolution of the Exodus Tradition* (B. Schwartz tr.), Jerusalem, 1992.

—, Reuben and Judah in the Cycle of Joseph Stories, in *From Babylon to Canaan* (S. E. Loewenstammm ed.), Jerusalem, 1992, 35-41.

B. O. Long, *The Problem of Etiological Narrative in The Old Testament* (BZAW 108), Berlin, 1967.

J. Loza Vera, Exode 32 et la Redaction JE, *VT* 23 (1973): 31-55.

H. Lubsczyk, Elohim beim Jahwisten, *SVT* 29 (1978): 226-253.

J. D. Macchi, Die Stämmesprüche in Gen. 49, 3-27, *ZAW* 96 (1984): 333-350.

—, Les Interpretations Conflictuelles d'une Narration, Genèse 34, 1-35 et 49, 5-7, in *Narrativity in Biblical and Related Texts* (G. J. Brooke and J. D. Kaestli eds), Leuven, 2000, 3-15.

T. W. Mann, The Pillar of Cloud in the Reed Sea Narrative Ex. 13,21, *JBL* 90 (1971): 15-30.

S. E. McEvenue, The Elohist at Work, *ZAW* 96 (1984): 315-332.

A Return to Sources in Genesis 28,10-22, *ZAW* 106 (1994): 375-389.

A. H. McNeile, *The Book of Exodus with Introduction and Notes (Westminster Commentaries)*, London, 1908.

—, *The Book of Numbers* (Cambridge Bible), Cambridge, 1911.

J. Milgrom, The Strucutres of Numbers 11-12 and 13-14 and their Redaction, Preliminary Gropings, in *Judaic Perspectives on Ancient Israel* (J. Neusner ed.), Philadelphia, 1987, 49-61.

P. D. Miscall, The Jacob and Joseph Stories as Analogies, *JSOT* 6 (1978): 28-40.

S. Molen, The Identity of Jacob's Opponent; Wrestling with Ambiguity in Gen. 32:23-32, *Shofar* 11 (1993): 16-29.

G. F. Moore, *A Critical and Exegetical Commentary on Judges* (ICC), Edinburgh, 1895.

S. Mowinckel, Der Ursprung der Bil'amsage, *ZAW* 48 (1930): 233-271.

—, *Erwägungen zur Pentateuchquellen Frage*, Oslo, 1964.

S. Mowinckel and S. Michelet (eds.), *Det Gamle Testament*, Oslo, 1935.

J. Muilenburg, The Birth of Benjamin, *JBL* 75 (1956): 194-201.

N. Neeman, *The Past as a Foundation for the Present, The Creation of Biblical Historiography at the end of the First Temple Period and after the Destruction* (Hebrew), *Yeriot* 3, Jerusalem, 1988.

E. Neufeld, The Anatomy of the Joseph Cycle, *JBQ* 22 (1994): 38-46.

E. Nicholson, The Antiquity of the Tradition in Ex. 24:9-11, *VT* 25 (1975): 69-79.

—, The Pentateuch in Recent Research: A Time For Caution, *SVT* 43 (1991): 10-21.

—, Story and History in the Old Testament, in *Barr Festschrift* (S. E Balentine and J. Barton eds.), Oxford, 1994, 135-150.

—, *The Pentateuch in the Twentieth Century*, Oxford, 1998.

E. Nielsen, *The Ten Commandments in New Perspective* (Studies in Bible: the Second Series 7), London, 1968.

S. B. Noegel, The Significance of the 7th Plague, *Biblica* 76 (1995): 532-539.

M. Noth, *Exodus, A Commentary* (J. S. Bowden tr.) (OTL), Philadelphia, 1962.

—, *Numbers, A Commentary* (OTL), London, 1968.

—, *A History of Pentateuchal Traditions*, (trnsl by B.W. Anderson tr.), Englewood Cliffs, New Jersey, 1972.

M. A. Obrien, The Contribution of Judah's Speech, Gen. 44: 18-34, to the Characterization of Joseph, *CBQ* 59 (1997): 429-447.

M. Paran, *Priestly Style in the Pentateuch, Formulae, Grammatical Usages, and Structures* (Hebrew), Jerusalem, 1983.

R. Parry, Source Criticism and Gen. 34, *TynB* 51 (2000): 121-138.

J. Pedersen, Die Auffassung vom Alten Testament, *ZAW* 49 (1931): 161-181.

L. Perlitt, *Bundes Theologie im Alten Testament* (WMANT 36), Neukirchen-Vluyn, 1969.

D. L. Petersen, The Yahwist on the Flood, *VT* 21 (1971): 197-208.

A. + L. Philips, The Origin of "I am" in Ex 3.14, *JSOT* 78 (1998): 81-84.

W. Plein, Ort und literarische Funktion der Geburtgeschichte des Mose, *VT* 41 (1991): 110–118.

J. D. Pleins, Sonslayers and their Sons, *CBQ* 54 (1992): 29-38.

J. B. Pritchard (ed.), *Ancient Near Eastern Texts Relating to the Old Testament*, Princeton, 1955.

O. Proksch, *Die Genesis Übersetzt und Erklärt*, Leipzig, 1924.

W. H. C. Propp, *Exodus 1-18, A New Translation with Introduction and Commentary* (Anchor Bible), New York, 1998.

K. Rabast, *Das Apodiktische Recht im Deuteronomium und im Heiligkeitgesetz*, Berlin, 1949.

D. B. Redford, *A Study of the Biblical Story of Joseph*, SVT 20, Leiden, 1970.

G. A. Rendsburg, Notes on Gen. 35, *VT* 34 (1984): 361-364.

—, David and His Circle, *VT* 36 (1986): 438 –446.

—, Redactional Structuring in the Joseph Stories, Gen. 37-50, in *Mappings of the Biblical Terrain* (V. L. Tollers and J. Maier eds.), Lewisburg, Philadelphia, 1990, 215-232.

—, Israelian Hebrew Features in Gen. 49, *Maarav* 8 (1993): 161-170.

—, An Additional Note to the Recent Articles on the Number of People in the Exodus from Egypt and the Large Numbers in Num. I and XXVI, *VT* 51 (2001): 396-401.

R. Rendtorff, Der "Jahwist" als Theologe, zum Dilemna Der Pentateuchkritik, *SVT* (Congress Volume), Leuven 1975, 158-166.

—, *Die Überlieferungsgeschichtliche Probleme des Pentateuch* (BZAW 147), Berlin, 1977.

—, Jakob in Bethel, Beobachtungen zum Aufbau und zur Quellenfrage in Gen 28:10-22, *ZAW* 94 (1982): 511-523.

—, *The Old Testament: An Introduction* (J. Bowden tr.), London, 1985.

—, *The Problem of the process of Transmisssion of the Pentateuch* (J. J. Scullion tr.), *JSOTS* 89, 1990.

—, Der Text in seiner Endgestalt; Überlegungen zu Ex. 19, in *Ernter was man Sät* (D. D. Daniels, U. Glessner, M. Rösel eds.) Neukirchen-Vluyn, 1991, 459-470.

—, Two Kinds of P? Some Reflections on the Occasion of the Publishing of J. Milgrom's Commentary on Leviticus 1-16, *JSOT* 60 (1993): 75-81.

—, *Die Bundesformel: eine Exegetische Theologische Untersuchung*, Stuttgart, 1995.

B. P. Robinson, Symbolism in Ex. 15:22-27 Marah and Elim *RB* 94 (1987): 376-388.

A. Rofe, *"The Book of Bilaam" (Numbers 22:2-24:25), An Inquiry employing the Critical Method and Transmission & Religion History with an Appendix: Bilam in the Deir Alla Inscription* (Hebrew), Jerusalem, 1980.

—, *Introduction to the Book of Deuteronomy* (Hebrew), Jerusalem, 1988.

—, *Introduction to the Composition of the Pentateuch* (Hebrew), Jerusalem, 1994

—, *Introduction to Prophetic Literature* (tr. J. A. Seeligman), London, 1997.

T. Römer, *Israels Väter: Untersuchungen zur Väterthematik im Deuteronomium und in der deuteronomistischen Tradition* (OBO 99), Freiburg, 1990.

—, Nombre 11-12 et la Question d'une Redaction Deuteronomique dans le Pentateuque in *Deuteronomy and Deuteronomistic Literature* (M. Vervenne and J. Lust eds.), Leuven, 1997, 481- 498.

—, La Narration, une Subversion; l'Histoire de Joseph Gen. 37-50 et les Romans de la Diaspora, in *Narrativity in Biblical and Related Texts* (G. J. Brooke and J. D. Kaestli eds.), 2000, 17-30.

T. Römer and M. Brettler, Deuteronomy 34 and the Case for a Persian Pentateuch, *JBL* 119 (2000): 401-419.

M. Rösel, Wie einer vom Propheten zum Verführer werde; Tradition und Rezeption der Bileamgestalt, *Biblica* 80 (1999): 506-524.

M. Rose, *Deuteronomist und Jahwist: Untersuchungen zu den Berührungspunkten beider Literatur,* Zürich, 1981.

H. Rouillard, On Alexander Rofe, The Book of Balaam, 1979, *RB* 89 (1982): 268-270.

W. Rudolph, *Der Elohist von Exodus bis Josua* (BZAW 68), Giessen, 1938.

L. Ruppert, *Die Josepherzählung der Genesis: Ein Beitrag zur Theologie der Pentateuch,* München., 1965.

—, Die Aporie der gegenwärtigen Pentateuchdiskussion und die Josefserzählung der Genesis, *BZ* 29 (1985): 31-48.

—, Zum Neuren Diskussion um die Josefsgeschichte der Genesis, *BZ* 33 (1989): 92-97.

J. D. Safren, Ahuzzath and the Pact of Beer-Sheva, *ZAW* 101 (1989): 184-198.

N. M. Sarna, Abraham in History, *BA Rev* 3,4 (1978): 5-9.

A. Saviv, ‫ה׳ יראה = המקום אשר יבחר‬, *Beit Miqra* 26 (1981): 279-281.

H. H. Schmid, *Der Sogenannte Jahwist, Beobactungen und Fragen zur Pentateuch Forschung,* Zürich, 1976.

—, In Search of New Approaches in Pentateuchal Research, *JSOT* 3 (1977): 33-42.

K. Schmid, *Erzväter und Exodus : Untersuchungen zur doppelten Begründung der Ursprünge Israels innerhalb der Geschichtsbücher des Alten Testaments* (WMANT 81), University of Zurich, 1999.

L. Schmidt, Die Alttestamentliche Bileamüberlieferung, *BZ* 23 (1979): 234-261.

—, Mose, die 70 Ältesten und die Propheten in Num 11 und 12, in *Gesammelte Aufsätze zum Pentateuch* (BZAW 263), Berlin, 1998, 251-279.

—, Israel und das Gesetz; Ex. 19, 3b-8 und 24, 3-8 als Literarischer und Theologischer Rahmen für das Bundesbuch, *ZAW* 113 (2001): 167-185.

W. H. Schmidt, *Exodus,* Neukirchen-Vluyn, 1974.

—, Die Intention der beiden Plagenerzählung (Ex. 7 -10) in ihrem Kontext in *Studies in the Book of Exodus* (M. Vervenne ed.), Leuven, 1996, 225-243.

H. C. Schmitt, "Priesterliches" und "prophetisches" Geschichtsverstädnis in der Meerwundererzählung Ex. 13,17-14,31, in *Textgemäss* (A. H. J. Gunneweg and O. Kaiser eds.), Göttingen, 1979, 139-155.

—, *Die Nichtpriestliche Josephgeschichte* (BZAW 155), Berlin, 1980.

—, Die Erzählung von der Versuchung Abrahams Gen. 22, 1-19 und das Problem einer Theologie der elohistischen Pentateuchtexte, *BN* 34 (1986): 86-109.

—, Die Hintergrunde der "neuesten Pentateuchkritik" und der literarische Befund der Josefsgeschichte Gen. 37-50, *ZAW* 97 (1985): 161-179.

—, Tradition der Prophetenbücher in den Schichten der Plagenerzählung Ex.7,1-11,10, in *Prophet und Prophetenbuch* (BZAW 185), Berlin, 1989, 196-216.

—, Das sogenannte vorprophetische Berufungsschema: zur "geistigen Heimat" des Berufungsformulars von Ex 3,9-12, Jdc 6,11-24 und I Sam 9,1-10,16, *ZAW* 104 (1992): 202-216.

—, Der heidnische Mantiker als Eschatoligischer Jahweprophet, zum Verständnis Bileams in der Endgestalt von Num. 22-24, in *Studien zur Theologie und Religiongeschichte Israels für Otto Kaiser zum 70 Geburtstag* (I. Kottsieper ed.), Göttingen, 1994, 180-198.

—, Der Kampf Jakobs mit Gott in Hos. 12, 3ff und in Gen. 32, 23ff: zum Verständnis der Verborgenheit Gottes im Hoseabuch und im Elohistischen Geschichtwerk, in *"Ich Bewirke das Heil und erschaffe das Unheil"* (B. Willnes and F. Diedrich eds.), Würzburg, 1998, 397-430.

—, Die Erzählung vom goldenen Kalb Ex. 32 und das Deuteronomistische Geschichtwerk, in *Rethinking the Foundations: Historiography in the Ancient World and in the Bible* (S. L. Mckenzie, T. Römer, and H. H. Schmid eds.), 2000, 235-250.

B. Schwartz, The Priestly Account of the Theophany and Lawgiving at Sinai, in *Text Temples and Tradition - A Tribute to Menachem Haran* (M. V. Fox ed.), Winona Lake, 1996, 103-134.

J. Schüpphaus, Volk Gottes und Gesetz beim Elohisten *ThZ* 31 (1975): 193-210.

H. Seebass, Num 11:12 und die Hypothese des Jahwisten, *VT* 28 (1978): 214-233.

—, The Joseph Story, Gen. 48, and the Canonical Process, *JSOT* 35 (1986): 29-43.

—, LXX und MT in Gen. 31,44-53, *BN* 34 (1986): 30-88.

—, Zur Literarischen Gestalt der Bileam-Perikope, *ZAW* 107 (1995): 409-419.

—, Zur Quellenscheidung in den Josephsgeschichte, in *Joseph- in den Bibel und Literatur* (F. W. Golka and W. Weiss eds), Oldenburg, 2000, 25-36.

S. K. Sherwood, *"Had God not Been on My Side", An Examination of the Narrative Technique of the Story of Jacob and Laban: Gen. 29.1-32.2* (European Union Studies 23/400), Frankfurt am Main, 1990.

J. C. Siebert-Hommes, Die Geburtgeschichte des Mose innerhalb des Erzählzusammenhangs von Ex I und II, *VT* 42 (1992): 398-404.

C. A. Simpson, *The Book of Genesis* (Interpreters Bible), New York, 1952.

J. L. Ska, Récit et Récit Métadiégétique en Ex. 1-15, Remarques Critique et Essai d'Interprétation de Ex. 3:16-22, in *Le Pentateuque: Débats et Recherches* (P. Haudbert ed.), Paris, 1992, 135-171.

—, Sommaires Proleptique en Gen. 27 et dans l'Histoire de Joseph: *Biblica* 73 (1992): 518-527.

—, Le Repas de Ex. 24: 11, *Biblica* 74 (1993): 305–327.

—, Notes sur la Traduction de "welo'" en Exode III 19b, *VT* 44 (1994): 60-65.

—, Exode 19,3b-6 et l'Identité de l'Israel Postexilique in *Studies in the Book of Exodus* (M. Vervenne ed.), Leuven (1996): 289-317.

J. Skinner, *Genesis, A Critical and Exegetical Commentary* (ICC), Edinburgh, 1910.

R. Smend, *Die Erzählung des Hexateuch auf ihre Quellen Untersucht*, Berlin, 1912.

J. Soggin, Jacob in Shechem and in Bethel Gen. 35, 1-7, in *Shaarei Talmon* (M. Fishbane and E. Tov eds.), Winona Lake, 1992, 195-198.

—, Dating the Joseph Story and Other Remarks, in *Joseph- Bibel und Literatur* (F. W. Golka and W. Weiss eds.), Oldenburg, 2000, 13-24.

B. D. Sommer, Reflecting on Moses – The Redaction of Num. 11 *JBL* 118 (1999): 601-624.

E. Speiser, People and Nation of Israel, *JBL* 79 (1960): 157-165.

—, *Genesis, Introduction, Translation and Notes* (Anchor Bible), New York, 1964.

S. Spiegel, *The Last Trial, on the Legends and Lore of the Command to Offer Isaac as a Sacrifice*, New York, 1967.

J. J. Stamm and M. E. Andrews, *The Ten Commandments in Recent Research* (Studies in Biblical Theology Second Series), London, 1967.

H. J. Stöbe, Gut und Böse in den J Quelle des Pentateuch, *ZAW* 65 (1953): 188-204.

H. P. Stähli, "Da schickte sie ihre Magd..." (Ex. 2,5); zur Vokalisation eines hebräischen Wortes, ein Beispiel des Ringens um das richtige Textverständnis, *Wort und Dienst* 17 (1983): 27-54.

C. Steuernagel, *Lehrbuch der Einleitung in das Alte Testament mit einem Anhang über die Apokryphen und Pseudepigraphen*, Tübingen, 1912.

A. Strus, Étymologie des noms propres dans Gen. 29,32 - 30,24, *Salesianum* 40 (1978): 57-72.

E. J. Sutcliffe, De Unitate Litteraria Num xxii *Biblica* 7 (1926): 3-9.

T. L. Thompson, *The Historicity of the Patriarchal Period* (BZAW 133), Berlin, 1977.

—, A New Attempt to Date the Patriarchal Narratives, *JAOS* 98 (1978): 76-84.

—, How Yahweh Became God: Ex: 3 and 6 and the Heart of the Pentateuch, *JSOT* 68 (1995): 57 – 74.

A. Tosato, The Literary Structure of the First Two Poems Num.23:7-10, 18-24, *VT* 29 (1979): 98-106.

E. Tov, *Textual Criticism of the Hebrew Bible (Hebrew)*, Jerusalem, 1990.

F. Tuch, *Kommentar über die Genesis*, Halle, 1838.

J. Van Seters, Confessional Reformulation in the Exilic Period, *VT* 22 (1972): 448-459.

—, The Conquest of Sihon's Kingdom: A Literary Re-examination, *JBL* 91 (1972): 182 – 187.

—, The Terms "Amorite" and "Hittite" in the Old Testament, *VT* 22 (1972): 64 - 81.

—, *Abraham in History and Tradition*, Yale University, 1975.

—, The Religion of the Patriarchs in Genesis, *Biblica* 61 (1980): 220-233.

—, *In Search of History, Historiography in the Ancient World and the Origins of Biblical History*, Yale University, 1983.

—, The Place of the Yahwist in the History of Passover and Massot, *ZAW* 95 (1983): 167-182.

—, The Plagues of Egypt, Ancient Tradition or Literary Invention, *ZAW* 98 (1986): 31-39.

—, *Der Jahwist als Historiker* (Theologisch Studien 134), Zürich, 1987.

—, Law and the Wilderness Rebellion Tradition, *SBSLP* 29 (1990): 583-91.

—, *Prologue to History: The Yahwist as Historian in Genesis*, Louisvile, Kentucky, 1992.

—, *The Life of Moses, The Yahwist as Historian in Exodus – Numbers*, Kampen, 1994.

—, A Contest of Magicians? The Plague Stories in P, in *Pomegranates and Golden Bells* (D. P. Wright, D. N. Freedman, and A. Hurvitz eds.), Winona Lake, 1995, 569-580.

—, Cultic Laws in the Covenant Code and their Relationship to Deuteronomy and the Holiness Code, in *Studies in The Book of Exodus* (M. Vervenne ed.), Leuven, 1996, 319-345.

—, The Law of The Hebrew Slave, *ZAW* 108 (1996): 534-546.

—, From Faithful Prophet to Villian; Observations on the Tradition History of the Bilaam Story, in *A Biblical Itinerary* (JSOTS 240), 1997, 126-132.

—, Divine Encounter at Bethel Gen. 28, 10-12, in Recent Literary Critical Study of Genesis, *ZAW* 110 (1998): 503-513.

—, The Law on Child Sacrifice in Exodus 22, 28b-29, *ETL* 74 (1998): 364-372.

—, In The Babylonian Exile With J, Between Judgement in Ezekiel and Salvation in Second Isaiah, in *The Crisis of Israelite Religion* (B. Becking and M. C. A. Karpel eds.) (Oudtestamentische Studien 42), Leiden, 1999, 71-89.

—, *The Pentateuch, A Social Science Commentary* (Trajectories), Sheffield, England, 1999.

—, The Silence of Dinah, in *Jacob – Commentaire a Plusiers Voix de Gen. 25-36* (J. D. Macchi and T. Römer eds.), Labor et Fides, 2001, 239-247.

F. Van Trigt, La Signifacation de la Lutte de Jacob Pres de Yabboq, *Oudtestamentische Studien* 12 (1958): 280-309.

J. Vermeylen, L'Affaire du Veau d'Or (Ex. 32-34); Une Clé pour la "Question Deuteronomiste"?, *ZAW* 97 (1985): 1-23.

—, Les Section Narrative de Deut. 5-11 et leur Relation a Ex. 19-34, in *Das Deuteronomium* (N. Lohfink ed.), Leuven, 1985, 174-207.

M. Vervenne, The "P" Tradition in the Pentateuch - Document or Redaction? "The Sea Narrative" Ex.13,17-14,31 as a Test Case in *Pentateuchal and Deuteronomistc Studies* (C. Breklemans and J. Lust eds.) Leuven, 1990, 67-90.

—, Exodus Expulsion and Exodus Flight; the Interpretation of A Crux Critically Reassessed, *JNSL* 22 (1996): 45-58.

P. Volz and E. Rudolph, *Der Elohist als Erzähler; ein Irrweg der Pentateuch Kritik* (BZAW 63), Berlin, 1933.

G. Von Rad, *Das Formgeschichtliche Problem des Hexateuch* (BWANT 4,26), 1938.

—, *Joseph Geschichte und Ältere Chokma*, SVT 1, Copenhagen, 1953, 121-127.

—, The Joseph Narrative and Ancient Wisdom, in *The Problem of the Hexateuch and Other Essays* (E. W. Trueman Dicken tr.), Edinburgh and London, 1966.

—, *Genesis: A Commentary* (J. H. Marks tr.) (Old Testament Library), Philadelphia, 1972.

H. Vorländer, *Die Entsehungszeit des Jehowistischen Geschichtswerkes*, Frankfurt am Main, 1978.

J. R. Wagenaar, Crossing the Sea of Reeds Ex. 13-14 and the Jordan Josh.3-4; a P Framework for the Wilderness Wandering, in *Studies in the Book of Exodus* (M. Vervenne ed.), Leiden, 1996, 461-470.

N. Wagner, Pentateuchal Criticism No Clear Future, *Canadian Journal of Theology* 13 (1967): 225-232.

—, A Response to Professor Rolf Rendtorff, *JSOT* 3 (1977): 57-63.

S. M. Warner, The Patriarchs and Extra-Biblical Sources, *JSOT* 2 (1977): 50-61.

P. Weimar, *Untersuchungen zur Redaktiongeschichte des Pentateuch* (BZAW 146), Berlin, 1977.

—, Beobachtungen zur Analyse von Gen. 32, 23-33, *BN* 49: 53-81, *BN* 50 (1989): 58-94.

—, Das Goldene Kalb; Redaktionkritische Erwägungen zu Ex. 32, *BN* 38-39 (1987): 117-160.

M. Weinfeld, *Deuteronomy and the Deuteronomistic School*, Oxford, 1972.

—, Sarah in the House of Abimelech (Hebrew), *Tarbiz* 52 (1983): 639-642.

—, The Traditions regarding Moses and Jethro at the Mountain of God (Hebrew), *Tarbiz* 56 (1987): 449-460.

Z. Weisman, The Interrelationship between J and E in Jacob's Narrative, *ZAW* 104 (1992): 177-197.

J. Wellhausen, *Die Composition des Hexateuchs und der Historischen Bücher des Alten Testaments,* Berlin, 1899.

—, *Prolegomena zur Geschichte Israels*, Berlin, 1905.

G. Wenham, Review of : H. Schmid, *Der sogenannte Jahwist, JSOT* 3 (1977): 57-60.

—, *Genesis 16-50* (World Biblical Commentary Vol. 2), Dallas, 1994.

—, The Priority of P, *VT* 49 (1999): 240-248.

C. Westermann, *The Promises to the Fathers: Studies on the Patriarchal Narratives,* Philadelphia, 1980.

—, *Genesis 1-11: A Commentary* (J. J. Scullion tr.), Minneapolis, 1984.

—, *Genesis 12-36: A Commentary* (J. J. Scullion tr.), Minneapolis, 1985.

—, *Genesis 37-50: A Commentary* (J. J. Scullion tr.), Minneapolis, 1986.

J. W. Wevers, The Balaam Narrative according to the Septuagint, in *Lectures et Relectures* (J. M. Avwers and A. Wenin eds.), Leuven, 1999, 133-144.

M. White, The Elohistic Depiction of Aaron; a Study in the Levite Zadokite Controversy, in *Studies in the Pentateuch* (J. A. Emerton ed.), Leiden, 1990, 149-159.

R. N. Whybray , *The Making of the Pentateuch - a Methodological Study* (JSOTS 53), Sheffield, 1987.

H. G. Williamson, The Life of Moses: Review, *VT* 45 (1995): 431-432.

E. V. Winnet, Re-examining the Foundations, *JBL* 84 (1965): 1-19.

H. W. Wolff, The Elohistic Fragments in the Pentateuch, *Interpretation* 26 (1972): 158-173.

D. J. Wynn-Williams, *The State of the Pentateuch* (BZAW 249), Berlin, 1997.

D. Yellin, *Biblical Inquiries, New Insights into the Text of Isaiah* (Hebrew), Jerusalem, 1938.

T. Yoreh, The Struggle, *ZAW* 117 (2005): 95-97.

—, How Many Sons Did Jacob Have According to E?, *ZAW* 118 (2006), 264-268.

I. M. Young, Israelite Literacy: Interpreting the Evidence, *VT* 48(1998): 239 –253, 408-422.

Y. Zakovitch, *Abram and Sarai in Egypt, Genesis 12:10-20, in the Bible in the Translations and in Early Jewish Commentaries* (Hebrew), Jerusalem, 1983.

—, Silhouette Narratives, Another Dimension for Evaluating Characters in Biblical Narrative (Hebrew), *Tarbiz* 54 (1983): 165-176.

Y. A. Zeligman, Inquiries into the Biblical Text (Hebrew), *Tarbiz* 25 (1956): 118-139.

B. Ziemer, *Abram - Abraham kompositionsgeschichtliche Untersuchungen zu Genesis 14, 15 und 17*, Berlin, 2005.

F. Zimmer, *Der Elohist als weisheitlich-prophetische Redaktionsschicht: Eine literarische theologiegeschichtliche Untersuchung der sogenannten elohistischen Texte im Pentateuch,* (European University Studies, Series 12, Vol. 656), Frankfurt, 1999.

M. Zippor, The Story of Laban's pursuit of Jacob as Reflected in the Septuagint (Hebrew), *Beit Miqra* 46 (2001): 1-27.

W. Zimmerli, Ich bin Jahwe, in *Geschichte und Altes Testament* (W. F. Albright ed.), Tübingen, 1953, 179-209.

H. J. Zöbel, Bileam Lieder und Bileam Erzählung, in *Die Hebräische Bibel und ihre zweifache Nachgeschichte, Festschrift fur R. Rendtorff* (ed. E. Blum *et al*), Neukirchen-Vluyn, 1990, 141-54.

W. Zwickel, Der Alterbau Abrahams Zwischen Bethel und Ai, Gen 12f: Ein Beitrag zur Datierung der Jahwisten, *BZ* 36 (1995): 207-219.

Index of Authors